HOME AND HEGEMONY

HOME AND HEGEMONY

Domestic Service and Identity Politics
in South and Southeast Asia

Edited by Kathleen M. Adams and Sara Dickey

Ann Arbor
THE UNIVERSITY OF MICHIGAN PRESS

Copyright © by the University of Michigan 2000
All rights reserved
Published in the United States of America by
The University of Michigan Press
Manufactured in the United States of America
∞ Printed on acid-free paper

2003 2002 2001 2000   4 3 2 1

A CIP catalog record for this book is available from the British Library.

Library of Congress Cataloging-in-Publication Data

Home and hegemony : domestic service and identity politics in South and Southeast Asia / edited by Kathleen M. Adams and Sara Dickey.
    p. cm
    Includes bibliographical references and index.
    ISBN 0-472-11106-X
    1. Domestics—Asia, South. 2. Domestics—Asia, Southeastern.
3. Minorities—Employment—Asia, South. 4. Minorities—Employment—Asia, Southeastern.
5. Asia, South—Ethnic relations. 6. Asia, Southeastern—Ethnic relations. I. Adams, Kathleen M., 1957– II. Dickey, Sara.

HD8039.D52 S694 2000
305.8'00954—dc21   99-055617

For our parents

CONTENTS

INTRODUCTION
Negotiating Homes, Hegemonies, Identities, and Politics
Sara Dickey and Kathleen M. Adams   1

MUTUAL EXCLUSIONS
Domestic Workers and Employers on Labor,
Class, and Character in South India
Sara Dickey   31

TRANSFERS OF KNOWLEDGE AND
PRIVILEGED SPHERES OF PRACTICE
Servants and Employers in a Madras Railway Colony
Rachel Tolen   63

SERVICE OR SERVITUDE?
The Domestication of Household Labor in Nepal
Saubhagya Shah   87

ALWAYS HOME, NEVER HOME
Visayan "Helpers" and Identities
Jean-Paul Dumont   119

INSIDE THE HOME AND OUTSIDE THE FAMILY
The Domestic Estrangement of Javanese Servants
G. G. Weix   137

NEGOTIATED IDENTITIES
Humor, Kinship Rhetoric, and Mythologies
of Servitude in South Sulawesi, Indonesia
Kathleen M. Adams   157

NURTURE FOR SALE
Sri Lankan Housemaids and the Work of Mothering
Michele Ruth Gamburd   179

DEPENDENTS IN THE MASTER'S HOUSE
When Rock Dulls Scissors
    Louise H. Kidder   207

DOLLS, T-BIRDS, AND IDEAL WORKERS
The Negotiation of Filipino Identity in Hong Kong
    Nicole Constable   221

GENDER, ISLAM, AND NATIONALITY
Indonesian Domestic Servants in the Middle East
    Kathryn Robinson   249

AMBIGUOUS HEGEMONIES
Identity Politics and Domestic Service
    Karen Tranberg Hansen   283

CONTRIBUTORS   293

INDEX   295

SARA DICKEY AND KATHLEEN M. ADAMS

INTRODUCTION
Negotiating Homes, Hegemonies,
Identities, and Politics

This is the difference between rich and poor people. Only if we work can
we have *kanji* [rice water]. But they could eat meat and rice even if they
stay at home for two to ten days. . . . If we don't have work, we couldn't
have even *kanji* to drink. That's the difference between rich and poor
people. *(Vasanthi, a domestic worker in Tamil Nadu, India; cited in Dickey,
this volume)*

If we still have the . . . feelings of a true Filipino, let us join hands to
prove to the whole world that Filipino maids still have moral values
though how lowly we are in this foreign land. *(Oly Rueda 1992, 16, Filipina domestic worker in Hong Kong; cited in Constable, this volume)*

These days you can't depend on helpers. Food and a roof are no longer
enough for them. They are all taking off to go to school or demanding
more wages . . . things were different in the old days. We had lots of
slaves around the house—whole families who were loyal and understood
their place. Back then they wouldn't dare sit on chairs to watch TV—
they knew their place was on the floor. Today they are so brazen. *(Indo
Rura, an employer in the highlands of Sulawesi, Indonesia; cited in Adams, this
volume)*

[My maid] said to me, "The same blood runs through my veins as yours." I
said to her, "If I said the same blood runs through my veins as [the Prime
Minister's] everyone would just laugh at me." My idea of socialism is to
feed the workers so they will work well. Their idea is to live like us. . . .
They want to live like us but they can't. It's . . . something about a person.   (Sita, an employer in Tamil Nadu, India; cited in Tolen, this volume)

These commentaries invite us to recognize the efforts of both domestic
workers and employers to create opposing identities out of their experiences
with one another. Here, a south Indian domestic worker critiques the class
basis of difference that creates hardship for her and privilege for her
employers. A Filipina domestic worker in Hong Kong struggles to prove her
morality to a skeptical audience, deploying native and adopted images of
femininity to demonstrate Filipina workers' righteousness. For their parts,
Sulawesi and south Indian householders argue that they are exploited by
their servants. Perceiving workers' claims to status as diminishing their own
standing, these employers reinforce their superiority by making claims of
inherent difference. These commentaries produce relational images of identity—notions of self and other that are constructed in relation and opposition to one another within hegemonic social systems. Such identities are
necessarily fluid, positioned, and contingent (cf. Alonso 1994; Butler 1995).
Like the relationships that give rise to them, they are also continuously
negotiated and constructed in tandem through "we-they" contrasts. Systems
of power cannot be understood as *systems*, we argue, unless we include
multiple and simultaneous points of view.

Given such a perspective, examining the interactive processes of identity
requires spotlighting multiple hegemonic positions, something few ethnographic studies have endeavored. Domestic service provides a particularly apt
arena for this enterprise. Unlike most other types of labor, the work takes place
in the employer's home, and relationships between domestic workers and
employers are developed at close range, creating a more intense dynamic of
self-other contrast than is found in most work settings. As a form of labor,
domestic service is household work carried out by someone who is remuner-
ated by wages or in-kind payment; the most common tasks include cooking,
washing dishes, doing laundry, cleaning and dusting household surfaces,
caring for children, and tending to animals. As a social setting, domestic
service is a highly personalized and often contested arena in which many
inequalities are brought to bear, including nationality, race, ethnicity, class,
gender, and/or sexuality, among others. Unfortunately, the majority of previous work on domestic service has focused separately on either workers or

employers. In contrast, most of the authors here take advantage of the possibilities afforded by the close contact of domestic service, and they address the experiences and interactions of both workers and employers. We have found that examining domestic service *relationships* allows a focus on the mutual constructions of identity, and especially their reliance on the process of differentiating self and other.

Literature about domestic service in societies around the world suggests that similar tensions appear widely because of the combination of an intimacy based on the worker's closeness to the family and a distance based on class and other hierarchies, hierarchies that are reproduced through the work and must be maintained in the home (e.g., Gill 1994; Hansen 1989; Rollins 1985; Romero 1992). It is important to note the power of domestic service in constructing such hierarchies and the identities associated with them. Domestic service not only reproduces preexisting inequalities; it may also contribute directly to the creation of inequalities, due to the stigma frequently associated with paid household work. Rollins makes this point powerfully:

> An employer passing on her dirty work to a woman who is also lower class, often of a subordinate racial/ethnic group, a woman who is asked to demonstrate various kinds of inferiority, further allows the employer to devalue the person of the worker. This overall "inferiority" of the household worker (an inferiority which is, in fact, created by the employer) not only justifies paying her low wages. More important, it suggests to the employer and her family that entire categories of people (the lower classes, people of color, etc.) may indeed be inferior. And if that is true, a social structure that maintains such people at a disadvantage may be a justifiable and legitimate structure. (Rollins 1990, 85)

Domestic service exhibits similar structural and logistical features across a wide variety of cultures. Nonetheless, the intricate details of power and inequality remain rooted in local circumstances, as the particularities of hierarchy are always culturally constructed (Colen and Sanjek 1990b, 177). Recent studies by anthropologists, sociologists, and historians have begun to suggest ways in which identities are influenced by locally determined hierarchies in combination with the intensely personal interactions of domestic service. Cooke (1990), for example, argues that Nyishang employers in Nepal use the knowledge they gain of their Tibetan and other non-Nyishang servants to help produce their own ethnic identities; while Colen and Sanjek (1990a, 8) point out that the associations of African-American women and of Chinese-American and Japanese-American men with domestic service in popular media have helped "to build racist stereotypes" in the United States. (For other work on race and ethnicity in domestic service, see, e.g., Cock 1980; Colen 1990; Gill 1994; Glenn 1986; Rollins 1985; Romero 1992; Tucker 1988.) Similar points have been made about domestic service and the construction of gender (Bujra 1992; Bunster and Chaney 1985; Chaney and García Castro 1989; Cock 1980; Gill 1994; Hansen 1989, 1990; Tucker 1988; Watson 1991), caste (Tellis-Nayak 1983), and class (Dickey forthcoming). Other ways in which domestic service contributes to hierarchies and identities have been noted as well. Constable, for example, argues that Hong Kong residents' nostalgic glorification of Cantonese amahs, when contrasted with stereotypes of Filipina workers "as loud, aggressive, boisterous, and brash," helps to address fears about reunification with China by invoking "a time and place—well away from Communist China—where there was no guilt about wealth, power, or class differences" (1997, 58). In a different vein, numerous authors have pointed out the crucial symbolic roles that domestic workers play in signaling the class standing of employers (e.g., Constable 1997, 96; Dickey forthcoming; Gill 1994). We build on this work by taking the interactive construction of identity and hegemony as our primary focus.

As these and other studies demonstrate, domestic service is hardly a new phenomenon. In Asia, James L. Watson's (1980) landmark exploration of systems of slavery shows us that markets in slaves and servants predate global capitalist economies. Others have documented colonialists' common practices of hiring local servants (Hansen 1989, 1990; Stoler 1985, 1995, 1996). However, as Louise Tilly (1978) and others have observed, industrialization, transnational capitalism, and the global economy have dramatically accelerated the expansion of the domestic worker phenomenon. Specific figures are difficult to obtain, given the frequently "casual" and unorganized nature of this private sector work, as well as the often undocumented status of migrant domestic workers. The numbers, however, are large and ever growing. There are, for example, more than a million and a half overseas Filipino contract workers (Constable 1997, 20), many of whom are employed as domestic workers. And, at this writing, as the Indonesian rupia spirals downward and unemployment soars, thousands of Indonesians are desperately seeking jobs in households in Singapore, Malaysia, Australia, and elsewhere. In short, domestic work is part and parcel of the global political economy. Like Colen and Sanjek (1990b), Hansen(1990), Constable (1997), and others, we wish to underscore the importance of viewing household work "historically, locally, and contextually within a capitalist world system" (Colen and Sanjek 1990b, 177). As many of the essays in this volume demonstrate, flows of capital, economic and political shifts, and transformations in the global economy spark migration and emigration and have multiple reverberations on the conditions of domestic work.

The authors of this volume are part of this transnational flow, taking part in both the colonial legacy of anthropology and in contemporary political and economic relations within and between nations. In addition to observing the processes of identity negotiation in domestic service, we have also participated in them directly. While some of us set out to conduct field research on domestic service, others became interested when we entered or formed field-site households that employed domestic workers. For all of us, this experience of negotiating unfamiliar household hierarchies has prompted troubling questions about our own identities and uneven relations with those whose worlds we step into and attempt to chronicle. As outsiders in local households we shared a liminal status with the domestic workers whose toil made our fieldwork lives so much more comfortable. And yet, as comparatively wealthy, educated, and privileged guests or heads of households, we were forced continually to recognize our own undeniably powerful positions in the hierarchies of these households. For a number of us reared to embrace the feminist or humanitarian rhetoric of equality (a rhetoric that is at the core of our disciplines), our daily interactions with domestic workers in our temporary fieldwork homes raised troubling awarenesses of the ways in which intersecting hierarchies of class, race, age, and gender color our own attempts at cultural understanding. As researchers and as individuals we were intimately and undeniably complicit in these hierarchies of the home, and our complex positions within them are apparent in our writing.

Most fieldworkers, in anthropology and other disciplines, have viewed the so-called public world outside their domestic space as the "real" research arena, and their private home space as a neutral, and intellectually uninteresting, launching pad for the rest. By contrast, we take the domestic as our focus and examine private and personal space as not only our own but others' workspace. As Colen and Sanjek point out, studies of domestic service "force us to acknowledge . . . that, worldwide, millions of homes are workplaces, and millions of workplaces are homes" (1990b, 179). The public/private distinction may not be relevant in all the societies we work in; and it is problematic in domestic service in any case since, as Gill similarly notes, "the private sphere of the employer is the public sphere of the employee" (1994, 9). Yet it is certainly embraced in most of our home societies and has been reproduced in most ethnographic work. In devoting attention to our own fieldwork homes, we problematize this classic dichotomy.

THE SOUTH AND SOUTHEAST ASIAN CONTEXT

This volume provides the first extensive documentation of domestic service in South and Southeast Asia. Although much material has been published on domestic service elsewhere in the world (particularly regarding Europe and the Americas, with a significant concentration on southern Africa as well),[1] such studies on Asia are almost nonexistent (Colen and Sanjek 1990b, 194). With some notable exceptions (including Armstrong 1990, 1996; Brandewie 1973; Constable 1997; Cooke 1990; Dias and Weerakoon-Gunawardene 1991; Margold 1995; Robinson 1991; Tellis-Nayak 1983), domestic work has been a largely overlooked topic of inquiry in South and Southeast Asia.[2]

Examining these two regions together may initially strike some readers as perplexing, given the classic Euramerican academic categorization of and division between the two regions. There is, however, a long and richly documented history of ties and movements of peoples between South and Southeast Asia, including expressive traditions, internal colonizations and migrations, shared experiences of European colonialism, and parallels in social and economic developmental projects (cf. Flueckiger and Sears 1991; Hall and Whitmore 1976). Moreover, the historic linkages between these two regions have intensified in the contemporary era of globalized economies. These on-the-ground linkages across "regional" boundaries often make such boundaries appear contrived at best, and we have found it more illuminating to view this area as a whole.[3]

While it is not our intention to conflate the experiences of rural Torajans with urban Filipinos or migrant Sri Lankans, the postcolonial world has fostered new intersections of different "locales" with one another. In the nations of Asia, satellite dish television, films, international religious organizations, political alliances such as the Association of Southeast Asian Nations (ASEAN), and transnational worker agencies offer new, broader frameworks for reflecting on home and work and for imagining new possibilities and new identities elsewhere (cf. Appadurai 1991). Today's rural Torajan domestic "helpers" watch *Brady Bunch* reruns and imagine migrating to urban areas so that they too can enjoy the ease with which the servant Alice whips through her tasks, thanks to dishwashers and vacuum cleaners. Large numbers of Muslim Indonesian domestic workers are drawn to Malaysia and the Middle East, in part as a result of the growing emphasis on their shared identities as Malays or as Muslims. Indian professionals move to Singapore and Malaysia for career opportunities and find they must deal with new markets, kitchens, and domestic service practices. In short, the postcolonial world has greatly transformed the nature and meaning of domestic work in South and Southeast Asia. We hope that the questions raised by this volume will prompt further research in this neglected area.

HEGEMONIES AND HOMES

The concept of hegemony is a useful starting point for unraveling the complex negotiations of identity and power that take place in domestic service. We approach hegemony, which Roseberry describes as "a problematic, contested political process of domination and struggle" (1994, 358), both holistically and processually. Our view is holistic in that we see hegemony as constructed by all who take part, rather than imposed by the holders of a dominant ideology that accounts either entirely or in part for the ideologies of other social groupings in any straightforward way. Furthermore, we see hegemony as inhering in everyday, informal, and often relatively inchoate aspects of living, as well as in formal and articulable ideological systems (Williams 1977, 109–110). The "relations of domination and submission" that comprise hegemony are, to use Williams's evocative phrase, "a saturation of the whole process of living" (Williams 1977, 110). In addition, our approach emphasizes process by recognizing hegemony as continuously remade through interaction and negotiation. As Gramsci (1957) maintained, hegemony entails both coercion and consent and requires frequent rejuvenation, fortification, and modification.

Just as our approach implies avoidance of simplistic and unilateral notions of domination and subordination, it also lacks frequent reference to subaltern resistance or accommodation, especially the reactive, unambivalent, romanticized, or "thin" senses of these terms (cf. Abu-Lughod 1990; Brown 1996; Ortner 1995). Rather, we examine hegemonies and their multiple hierarchies as constantly negotiated (a process we discuss in the following), and originating from multiple sides. Similarly, we see multiple vulnerabilities and dependencies, axes of opposition, and contestations of representations on all sides. The cases presented in this collection convey a sense of the fragility of hegemonies, and, as Karen Tranberg Hansen notes so aptly in her concluding essay, of their ambiguities.

Where does the construction of hegemony occur? If it requires frequent remaking and alteration, where do these processes take place? Of the many social, cultural, and political sites in which hegemony is reproduced, we focus on one site that has received relatively little attention in this vein, the household. Having stated this, we must note two complications immediately. Because the household—or "home" more broadly constituted—that we examine is usually the employer's, the overall picture we produce is not symmetrical in its representation of sites. This is of course a reflection of the economic structures we are examining. And yet the picture is not quite so simple, nor so skewed. Although most of these essays examine employers' households, many of them also include other arenas. Several consider the impact of the practices and ideologies inculcated by domestic service on the homes of workers. Others examine arenas that are "public" but nonetheless part of, or directed to, the home. Thus the home as we understand it is not narrowly defined. It is rather a fairly problematic area, one that is often made more so by the fact of domestic service, and which often results in a kind of "borderzone" (Lavie and Swedenburg 1996). It is a symbolic and ideological sphere at least as much as a physical one.

This recognition leads to the second complication in our notion of "home" and "household." Our interest in expanding our notion of the home and its political significance dovetails with recent work on the relationship between the household and other social spheres and the role of the domestic in the construction of power relations (e.g., Bourdieu 1984; Comaroff and Comaroff 1992; Moran 1992). In viewing the realm of the domestic—which is related but not restricted to the physical boundaries of the home—as a site of the production of societal power structures, we concur with Moran's definition of the "domestic" as referring not only to a space but also to "the meaningful practices that take place there." Moreover, we recognize that "the domestic, even when ideologically separated from other aspects of human life, is inextricably bound to and mutually constitutive of broader political and economic structures" (Moran 1992, 98–99). The home is integrally and reciprocally related to the creation of social and political structures outside (and inside) of it. This point constitutes one of the major thrusts of this volume. Conversely, we also note the impact of larger social, economic, and political processes on the domestic realm, including in particular the impact of international labor flows on local relations. In taking on these issues, the analyses in this volume exemplify the ways in which a very particular examination of identities allows close scrutiny of the impact of macrolevel forces at the microlevel and vice versa.[4]

Finally, recognizing the role of language in constructing hegemony, we think it important to consider the terminology we use to refer to people and labor in this volume. In our analyses of domestic service, we have chosen to use local terms and explore the local meanings of positions and relationships. Although we are sensitive to the often negative connotations of terms such as *servant* and *domestic worker*, we find ourselves unable to follow the advice of Colen and Sanjek (1990a) to restrict ourselves to the terms *household worker* and *employer*. Despite their persuasive argument that terms such as *servant*, *domestic worker*, *master*, or *patron* carry connotations of stigma or its opposite, and that terms such as *household worker* and *employer* may more adequately describe "the situation of workers in homes" and avoid mystifying the employment relationship (Colen and Sanjek 1990a, 1, 4), we prefer the opposite strategy of relying primarily on specific indigenous terms (or their English-language glosses). While we agree that *household worker*, for example, may lack the negative connotations that many readers would associate with terms like *servant* or *domestic*, this term rarely provides an adequate reflection of the circumstances of the people whom it portrays. As Shah points out, for instance, replacing the Nepali term *malik* with *employer* would erase the connotations of "total loyalty and fidelity in an asymmetrical relationship" that also apply when a woman uses this same term to refer to her husband (Shah, in this volume). Moreover, while the more neutral term *employer* reminds us that kin-based euphemisms can obfuscate the labor basis of this relationship, such terminology may add its own unwarranted denotations by implying a formal wage relationship where there is none, as Shah also notes. Thus, recognizing that either choice carries conceptual and political gains and losses, we have by and large chosen the route of greater specificity, opting to convey the local nuances of power that such terms reveal.

IDENTITIES AND POLITICS

Identity politics are central to each of the cases in this volume. In recent years the phrase "identity politics" has been applied to such a wide range of phenomena that we find it necessary to clarify our use of the concept. Recent writers share a concept of identity as a dynamic, ongoing process that is "politically contested and historically unfinished" (Clifford 1988, 9). This understanding contrasts with older construals of identity (particularly ethnicity) as inert, primordial inheritances constructed in isolation. Newer, more dynamic conceptions stress the conceptual processes of contrast through which identities take form (Kipp 1993; Norton 1988).[5] As Kipp elaborates, "the contrasts mark not merely differences, but hierarchies of value and power" (1993, 5–6). That is, identity politics often embody claims of cultural or moral supremacy. Moreover, they frequently entail struggles over challenges to a group's power, or attempts on the part of subordinated groups to reaffirm a sense of self-worth. Appadurai also notes that although emerging perspectives on identity come close to "instrumental" conceptions of ethnicity (cf. Barth 1969; Southall 1976), they differ in their recognition that claims of group difference are not always motivated solely by the pursuit of economic, political, or emotional gains (Appadurai 1996, 14). As Appadurai suggests, "the mobilization of markers of group difference may itself be part of a contestation of values *about* difference, as distinct from the consequences of difference for wealth, security or power" (Appadurai 1996, 14). That is, the construction of group identities may not always be tied to instrumental or emotional objectives but may be, in some instances, simply about the valorization of "difference" itself. Our use of the expression identity politics emerges from these and other recent reformulations of concepts such as "ethnicity," "person," "class," and so forth by Nagata (1981), Clifford (1988), Linnekin (1983, 1990, 1992), White (1991), Keesing (1989), and others.

Central to our use of the expression identity politics are contrast sets, or "we-they" distinctions. In articulating their identities, domestic workers and employers draw on such contrast sets, situating themselves in counterdistinction to others. As the opening quote from a south Indian domestic worker explains, "This is the difference between rich and poor people. Only if we work can we have *kanji* [rice water]. But they could eat meat and rice [good food] even if they stay home for two to ten days. . . . If we don't have work, we couldn't even have *kanji* to drink. That's the difference between rich and poor people."[6] In short, such we-they distinctions are part and parcel of the construction of identities.

Rather than exploring forms of identity in isolation, the contributors to this volume are concerned with the ways in which *multiple* dimensions of identity interact and come into play in settings where competing hierarchies are manifest. In drawing on the concept of identity politics we use the term *politics* to refer to the social processes whereby people articulate, assert, challenge, suppress, realign, and co-opt varying hierarchies of identity. As our essays illustrate, these verbal and nonverbal processes are varied and entail drawing on an array of facets of identity. However, it is worth noting that although these essays attempt to convey negotiations of multiple dimensions of identity in the context of domestic service, certain types of identities tend to be foregrounded. Rank and/or class identities are a core concern of many of these papers (cf. Dickey, Tolen, Shah, Adams, Dumont, Weix). Likewise, ethnic and national identities are also highlighted in much of this work (cf. Constable, Gamburd, Robinson, Adams, Kidder). Surprisingly, gender receives less attention in these essays than the preceding identity categories. It is also noteworthy that familial identity, sexuality, and age, which are less standard in the contemporary literature on identity, appear often in this volume. These last two points merit further discussion.

Because of the frequently gendered nature of domestic service (for both employers and workers), it is interesting to note that gender identities are more often implicit than explicit in this work. Hansen's (1990) crucial point that the gendering of domestic service is not to be taken for granted is, however, strikingly demonstrated in several of these essays (see especially Gamburd, Constable, and Robinson). Nonetheless, we find it interesting that gender is not a central feature of analysis in more of these papers and speculate that this is due in part to many Western and other academics' continued assumptions about the gendering of domestic work. This phenomenon may also be due to what some have suggested is the greater salience of other dimensions of identity in the Asian context. As Sears observes for Indonesia, "gender may be one of the least contested sites of discontent in contemporary Indonesia, where poverty, ethnic tensions, persecution and disease coexist in global networks of late capitalism" (1996, 5).

Sexuality is also a facet of the identity politics at play in a number of these essays. In the Toraja households described by Adams, "helpers" often level rank hierarchies by slyly teasing their employers about sexual matters. Employers, in turn, strive to reaffirm these hierarchies by invoking imagery of lower-ranking people as (hetero-)sexually promiscuous. Likewise, Constable's essay portrays the intertwining of sexuality with identity politics and Philippine national imagery in Hong Kong. As she illustrates, the visibility of lesbian Filipina domestic workers has prompted media debates about what constitutes the "proper" display of sexuality and sexual orientation for Filipina women representing their country abroad. As some have recently observed (e.g., Murray 1997), sexuality in general, and same-sex sexuality in particular, have been underrepresented in the anthropological literature—as in, we would argue, the domestic service literature.

Age and generational identities are also touched on in several of these papers. This is not surprising given that, throughout South and Southeast Asia, age-status is an essential determinant of hierarchy and plays an important role in structuring interactions between people. In fact, pronouns in many Malay-based languages tend to convey relative age rather than gender. Moreover, social relations tend to be structured in terms of a younger/older axis. For instance, in Indonesia, ideally younger siblings are expected to defer to older siblings, and relations between wives and husbands, and servants and employers, are often spoken of in terms of this age-based model. In recent years, aged-based groupings have fallen out of favor as a category of anthropological focus in the identity literature. Likewise, family-based identity is often overshadowed by the popularity of the categories of race, ethnicity, gender, and class. The cases presented by Adams, Dumont, Shah, and Weix prompt us to encourage attention to these neglected "categories." In short, we find value in problematizing the "classic" dimensions of identity that have been celebrated to the exclusion of other categories of identity. As the cases presented in this volume suggest, it is time to expand the range of identities that we recognize as under negotiation.

NEGOTIATIONS OF IDENTITIES:
OVERVIEW OF THE VOLUME

All of the essays in this volume illustrate the ways that identities are constructed through everyday negotiations. The forms of these interactions
vary significantly according to local idioms of hierarchy and exchange. In
the remainder of this introduction, we highlight the identity negotiations
discussed in the essays that follow.

Sara Dickey's opening essay examines the images that workers and
employers in Madurai (a city in southern India) produce of themselves and
one another in narratives about domestic service. The simultaneous focus
on narratives as tools for creating coherence and meaning out of lives, and
as ideological forms, allows Dickey to examine the construction of identity
as a social process. Each speaker sees her own class as morally upstanding
and the other as morally reprehensible. In particular, each cites the other's
inability to see people in their full humanity, making material demands at
the expense of human relations. The narratives reveal strikingly reciprocal
moral images. Servants' and employers' accounts diverge, however, in their
definitions of "class" and the links they portray between social class and
personal character. As Dickey argues in her conclusion, "Domestic workers'
and employers' narratives reveal the terms in which their speakers conceptualize, enjoin, and negotiate an urban Indian identity politics of class."

In her analysis of class in the railway colony of the nearby city of
Madras, Rachel Tolen provides a complementary focus on the ways that
class-specific knowledge and practices are transferred from employers to
workers, and on the contestation that accompanies such transmission. Thus
she examines not only the construction of difference, but also the perme-
ability of the boundaries created in this construction. Focusing on the transmission of practices such as hospitality, manners, and language between the
employer's "bungalow" and the servant's "outhouse," she reveals the contested nature of learning. Domestic workers strive to take on the practices of
their employers, but their limited resources restrict them to piecemeal
adoptions. Employers, for their part, argue that servants will never be able to
change their class because they do not possess the "understanding" required
for wielding these practices properly. Tolen suggests that this emphasis on
understanding, communicated by employers' mockery of servants' attempts
to speak English or to adopt genteel manners, constructs a deep difference
that by implication can never be erased. But as employers work to reify the
boundaries that mark difference, servants strive to narrow the latitude of
that difference. Overall, Tolen concludes, "the railway colony represents a

distinctive context in which . . . domestic service has come to operate as a medium of class identity negotiation *and* class identity transformation."

Saubhagya Shah focuses on child and youth servants and their masters in Nepal, to examine the construction of class and urban-rural identities. The two lenses he uses are schooling and fictive kinship. Education can help servants to raise their socioeconomic status in the future, but it also draws stark class lines in Nepal, since servants attend free government schools while employers' children largely attend private schools. The servants are teased about their work at school, and when they return home at the end of the day, they (unlike the other children of the household) must focus on household chores rather than homework. Thus there are tensions between their identities as students and as servants. Schooling also leads to tensions between rural and urban or lower- and middle-class values (e.g., differences in attitudes toward marriage, patterns of consumption, and work aspirations), splitting servants from their natal households. The practice of "kinship" also influences servants' identities. In rural households, both workers and employers use kinship terminology to refer to one another. In the city, however, there is a more "ephemeral domestic-familial rhetoric," via which the worker "will often be reminded that he or she is a 'member of the family' without specifying the kinship position, or a 'person of the home,' in order to inculcate a sense of loyalty and diligence." In both rural and urban cases, however, Shah argues that the framework of kinship, however shallow, provides a sense of identity and meaning for young servants cut off from their own families. Both schooling and kinship offer ambiguities that workers and employers alike can manipulate in their self-representations. Servants may claim service as their fate, or explain it as a means to survival, or deny their servitude altogether, instead portraying themselves as working students or family helpers. Shah points out that "the same person may construct different identities at different times and to different audiences." But all these representations are reactions to the euphemizing power enjoyed by masters, whose ability to manipulate the definition of relationships and situations (such as calling a worker a "family member" in one context and a "servant" in another) gives them leverage over servants, and the capacity to grant or deny legitimacy to interpretations of ambiguity. But servants also cooperate in these constructions, since the fiction of family is in their interest, "however fragile and susceptible to arbitrary redefinition the negotiated identity may be."

Jean-Paul Dumont provides a similar focus on language in the Philippines. Examining the uses of (and identities wrought by) the terms *domestic worker*, *helper*, and *nursemaid*, he explores the situation of Visayan workers whose lives are colored by their liminal identities in and ambiguous associations with the families of their employers. Dumont is concerned with the ways in which movement into and out of these three categories of employee identity often fits into the overall life trajectory of rural, impoverished Visayan women. Initially, these young women find positions with urban bourgeois families as helpers, a status that they generally retain until marriage. Long-term bonding with these urban families occurs for some of these women when their identities are transformed from helpers into nursemaids, an identity that entails both increased respect and increased intimacy. Furthermore, as nursemaids, Dumont suggests, these women are anticipating their own future identities as mothers. His discussion underscores the often transitory nature of each of these identities, as part of a larger set of shifting identities in the life course (from daughter, to helper, to nursemaid, to mother).

G. G. Weix also addresses the betwixt-and-between identities of Javanese domestics, who are incorporated into the families of their employers through idioms of adoption and simultaneously estranged by distinctions of social rank. Examining domestic work from the perspective of both employers and employees, Weix's essay offers a sensitive exploration of the paradoxes and tensions embodied in the rhetoric of fictive kinship. She observes that servants working in elite Javanese homes express the paradox of their social identities in Javanese cultural terms which underscore the contrast between "external and internal" experience. Moreover, Weix points out that employers' gifts to servants traverse the boundaries between kin and nonkin, creating the possibility of "feeling like kin" while underscoring servants' moral obligations to their employers. In short, both emotional ties and enduring social differences between servants and employers are marked by gifts. On Java, then, gifts shape the emotional texture of servitude, implying both engagement with and estrangement from a familial order and paternal relations.

The essay by Kathleen Adams also discusses the use of kinship rhetoric to bind servants while simultaneously marking hierarchies within the home. As on Java, in the Toraja highlands of Sulawesi (Indonesia), metaphors of kinship pervade servant-employer relations. Spotlighting the understudied role of humor in negotiating unequal household relations, Adams observes that metaphors of kinship frequently emerge in jesting encounters between Toraja employers and servants. In such mirthful interactions, when household workers strive to erase the hierarchies and social distance between themselves and their employers by playfully stressing their commonalities as human beings (or women, or Torajas), elite employers frequently counter with jests that rely on kinship rhetoric and underscore their servants' lower-ranking positions as metaphoric "grandchildren." As Adams illustrates, humorous interactions between employers and helpers have a political dimension, as they embody the negotiation of multiple facets of identity as well as realignments of identities.

Michele Gamburd analyzes the shifts in motherhood and gendered divisions of labor that occur when Sri Lankan women migrate to the Middle East. Noting that in Sri Lanka, female migration highlighted "conceptual dissonances in the taken-for-granted categories of 'work' and 'home,' challenging the 'naturalness' of mothering and the power structures that surrounded it," Gamburd explores the fragmentations of motherhood and the negotiations of gender roles that they have generated. Abroad, she finds that the migrant domestic worker holds a precarious position as a marginal outsider and intimate insider; the housemaid mothers the children but is not their father's sexual partner. Back at home the woman, who has migrated to a paid job in order to provide material support for her children and husband, becomes vulnerable to accusations of "abandoning" them, and to feelings of failure if she returns to find that her family members have been running wild and her remittances have been spent unwisely. Gamburd sets these new experiences in the context of older patterns of family association, focusing on how new behaviors both challenge and reinforce accepted thinking about motherhood, gender hierarchies, personal identity, and women's work. Her detailed analysis demonstrates that while migration often forces women to question standard gender roles, the men in their families—as well as nonmigrant women—are not yet inclined to support serious changes. Similarly, she also finds that migration rarely has the more consciously intended effect of increasing the family's wealth and class status in Sri Lanka.

Louise Kidder addresses the flip side of these transnational negotiations of identity in her examination of relationships between U.S./British expatriate employers and Indian servants in Bangalore, India. In her essay, Kidder notes a variety of ways in which the hierarchy of skills, knowledge, and dependence is anything but straightforward and linear. Expatriates have money, while servants possess skills and knowledge of daily living; expatriates are dependent for food, water, and hygiene, while servants are dependent for livelihood; expatriates are the bosses but are helpless in the kitchen or market, while servants are subordinate but are competent in these places. The tensions expatriates feel because of their dependence on servants to help them live in India lead to a variety of themes in expatriate conversations, which reveal several of the ironies of the situation. For example, employers often portray servants as children because of their incompetent responses to requests and commands, but Kidder argues that it is the employers who are childlike in their dependence on servants. Similarly, "communication problems" are inherent in situations in which someone else is asked to do the work for which the employer is responsible. Employers may wish they could "do it themselves," but they are largely unable to. All of this suggests that power is neither held nor deployed unilaterally.

The construction and articulation of ethnicity and nationality are additional dimensions of identity explored by many of the papers in this collection. Two essays address constructions of national identity in the context of transnational labor migration. Nicole Constable is concerned with the ways in which Hong Kong Filipino domestic workers originating from diverse regions in the Philippines come to express themselves as Filipino or Filipina. As Constable observes, these domestic workers articulate, embrace, and reject a variety of images of their national identity, depending on particular audiences and objectives. Moreover, through examining domestic worker dolls, articles published in newspapers oriented to overseas Filipino domestic workers, and ceremonies honoring exceptional employers and workers, Constable illustrates how the assorted images of Filipino national identity are variably entwined with gender and class identity. For example, her discussion of an award ceremony honoring Filipino domestic workers in Hong Kong addresses the ways in which these workers both celebrate and contest idealized images of Filipino womanhood. While many of the awardees donned glamorous, ultrafeminine attire, the lesbian "T-birds" in attendance clearly challenged the "official" image of Filipino femininity (and thus morality) being promoted for Hong Kong consumption.

Kathryn Robinson also examines the ways in which gender, along with family and religion, is called upon in constructing national identities and transnational relations. Noting that the Indonesian government relies on the "family principle" as an important cornerstone of its national identity, Robinson illustrates how, in public discussions concerning Javanese housemaids in the Middle East, this principle is entwined with other discourses concerning Muslim identity and femininity. For instance, central to Robinson's analysis of news reports concerning the "problem" of Indonesian housemaids in the Middle East are debates about whether overseas migration is an acceptable activity for Indonesian Muslim women. Robinson's essay illustrates how these various dimensions of identity (religion, gender, family, nationality) are drawn upon in different ways by different parties in highly publicized debates regarding the Indonesian government's obligations to prevent the mistreatment of Indonesian housemaids in the Middle

East. Robinson's essay also spotlights an underexplored topic in the domestic work literature: the sexual harassment and abuse of housemaids. As she notes, due to reports of abuse, public support for the continued export of Indonesian housemaids to the Middle East began to erode and a new move to send these women to work in Malaysia emerged. Interestingly, the media rhetoric celebrating this new destination as a more appropriate "home" for Javanese housemaids highlighted not only the Muslim orientations shared by Indonesia and Malaysia but also the two countries' shared Malay identities.

In the final essay of this volume, Karen Tranberg Hansen, a pioneer in domestic service research, discusses these South and Southeast Asian cases in the larger global and transhistorical context and raises questions for future studies of domestic service. Hansen emphasizes how domestic service inequalities are "deeply embedded in the overall processes of state formation and nationalism." Moreover, focusing in particular on hegemony, she underscores the ambiguous, fragile nature of hegemonies. As she notes, it is the "very lack of consensus, the possibility of opposition, and the tolerance of alternative meanings that may make the concept of hegemony of some use in relationship to domestic service." Hansen's apt observations about the ambiguity and fragility of hegemony prompt further reflection. For not only is hegemony fragile, but as some have recently begun to suggest (cf. Sears 1996), so is identity, a point implicit in many of the essays offered here.

What lessons do these essays offer us? One of the opportunities they present is the chance to compare identity construction in different domestic service settings. To our minds, the most interesting contrasts are to be drawn not along national and cultural lines, but among different structural situations. This is reflected in the organization of our essays. The first six studies, beginning with Sara Dickey's essay, focus on domestic workers and employers within their own nations. While domestic service in these examples may entail crossing regional or ethnic boundaries, it does not require negotiating national identities in the place of employment (except vis-à-vis the foreign researcher). Often, in fact, workers and employers are members of what many scholars would recognize as the same "culture," and yet they must find a way to create difference and otherness in order to justify workplace hierarchies. Of course, this process feels "natural" to most of those involved, even if the tenets of hierarchy are questioned by participants, but the extent of the energy that goes into constructing and maintaining otherness raises interesting questions about diversity and difference within cultures and hegemonies.

The remaining four studies examine situations in which employers and employees are of different nationalities. In three of these cases, workers have migrated; in the fourth, employers have done so. Here, differences are even more striking to participants, thanks to the division of nationality, which often coincides with religious, racial, and language distinctions as well. Questions about differences may be either more contested (since there is rarely a shared knowledge of the cultural assumptions generating them, at least at the outset), or less so (since difference is assumed a priori), but they are certainly more far-flung, because transnational domestic labor results in concerns about servants' identities both at home and abroad. In all three chapters about migrant domestic workers, those workers are women, and questions about their status as women are raised at home, in the "host" country, or both. In all these settings, impassioned discussions take place about what happens when women go to work in foreign households, away from the "protection" of their own cultures and families; similar concerns may be raised by employing households. Sometimes, interestingly, such questions lead to an emphasis on *similarities* across nations (as when Indonesian women are encouraged to work in Muslim countries). (Note that if men were migrating to do domestic labor, the questions might be less urgent, and in any case they would surely be different.) Finally, at least in the cases represented here, domestic service involving transnational migration is also more likely to include what Kidder refers to as "nonlinear hierarchies," since migrants' drive to earn capital can result on the one hand in situations in which servants have higher educations or greater prestige in their native hierarchies than do their overseas employers, or in which migrant employers are highly dependent on the cultural expertise of their servants.

As these observations suggest, the stories of domestic service presented here are often diverse in their particulars. Taken together, however, they also offer some broader substantive and methodological observations, and we invite our readers to think about the complex process of the construction of identities as they are created in response to others' identity claims. As we have argued throughout this introduction, identities are constantly renegotiated in domestic service interactions and accounts. Micropolitical examinations of relations between employers and employees allow us to see how different dimensions of identity are comingled and intertwined, so much so that it is often challenging to speak of these separately. Moreover, these essays enable us to see how the "categories" of identity celebrated in the anthropological literature tend to obscure alternative facets of identity at play in these situations (including sexuality, age, and family). Perhaps most significantly of all, they remind us that identity in general and the specific identities that cultures prescribe—be they class, ethnicity, gender, sexuality, or any other—are processes rather than static categories. Identity is a "process" rather than a state in the sense that it changes over time throughout an individual's life course; it involves multiple shifting pieces and often divergent faces to be presented to different interlocutors in different situations; and, once again, it involves the shared work of negotiations among people who are at once audiences and actors of identity. Finally, these negotiations simultaneously address not only the varieties of identity we have noted, but also who "servants" and "employers" are. This latter point is perhaps so obvious as to be overlooked, but it remains a crucial issue that this volume's essays are especially well situated to address. Close attention to domestic service interactions allows us to examine what the rights, obligations, and "place" of each participant is, and the intricate ways in which each of these is determined.

In this collection, the domestic comes fully to the fore. This focus adds to our systemic understanding of societies by allowing examination of the ways in which domestic interactions have broader consequences—on the community, ethnic group, class structure, or nation. Methodologically, in making homes (including our fieldwork homes) the object of study and observing our own complicity in the hierarchies of the home, this work helps further dismantle the classic artificial divides between the "private" dimensions of fieldwork and the more public object of research, as well as the long-embedded dichotomy between researcher and subject. In conclusion, we hope that the accounts presented here will humanize both workers and their employers.

Acknowledgments

Copious thanks are due to Susan Whitlock, Susan Bell and Judith Wittner for reading, commenting on, and clarifying multiple earlier versions of this chapter. Thanks also to Nancy Riley and Karen Tranberg Hansen for helpful discussions, as well as to Selvan Maria Augustine, Tamara Smith and Caryn Aviv for their assistance in formatting the manuscript.

Notes

1. In addition to numerous works cited elsewhere in this introduction, examples include Bujra 1992; Coser 1973; Dill 1988; Fairchilds 1984; Gaitskell et al. 1984; Graham 1988; Gregson and Lowe 1994; Jelin 1977; Katzman 1978; Maza 1983; Palmer 1989; Smith 1978; and Taussig and Rubbo 1983. For extensive reviews of domestic service literature, see Sanjek and Colen 1990 and Smith 1989.

2. Although a number of historical accounts directly address the topic of Asian servants (e.g., Gaw 1988; Gin 1992; Leupp 1992; Stoler 1995, 1996; Taylor 1983; Watson 1991), studies of contemporary domestic service in South and Southeast Asia remain limited.

3. Any division is inevitably at least partly artificially bounded. Indeed, our original intent in organizing this volume was to focus on "Asia" as a whole, which has its own academic history as a "region." As we pursued the project, however, we encountered great difficulty in locating contributors for essays addressing domestic service in a variety of Asian nations, including Japan, Korea, China, and even Thailand. In part this dearth of research appears due to structural and cultural factors, such as in Japan, where reluctance to have strangers in the home, and entrenched ideas about wives' traditional duties, make domestic service rare; or China, where until recently, state control over income has prevented the income disparities and other sources of class differentiation that are generally correlated with domestic service. In other cases, such as Thailand, where domestic service is certainly common, we speculate that research efforts have been directed elsewhere for a variety of interesting reasons related to local political economies and international academic currents.

4. For an excellent model of the ways in which microlevel analysis of domestic service can reveal societal patterns, see M. Jocelyn Armstrong's work (1990, 1996).

5. Historically, the ethnic identity literature was framed in terms of a debate between primordialists, who conceived of ethnicity as based on the irreducible "givens" of birth (cf. Geertz 1963; van den Berghe 1978) and the situationalists (or constructionists) who argued that ethnicity is invented in the context of competition over material and abstract resources (cf. Barth 1969). A somewhat parallel debate developed in the gender literature between essentialist approaches, which emphasized inherent biological sources of gender difference, and social constructionist approaches, which argued that gender differences and inequality are primarily social and cultural constructs (for discussions of these perspectives, see Fausto-Sterling 1985; Kessler and McKenna 1978; Lorber 1994).

6. As this quote suggests, individual and collective identities often involve stories that embody and valorize distinctive qualities, customs, affinities and histories. Such narratives of identity are continually retold and reshaped as individuals make cultural meaning out of changing social and political situations (White 1991). Dickey, who takes these narratives as her primary focus, argues that narratives create coherence and give meaning to disparate life experiences, help shape an integrated sense of self, communicate moral stances, and reveal the social structures from which they derive. For examples of other work on narrative, identity, and life experience, representing a variety of schools of narrative analysis, see Atkinson 1997; Bell 1988, forthcoming; Frank 1995; Gergen and Gergen 1997; Kleinman 1988; Personal Narratives Group 1989; and Somers and Gibson 1994.

REFERENCES

Abu-Lughod, Lila

1990   The Romance of Resistance: Tracing Transformations of Power through Bedouin Women. *American Ethnologist* 17 (1): 41–55.

Alonso, Ana Maria

1994   The Politics of Space, Time and Substance: State Formation, Nationalism, and Ethnicity. *Annual Review of Anthropology* 23:379–405.

Appadurai, Arjun

1991   Global Ethnoscapes: Notes and Queries for a Transnational Anthropology. In Richard G. Fox, ed., *Recapturing Anthropology: Working in the Present*. Santa Fe, NM: School of American Research Press.

1996   *Modernity at Large: Cultural Dimensions of Globalization*. Minneapolis: University of Minnesota Press.

Armstrong, M. Jocelyn

1990   Female Household Workers in Industrializing Malaysia. In Roger Sanjek and Shellee Colen, eds., *At Work in Homes: Household Workers in World Perspective*, 146–63. American Ethnological Society Monograph Series, No. 3. Washington, DC: American Anthropological Association.

1996   Twenty Years of Domestic Service: A Malaysian Chinese Woman in Change. *Southeast Asian Journal of Social Science* 24 (1): 64–82.

Atkinson, Paul

1997   Narrative Turn or Blind Alley? *Qualitative Health Research* 7 (3): 325–44.

Barth, Fredrik

1969   Introduction. In Fredrik Barth, ed., *Ethnic Groups and Boundaries*. Boston: Little, Brown.

Bell, Susan E.

1988   Becoming a Political Woman: The Reconstruction and Interpretation of Experience Through Stories. In Alexandra Dundas Todd and Sue Fisher, eds., *Gender and Discourse: The Power of Talk*, 97–123. Norwood, NJ: Ablex.

Forthcoming   Experiencing Illness In/And Narrative. In Chloe Bird, Peter Conrad, Allen Fremont, and Sol Levine, eds., *Handbook of Medical Sociology* (5th ed.). Englewood Cliffs, NJ: Prentice-Hall.

Bourdieu, Pierre

1984   *Distinction*. Trans. Richard Nice. Cambridge: Harvard University Press.

Brandewie, Ernest
1973   Maids in Cebuano Society. *Philippine Quarterly of Culture and Society* 1:209–19.

Brown, Michael F.
1996   On Resisting Resistance. *American Anthropologist* 98 (4): 729–34.

Bujra, Janet M.
1992   Men at Work in the Tanzanian Home: How Did They Ever Learn? In Karen
        Tranberg Hansen, ed., *African Encounters with Domesticity*, 242–65. New
        Brunswick, NJ: Rutgers University Press.

Bunster, Ximena, and Elsa M. Chaney
1985   *Sellers and Servants: Working Women in Lima, Peru*. New York: Praeger.

Butler, Judith
1995   Collected and Fractured: Response to *Identities*. In Kwame Anthony Appiah
        and Henry Louis Gates, eds., *Identities*. Chicago: University of Chicago Press.

Chaney, Elsa M., and Mary García Castro, eds.
1989   *Muchachas No More: Household Workers in Latin America and the Caribbean*.
        Philadelphia: Temple University Press.

Clifford, James
1988   *The Predicament of Culture: Twentieth Century Ethnography, Literature and Art*.
        Cambridge: Harvard University Press.

Cock, Jacklyn
1980   *Maids and Madams: A Study in the Politics of Exploitation*. Johannesburg:
        Ravan Press.

Colen, Shellee
1990   "Housekeeping" for the Green Card: West Indian Household Workers, the
        State, and Stratified Reproduction in New York. In Roger Sanjek and Shellee
        Colen, eds., *At Work in Homes: Household Workers in World Perspective*, 89–118.
        American Ethnological Society Monograph Series, No. 3. Washington, DC:
        American Anthropological Association.

Colen, Shellee, and Roger Sanjek
1990a   At Work in Homes I: Orientations. In Roger Sanjek and Shellee Colen,
        eds., *At Work in Homes: Household Workers in World Perspective*, 1–13. Ameri-
        can Ethnological Society Monograph Series, No. 3. Washington, DC: Ameri-
        can Anthropological Association.
1990b   At Work in Homes II: Directions. In Roger Sanjek and Shellee Colen, eds.,
        At Work in Homes: Household Workers in World Perspective, 176–88. American

Ethnological Society Monograph Series, No. 3. Washington, DC: American Anthropological Association.

Comaroff, Jean, and John L. Comaroff
1992   Home-Made Hegemony. In KarenTranberg Hansen, ed., *African Encounters with Domesticity*, 37–74. New Brunswick, NJ: Rutgers University Press.

Constable, Nicole
1997   *Maid to Order in Hong Kong: Stories of Filipina Workers*. Ithaca: Cornell University Press.

Cooke, M. T.
1990   Household Workers in Nyishang, Nepal. In Roger Sanjek and Shellee Colen, eds., *At Work in Homes: Household Workers in World Perspective*, 63–73. American Ethnological Society Monograph Series, No. 3. Washington, DC: American Anthropological Association.

Coser, Lewis
1973   Servants: The Obsolescence of an Occupational Role. *Social Forces* 52:31–40.

Dias, Malsiri, and Nedra Weerakoon-Gunawardene
1991   Female Labour Migration to Singapore and Hong Kong: A Profile of the Sri Lankan Housemaids. Colombo, Sri Lanka: Centre for Women's Research.

Dickey, Sara
Forthcoming   Permeable Homes: Domestic Service, Household Space, and the Vulnerability of Class Boundaries in Urban India. *American Ethnologist*.

Dill, Bonnie Thornton
1988   "Making Your Job Good Yourself": Domestic Service and the Construction of Personal Dignity. In Ann Bookman and Sandra Morgen, eds., *Women and the Politics of Empowerment*, 33–52. Philadelphia: Temple University Press.

Dumont, Jean-Paul
1994   Matrons, Maids, and Mistresses: Philippine Domestic Encounters. *Philippine Quarterly of Culture and Society* 22:174–91.

Fairchilds, Cissie
1984   *Domestic Enemies: Servants and Their Masters in Old Regime France*. Baltimore: Johns Hopkins University Press.

Fausto-Sterling, Anne
1985   *Myths of Gender: Biological Theories about Women and Men*. New York: Basic Books.

Flueckiger, Joyce B., and Laurie J. Sears

1991   *Boundaries of the Text: Epic Performances in South and Southeast Asia*. Michigan Papers on South and Southeast Asia, No. 35. Ann Arbor: Center for South and Southeast Asian Studies.

Frank, Arthur W.

1995   *The Wounded Storyteller: Body, Illness, and Ethics*. Chicago: University of Chicago Press.

Gaitskell, Deborah, Judy Kimble, Moira Maconachie, and Elaine Unterhalter

1984   Class, Race and Gender: Domestic Workers in South Africa. *Review of African Political Economy* 27/28:86–108.

Gaw, Kenneth

1988   *Superior Servants: The Legendary Cantonese Amahs of the Far East*. Oxford: Oxford University Press.

Geertz, Clifford

1963   The Integrative Revolution: Primordial Sentiments and Civil Politics in New States. In Clifford Geertz, ed., *Old Societies and New States: The Quest for Modernity in Asia and Africa*, 105–57. New York: Free Press.

Gergen, Kenneth J., and Mary M. Gergen

1997 [1983]   Narratives of the Self. In Lewis P. Hinchman and Sandra K. Hinchman, eds., *Memory, Identity, Community*, 161–84. Albany: State University of New York Press.

Gill, Lesley

1994   *Precarious Dependencies: Gender, Class, and Domestic Service in Bolivia*. New York: Columbia University Press.

Gin, Ooi Keat

1992   Domestic Servants Par Excellence: The Black and White Amahs of Malaya and Singapore with Special Reference to Penang. *Journal of the Malaysian Branch of the Royal Asiatic Society* 65 (2): 69–84.

Glenn, Evelyn Nakano

1986   *Issei, Nisei, War Bride: Three Generations of Japanese American Women in Domestic Service*. Philadelphia: Temple University Press.

Graham, Susan Lauderdale

1988   *House and Street: The Domestic World of Servants and Masters in Nineteenth-Century Rio de Janeiro*. Cambridge: Cambridge University Press.

Gramsci, Antonio

1957   *Selections from the Prison Notebooks of Antonio Gramsci*. Quinton Hoare and Geoffrey Nowell Smith, eds. New York: International Publishers.

Gregson, Nicky, and Michelle Lowe

1994 *Servicing the Middle Classes: Class, Gender and Waged Domestic Labour in Contemporary Britain*. London: Routledge.

Hall, Kenneth R., and John K. Whitmore

1976 *Explorations in Early Southeast Asian History: The Origins of Southeast Asian Statecraft*. Michigan Papers on South and Southeast Asia, No. 11. Ann Arbor: Center for South and Southeast Asian Studies.

Hansen, Karen Tranberg

1989 *Distant Companions: Servants and Employers in Zambia, 1900–1985*. Ithaca: Cornell University Press.

1990 Domestic Trials: Power and Autonomy in Domestic Service in Zambia. *American Ethnologist* 17 (2): 360–75.

Jelin, Elizabeth

1977 Migration and Labor Force Participation of Latin American Women: The Domestic Servants in the Cities. *Signs* 3:129–41.

Katzman, David

1978 *Seven Days a Week: Women and Domestic Service in Industrializing America*. New York: Oxford University Press.

Keesing, Roger

1989 Creating the Past: Custom and Identity in the Pacific. *The Contemporary Pacific* 1/2:19–42.

Kessler, Suzanne, and Wendy McKenna

1978 *Gender: An Ethnomethodological Approach*. New York: John Wiley.

Kleinman, Arthur

1988 *The Illness Narratives: Suffering, Healing and the Human Condition*. New York: Basic Books.

Kipp, Rita

1993 *Dissociated Identities: Ethnicity, Religion, and Class in an Indonesian Society*. Ann Arbor: University of Michigan Press.

Lavie, Smadar, and Ted Swedenburg

1996 Introduction: Displacement, Diaspora, and Geographies of Identity. In Smadar Lavie and Ted Swedenburg, eds., *Displacement, Diaspora, and Geographies of Identity*, 1–25. Durham: Duke University Press.

Leupp, Gary P.

1992 *Servants, Shorthands, and Laborers in the Cities of Tokugawa Japan*. Princeton: Princeton University Press.

Linnekin, Jocelyn

1983   Defining Tradition: Variations on the Hawaiian Identity. *American Ethnologist* 10:241–52.

1990   The Politics of Culture in the Pacific. In Jocelyn Linnekin and Lin Poyer, eds., *Cultural Identity and Ethnicity in the Pacific*, 149–73. Honolulu: University of Hawaii Press.

1992   On the Theory and Politics of Cultural Construction in the Pacific. *Oceania* 62:249–63.

Lorber, Judith

1994   *Paradoxes of Gender*. New Haven: Yale University Press.

Margold, Jane A.

1995   Narratives of Masculinity and Transnational Migration: Filipino Workers in the Middle East. In Aihwa Ong and Michael G. Peletz, eds., *Bewitching Women, Pious Men: Gender and Body Politics in Southeast Asia*, 274–98. Berkeley: University of California Press.

Maza, Sarah

1983   *The Uses of Loyalty: Domestic Service in Eighteenth Century France*. Princeton: Princeton University Press.

Moran, Mary H.

1992   Civilized Servants: Child Fosterage and Training for Status among the Glebo of Liberia. In Karen Tranberg Hansen, ed., *African Encounters with Domesticity*, 98–115. New Brunswick, NJ: Rutgers University Press.

Murray, Stephen O.

1997   Explaining Away Same-Sex Sexualities When They Obtrude on Anthropologists' Notice at All. *Anthropology Today* 13 (3): 2–5.

Nagata, Judith

1981   In Defense of Ethnic Boundaries: The Changing Myths and Charters of Malay Identity. In Charles F. Keyes, ed., *Ethnic Change*, 81–116. Seattle: University of Washington Press.

Narayan, Kirin

1989   *Storytellers, Saints, and Scoundrels: Folk Narrative in Hindu Religious Teaching*. Philadelphia: University of Pennsylvania Press.

Norton, Anne

1988   *Reflections on Political Identity*. Baltimore: Johns Hopkins University Press.

Ortner, Sherry

1995   Resistance and the Problem of Ethnographic Refusal. *Comparative Studies in Society and History* 37 (1): 173–93.

Palmer, Phyllis

1989   *Domesticity and Dirt: Housewives and Domestic Servants in the United States, 1920–1945.* Philadelphia: Temple University Press.

Personal Narratives Group, eds.

1989   *Interpreting Women's Lives: Feminist Theory and Personal Narratives.* Bloomington: Indiana University Press.

Robinson, Kathryn

1991   Housemaids: The Effects of Gender and Culture on the Internal and International Migration of Indonesian Women. In Gill Bottomley, Marie De Lepervanche, and Jeannie Martin, eds., *Intersexions*, 33–51. Sydney: Allen and Unwin.

Rollins, Judith

1985   *Between Women: Domestics and Their Employers.* Philadelphia: Temple University Press.

1990   Ideology and Servitude. In Roger Sanjek and Shellee Colen, eds., *At Work in Homes: Household Workers in World Perspective*, 74–88. American Ethnological Society Monograph Series, No. 3. Washington, DC: American Anthropological Association.

Romero, Mary

1992   *Maid in the U.S.A.* New York: Routledge.

Roseberry, William

1994   Hegemony and the Language of Contention. In Gilbert M. Joseph and Daniel Nugent, eds., *Everyday Forms of State Formation: Revolution and the Negotiation of Rule in Modern Mexico*, 355–66. Durham: Duke University Press.

Rueda, Oly

1992   Some Food for Thought. *Tinig Filipino*, April, p. 16.

Sanjek, Roger, and Shellee Colen, eds.

1990   *At Work in Homes: Household Workers in World Perspective.* American Ethnological Society Monograph Series, No. 3. Washington, DC: American Anthropological Association.

Sears, Laurie J., ed.

1996   *Fantasizing the Feminine in Indonesia.* Durham: Duke University Press.

Smith, Margo L.

1978   The Female Domestic Servant and Social Change: Lima, Peru. In Richard
        Schaedel, ed., *Urbanization in the Americas from the Beginnings to the Present*,
        569–85. The Hague: Mouton.

1989   Domestic Service in Cross-Cultural Perspective: A Computerized Data Base.
        In Elsa M. Chaney and Mary García Castro, eds., *Muchachas No More: Domes-
        tic Workers in Latin America and the Caribbean*, 451–80. Philadelphia: Temple
        University Press.

Somers, Margaret R., and Gloria D. Gibson

1994   Reclaiming the Epistemological "Other": Narrative and the Social Constitu-
        tion of Identity. In Craig Calhoun, ed., *Social Theory and the Politics of Identity*,
        37–99. Cambridge: Blackwell.

Southall, Aidan

1976   Nuer and Dinka Are People: Ecology, Ethnicity and Logical Possibility. *Man*
        11 (4): 463–91.

Stoler, Ann Laura

1985   *Capitalism and Confrontation in Sumatra's Plantation Belt, 1870–1979*. New
        Haven: Yale University Press.

1995   *Race and the Education of Desire: Foucault's History of Sexuality and the Colonial
        Order of Things*. Durham: Duke University Press.

1996   A Sentimental Education: Native Servants and the Cultivation of European
        Children in the Netherlands Indies. In Laurie J. Sears, ed., *Fantasizing the Fem-
        inine in Indonesia*, 71–91. Durham: Duke University Press.

Taussig, Michael, and Anna Rubbo

1983   Up Off Their Knees: Servanthood in Southwest Colombia. *Latin American
        Perspectives* 10 (4): 2–23.

Taylor, Jean Gelman

1983   *The Social World of Batavia: European and Eurasian in Dutch Asia*. Madison:
        University of Wisconsin Press.

Tellis-Nayak, V.

1983   Power and Solidarity: Clientage in Domestic Service. *Current Anthropology*
        24:67–79.

Tilly, Louise

1978   Introduction and Overview. In Louise Tilly, Susan Berkowitz Luton, and
        Andrea Sankar, eds., *Female Servants and Economic Development*, 1–4. Michigan
        Occasional Paper. No. 1. Fall. Ann Arbor: University of Michigan.

Tucker, Susan

1988   *Telling Memories among Southern Workers: Domestic Workers and Their Employers in the Segregated South*. New York: Schocken Books.

Van den Berghe, Pierre

1978   Race and Ethnicity: A Sociobiological Perspective. *Ethnic and Racial Studies* 1:401–11.

Watson, James, ed.

1980   *Asian and African Systems of Slavery*. Berkeley: University of California Press.

Watson, Rubie S.

1991   Wives, Concubines and Maids: Servitude and Kinship in the Hong Kong Region, 1900–1940. In Rubie S. Watson and Patricia Buckley Ebrey, eds., *Marriage and Inequality in Chinese Society*, 231–55. Berkeley: University of California Press.

White, Geoffrey

1991   *Identity Through History: Living Stories in a Solomon Island Society*. Cambridge: Cambridge University Press.

Williams, Raymond

1977   *Marxism and Literature*. Oxford: Oxford University Press.

MUTUAL EXCLUSIONS
Domestic Workers and Employers on Labor, Class, and Character in South India

[Employers] can survive only by beating the stomachs of those who don't have. *(Vasanthi, a domestic worker in several employers' homes)*

And without our knowledge we start giving [servants] more and more of freedom and finally, suddenly, we get a shock when we realize that we've been thoroughly exploited. *(Padma, an employer of several domestic workers)*

Class identities in urban south India are frequently oppositional and always morally charged. When people of different classes work together, these identities are shaped both by the negotiations of daily interactions and by the narrative accounts told about these interactions. This essay examines the opposing images of labor, poverty, wealth, and class that domestic workers and their employers in the city of Madurai, Tamil Nadu, create in narratives about their experiences with one another. Such narratives offer a window onto relational aspects of class, which, as White (1992, 37) has argued, are crucial for grasping the nature of class as a system. They also encourage attention to the negotiation of identity, enhancing our understanding of the construction of identity as a social process (Ginsburg and Tsing 1990).

Domestic service provides an ideal domain for examining the production of class relations and identities. It is an arena in which class is reproduced and challenged on a daily and intimate basis. Moreover, domestic service interactions constitute the most intense, sustained contact with members of other classes that most of its participants encounter. Most critical for my research, the participants perceive themselves to be on different sides of class lines, and their reciprocal perspectives enable a relational focus to the research rather than an emphasis on only one side or the other.[1] If class relations are to be grasped in full, it seems to me we must give equal weight to each side's perspective. Narratives about domestic service enable a close examination of concepts of labor and class, the oppositional and moralizing images that constitute notions of self and other in class terms, and the ways that these develop out of daily interaction.

Class is a salient but ambiguous concept in urban south India. It is recognized as a distinct form of hierarchy, possessing its own signs and sources. Differences between classes are signified by a range of markers, including clothing and other items of fashion, consumer goods and their display, manners and sophistication, education, and language, among others. And class standing is understood to derive primarily from income, assets, occupation, and education. Yet there is no unambiguous term for class in either Tamil or English, and class often merges into caste in local understandings. The term *class* in fact can mean *caste*, as when disprivileged castes are grouped for government purposes as "Backward Classes." And in common usage, although class-specific attributes are sometimes spoken of as coming from such environmental influences as a rural or urban setting or family upbringing, they are more often spoken of as being essential and possessing inherent sources such as "genes" or "blood," much as does caste.[2]

Despite clear socioeconomic divisions in Indian society, class in India has received relatively little scholarly attention. In the past decade, scholars inside and outside of India have taken to task a long-standing academic emphasis on caste, pointing to other hierarchies that provide competing frames of reference to the purity-pollution scale underlying most models of caste (Appadurai 1986; Dirks 1987; Raheja 1988; Ram 1991); yet little direct attention has been focused on class structures and relations. Class, which is more mutable than caste and derives more directly from both economic and social standing, has become one of the most potent idioms of identity, rank, and political power in contemporary India, particularly in urban areas (Dickey 1993; Fernandes 1997; Kapadia 1995; Kumar 1988; Manor 1989).

Very little work has attended to the precise formations of class in India, especially its urban manifestations (Dickey 1993; for exceptions, see L. Caplan

1987; Holmström 1984). For the purposes of this essay I rely on the major divisions that Madurai residents use, since it is in any event a clearer grasp of indigenous conceptions of class that I am after. In this city, the people I refer to as "poor" or "lower class" include skilled and unskilled laborers or low-level office workers, and their household members, who possess or con-trol little in the way of land and other property and endure a general lack of economic security. Almost all have incomes at or near the Indian poverty line.[3] These people refer to themselves as "poor people," *eezhai makkal;* "laborers," *tozhilaalikal;* "people who suffer," *kashtappattavarkal;* or "people who have nothing," *illaatavarkal.* They are referred to as "the lower class" or "the mass" (usually in English) by members of higher classes (cf. L. Caplan 1987, 11).

The poor lump all more privileged people together as "rich people," *panakkaararkal,* or "big people," *periyavarkal.* These wealthier people, on the other hand, tend to identify themselves (in English) as "middle-class" or "upper-class" people. They include merchants, shopowners, professionals (such as doctors or lawyers), teachers, and government officials, and the members of their households. Although some differences exist between those who identify themselves as middle or upper class in terms of lifestyle, values, and income, they also share significant attributes. Both the middle and the upper classes can be distinguished from the poor by their awareness and expectation of personal opportunities in education and employment, a sense of hope and potential much unlike the resignation expressed by the urban poor—who are often struggling to maintain a grasp on what they have, rather than expecting or achieving improvement. Both hold a common view of the poor as shortsighted, narrow-minded, and often morally misguided, as will be clear in the following. Members of the higher classes tend to receive substan-tial education (at least through secondary school) and share a set of values learned in schools. Finally, domestic service itself provides one of the clearest markers of class distinctions. The ability to hire servants is a sign of having achieved middle- or upper-class status; poorer people, on the other hand, may work as servants but cannot afford to employ them.

Because household work is labor intensive and largely manual, and wages for hired domestic service very low, most middle- and upper-class households hire lower-class servants. Housework in Madurai is the domain of women. The alignment of women and domestic service must not be taken for granted, however, but should be understood as the result of specific eco-nomic and social forces (Hansen 1990, 1991). Although many poor women cannot afford to remain at home as they "properly" should, their work options are limited by a lack of education, perceived lack of physical strength, and/or the need to do protected (i.e., nonpublic) work (P. Caplan

1985; Raju 1993a, 1993b). Domestic labor satisfies these criteria and, moreover, is eschewed by men and higher-class women due to low pay and stigma. By taking it on, poor women free both themselves and their employers from gendered expectations—employers from the most onerous household tasks, and themselves from the restrictions of staying at home—though each is a most complicated "freedom."

Domestic workers and their employers come from a variety of castes and religions and are of all ages. In Madurai, unlike some other cities in India, almost all domestic workers are women, as are their employers. Most employers do not hold paid jobs, but some do, and many carry out other formal responsibilities outside the home, such as charitable, social service, or religious work. These women and their families enjoy relative financial security; at least one household member generally has reliable employment, and most have some level of savings or other assets. Their homes, almost always solid structures built of brick and plaster, can vary from tiny apartments with no indoor plumbing to grand houses with luxurious furnishings. These homes prominently display modern consumer goods—an important sign of a certain class standing—from metal bureaus to televisions to washing machines. The homes of domestic workers, on the other hand, are usually single-room houses with mud or brick walls, often built in rows or "lines" of adjoining homes that share a long thatch roof. Sparsely furnished, none have indoor plumbing, and some have no electricity. Most domestic workers provide the primary economic support of their families, even when living with a husband, because a man generally keeps most of his earnings for his own needs (cf. Agarwal 1994, 28–29; Kapadia 1995, 205). Most of them live at a level of such poverty that a day without work means a day without food. Whereas employers depend on workers' labor to maintain their labor-intensive homes and to demonstrate their class standing, for workers the employment is necessary for physical survival.

Today, most domestic service in Madurai is part-time. "Part-time" workers may put in a full day's labor, but in multiple homes, often at a single task—such as washing pots, dusting and scrubbing, doing laundry, or cleaning latrines. Other workers will do some or all of these tasks, along with cooking, in a single home. In either case, it is now fairly rare for servants to live in the homes of their employers. (Wealthy families have also become less likely to employ large retinues of servants.) This notable change, which has taken place over the past several decades, represents increased independence for workers, who are now less vulnerable to demands for long or irregular working hours, have greater power to negotiate wages and tasks, and retain greater control over their own family lives than when they were essentially dependents of a wealthy patriarch. At the same time the change

can mean greater insecurity, since employers no longer feel as much obligation to provide assistance with such needs as education or health or life-
cycle rites, or to provide continued care in lean times. Nor, however, are
their relations fully contractual; both sides feel some moral obligations to
one another, and "affection" remains a quality cultivated in the other by
workers and employers alike. These qualities befit a relationship that is often
described and enacted in familial terms. Domestic workers address their
employers and their families in kin terms denoting simultaneous respect and
closeness, such as "mother," "older sister," and "older brother." Employers
(who often refer to a worker as "younger sister" or "aunt," depending on the
servant's age, but may also dispense with kinship terms if they create more
closeness than is desired) define themselves as good employers by saying
they treat their servants as "one of the family." These idioms continue to
shape the expectations that workers and employers have of one another,
despite the decreasingly patrimonial nature of their relationship.

To learn about the perspectives of these different actors, I spoke with
domestic workers and employers who differed in gender, religion, caste, age,
socioeconomic status, and household size. This included formal interviews
with twenty-seven servants and twenty-eight employers. Interviews always
took place in the primary respondent's home, but other details of the setting
varied. When I interviewed employers, we were almost always alone, and
usually seated on furnishings such as couches and chairs in rooms whose
main purpose was to entertain guests; most of these interviews were primarily in English. Interviews with workers were held seated on the floor in
houses that most often consisted of one room, and they always included
other people—friends, neighbors, sometimes spouses—who frequently
joined in but occasionally constituted a more separate audience; we always
spoke in Tamil. To have carried out the interviews in any other way would
have felt "unnatural" for both groups. I also spent large amounts of more
informal time in workers' and employers' homes, talking, observing, and
sometimes joining in the household work. For ethical and methodological
reasons, I avoided interviews with employers and servants who work in the
same households. Meeting with both would have put domestic workers in
jeopardy had the employers become suspicious of what the workers were saying, and neither side was likely to speak fully if they feared I would repeat
what they said in later conversations with the other. Finally, I have also
employed domestic workers myself during some of the time I have lived in
Madurai, and at other times I have carried out domestic tasks alone. Both
servants and employers were as interested in my domestic arrangements as I
was in theirs, and they identified (and sometimes criticized) the similarities
and contrasts between our situations and sympathies.

In this essay, I focus on the narrative accounts that workers and employers tell about one another. Not all discourse takes the form of narrative, and a definition of this type of talk is in order here. Analysts often take "narrative" to be synonymous with "story." My definition is at once broader and more specific. I define *narrative*, following Riessman (1993, 3, 18), as talk that is sequentially organized "around consequential events." The sequence within a narrative is often understood by scholars to be chronological, or otherwise based on time (Labov and Waletzky 1967; Polkinghorne 1988; Ricoeur 1984; Rosaldo 1989), with some recognition that "time may be perceived as linear, circular, or spiraling depending on cultural context" (Narayan 1989, 243). But it has also been argued that narratives can be organized thematically, "stitched together by theme rather than by time" (Riessman 1993, 17; also see Michaels 1981). Such questions of form are crucial in narrative analysis in the social sciences, which focuses on structure in addition to context and content. Narrative analysis may identify structural patterns anywhere from the level of phonemes and clauses to the thematic organization found within and between narratives. The focus on structure helps to identify a speaker's intent and interests in telling the account in a way that attention to content alone cannot: our understanding of what a speaker says is enhanced by attending to how she says it.

Narratives serve particular purposes for their speakers. By linking events or situations, they help create coherence and meaning out of the discrete experiences of human lives (Gee 1985; Mishler 1986; Polkinghorne 1988). They are especially useful for creating an integrated sense of self; in narratives, speakers are "composing impressions of themselves, projecting a definition of who they are, and making claims about themselves and the world that they test and negotiate in social interaction" (Riessman 1990, 74; see also Bell 1988; Mishler 1986). They are also particularly effective at communicating moral stances, since "the impression of lifelikeness . . . can recruit imaginative empathy" (Narayan 1989, 243) and promote identification with the speaker (Riessman 1990). Tellers are often motivated to persuade their listeners that they are moral selves, that is, good people, and narratives provide an effective vehicle for such representation (Riessman 1990, 1993).

Finally, narratives also reveal much about the social structures in which their tellers are embedded. Whether hegemonic or counterhegemonic, narratives pose "responses to the system in which they originate and thus reveal its dynamics" (Personal Narratives Group 1989, 8). My analysis treats narratives as "political praxis" (Langellier 1989; also see Daniel 1993), constructing meanings to serve the speaker's interests. The servant-employer relationship is an interactive one, its power constructed and contested by both sides, and the narratives spoken about it are not simply descriptions of the relationship but a constituent part of it (Giddens 1983; Raheja and Gold 1994; Rosaldo 1989).

The narratives that follow were chosen because they reveal how images of the other and the self are built out of the experiences of working together. In analyzing them I pay attention to the context in which they are told and the interaction of speakers, to the structure of the accounts, and to content, in order to examine the ideological message that each narrative conveys. Content and structure are analyzed together, rather than strictly di-chotomized, just as listeners feel their impact simultaneously when a narra-tive is told. All these narratives share specific structural and thematic fea-tures. In particular, all are oppositional, creating repeated contrasts, such as "us" versus "them," "past" versus "present," and "home" versus "business." They focus on differences between the wealthy and the poor, and in partic-ular the rejection by the other of human consideration and decency. The following discussion opens with an employer's narrative that examines labor and character and their connections to caste and class, followed by the nar-rative of two domestic workers who critique employers' perceptions of the labor-character nexus. Next I discuss three narratives from one domestic worker who describes the hardships of poverty and their impact on the poor, the moral failings of employers, and the systemic nature of class. Finally, these are contrasted with the narratives of two employers who emphasize the moral failings of workers, the moral strengths of employers, and differ-ences between past and present servants. (All of the employers' narratives were told in English, all of the workers' narratives in Tamil.) Together these narratives help us to comprehend how reciprocal oppositional images are constructed and take on a moral force.

DOMESTIC SERVICE, WORK, AND CHARACTER

To apprehend what domestic workers and employers say about one another, we need a sense of the cultural meaning of labor. I begin with a narrative[4] told by Raman, a Brahman physician, about the societal division of labor and the inherent link between occupation and personal character. The nar-rative comes from a discussion that began as an interview with Raman's wife, Usha. Usha and I had been talking alone in their small but comfortably furnished apartment, and we were waiting for Raman to return from his office so that we could have lunch. Usha was describing her servant, a woman from the middle-caste Thevar community, and began to speak about differences among social classes. Comparing the servant's class with her own, she said:

I'd suppose like, say, this Thevar community. They wouldn't stop twice to pick up a fight, right? They are just waiting. They are the servant class. They just drop in the road and they have no prestige at stake. Right? But once you reached the upper class, you do have a position in the society, you wouldn't stoop down to a street fight. Though they belong to the same community [i.e., caste], they/ they'll have these restrictions because they have a social standing, whereas these [lower-class] people don't have [this standing or restrictions].

In Usha's mind, behavioral differences among classes are economically based; she emphasized the possibility of movement between classes, arguing that once people "reached" a higher class, they would adopt the behaviors expected of that class.

At this point Raman walked in and joined our conversation. At first he appeared to agree with his wife, saying, "Yes, even when people of the lowest standard or lower strata get affluent, you know, they slowly start changing their lifestyle. So it is money that makes the difference"; in other words, class is mutable, and distinguishable from caste. Shortly thereafter, however, Raman reversed himself. He began by describing the classical model of the Hindu city (cf. Lewandowski 1977), which is organized from its center outward in residential rings of decreasing caste status. At the city's center is the temple, around which live Brahmans—the purest castes who, Raman said, "do the temple work [and] who are supposed to be more patient, who are people who guide others," then other high castes, and then the lower castes. Raman ended his description by saying, "They [the society] classified people according to their work, according to their work, and depending upon that only they classified the society. And the class will be also only that much. The class will be also only that much." His repetition that "class will be also only that much" emphasizes the correspondence between class and caste (note that in Indian English, *only* is a speech particle marking emphasis or exclusivity). Having established this equation, Raman eagerly launched into a narrative linking caste, work, class, and character.

RAMAN: I can't go out doing a butcher's job. I can't go and cut a goat and do a butcher's job. A butcher cannot come and sit with a big *miicai* [mustache] in my office and start treat/ treating patients. Both are not possible. So basic attitude itself in life is different. It's different. They are not the same, and behavior will be totally different. We are supposed to be soft. Upper-class people are supposed to be soft, tolerant, intelligent in approaching problems; they reason out; they don't just like that pick up quarrels or fights. You know, they, they forgive. You know, this is that type of class. The other people, the lower-middle-class people, they, um, because of poverty, because of poor education—education is the—because of poor education, because of poor brought-up, right? In the childhood if this boy sees, if my son sees me treating heavily and beating my wife, you know what'll be the mental impact he will have? He will do the same thing to his wife. So, the same way, the attitude of that lower class is from childhood. You know they are brought [up] in a hard way. So they will inherit only those qualities or tendencies from their parents. They cannot suddenly change, I mean, overnight. And they are rough, they are more impulsive, they don't reason out things; they don't forgive, they punish. You know, it's that type of / That is the basic difference between the upper class and the lower class. And the, the, upper class is a general term, even in the upper class there are differences, even in the lower class there are differences. Right. But this is the gross difference between [them].

Here Raman develops a formulation in which work is tied to caste (as a Brahman, he says, "I can't go and cut a goat"); and class, which he has already equated with caste, is tied in turn to character ("upper-class people are supposed to be soft"). He establishes the naturalness of the link between individual character and occupation by twice saying that neither can he do the butcher's job, nor can the butcher do his job. This opening to his narrative sets up a powerful contrast, since the bloody slaughter of animals provides a jarring juxtaposition not only to the healing work of a physician, but also to the stereotypical calm and nonviolence of Brahmans. (See Srinivas 1976, 316 for a similar contrast.) Butchers typically belong to low castes, and even their mustaches signify a virility that is opposed to the ideal passivity of higher castes. (Note how this opposition between roughness and softness echoes the one voiced by Usha earlier.) Anything else is impossible, that is, unnatural, and outside of the individuals' natures. Moving from this opening passage, Raman works to stress the distinctions between people of different classes, saying three times in succession that attitudes and behaviors are "different" depending on class. Upper-class people are soft, tolerant, intelligent, reasoning, forgiving, while members of lower classes fight, beat, punish, and otherwise act impulsively rather than reasoning things out. They use their bodies rather than their minds. Raman provides an explanation for this, pointing out that such behavior is learned, passed on from parents to children, "because of poor education, because of poor brought up." Yet he also speaks of such qualities being inherited—"they will inherit only those qualities or tendencies from their parents"—and makes this point even more clearly later in the interview.

This emphasis on the inborn nature of class is not the only perspective espoused by Madurai employers, some of whom like Usha state that behavior, character, and values may be mutable because they are affected more by upbringing and income, and their fruits (including education), than by "genes" or "blood" or other immutable influences. Yet even causes that occur after birth, which in the terms of Western scientific discourse are "environmental" influences, are usually considered to have permanent effects and thus produce "essential" differences. Raman's generalizing statements about class and personal nature are representative of the formulation voiced most often by the employers I spoke with, and the natural connection he perceives between work and character is widely assumed among people of his class.

In the model Raman develops, domestic service is not the work of higher-class people. Indeed, throughout Indian society, manual labor is often eschewed by high-caste and -class people, and doing paid manual labor for others is a sign of low status. Moreover, domestic workers' labor involves contact with the dirt and pollution of others, making theirs an especially low-prestige occupation. Servants frequently mentioned the ways in which their work influenced employers' perceptions of their character. They also noted differences between classes regularly; yet I never knew domestic workers to make global statements about work and character, and they were more likely to view class differences as based on economics than anything truly immutable. They held a strong and clearly articulated view that servants were seen by others as particular types of people because of their labor, and workers often mentioned comments or behaviors by employers that implied servants' inferior status.

This viewpoint is especially clear in the following narrative, which was told during an interview with a domestic worker named Rupa, a woman in her thirties with three young children. I talked to Rupa on a Sunday afternoon, a day when many workers have time off. Many of the women in this neighborhood are domestic workers, and about a dozen of them joined us, sitting on the floor of Rupa's one-room house. A couple of them, including Rupa's neighbor Mutthammal, were frequent contributors to the conversation. In the middle of the interview, Rupa was interrupted by Mutthammal, who had become irritated by Rupa's sanguine descriptions of employers, and the following discussion ensued:

MUTTHAMMAL: They [employers] think of us as slaves [atimai]. Just as slaves. You [Rupa] don't know how to say this. They ask us to do a lot of work. And even after we do all that, they keep finding faults with everything we do. There are people who think, "Okay. This woman works responsibly. We should treat her well." There are people who don't give anything. There are servants who do a lot of work and come home without anything. Their employers would say, "We don't have anything today," and send them off after making them do so much work. For we would come home without anything and send our children to school without giving them anything or just old rice. There are houses like that. There are very few who give. Some don't even mention food. They'd say, "We won't give you food. We will only give you salary." The servants would tell them, "That won't be enough for us. We would definitely need breakfast." If they don't agree to give that, we won't work there, and will keep looking for some good house. If there is a good house, we will go and work there.

SARA: What do employers think about that?

MUTTHAMMAL: They think we are vulgar [kiizhtaram]. Those people, because they give wages, they think we are disgusting [mattam] and order us to work.

SARA: They think that way? Like that / Why do they think like that?

RUPA: We go to their houses and wash their plates. We wash the clothes that they wear. Then we clean their houses and wipe the floors. Because we do lowly work like that, they think of us as slaves. As bonded slaves. They think we are lowly. They would give if they have anything left over. They won't give thinking that it is their duty. There are people who would give only if there is something left over. There are also people who think, "We should give to that servant," and do it. People are of various types.

SARA: About poor people they don't—

RUPA: They don't sympathize. They interact with us thinking, "We give them wages and they work." They won't have a sympathizing heart. When they consider us to be cheap, where would they get sympathy? They'd only think, "We give wages. And she comes and washes the dishes."

SARA: Like that—

RUPA: That's exactly how they would think. In addition to thinking of us as very vulgar and cheap, they would put a huge amount of clothes out for us to wash. They would give us two buckets, three buckets full of clothes. They won't think, "She is also human like us, poor thing."

Mutthammal and Rupa jointly deliver a searing castigation of employers' perceptions and treatment of workers. Mutthammal charges, "They think of us as slaves," then illustrates her claim by moving back and forth from employers' perspective to workers'. She frequently speaks in the voice of her subject ("'We will only give you salary'"; "'We would definitely need breakfast'"), a narrative device that lends concrete immediacy to her general points. After I have interjected questions twice, Rupa returns to the conversation and finishes out this narrative with a continuing focus on employers. She elaborates on the image of slavery, providing examples both of employers' attitudes and of the sources of these attitudes, such as the dirty, polluting, menial, "cheap" tasks that servants perform, which in this depiction serve both to identify workers' natures with their dirty and polluting work (for employers) and to act as signs of employers' contempt toward workers. Servants are understood to be a particular kind of person, and treated in particular ways, because they sell their labor to employers for a wage ("Because we do lowly work like that, they think of us as slaves"; "They interact with us thinking, 'We give them wages and they work' "). When employers buy servants' labor, they also buy and construct their subservience. Even though both women complicate the picture by pointing out differences among employers (which also serves to demonstrate the speakers' comparative open-mindedness), the overall impact of their words is an indictment of employers' behavior.

Because having to work for a daily wage is one of the elements of being poor, and having to do manual labor is a sign of low status in Tamil culture, commentaries such as this on the treatment of workers constitute part of a larger discourse about poverty, wealth, and class. Connections among these topics were examined frequently and at length by Vasanthi, a domestic worker who is highly articulate about the exigencies of poverty and of the class system as a whole. Vasanthi is in her mid-twenties, a Christian and member of a scheduled caste, and lives in a slum not far from Rupa's neighborhood. She has three children; her husband occasionally works in a nearby tea stall, but he rarely makes much money and does not share most of what he makes. Vasanthi is quite vocal about the inequities of class. Her narratives not only utilize workers' and employers' speech, they also construct conversations between rich and poor and between servants and employers and use the dynamic revealed to illustrate class relations and class images. The following selections come from the first of two long interviews, both of which took place in Vasanthi's single-room home. In this first interview, we were joined by four other women, all domestic workers, who sat with us and occasionally joined in. The passion and power of her oratory, however, meant that Vasanthi held the stage for extended periods without interruption from anyone, including the interviewer.

Vasanthi's narratives focus on the greed of the rich, the stark contrasts between the lives of the poor and the wealthy, and the systemic connections between their lives. Her first narrative discusses how the wealthy behave, emphasizing their exploitation of the poor. Just prior to it, Vasanthi has been talking about upper-class people's hesitation to give loans or other assistance to the poor.

VASANTHI: Look at me. I have nothing at all. But they are loaded. If I go to them and say, "Please give me ten rupees. I'll give it back to you in the evening," they will say, "Would you give me a rupee as interest?" If I say, "Give me ten rupees, I'll return it in the evening," they will say, "I will definitely take one rupee in interest. Will you bring the whole ten rupees back in the evening?" Okay. What to do in that case? Even if I offer to give a pot [as collateral] and say, "I'll take it back soon," they'll give [the money] only after taking out their interest. Okay, let them take it. While we face such circumstances, some people would still say, "She is just fine." We are sitting here with difficulties and worrying [*pūl*] about them. But those who have would talk like that, because they need the extra income [of interest]. They can survive only by beating the stomachs of those who don't have.

At this point Vasanthi begins to talk about the corruption of social service organizations that are intended to aid the poor. After briefly discussing some of her experiences with these organizations, she turns to the hardships of poverty and the ways rich people respond to them.

VASANTHI: You are those who have. You could eat whatever you want. You could cook anything to eat. Nothing bad will happen if you fall ill. [Among us] there are three children in one house. There are six children in another house. What can be done for those children? Only if our husbands drive a rickshaw [i.e., are in good health], there will be money. If they don't drive a rickshaw one day, what can we do? We have to buy ten rupees from another person. We would ask for ten rupees as loan. They'd say, "Would you pay interest?" Okay, for the sake of the husband and children, we would get the money and boil the kanji [water left over from cooking rice]. Two days will pass by. The money-lender would say, "Why didn't you repay it? You have to pay interest, too. Even for that one rupee." What is there? Think about it. We are asked, "Why do you pawn? Why do you borrow money?" Can I bring my children to your house if they are starving? You could offer food to only one of my children. Can you feed them all? No. Because you'd say, "With the cost of things today, how can I feed you?" I myself have to incur debt. How can I do otherwise? Can my children come to your house? I could only get a little food for one of my children. If I say to someone, "My child asks for a little rice," he'd give [but only for that one]. Can all of the children go, sit and eat in a house? No one thinks like that [i.e., understands that].

Both of these narratives display a marked pattern. They are composed primarily of a series of couplets and occasional triplets that alternate matched statements about the rich and the poor, interspersed with statements addressed directly to the audience that call for reflection and moral judgment on what she has said. The first half of the first narrative, for example, follows this pattern:

If we say / they'd say
If I say / they'd say
Okay, what to do in that case?
Even if I offer collateral, they'll give only with interest
Okay, let them.

The second narrative works similarly, but instead of exploring back-and-forth responses, it paints sharp contrasts between the conditions of wealth and poverty. Employing a standard narrative device in Tamil that poses the speaker as addressing her intended "other"—here employers and other wealthy people, but in this case possibly directing her words to me as well—Vasanthi says that "you" have food and ease and health, whereas "we" have children (who must eat) and husbands (who may not work), and whereas "we" may have to ask for loans. "You" ask for interest, "we" take the money you give us and cook. The moneylender (her employer or any other person with money) insists on interest, even compounded on interest, and hounds the debtor. "Think about it," Vasanthi says. In the remainder of the second narrative, Vasanthi continues this pattern, using a question-response method again, and this time asking repeatedly whether something "can" happen, using the irony of her questions to show that indeed such basic things as feeding her entire family may not be possible.

Vasanthi constructs especially tight and stark contrasts between the rich and the poor in her narratives. The poor and the wealthy are always portrayed in relation to each other, with this systemic relation reaching its height in the final violent image of her first narrative. The rich do not give freely, despite their relative wealth. They make their money off the poor—those who have take from those who do not. This is not only a strong moral indictment of the failure to do charity and to be generous (important cultural values), but also a demonstration of how the employers' wealth is built directly on (and exacerbates) servants' poverty. In the second narrative

Vasanthi points out that for the poor, in contrast, money (and food, i.e., survival) comes only from labor: "Nothing bad will happen if you fall ill," she says, but "if [our husbands] don't drive a rickshaw one day, what can we do?" The statement that "for the sake of the husband and children, we would get the money and boil the kanji" is especially poignant, for two reasons. First is Vasanthi's reference to kanji, or rice water, a food considered to be the last resort against starvation and associated specifically with the poor. Second is her insistence that she borrows money only for her family's sake, stressing that in order to *provide*, she must do what she does not want to, or knows she should not (because she, like her wealthy critics, recognizes the economic costs of borrowing). She follows this with a related rejoinder to the rich, who in life as in her narrative often ask, "'Why do you pawn? Why do you borrow money?'" "How can I do otherwise?" she responds, drawing in her listeners. The employer, who has excess, asks, "With the cost of things, how can I feed you?"—which forces Vasanthi to borrow money. The employer is greedy and self-concerned, but also blind: she does not understand the circumstances of the poor, so she criticizes; she does not see need, so she does not give. She is possessed of both moral failing and social blindness.

Vasanthi examines the differences between the circumstances of the rich and the poor more thoroughly later in this same interview. Like the others, this narrative crafts tight oppositions between classes.

VASANTHI: If they [those who have money] get their daughter married, they offer some *pavuns* [8 gm of gold] of jewelry. But people like us will be holding our lives in our hands [feeling terrified] if someone comes to see our daughters. We will say, "Oh my god! A groom has come for my daughter. And we have to offer so many pavuns of jewelry. What can I do?" They look for "officers." But we look for house servants, rickshaw pullers, construction workers, etc. They'd have gotten their children educated. They'd have gotten their children to be lawyers or doctors. They'd have poured money / They'd have a lot of property. Their parents would have a lot of property. They could advance using those properties. They will be like, "Our family has this much property. Our parents give so much to us. They educated us to this degree. So, we should get into this job." But for poor people like us, we could not pay money for schools like "city" schools [private schools] and get our children educated there. We will search for government schools and we will get our children educated there. Sometimes, if our children don't have books, we say, "Wait. We will buy those books later" and the education of our children gets ruined. Education gets ruined. In the future, the lives of our children would be only like ours. Observe certain places

[i.e., families]. They keep their children neat and make them get educated, keep them strong and make them study for good jobs. Those children, in future, would get jobs as doctors, lawyers or teachers. They will
make 2,000/- or 3,000/- rupees [per month] as salary. When they get
2,000/- or 3,000/-, we have to be working in their house. They are those
who have. Now we get 60 rupees per month. If we get 60 rupees, we use
that to pay the rent for our house. If we work in another house, we
might buy soaps, coconut oil, etc. You could calculate. . . . We will
repay a debt, cook food, pay the house rent—that's how it is. How can
we progress with this money? If we don't go to work for a day, we have
to borrow money. But what do they do? Because they get salary only on
the first, they buy and stock rice, lentils, etc. If those provisions cost
1,500 rupees, they'd have 1,500 rupees on their hands. With those
1,500 rupees, they apply for loans, and they build big concrete houses.
We don't have such status. Only if we work can we have *kanji*. Even if
they are on leave for two days, they will get their whole salary. But if we
have to lie in our house due to ill health, they'll deduct money for those
two days from our salary. This is the difference between rich and poor
people. We are poor people. We go to houses for work. If we ask for ten
rupees from the employer, they would deduct it from our salary. They
are not going to give it for free. . . . In some houses, they wouldn't give
even five paise more even if we insist. This is the difference between
rich and poor people. Only if we work can we have *kanji*. But they could
eat meat and rice [good food] even if they stay at home for two to ten
days. . . . If we don't have work, we couldn't have even *kanji* to drink.
That's the difference between rich and poor people.

Vasanthi proceeds systematically and pointedly through contrasts
between rich and poor, always posing them in relation to one another,
revealing mutual connections and causative relations. She frames the differences of their experiences in the realms of marriage, including dowry and
grooms, education, and employment. While the upper class offers large
dowries of "some *pavuns* of jewelry" for grooms who are "officers," the lower
class can only cry, "What can I do?" when "servants, rickshaw pullers, [and]
construction workers" come asking for their daughters. While the wealthy
"have gotten their children educated" in private schools, the poor often
must "ruin" their children's education by delaying it beyond redress. Paired
constructions like these emphasize the confidence and ease of the wealthy
and the fear and constraints of the poor. But Vasanthi goes beyond this, noting repeatedly that their relationship is not static: the rich "advance" and
"progress"—using their money and capital—while poverty means "the lives

of our children would be only like ours." In the end of this narrative she returns to a focus on labor. The need to labor, and the consequences of not laboring, separate the poor from the rich. If the rich cannot work, they can go on leave, still receive salary, and eat "meat and rice." If the poor cannot work, they lose wages, borrow loans that create further deductions from wages, and "couldn't even have *kanji* to drink." Twice Vasanthi repeats the fact that the poor work in the homes of the wealthy; they are bound in mutual dependency, but while the poor reproduce the conditions of hardship for their children, the wealthy improve their lots without using their surplus to care for their workers.

Issues of exploitation, caring and altruism, and attention to real needs have their parallels in employers' domestic service narratives. Padma is a wealthy divorced Brahman woman and lives with her mother and adult son in a spacious home surrounded by carefully tended gardens. She and her mother employed a single family of servants for more than twenty-five years, and the now-adult daughter of that family had worked for them until the previous year. I interviewed Padma on the verandah of her home, without any listeners. Her new servant was not working that day. Padma opened our discussion by telling me that servants now dominate employers, and the following narrative occurred immediately after this. It highlights themes that appear frequently in employer interviews: the material-mindedness of servants, their exploitation of employers, and by contrast, the fair-mindedness and generosity of employers.

SARA: So you were saying that nowadays they have come to dominate us.
PADMA: It's not the question of domination alone, their requests are totally different, their wants are different nowadays. Before it wasn't that— they just wanted to work for one person and stick to one person and their needs were fulfilled. But nowadays their expectations are more. Whereas the employer's expectations vary from the servant's aspect. Before it was sort of an understanding between the employer and employee. And they were quite satisfied with what the employer was giving, and they wanted to stick to one place. But present-day people are totally different. They are just material-minded. They don't want the emotional support these days. They want a place to live in, [which] we are providing them with. And, uh, in the beginning they say, "We just want a room," and they come to stay with us. And, uh, presently the aristocracy creeps into them also. See, they want a two-in-one [radio/cassette player], so they want the power to be connected to their room. Then slowly they build up. We don't have the least hesitation to offer them [these things], provided they understand our problems and

accept what we give them also, you see. I had a servant at the backyard.
We gave them two rooms. Actually, when we employed them, we said
we'll give them only one room. And a bath and a toilet attached. And
water, running water facility and electricity. And, uh, after some time
she bought a big steel cupboard, so the room wasn't enough. So she took
the liberty to come and ask us, "I want another room." And if she has to
rent one room, it's about two hundred rupees when she goes out. She
doesn't add it up with her salary at all. And we too never bothered
about it. We think, "Oh, they have come to live with us, let them have
all the comforts." They take advantage of it. And they don't accept it
whole-heartedly, they think they can demand. You know what I mean?
{Sara: Yes.} The kindness is taken as weakness or worse. They start
exploiting us. And without our knowledge we start giving them more
and more of freedom, and finally, suddenly, we get a shock when we
realize that we have been thoroughly exploited. And we never have the
tendency to compare ourselves with other servants [i.e., with how their
employers treat them]. I never do that, because that has not been in our
nature.

Padma makes a case for the exploitation of employers by servants,
reversing the more predictable power relationship that stands as an implicit
contrast throughout her account. In the first half of her narrative, she
focuses on servants in general, alternating her depiction between past and
present—moving several times from the "wants" and "expectations" of
"nowadays" to the "needs" and "understanding" of "before." Having set up
the stark contrast between a past when both workers' and employers' needs
were satisfied and a present when workers reject emotional support for the
sake of greater material desires, Padma moves to a specific illustration of her
general point. In the second half she brings in the employer's perspective
more directly, in the form of herself, and describes the way in which contemporary conflicts develop. As she describes it, servants' expectations
build, but the employer remains ingenuous and generous. Padma comments
on the servants' wiliness and inconsiderateness while portraying herself as
naive and manipulated. Finally, with a "shock," she realizes the exploitation
taking place. Her dramatic development of this scene serves to re-create the
process of her own shocked discovery that she had been taken advantage of.
The impression she conveys of her initial ingenuousness and altruism is also
supported by the kinds of contrasts she makes, which are less tightly and, at
first, less starkly juxtaposed than are Vasanthi's, fitting Padma's portrayal of
herself as an open-minded, rather innocent employer.

Padma begins and ends this narrative with strongly moral statements about character, and the primary contrasts she develops are about past versus present and the nature of people. Now, servants want material goods at the expense of emotional support. Nor do they realize everything, tangible and intangible, that their employers give them. They neither think about nor realize these things—they are intellectually as well as emotionally unable to appreciate what they receive. Employers, on the other hand, give out of their altruism and considerateness without calculating the costs. This kindness is read as weakness and leads to exploitation. Reversing Rupa's formulation, Padma argues that while employers care for servants, servants dominate and exploit employers. Thus servants may not have the character or intelligence—what Padma later in this interview calls "IQ"—to recognize true value, but they are more cunning and crafty than their ingenuous employers.

The following short narrative further highlights the servant's narrow and interpersonally destructive focus on money, clarifying what Padma considers to be *true* liberties. After describing how the servant's husband threw out all his family's belongings and moved back to the village after a quarrel with Padma's family, despite all that the family had given their servant, Padma commented on the situation this way:

PADMA: Basically, the gene dominated, so she couldn't accept. Whatever was done to her was the best, [but] she couldn't take it that way. Whatever others were saying / See in that, the village concept only comes. Only the money mattered to her. She was yielding to anybody and everybody who was calling her and going out, and when we wanted her she won't be available. And that was irritating us also because we have given her all the freedom here. She could come and watch television whenever she wanted. And whenever the husband was away she was asked to sleep inside the house. We gave her all the liberties.

"Whatever was done to her was the best," Padma says, encapsulating the years of affectionate upbringing the family had given the servant; but despite the years of affection and luxury, the servant failed to act in the way a higher-class person would have. In Padma's mind, the inability to shed her lower-class character must therefore be explained by genetic influences and the "village concept," that is, the values espoused in the servant's ancestral village, to which the husband had returned her. Here Padma employs a typical mix of genetic and environmental causes, reminiscent of Raman's construction, and class and urban-rural contrasts. Having established this background succinctly, she lists some of her specific complaints. Padma treated her servant like a member of the family, she implies, giving her true consideration. The privilege of watching television and the concern that led to inviting her to sleep in the main house at night were not only "liberties," but signs of how much the family considered the servant part of them and felt a real personal attachment to her. To reject their offerings was to show not only insensitivity but a serious lack of judgment. Thus, despite her extended access not only to certain material privileges of the upper class, but especially to their values and outlook, the servant's true nature appears in her adoption of materialistic, short-sighted "village" values.

Janaki, a wealthy woman of the high-ranked Chettiar caste, employs four or five servants but considers this a small number compared with the retinue of workers her parents once employed. We spoke in her large living room, sitting on a plush sofa, as visiting relatives and their own servants came in and out of the room. Like Padma, Janaki emphasized recent changes in servants' behaviors and desires and argued that workers' unrealistic desires spark resentment, disloyalty, poor work, and irresponsible consumption. When I asked her whether a servants' union would ever appear in Madurai, she first responded by noting the comparisons that workers make between themselves and their employers and then moved on to examine the nature of domestic service work and employers' potential reactions to changes in servants' attitudes.

SARA: Do you think a union will ever come to Madurai?
JANAKI: See, the way the trends are going, I wouldn't be / Because now, uh, the feeling is, "Why should they only benefit, the upper class—we are slogging, we are working for them. Why should we also not get some benefits like the other unions and all that, the other employees in business houses and factories?" They [in the factory] have (unintelligible) and the hospital, this thing, you know, so many other purposes which they get. But here what we do in houses is we look after the needs ourselves. We take them to the doctor, we buy them medicines, we buy them injections and when their, uh, they have some family function we lend them the money. So the relationship is not like that in the factories and other offices. This is not an officer-employee relationship. It's something different. Because that sort of a relationship won't work here. And/But the feeling now is going a little more towards, "We are slogging for them twenty-four hours a day, we should raise our voices" and things like that. That is the general, this thing. But what they don't understand is, I feel that they don't understand is, one thing, we are feeding them all through the day and, morning two-three hours work

and again the evening two-three hours work. Maybe altogether about seven hours work. But whereas those people there work eight hours and they go away, these people work seven hours, yes, and then their time is their own. We don't give them strenuous work, it's all under, you know, the roof. And we're helping them out in so many other ways also. And, uh, another thing is, we go in, our businesswise we go into a lot of debts and things like that, and we try to work out. And out of what we get we would like to at least be relaxed at home and [therefore] we employ these people. And if the same mentality of union and that and this comes as like in the offices and factories, I mean this is going to be just another office-factory. This is not a home then. So then we wouldn't, we would also start changing our opinions, start applying more of the modern appliances, and cut short on these people. We wouldn't employ them.

Like Padma, Janaki is interested in ongoing changes in worker-employer relationships; but unlike Padma, she gives no impression of allowing herself to be exploited in this new era. She begins her narrative by stating that a union is unlikely to be organized, then explaining in the servant's voice why a union might be attractive. "Why should they only benefit, the upper class. . . . Why should we also not get some benefits like the other unions and all that, the other employees in business houses and factories?" she questions, portraying the resentment spawned not only by employers' privileges but also by the benefits earned by unionized factory workers. After demonstrating her empathy for servants' desires, however, she notes the more significant needs that employers look after. This pattern is repeated throughout the narrative, as Janaki moves from servants' feelings to employers' beneficence to further comparisons with the factory or business. She ends by noting how employers will have to respond if servants insist on creating a businesslike atmosphere in the home; as she says a few sentences later in the interview, "We would not want to have such people at home."

Janaki wields the contrast between home and business in two ways. The home and the factory signify alternative domains of work available to lower-class people, at the same time that they comprise two domains simultaneously present in employers' lives, especially for Chettiars, who are traditionally a mercantile caste. In the home, Janaki says, servants are looked after—employers take them to the doctor, pay for medicine, lend money for important rituals, give them food—and the relationship that enables this paternal beneficence is much more personalized than that of "an officer-employee relationship." Like Padma, she portrays herself treating servants like family members, which is the opposite of a contractual relationship.

And while workers complain about "slogging for [employers] twenty-four hours a day," in fact they work fewer hours than factory workers do, and the work is easier. Instead, it is employers whose work is difficult and stressful, and when they come home, they want to be able to relax in a nonbusiness environment. If this personal relationship is challenged sufficiently, Janaki predicts, then the labor of servants—of persons—will be replaced by machines. This is what will happen if the home is forced to become more like a factory, because it *is* a home, and if workers cannot see that *their* own interests are best served by keeping it as such, then employers at least will be clear about their interests. Janaki is arguing that servants need to see their employers as persons, with their own good hearts and good will as well as their own financial expenses, and not just as automaton-type employers; she is also arguing that servants are persons, but persons can be replaced by more reliable machines. She implies that if servants insist on thinking only in terms of money, so will employers.

CONCLUSIONS

The accounts that I have presented here are similar in both structure and content to others that these women told me, one another, and their families and friends. Narratives are always constructed in relation to an audience, including but not limited to the immediate listeners. Interactively produced and ideologically motivated, narratives provide pictures of the social world. Although told by individuals, they often represent those individuals' positions within social structures and institutions (Bell in press). Thus while the narratives I have interpreted here are spoken in unique ways and expound individual points of view, the images of the world that they create are similar to those produced by other domestic workers' and employers' narratives. Given workers' and employers' explicitly oppositional positions vis-à-vis one another, then, it is not surprising that these narratives—like countless others told to me and to other audiences—are closely related, despite their separation in time and space.

These narratives focus on the images of classes that develop from domestic service. Not surprisingly, labor is a frequent topic in them. As we have seen, discussions of labor suggest that whereas employers tend to see occupation as determining character, workers believe that it determines only the *perception* of a worker's character, not her actual nature. Nonetheless, both sides see themselves separated by the act of labor and the meanings ascribed to it. Because the survival of the poor depends on labor, as Vasanthi contends, the need to labor for a wage is a defining element of poverty. Vasanthi, Rupa, and Mutthammal describe a world in which workers' survival is based on the thinnest of threads, and in which a day without work can mean a day without food. This is not so, Vasanthi argues, for the wealthy, who can survive for days, or years, without laboring. Janaki and Padma charge, however, that servants neither labor enough themselves, nor respect the work of their employers. These employers describe a world in which workers desire only easy work and leisure and are resentful of being asked to do what servants once did willingly. The allusion to a golden past is not echoed by servants, for whom that past is either unfamiliar or undesirable.[5] For all domestic service participants, the pivotal role of labor creates both their relationship—it is employers' need for servants' labor and servants' need for a wage that brings them together—and one of the primary idioms for discussing that relationship.

Just as workers and employers disagree on whether labor determines character, so they differ about the relationship between class and character. Here, however, both agree that members of different classes tend to have corresponding characters: each sees their own class as morally upstanding and the other as morally reprehensible. To this extent, their views are strikingly parallel. There is nonetheless a systematic difference in the import of their injunctions, a difference rooted in opposed positions within the class structure. When employers discuss "class," they speak of both class standing and personal character. Often they combine the two meanings to produce an ambiguous and multivalent term, but when necessary, they will separate them, as they do when discussing poor people who gain wealth and therefore class standing, but retain their inherent "low-class" nature. Similarly, upper-class people in Madurai typically feel that they are better individuals than lower-class people, but they do not argue that their money makes them this way, and only rarely that a lack of money and privilege makes poor people the way they are. To suggest otherwise would weaken the "rightness" of the moral differences that keep the relatively privileged on their side of the class divide. Rather, their narratives reveal an implicit but unexamined assumption that something logically prior to income or other assets makes people what they are. For higher-caste employers, this prior feature might be caste (as Raman implies), but lower-caste employers' conceptions of just what justifies their standing in a moral-economic order is less clear.

Domestic workers, on the other hand, do not combine character and socioeconomic standing into a single concept (in part because Tamil terms are less accommodating of this ambiguity than is the English term *class*). Furthermore, as these narratives demonstrate, domestic workers focus equally on money and character as distinguishing people of different classes. They do not postulate what would happen to their employers' characters should the employers fall in class standing—since this possibility poses no parallel anxiety to that sparked by the upper-class fantasy of poor people who climb the class ladder. Thus while domestic workers do speculate, in narratives not reproduced here, about how more money might or might not change one's character, they of course do not worry about the problem of retaining their own character should they improve their class status, because that character is already an admirable one. Instead, they answer employers' charges of their moral inadequacy in two ways: first, by redefining the terms of difference as rooted in money (a commodity that can be acquired somewhat independently of character), rather than in a prior and inherent difference, and, second, by claiming their own moral superiority.

Moral differences provide one of the predominant vehicles for discussing class differences in south India, and not only in the realm of domestic service (Dickey 1993, forthcoming a; Hancock 1995). These moral critiques cast a wide net; in addition to the criticisms narrated here, they can cover hygiene, sexuality, honesty, and consumption habits, among other qualities (Dickey forthcoming b). In the narratives presented in this essay—with their focus on labor, character, and the domestic service relationship—the most consistent moral critique addresses workers' and employers' inability to see the other in his or her full humanity. Both sides highlight a lack of human concern in the other. Their narratives criticize the other's focus on money and materialism at the expense of needs less easily objectified and quantified—including less market-oriented concerns such as food, medicine, and pivotal life events—and a lack of recognition of what is most important in human relationships. Padma and Janaki feel unappreciated, and even exploited, by their servants because the latter do not appreciate the nonwage benefits they receive. More than this, these employers say, servants do not recognize what is most important about relationships between people, which is not an impersonal contract, but the provision of emotional support, loyalty, and commitment. They locate their own increased concern with calculating returns in servants' insistence on defining their relationship in financial terms. Rupa and Mutthammal, on the other hand, believe employers use money as a license to treat workers as polluted slaves. They, like Vasanthi, argue that if servants were instead seen as fully human, employers would provide food and other assistance, think about daily work and occasional crises from the worker's point of view, and thus realize that servants have the same needs and limits as employers do. Vasanthi argues, most cogently of all, that employers exploit the poor to become rich. Although domestic workers argue for an ideal relationship that poses workers and employers as more equivalent persons than do employers, all these speakers construct an ideal in which the asymmetrical needs of self and other would be reciprocally attended to by the domestic service relationship.

In doing so, both sides claim to prefer a relationship based not on a contract but on trust, affection, and concern.

Such desires are deeply rooted in the paternalistic and largely noncontractual nature of domestic service. Workers and employers generalize their comments, however, beyond the realm of domestic service to represent classes as a whole. In content as well as in structure, their narratives represent classes as opposed to one another and demonstrate this opposition. They make moral critiques about the other's class and stress the moral superiority of their own class's values and actions. Thus the other is portrayed as greedy, exploitative, and materialistic, while the self is generous, altruistic, and focused on values that transcend money. These images are intriguingly complementary, often very nearly the reverse of one another, suggesting that actors feel parallel stresses that are perhaps rooted in the class system as a whole. But these images also arise, crucially, from the negotiations of individual and intimate contact. This gives them, and the narratives that contain them, a forcefulness that highlights their utility in the construction and reproduction of class ideologies. In attending to such images, as I have begun to do in this essay, we can begin to understand the construction and significance of class identities in everyday interactions.

As I have argued here and elsewhere, moralizing across class lines is a frequent feature of discourse about class in India (Dickey 1993, forthcoming a; see also Tolen, this volume, and Kidder, this volume). In the context of domestic service, the reasons for moralizing are both specific to this arena and connected to a broader realm of class relations. In the first instance, they appear to derive from the familial idiom in which domestic service relations are frequently couched. Family members have moral obligations to one another, and all the members of this "family" believe the others to be failing them. These tensions have likely been exacerbated by the ongoing process of shifting from more thoroughly patrimonial relations to more nearly contractual ones (cf. Romero 1992). They are part of the struggle for control over the worker-employer relationship in this shifting terrain of social relations, which is itself a part of transitions in class relations as a whole. The moral tone of class images is likely to derive also from the need to rationalize or oppose each player's position in the hierarchy. Employers' insistence on the inherent nature of class may be a means both of justifying difference as morally right and of constructing distance as immutable. Members of higher classes need to justify their place in a hierarchical system, posing their position as rightful because they are inherently righteous and those below them are not. Because they also know that class standing is in theory (if rarely enough in actuality) mutable, they fear both an absolute loss of status caused by their own possible loss of financial assets, and a relative loss caused by poor persons' potential to attain higher-class status. They need to defend their position against feared encroachments by those below them, which would constitute an erasure of difference (cf. Tolen, this volume). By contrast, it is not in workers' interests to perceive difference as immutable. They do not do so, but because they also know the extreme difficulty of rising in the class hierarchy, they frequently pose the realm of morality as an alternative hierarchy to class in which they, not the wealthy, are enviably positioned (cf. Dickey 1993). As Kipp (1993, 6) comments, "identity politics are thus a contest to retain power, or else an assertion of value against the grain." Domestic workers' and employers' narratives reveal the terms in which their speakers conceptualize, enjoin, and negotiate an urban Indian identity politics of class.

Acknowledgments

Research for this essay was supported by an Advanced Research Grant from the Joint Committee on South Asia of the Social Science Research Council and American Council of Learned Societies (including funds from the National Endowment for the Humanities) and by faculty research funding from Bowdoin College, whose assistance I gratefully acknowledge. This essay has benefited from the generous comments of a number of people. Earlier versions were presented to the Conference on South Asia in Madison, Wisconsin; the New York University Department of Anthropology; and the Harvard University Anthropology Colloquium. In each of these venues, I received a number of thoughtful questions and suggestions that have contributed to this work. Fellow members of the MIDAS Narrative Studies Group read and critiqued the paper thoroughly, and I owe them many thanks for helping to clarify my understanding of narratives and narrative analysis over the years. Many thanks also to Kathleen Adams, whose reading and comments have been particularly helpful at crucial moments. And thanks especially to Susan Bell, who has followed the progress of this paper from its earliest form, and whose highly perceptive and thoroughgoing observations have played a substantial role in its development.

Notes

1. Most domestic service research focuses on the experiences of workers (e.g., Bossen 1980; Chaney and Garcia Castro 1989; Dill 1988; Glenn 1986; Rollins 1985; Romero 1992; Sanjek and Colen 1990), though a few studies provide a wider range of perspectives (e.g., Cock 1980; Gill 1994; and Hansen 1990).

2. Caste is hereditary (and thus cannot be altered), and castes are generally endogamous. Historically, most castes have had specific hereditary occupations (e.g., Barbers, Smiths, and Leatherworkers), though in this highly agrarian subcontinent, castes with a variety of hereditary occupations have also done agricultural labor. Today, most scholars view caste as a form of hierarchy based in part on gradations of inherent purity and pollution—with Brahmans the purest and thus highest-ranked castes, and a variety of "scheduled" or "Untouchable" castes marked as the lowest and least pure—and in part on economic factors. In addition to inherent levels of pollution, transient impurity can also be incurred by contact with polluting events or substances, such as death, childbirth, and bodily excretions.

3. Heston reports that 34 percent of the urban population in India is at or below the poverty level, which in 1988 was approximately Rs 90 per person per month; in southern India, 30 percent of the urban population lived in poverty according to these standards (1990, 103,106,109). Levels of poverty are relative, and Heston points out that over 95 percent of Indians would be considered poor by U.S. standards (1990, 103). It should be noted that the Rs 90 figure was determined for rural areas and is even less adequate in urban areas where a higher percentage of commodities must be acquired with cash.

4. My transcription conventions are as follows: Square brackets ([ ]) indicate words inserted by me for clarity, or, when in italics, the Tamil original; curved brackets ({}) indicate interjections by other speakers. Slashes (/) indicate an abrupt end to or switch in the statement under way. Dashes (—) at the end of a statement indicate that it was cut off by the next speaker. Words or passages that are unclear in the original are noted as "(unintelligible)."

5. Whereas many employers' families have had servants for generations, most servants' parents did not do service work.

REFERENCES

Agarwal, Bina
1994   A Field of One's Own: Gender and Land Rights in South Asia. Cambridge: Cambridge University Press.

Appadurai, Arjun
1986   Is Homo Hierarchicus? American Ethnologist 13 (4): 745–61.

Bell, Susan E.
In press   Narratives and Lives: Women's Health Politics and the Diagnosis of Cancer for DES Daughters. Narrative Inquiry 9 (2).
1988   Becoming a Political Woman: The Reconstruction and Interpretation of Experience Through Stories. In Alexandra Dundas Todd and Sue Fisher, eds., Gender and Discourse: The Power of Talk, 97–123. Norwood, NJ: Ablex.

Bossen, Laurel

1980   Wives and Servants: Women in Middle-Class Households, Guatemala City. In George Gmelch and Walter P. Zenner, eds., *Urban Life*, 265–75. New York: St. Martin's Press.

Bourdieu, Pierre

1984   *Distinction*. Trans. Richard Nice. Cambridge, MA: Harvard University Press.

Caplan, Lionel

1987   *Class and Culture in Urban India: Fundamentalism in a Christian Community*. Oxford: Clarendon Press.

Caplan, Patricia

1985   *Class & Gender in India: Women and Their Organizations in a South Indian City*. London: Tavistock Publications.

Chaney, Elsa M., and Mary García Castro, eds.

1989   *Muchachas No More: Household Workers in Latin America and the Caribbean*. Philadelphia: Temple University Press.

Cock, Jacklyn

1980   *Maids and Madams: A Study in the Politics of Exploitation*. Johannesburg: Ravan Press.

Daniel, E. Valentine

1993   Tea Talk: Violent Measures in the Discursive Practices of Sri Lanka's Estate Tamils. *Comparative Studies in Society and History* 35 (3): 568–600.

Dickey, Sara

1993   *Cinema and the Urban Poor in South India*. Cambridge: Cambridge University Press.

Forthcoming a   Opposed Faces: Fan Club Constructions of Class Identity in South India. In Christopher Pinney and Rachel Dwyer, eds., *Pleasure and the Nation: The History, Politics and Consumption of Popular Culture in India*. Delhi: Oxford University Press.

Forthcoming b   Permeable Homes: Domestic Service, Household Space and the Vulnerability of Class Boundaries in Urban India. *American Ethnologist*.

Dill, Bonnie Thornton

1988   "Making Your Job Good Yourself": Domestic Service and the Construction of Personal Dignity. In Ann Bookman and Sandra Morgen, eds., *Women and the Politics of Empowerment*, 33–52. Philadelphia: Temple University Press.

Dirks, Nicholas

1987   *The Hollow Crown: Ethnohistory of an Indian Kingdom*. Cambridge: Cambridge University Press.

Fernandes, Leela

1997 *Producing Workers: The Politics of Gender, Class, and Culture in the Calcutta Jute Mills*. Philadelphia: University of Pennsylvania Press.

Gaitskell, Deborah, Judy Kimble, Moira Maconachie, and Elaine Unterhalter

1984 Class, Race and Gender: Domestic Workers in South Africa. *Review of African Political Economy* 27/28:86–108.

Gee, James P.

1985 The Narrativization of Experience in the Oral Style. *Journal of Education* 167:9–35.

Giddens, Anthony

1983 *Central Problems in Social Theory: Action, Structure and Contradiction in Social Analysis*. Berkeley: University of California Press.

Gill, Lesley

1994 *Precarious Dependencies: Gender, Class and Domestic Service in Bolivia*. New York: Columbia University Press.

Ginsburg, Faye, and Anna Lowenhaupt Tsing

1990 Introduction. In Faye Ginsburg and Anna Lowenhaupt Tsing, eds., *Uncertain Terms: Negotiating Gender in American Culture*, 1–16. Boston: Beacon Press.

Glenn, Evelyn Nakano

1986 *Issei, Nisei, War Bride: Three Generations of Japanese American Women in Domestic Service*. Philadelphia: Temple University Press.

Hancock, Mary

1995 Hindu Culture for an Indian Nation: Gender, Politics, and Elite Identity in Urban South India. *American Ethnologist* 22 (4): 907–26.

Hansen, Karen Tranberg

1990 Domestic Trials: Power and Autonomy in Domestic Service in Zambia, *American Ethnologist* 17 (2): 360–75.

1991 Domestic Service. What's in It for Anthropology? *Reviews in Anthropology* 16 (1): 47–62.

Heston, Alan

1990 Poverty in India: Some Recent Policies. In Marshall M. Bouton and Philip Oldenburg, eds., *India Briefing, 1990*, 101–28. Boulder, CO: Westview Press. (Published in cooperation with The Asia Society.)

Holmström, Mark

1984 *Industry and Inequality: The Social Anthropology of Indian Labour*. Cambridge: Cambridge University Press.

Kapadia, Karin

1995   *Siva and Her Sisters: Gender, Caste and Class in Rural South India*. Boulder, CO: Westview Press.

Kipp, Rita

1993   *Dissociated Identities: Ethnicity, Religion, and Class in an Indonesian Society*. Ann Arbor: University of Michigan Press.

Kumar, Nita

1988   *The Artisans of Banaras: Popular Culture and Identity, 1880–1986*. Princeton: Princeton University Press.

Labov, William, and Joshua Waletzky

1967   Narrative Analysis: Oral Versions of Personal Experience. In June Helm, ed., *Essays on the Verbal and Visual Arts*, 12–44. Proceedings of the 1966 Annual Spring Meeting of the American Ethnological Society. Seattle: University of Washington Press.

Langellier, Kristin M.

1989   Personal Narratives: Perspectives on Theory and Research. *Text and Performance Quarterly* 9 (4): 243–76.

Lewandowski, Susan

1977   Changing Form and Function in the Ceremonial Port City in India: An Historical Analysis of Madurai and Madras. *Modern Asian Studies* 11:183–212.

Manor, James

1989   Karnataka: Caste, Class, Dominance and Politics in a Cohesive Society. In Francine R. Frankel and M. S. A. Rao, eds., *Dominance and State Power in Modern India: Decline of a Social Order*, 322–61. Delhi: Oxford University Press.

Michaels, Sarah

1981   "Sharing Time": Children's Narrative Styles and Differential Access to Literacy. *Language and Society* 10:423–42.

Mishler, Elliot G.

1986   *Research Interviewing: Context and Narrative*. Cambridge: Harvard University Press.

Narayan, Kirin

1989   *Storytellers, Saints, and Scoundrels: Folk Narrative in Hindu Religious Teaching*. Philadelphia: University of Pennsylvania Press.

Personal Narratives Group, ed.

1989   *Interpreting Women's Lives: Feminist Theory and Personal Narratives*. Bloomington: Indiana University Press.

Polkinghorne, Donald E.

1988   *Narrative Knowing and the Human Sciences.* Albany: State University of New York.

Raheja, Gloria Goodwin

1988   *The Poison in the Gift: Ritual, Prestation, and the Dominant Caste in a North Indian Village.* Chicago: University of Chicago Press.

Raheja, Gloria Goodwin, and Ann Grodzins Gold

1994   *Listen to the Heron's Words: Reimagining Gender and Kinship in North India.* Berkeley: University of California Press.

Raju, Saraswati

1993a   Gender and Caste Inequities in Workforce Participation in Urban India: A Sociospatial Interpretation. In Saraswati Raju and Deipica Bagchi, eds., *Women and Work in South Asia,* 74–98. London: Routledge.

1993b   Introduction. In Saraswati Raju and Deipica Bagchi, eds., *Women and Work in South Asia,* 1–36. London: Routledge.

Ram, Kalpana

1991   *Mukkuvar Women: Gender, Hegemony and Capitalist Transformation in a South Indian Fishing Community.* New Delhi: Kali for Women.

Ricoeur, Paul

1984   *Time and Narrative.* 3 vols. Chicago: University of Chicago Press.

Riessman, Catherine Kohler

1990   *Divorce Talk.* New Brunswick: Rutgers University Press.

1993   *Narrative Analysis. Qualitative Research Methods Series, Vol. 30.* Newbury Park, CA: Sage.

Rollins, Judith

1985   *Between Women: Domestics and Their Employers.* Philadelphia: Temple University Press.

Romero, Mary

1992   *Maid in the U.S.A.* New York: Routledge.

Rosaldo, Renato

1989   *Culture & Truth: The Remaking of Social Analysis.* Boston: Beacon Press.

Sanjek, Roger, and Shellee Colen, eds.

1990   *At Work in Homes: Household Workers in a World Perspective.* American Ethnological Society Monograph Series, No. 3. Washington, DC: American Anthropological Association.

Srinivas, M. N.

1976   *The Remembered Village*. Berkeley: University of California Press.

White, Sarah C.

1992   *Arguing with the Crocodile: Gender and Class in Bangladesh*. London: Zed Press.

Rachel Tolen

TRANSFERS OF KNOWLEDGE AND PRIVILEGED SPHERES OF PRACTICE
Servants and Employers in a Madras Railway Colony

The subject of domestic service seems inherently linked with the construction of social difference. The images that surround institutions of domestic service in the public sphere, from novels, movies, and TV programs (*The Remains of the Day, The Nanny*) to the contentious political discourse surrounding the conditions of employment of domestics by U.S. public officials (such as the "Nannygate" controversies surrounding Clinton's nominees for attorney general), play on our everyday notions of social difference and inequality. The linkage of domestic intimacy with often wrenching forms of social inequality provides a powerful set of everyday circumstances that continually spark the imaginations of writers, cinema producers, political commentators, and social scientists alike, all eager to explore (and sometimes exploit) the charged significance of institutions of household servitude.

Perhaps for these reasons, the context of domestic service itself has proven for scholars a rich and fruitful ground for exploring in microcosm the wider processes through which social difference is created, reproduced, and solidified. Anthropologists, sociologists, and historians have used domestic service as a window for focusing, in more concrete and intimate terms, on issues that often might be explored in more abstract theoretical terms, such as those involving race, class, and gender constructions. Indeed, wherever institutions of household service are found, they are linked with wider processes of social differentiation, whether based on ethnicity, race, caste, status, or gender.[1]

Although many of these studies demonstrate the capacity for institutions of domestic service to illuminate the processes through which the construction of difference is carried out, the question still arises whether in such contexts difference is only created, solidified, and achieved once and for all or whether the parties involved are not themselves transformed through their interactions. While domestic service provides a context for the construction of social difference, it also provides a fertile ground for the transmission of knowledge and practice across boundaries of social difference, as servants gain intimate knowledge of their employers' lives.

In this essay I explore some of the links between class and different forms of knowledge, and the transmission of knowledge and practice across class boundaries. Based on fieldwork that focused on the lives of families of officers of the Indian Railways and the families of the servants who work for them, this essay looks both at the construction of class difference in the everyday setting, and the processes of transformation of class difference that occur as servants seek to re-create themselves. The concrete setting for the study was a railway colony in Madras, south India, a residential community for employees of the government-run Indian Railways, where I conducted fieldwork from October 1991 to June 1993.[2] Railway colonies, built during the period of colonial rule in India, were intended to provide a distinct social world for the British officials who built and managed railway enterprise from the mid–nineteenth century, and their architectural features reflect the race and labor relations upon which colonial rule was built. Today, Indian railway officers are provided with spacious bungalows in the railway colony, and each bungalow-compound contains separate servants' quarters, or "outhouses," where servants who work in the bungalow live, sometimes along with their families. Some of these servants are hired by private arrangement with the officer's household, whereas others are official employees of the Indian Railways hired to work in the officer's house.

In India, as perhaps in other areas of the world with the colonial past still lingering in their administrative structures, institutions of servitude have evolved into varied forms within state bureaucracies. In the railways, the position of the "bungalow peon" evolved as an officer's personal attendant, who served him in his bungalow. Although their duties at one time appear to have been primarily clerical in nature, the bungalow peons' duties today have been expanded to include all manner of household help. Bungalow peons are official employees of the Indian Railways, receiving salaries and benefits as do other government workers.[3] While the bungalow peon's salary is modest in comparison with an officer's, it can mean for a poor family that they will no longer have to be concerned on a daily basis about whether there will be money to buy enough food to feed the whole household. In addition, it can provide the security to plan for some larger expenditures in the future, such as weddings or purchases of more expensive, durable goods. Bungalow peons are invariably male and are usually under the daily supervision of the senior woman of the bungalow household, who is known as the 'bungalow' ammā, meaning "woman of the bungalow" (usually the wife of a male railway officer, or in a few cases, a female railway officer herself). Most railway officers' families employ at least one other servant, usually a woman, who is not an official employee of the railways, but works for the right to occupy the outhouse rent-free (along with her family members) and sometimes for a minimal monthly salary, of perhaps fifty rupees.[4] While these women work for a "house without rent" they invariably seek more: to gain a permanent job for a male family member in the railway workshops or offices (which offers higher pay and increased security) through the help of an officer's family, in the hopes that they might one day escape servitude altogether.

In this context, systems of domestic service link with bureaucratic state structure, both in forms of service to public officials that transcend public/private distinctions, and in systems of patronage through which subordinates seek to use private service to officials to gain entrance into the permanent ranks of state employment. It is common for people to work as household servants for powerful officials or factory managers in order to obtain a job for oneself or a family member in such state enterprises as the railways, as well as in private industries (Breman 1979, 133; Holmström 1985, 111; Tolen 1996). These conditions in the bureaucratic village of the railway colony provide a distinct, yet fertile, set of circumstances for viewing not only the processes through which social difference is constructed, created, and reproduced, but also the processes through which servants seek to transform themselves and seek social mobility.

Together the railway colony forms a kind of community, but it is in many ways one that is bifurcated by class. Officers' families and servants' families form two distinct classes in this community, and in some respects, two distinct social worlds. Most of the railway officers are highly educated, with degrees in competitive fields like engineering and medicine. Their spouses are similarly educated, and their children attend prestigious English-medium schools in Madras. Due to frequent transfers in the Indian Railways, the officers' community in the railway colony is particularly cosmopolitan and multiethnic, composed of families of different castes (although a significant number are Brahmin or of other high castes) from many different regions of India, speaking various north and south Indian languages, as well as English. The officers' class constitutes part of the spatially mobile class of professionals, whose styles of life are particularly cosmopolitan and influenced by Western tastes (Appadurai 1988, 6). Although their divergent regional and ethnic origins create some cleavages within the officer's rank, commonalities of education, upbringing, and orientation toward a cosmopolitan national culture create a great deal of coherence among their community. The servants' community, in contrast, is primarily composed of families from Madras or other parts of Tamil Nadu or one of the adjacent south Indian states. Most are speakers of Tamil or one of the related south Indian languages; they also are of various castes, both Brahmin and non-Brahmin. Some are migrants from rural areas of south India who flock to Madras in search of work. While most of the maids occupy outhouses along with their families, a number of the bungalow peons are young bachelors residing in outhouses away from kin in other parts of south India.

As its theoretical subject, this essay looks at the conjuncture of class, as a relation between rich and poor generated in the contradictory circumstances of social and material production and experienced both symbolically and materially in the everyday world, and practice, as the mode through which class structures action in, and orientations to, this world. As Pierre Bourdieu (1984) has argued in his work *Distinction*, class conditions produce orientations and dispositions (what he terms "habitus," or structured and structuring structures) toward practices, resulting in a correspondence between particular lifestyles, distinctive tastes, and class conditions. Bourdieu draws attention to the regularities with which people sharing a particular class condition select in similar ways from the world of practice around them. Agents and agents' actions are both structured and productive of structure (Bourdieu 1977, 1984), or, as Anthony Giddens puts it, structure and agency are mutually dependent; structure is both the "medium and outcome of the reproduction of practices" (Giddens 1979, 5, 69). Drawing also on the work of Jean Lave (1988, 1993), I understood knowledge to be a "situated practice," linked to the experience of particular class conditions and practical spaces of activity. In the context that I explore, knowledge and practice become the subject of negotiation and conflict, and media in the construction of class identity.

Many scholars, finding no central cultural discourse in Indian society (outside of scholarship or specifically political rhetoric) that makes direct reference to "class," have argued that class is not relevant to Indian society, that India is a caste society organized according to fundamentally different "value" orientations than Western societies, in essence, that in India, class does not exist. The major proponent of this view is Louis Dumont, who argues that class is subordinated to caste in Indian society (Dumont 1970, 366). Yet the people that I knew in Madras talked frequently and with great intensity about the differences that wealth makes, about rich people and poor people as well as those in between. This talk could be bitter, angry, or frustrated; it could also be lurid and graphic in its detail. As Sara Dickey has noted in her study of cinema in the south Indian city of Madurai: "Class is essential to urban residents' identity; when Madurai residents talk about 'people like us,' they are much more likely to be identifying themselves with a socioeconomic category such as 'poor people' than with forms of identity that have historically received more frequent consideration by analysts, such as caste or religion" (Dickey 1993, 7). Dickey found that while people may not often talk about class in the terms that scholars use, there is widespread *awareness* of the differences between rich and poor in south India (Dickey 1993, 10).

In the context of the railway colony, these class differences are particularly encoded in spatial relations. The two primary class referents that people use in this context are "bungalow people" (*'bungalow'-kārarkaḷ*) and "outhouse people" (*'outhouse'-kārarkaḷ*), and the main class categories that are used in everyday talk index the spatial relationship between bungalow and outhouse. These spatial referents overlap in everyday talk with the categories of "rich people" (*paṇakkārarkaḷ*) and "poor people" (*ēḻaikaḷ*). Thus it is that class relations are explored here as they are situated in the concrete context of the railway colony through the relation between outhouse people and bungalow people.

The proximity of the servant families to the officers' families who employ them and the particularly intense daily interaction between these sets of families made the railway colony setting a particularly fruitful place to study the flow of knowledge and practice across class boundaries. One of my main concerns in the railway colony was to explore the links between social class and particular forms of knowledge and how forms of knowledge are transmitted between outhouse and bungalow. In more concrete terms, I was interested in what servants learn from their employers and what employers learn from their servants, and the implications of this exchange of knowledge for class relations. In this exchange, practice itself becomes a subject of contentious debate between servants and employers, laying bare the nature of the very links between class and practice.

THE POLITICS OF KNOWLEDGE TRANSFER

For servants, entering into the bungalow for domestic work provides a context for encountering a whole new world of practice situated in the upper-class household, a context for social learning. Some part of what is learned in the bungalow becomes part of servants' practical repertoire and is transferred back to life in the outhouse. Servants do not simply learn work procedures while performing domestic service, but encounter an entire lifestyle, leading to improvisations in their own lifestyles (within the means available to them) and the transfer of practices/knowledge from employers' households to servants' households.

As practical spaces of situated activity, the employer's bungalow and the servant's outhouse reveal the working out of different plans, schemes, and models in the use of social space and the structuring of activity. Looking at how knowledge and practice move between these practical spaces, bungalow and outhouse, can illuminate the relation between knowledge/practice and class. Jean Lave's study of how, based on pragmatic context, U.S. grocery store shoppers alternately use and abandon the use of mathematical principles learned in school, suggests that whether practice does indeed move across different contexts of everyday life depends on the pragmatic orientations of actors in specific settings (Lave 1988). Lave's observations concerning learning-transfer are particularly relevant to studying how practices both *do* and *do not* travel between bungalow and outhouse. As will be shown, learning is never socially neutral, and learning-transfer in this context is conditioned by the power relations between bungalow and outhouse, by material circumstances that may facilitate or constrain the transfer of practices, and the particular improvisational character of everyday life.

Although learning pervades the encounter of servant and employer, this kind of learning is only half perceived as such by many people in the railway colony. As one maid said when I asked her whether she had learned anything from her employers: "We have come only to do the work, not to learn anything." Reflection on the transfer of knowledge in itself is shaped by the politics of knowledge and the particular positions of actors: employers comment often on what servants pick up from them, but servants rarely comment on this process. The many new tasks that servants learn to perform are obvious to many employers as a point of transfer of knowledge, as one officer outlined: "The bungalow peons learn to answer phones, take messages, clean house, attend to office, take papers back and forth, prepare for camp, arrange transport. They learn cooking and setting the dining table and attending guests." I believe there is indeed only a partial recognition of carrying out these transfers, but, regardless of what servants are or are not "taught" by their employers, the bungalow household inevitably provides a context for exposure to a different kind of life and household practice.

The primary kinds of learning that take place between servants and employers involve housework itself. For the most part, learning domestic work is a formative process that takes place while doing rather than a process of self-conscious pedagogical instruction in which employers teach servants. Most of the forms of housework that are learned in the bungalow are "*kaṇ pātru kai vēlai*," "eye-seeing hand-doing work," that is, work that is learned by seeing and doing rather than through oral description of techniques. When I asked employers how they trained their servants, most responded like the bungalow amma who said, "There is no training, they just come and do the work." Most employers said they simply tell the servants what work to do, and then if they do it the wrong way, the employers correct the servants' mistakes. The technique for performing each kind of task is gradually negotiated by trial and error, day by day, between employer and servant.

For their part, employers have a litany of complaints about the tedium of correcting servants' mistakes. The formative process of correcting becomes particularly antagonistic in some instances between the bungalow ammas and the male bungalow peons, who through the course of their work must learn about a whole world of domestic practice that is conventionally only the purview of women. As one bungalow amma put it when I asked her whether it is more difficult to train the (male) bungalow peon than the (female) maid, "Naturally, they are boys. They don't know how to do the housework!" Most of the bungalow ammas said they have less difficulty managing their female maidservants than their male bungalow peons. They complained frequently of the difficulties of training the male bungalow peons, of teaching them how to do the most simple tasks in the proper way. A constant struggle sometimes ensues to teach the bungalow peons proper domestic technique, although on the part of the peons, what sometimes appears as incompetence overlaps with recalcitrance about doing certain tasks, particularly those that are from their perspective more onerous, feminine, dispensable, or useless.

In part the greater difficulty in managing bungalow peons results from structural contradictions in their position in the Indian Railways. As bona fide employees of the Indian government, who work as personal household servants for particular officers, intrinsic contradictions result from the mixing of the private and personal nature of their positions. But the difficulty in managing bungalow peons is also shaped by gender, and part of the resistance of the male bungalow peons to working as servants derives from the fact that the women of the bungalow household are the ones primarily in charge of the management of the bungalow peons, a situation that reverses conventional gender roles.

A whole repertoire of new tasks to be carried out are encountered in the bungalow. Many new tasks are learned that are not common among the working classes, from ironing, mopping, and using certain appliances to making beds and driving cars. As one bungalow amma explained:

> [The bungalow peon] comes from a *totally* different background. We have had to teach him how to behave, how to talk, how to answer the phone, note messages, how to behave with officers. It is most difficult to make him understand. We have to tell him how to serve tea—"Make sure the tray is clean"—or else he brings it out with water on it. When we are tired or don't want to talk to someone we say to say we are not here, but he tells them, "Master says to say he is not here."

Thus, the learning of new tasks, as well as the learning of new modes of interaction and the renegotiation of class identities, is critical to the education of the bungalow peon. Knowledge must be shared with servants to ensure the proper performance of their duties, yet as we shall see, the transfer of knowledge/practice across class boundaries creates problems, and employers may seek to control servants' use of such knowledge and maintain social differences.

Much of this process of learning involves gaining familiarity with the particular technologies of the bungalow and learning to use its specialized *vacati*, or conveniences. The polysemous Tamil word *vacati* can refer to both money as well as all the things that money can buy and is used very often by servants in speaking about the space of the bungalow and the wealth of modern household conveniences and furnishings that fill it. The word is often glossed in Indian English as *facilities*, but its meanings in everyday Tamil discourse are more complex.[5] Sometimes the word refers more literally to money or wealth. Sometimes the word is used in a way that means something like *resources*, as on the many occasions when I was told by outhouse people in exasperation that a certain child could not attend school, that a marriage could not yet be arranged, or that a particular favor could not be procured at a government office, because "We don't have *vacati*" ("*Vacati illai mā*"). At other times *vacati* refers to particularly marked objects, key commodities that serve as particularly salient class signifiers. Many times servants said their employers had "all *vacati*," and when I inquired what "all *vacati*" they had, the response was frequently along the lines of "Oh *all vacati*: car, TV, bungalow." As key commodities, *vacati* figure prominently in the construction of social spaces in the bungalow and in negotiations of class identities between servants and employers. It is telling that in my conversations with servants in the railway colony, they regularly used the word *vacati* in discussing the differences between them and their employers.

The particular care of the *vacati* of the bungalow household, its furnishings and appliances, often involves unfamiliar practices, as one bungalow amma commented: "The bungalow peon is from a poor family and they didn't have all this furniture, so we had to teach him to put the sheets on the bed and dust the furniture." The particular techniques for making beds, dusting furniture, and setting the table all involve technical details linked to the particular objects of the upper-class household. Many employers mentioned that they have to remind the servants to be gentle with the blender ("mixie") and clean it immediately after using it, and to put the lid on it before turning it on. Many bungalow peons who are hired do not know how to operate the gas stove of the bungalow, having grown up using only kerosene stoves in their homes. Employers also complain that they must remind the bungalow peons to close the refrigerator door, which is often left standing open. The glass and ceramic dishes used in the bungalow break easily and are not as durable as the stainless steel utensils used in the outhouse, but the need for caution is sometimes impressed only through trial and error and a few broken dishes. All these areas of negotiation of practice serve as points of transfer of knowledge.

Particular technologies of hospitality in the bungalow are also points of transfer of knowledge, as well as foci of negotiation and occasional disputes between servant and employer. How to set a table properly with tablecloth and crockery and how to serve guests properly at tea or at the dinner table comprise a vast area of etiquette that is an important part of household pedagogy. Many employers complain that the servants do not know how to serve properly; on my visits to bungalows I frequently witnessed employers correcting the technique with which a bungalow peon served me tea, as on one occasion when the peon came in and put the tray down on the coffee table with the cup on it and the bungalow amma instructed him to hold the tray out and allow me to take the cup from it before setting the tray down.

Unfamiliarity with the intricacies of certain techniques and technologies on the part of servants is often strategically transmuted by employers into simplemindedness.[6] Recounting an incident where the peon had turned on the mixie (blender) without holding down the lid, splattering chutney all over the kitchen, one bungalow amma said, "We don't let the servants run the gadgets. Because of ignorance they don't know how to use them." On another occasion, a woman told me of the young girl she had just hired to work in her house: "She's not very smart. She stands there and looks at me until I tell her what to do. She doesn't even know how to make a bed!"

Most likely obeying the one rule repeated among servants about how to conduct themselves in the bungalow—"do whatever they ask you to do"—the
girl's natural curiosity at the different lifestyle encountered in the bungalow,
and her unfamiliarity with its household techniques, is strategically interpreted by the bungalow amma as a sign of weak intellect.

While new skills may be learned in the bungalow, the importance of
doing certain tasks is never self-evident to anyone unaccustomed to them.
Most employers require the servants to mop the hard cement floors of the
bungalow floor every day, but many of the servants have grown up in houses
with mud floors, which are swept but cannot be mopped, and are instead
smeared with cow dung. Mopping is mentioned most often by servants as a
newly learned task, and to some it appears a useless task once the floor has
been swept to remove the dirt. Likewise, in many households the servants
are expected to polish the shoes of the officer and the children before they
leave in the morning, but for many servants, who may wear only sandals or
go barefoot, these techniques of polishing shoes are new.

Household practices, like other practices, are context-linked, anchored
to specific spaces, and while many kinds of household practice are common
to both bungalow and outhouse, the specificity of activity may vary in different spaces (Lave 1988, 144). Certain kinds of activity may be associated
with one kind of space rather than another and the same kinds of activity
may be carried out through different procedures in different contexts, so that
work procedures carried out in the bungalow often vary from the way work
is carried out in the outhouse. Even the ordinary tasks that are carried out in
the bungalow that are familiar to servants from working in their own households may be carried out according to different techniques in the bungalow.
In the outhouse, clothes are beaten on stones and scrubbed hard with a
brush to get them clean, but the bungalow people may complain that washing the clothes in this way makes the clothes become threadbare in no time
and ask the maid not to scrub and beat the clothes so hard. The general
everyday strategy of the outhouse of economizing by not wasting soap, and
instead using human muscle to clean clothes, when carried over to the bungalow can lead to problems, as when employers complain that the maid
scrubs the clothes too hard, so she takes it easy on them, and then they complain that the clothes are not clean.

Many employers say that the servants learn only the work they are
asked to do by their employers. The specific kinds of work activities and the
specific methods for carrying them out provide a context for learning, as servants learn to perform new work tasks and learn new methods of performing
old ones. But learning within the bungalow is in no way confined to the limited tasks that servants are called on to perform in the course of their work.

Servants not only learn work procedures in the bungalow; they also gain familiarity with a whole lifestyle and its material condition. The bungalow provides a space for the study of a whole universe of practice of the upper classes. A world of habits, language, manners, dress, and dispositions is observed within the bungalow by servants, and some of this world becomes a part of their own repertoire. We will see, however, how contradictions arise as a result of this transformation in servants' lives, leading to conflicts over symbolically valued practices that serve as signs of class distinction.

Modes of dress play an important part in this transformation in habit and figure prominently in the renegotiation of class distinctions between servants and employers. Many bungalow ammas do not like it when the bungalow peons wear any clothing that is fancy or "showy"; they tell them to wear only a plain white dress shirt and dark pants to work in the bungalow, rather than the more fashionable styles of patterned fabrics in shiny synthetics. Many of the officers and bungalow ammas ask the bungalow peons to come to work dressed in shirt and pants rather than the more traditional forms of dress such as *dhoti* or *lungi* (both forms of wrapped garments similar to a sarong). One bungalow amma told me she took the bungalow peon with his first month's salary to select the material for two pairs of pants and two shirts so that he would have "decent" clothes to wear to work in the bungalow. The bungalow peon who comes dressed in a *lungi* or *dhoti* and is told to go home and change into pants, not only changes his clothes, but is impressed with the knowledge that these garments are not considered appropriate by the bungalow people. Maids too may be told to come to work dressed neatly, to tuck the ends of their saris inside the skirt while they are working rather than letting them swing freely, or to comb their hair neatly. But if a maid goes too far and wears clothing deemed too fancy by her employers, they may also subtly criticize her dress.

Employers especially comment on the adoption of new manners. As one bungalow amma commented:

> With the outhouse lady there has been a drastic change. When she came she did not know how to talk nicely but now she is getting the habit. She did not know how to show respect, and she did not know manners. She did not know how to greet people and say "*Ammā* [the woman of the house; 'Madam'] will come." But she is learning.

Learning to uphold the formal code of hospitality that prevails in the bungalow is an important part of this process of learning manners. Learning the particular procedures of setting the table and serving are only one part of this process, for more generally servants must be impressed with the merits of formality over informality and learn a new mode of presentation of self (Goffman 1959). But the more informal code of hospitality in the outhouse may conflict with the code of hospitality of the bungalow, and it is gradually negotiated as servants learn that guests are not to be treated as friends or kin might be treated in the outhouse, with a degree of friendly familiarity or informality. As we learned from one bungalow amma, the importance of standing on formality must be impressed on the bungalow peon who brings the wet tray out to serve tea to guests, or tells the caller that "Master says to say he is not here."

Language is another area in which servants learn from employers. English is used with frequency in the bungalow, and in many respects it has a deictic presence in this space, with the many modern conveniences (*vacati*) that are spoken of with English words. Some of the bungalow families speak most of the time in a mixture of English and Tamil or other Indian languages.[7] Servants adopt a good deal of the English vocabulary, and English words are used often in everyday speech in the outhouse (typical, in fact, in much of Madras). Non-Brahmin maids who work in Brahmin households sometimes pick up some of the Brahmin dialect and use it.[8] It is not just any words, but particular ones that find their way into servants' talk, especially those that refer to things such as vegetables and household things in the bungalow, as well as to personal qualities and values. Most of the *vacati* (conveniences) are known by their English names, many of which do not have Tamil names (*fridge, TV, grinder, mixie*) but also some that do (*table, chair*). Particular words in English for qualities (*discipline, condition, correct*) especially find their way into servants' everyday speech. Bungalow peons speak often of "discipline" while maids speak often of "condition" (rules or conditions of employment) and "detail" (prescriptions). "Manners," "prestige" and "style" also are prominent matters of everyday discourse among the outhouse community, as they are to some extent among Tamil speakers more generally in Madras. Tamil servants also learn other Indian languages in this way, and most who work for Hindi-speaking families know at least all the names of vegetables in Hindi, as well as polite phrases that may be used with Hindi-speaking guests. Although some employers may encourage the acquisition of new linguistic skills by their servants, as we shall see, language frequently becomes the site of conflicts between servants and employers in their negotiation of class distinctions.

While so many English words move from bungalow to outhouse, language crosses these barriers more consistently in lexicon than in grammatical structure. Lexical items from English are adopted into everyday speech in Tamil, through the use of loan words or "borrowing," rather than English becoming the medium of discourse in itself (Gumperz 1982, 66–68). In a few cases, where children of the outhouse have obtained some formal schooling in English that is backed up by exposure to conversation in the bungalow, they do become conversant in English. But in the absence of such formal schooling backed up by exposure to conversation in the bungalow, it is primarily lexical knowledge that is transmitted.

Just as it is with respect to language that lexical items move more consistently than do grammatical structures, to some extent something similar might be said to take place with respect to all practices that travel from bungalow to outhouse: the world of practice travels not as a whole but in parts, as practice is transferred through an active process of improvisation by outhouse people. It is not that the outhouse people adopt the *habitus* (or a generalized orientation toward practice) of the bungalow people but that practices are adopted in a piecemeal fashion. Practice travels rather sporadically between the actual spaces of bungalow and outhouse. Learning to do different work and carry out different techniques in the bungalow, and gaining familiarity with its different *vacati*, do not in themselves also directly lead to the carrying out of such techniques within the outhouse.

Work in the bungalow provides a context for the transfer of knowledge and practice across class lines, and for the transformation of lifestyles, but for outhouse people with only limited material resources there are constraints in the extent to which this transformation in lifestyle can take place. For those families who gain access to an official job in the railways through an officer's family, the increased salary provided by a railway job allows for an increasing capacity to transform their way of life. Even for those families who do not gain a railway job, the freedom from paying rent sometimes creates a situation of slightly increased disposable income that can be used for the consumption of new durable goods. In the outhouse, a separate sphere of improvisation is carried out that combines elements of the lifestyle of convenience of the bungalow, even where the material resources for reproducing it are sometimes in short supply. For example, a bungalow peon stacks crates and covers them with blankets to construct "sofa" and "chairs" in his outhouse for entertaining guests and buys a silver tray from which to serve them tea in the proper manner as he has been taught to do by the bungalow people; a maid recovers a discarded cabinet from the bungalow and transforms it into a "showcase" for displaying dolls and souvenirs just as the bungalow people have in their houses. Behind their employers' bungalows, the servant families seek to create for themselves a domestic space of comforts within the means available to them, such as by purchasing a TV, or at least a cassette recorder (even if it means pawning jewels and cooking vessels and taking loans), or by salvaging some pictures discarded by the bungalow to decorate the outhouse.

The transfer of practices as well as the nontransfer of practices, that one practice is chosen but not another, are all socially significant. As Lave has noted, *nonlearning* and *mislearning* are socially constructed just as much as is learning (Lave 1993, 16). Material circumstances of course remain an impediment to the transfer from bungalow to outhouse of many kinds of practices that from the perspective of servants may be an inconceivable luxury, as in the case of the outhouse maid who told me that she has learned to make *aloo paratha*[9] from her officer, and although she likes it, she said she does not make it for her family because she does not have the *vacati* (money or resources) to do so. For the most part, the process of learning practices is of an improvisational nature, shaped by the context of life in the outhouse and the particular social and material circumstances of outhouse people. Within the means available to them, outhouse people improvise their own space of *vacati*, and practices travel, not so much as a total orientation but as occasional improvisations.

While most people in the railway colony generally assume that employers have a greater role in passing on knowledge to their servants than the reverse, knowledge clearly flows in both directions between outhouse and bungalow. But the flow of knowledge is profoundly conditioned by power relations. Although employers do learn from servants, there are many different kinds of constraints on the extent to which they do so. As there is a certain specificity of the link between activity and setting, many kinds of knowledge/practice are constrained from moving from outhouse to bungalow. Outhouse people are constrained, for instance, from carrying out even the work tasks that they perform in the bungalow in accordance with the way they are accustomed to doing them in the outhouse, so that particular techniques of washing clothes and cooking are hindered from moving from outhouse to bungalow. The politics of learning-transfer and the ways in which difference is constructed and imposed are critical not only to the understanding of learning, but to the links between class and knowledge. As forms of knowledge are always bound to forms of power, transfer of knowledge and practice across class lines is never a neutral, socially undifferentiated process, but one always inflected by the dynamics of power relations.

In this section we have seen how knowledge travels between outhouse and bungalow. Servants in the railway colony do adopt many elements of their employers' lifestyle, within the material circumstances of their lives. But transfers of practice and knowledge take place in a partial and improvisational manner, and outhouse people do not so much transform the outhouse into the bungalow as improvise their own provisional space of *vacati* within their own means. As we will see, employers sometimes attempt to delimit this process of transformation of their servants' lifestyle, as well as servants' social mobility.

PRIVILEGED SPHERES OF PRACTICE AS SITES OF STRUGGLE

We have seen how work in the bungalow provides a context for the transfer of practice and knowledge and for the transformation of servants' lifestyles. This process of learning a new lifestyle, however, is not a neutral process, but one bound to the relations of power between outhouse and bungalow, servant and employer. Servants' improvisational ventures into privileged spheres of practice are sometimes met with disapproval by employers, who may act to limit servants' mobility, not only in material terms, but through control over symbolically valued practices. Not only do employers delimit servants' attempts at experimentation with new symbolically valued practices, but they sometimes attempt to curtail and slow servants' mobility through railway structures.

While employers may see a positive transformation taking place through their servants' adoption of singular elements of their own lifestyle (imitation after all can be construed as a form of flattery), in many respects they attempt to delimit the effects of these processes. Employers seek to maintain an upper hand through claiming greater mastery of symbolically valued practices. For instance, although English has a pervasive presence in Madras, it functions across many different contexts and situations as a privileged code, whose monopoly is claimed by the upper classes, so that the servant who attempts to use the code is denigrated for lack of sophistication in its use, as in the following incident that I witnessed one day when Raj,[10] a bungalow peon, was helping Sita, a bungalow amma, to make a telephone call. Sita was holding the receiver of the phone while Raj was preparing to dial it, and he turned to ask her "'*Dial*' *irukkā?*" ("Is there a 'dial'?"). She shouted (in English), "Stupid! Just dial the phone." Later Sita told me that Raj "tries to be smart" by speaking English to her, but she tells him just to speak in Tamil, which both she and he can understand. She said, "You should either use the right word, 'dial *tone*,' or don't speak in English." The extent to which English functions in the servant-employer relation as a privileged code in Madras is further exemplified in the case of an Anglo-Indian maid (whose mother tongue was English) who was forbidden to speak English in front of her Anglo-Indian employer, with the injunction "Servants must speak in Tamil."

Thus, many employers try to delimit their servants' attempts to encroach on privileged spheres of practice, and practice itself becomes the site for imposing difference, even while the flow of knowledge between bungalow and outhouse threatens to blur class distinctions. As servants' lives are transformed, consumption, dress, and objects become contested sites for the production of difference in struggles between bungalow and outhouse, and in many cases encroachment by servants on privileged spheres of practice is met with indignation or even outright anger from employers. Employers tell their servants to be thrifty and save money, but what servants see firsthand in the bungalow impresses them more, transmitting styles and orientations that result to some extent in improvisations that replicate the lifestyle of the bungalow and its space of *vacati*. Disputes over some other matter may give rise to employers' comments on servants' consumption, and their obtaining *vacati* provides a context for the dispute of their proper standing. If servants wear a new sari or buy a new household good, employers may inquire where they got the money to buy it. The sari in particular is highly fetishized as a powerful object, and given the focal place of the sari as a supreme marker of value and of status differences between women, it comes as little surprise that the sari, along with the *vacati* of the household, often become the loci of dispute between servants and employers. The adoption of new privileged elements of lifestyle and the use of objects and accoutrements that serve as potent class signifiers are not only matters of class distinction, but of *mariyātai*, the respect that employers expect from servants, as Jayashree explained:

> If we don't stand bowing and give respect, this way [bowing], stand bent, respectfully. . . . [They will say] "Why are you not giving me respect? Am I not an officer? Why are you not giving me respect? Then what's the difference between you and me? I am a big officer. You are a servant. What is the difference between you and me?" That's the reason why they didn't give us electricity. "If I give electricity now, you will buy a TV, buy radio and there will be no difference between you and me. I am a rich person. You are a poor person. The difference will not be there." Thinking that way [the officer] spoke.

Later Jayashree continued:

> Then [the bungalow people think] in our house we shouldn't eat well, shouldn't wear good clothes, shouldn't buy and have anything. In their eyesight we can't wear a nice sari, we can't wear a nice blouse, we shouldn't

wear lots of flowers in our hair and comb our hair and go in front of them.
[The bungalow people will say] "Then what's the difference between you
and me? What's the difference between the people in the outhouse and us?"
They will ask how did you get this nice sari? How did you buy it? For buying
all this, how did you get the *vacati* [money]? That way they will ask. They
say there should be difference between working people and rich people.

In Jayashree's adoption of the bungalow people's voice, the radio, TV,
nice sari, even flowers worn in the hair all serve as potent class signifiers and
objects of struggle in the relation between bungalow and outhouse, rich and
poor. Even practices such as the use of electricity and combing the hair
threaten to blur the unqualified character of class distinction. In Jayashree's
account, for the bungalow people, *mariyātai*, or respect, is linked to class difference, and the consumption of special *vacati* that threaten to blur class distinctions is an affront to the respect that employers expect from servants.
Jayashree's officer would not allow her family to use electricity in the outhouse, and she felt that the reason was that she would then have the potential to buy appliances, the special *vacati*, that serve as potent signifiers of
their difference. According to Jayashree, the bungalow people think that
there should be difference between working people and rich people, and the
possession by servants of privileged signs of class distinction threatens to
negate these differences.

From the bungalow people's perspective, the contradiction appears as
one of gaining the objects of a lifestyle without gaining the life or the position appropriate to them. In the words of Uma, a bungalow amma:

> Not all [the servants] learn is good. They see us living a lavish life. They
> want to be like us, like their manager, their owner. They don't want to live
> within their means. They see us having TV. Then they want also to have
> a TV. But they don't want to work to get the TV. They learn wearing fancy
> sari and going out. Some of what they learn from us is bad. They pick it up
> without really understanding.

The statement by Uma highlights some of the contradictions of learning a lifestyle in the bungalow. Uma sees the servants as gaining only a partial knowledge through this process of learning, and in particular of learning
only a mode of consumption of luxurious goods like TVs and fancy saris,
without an incorporation of the entire world of practice associated for her
with the life represented by these goods and its purported work ethic. She
highlights what she sees developing in the servants: a desire for these luxury

goods, a process she views as negative. As special *vacati* serve as potent class signifiers, their ownership by the poor are seen as inappropriate to their station and out of place in their lives. The rich may consume what the poor are told is beyond their means to consume. Sita expressed a similar sentiment:

> They [her bungalow peon and maid] talk of socialism. . . . She said to me, "The same blood runs through my veins as yours." I said to her, "If I said the same blood runs through my veins as P. V. Narasimha Rao's,[11] everyone would just laugh at me." My idea of socialism is to feed the workers so they will work well. Their idea is to live like us. She complains about the price rises . . . well, the price rises affect me just as much as her. They want to live like us but *they can't*. It's . . . something about a person. It's . . . *education*. There's something you can see, in a person's eye, it comes from inside, that they *know*, that they're not just . . . *bragging*.

Sita too sees the servants as gaining only a partial knowledge, as gaining a desire to live like the bungalow people. But she sees this partial knowledge as limited, illegitimate, and tellingly incomplete, as servants reveal in their demeanor their imperfect mastery of symbolically valued practice (as we saw when she criticized Raj's attempts to use English). But Sita says something more: that even if the servants gain some part of the lifestyle, they can never truly assume the position taken as congruent with that lifestyle. Whatever they can gain materially cannot give the education of one who truly can take one's knowledge for granted, the lifelong pedagogy of a privileged upbringing. At issue, then, is the process through which one may gain a lifestyle without gaining the life.

In this section we have seen how when talking about struggles carried out over these privileged spaces of consumption and practice, servants may assume the voice of the bungalow people in expressing explicitly and directly the principles they see operating more implicitly in everyday life. In her account, Jayashree's officer forthrightly stated the idea that there should be difference between bungalow people and outhouse people. Employers may indeed occasionally baldly accuse servants of trying to act like them and attempt to directly enforce distinctions. Sita and Uma accused the servants of wanting to live like the bungalow people. Yet even in the absence of such bald statements by employers, questions and comments about servants' attire and consumption habits communicate that the bungalow people give credence to this difference. In assuming bungalow people's voices when talking about these attitudes, servants make explicit the distinctions that are sometimes enforced more subtly in everyday life.

CONCLUSION

Forms of knowledge are always bound to forms of power. The transfer of knowledge across class boundaries is never a neutral process but is always inflected by the dynamics of power relations. Domestic service has been revealed to be a site not only for the creation of social difference but also for social learning and a channel for the flow of knowledge/practice across class boundaries. This flow of knowledge problematizes the class identities of servants and employers, creating contradictions for both in some respects. Domestic service is revealed to be not only a pedagogical site but also a site of struggle over practice. Practices become a site of struggle between employers and servants, as employers seek to delimit servants' encroachment on privileged spheres of practice. We have seen how the adoption by the poor of singular elements of the bungalow lifestyle—the purchase of a TV or the wearing of a fancy sari—is viewed from the upper-class perspective as ridiculous, absurd, or out of place. Whereas from outhouse people's perspective such practices and things may be valued in singularity, from bungalow people's perspective they appear as mere signs of the partial adoption of a lifestyle without achieving the life.

It may be tempting to see such examples of the adoption of new consumption practices by servants as instances of resistance. Yet baldly labeling them as such risks overlooking the often contradictory nature of social action, the way in which it may reproduce meaning even as it alters it. Both hegemony and resistance are fragile and ambiguous, as has been argued elsewhere in this volume (Dickey and Adams this volume; Hansen this volume).

This essay has focused on the exchange of knowledge/practice between servants and employers, but this form of exchange is part of a larger story, involving systems of patronage through which servants seek social mobility, and an escape from servitude, by gaining access to permanent employment in the railways. The pedagogy of the bungalow through which servants learn a new lifestyle still leaves little scope for mobility without an increase in material resources, but for those outhouse families who gain a railway job, with its greater economic benefits and social prestige, structural contradictions arise between accepting this increased social position with all its ramifications and the continued pressure to serve. As long as a family continues to reside in an outhouse, under the watchful eye of the officer's family, there are constraints in the extent to which they can begin to transform their way of life befitting their increased economic resources and social position. It is not only through the imposition of symbolic class distinction by seeking to control spheres of privileged practice that employers seek to delimit servants' social mobility. For those outhouse families who have gained a railway job, as the primary personal link with the railway power structure, the officer who has helped them to get the job (and his family) may continue to exercise control over mobility within the railway structure in more explicit ways, by influencing future promotions in the railways. Not only do employers seek to delimit servants' encroachment on privileged spheres of practice, but they may subtly act to impede servants' upward mobility. These structural contradictions carefully must be negotiated, as servants may gradually seek to assume the role of independent railway worker and lessen their role of service to the officers and their families, but a number of outhouse families have succeeded in achieving this transition.

Domestic service may be both a medium for the creation of social difference and one through which social difference may be transformed. If actors are not to be construed as having preordained statuses that are given once and for all, then from a theoretical standpoint one must assume that actors are always transformed by their action in the world and that the circumstances of agents are structured by their world as they also structure it through their action. As an empirical case, the railway colony represents a distinctive context in which domestic service itself has to some extent gained the capacity to serve as a medium of social mobility. In this context, domestic service has come to operate as a medium of class identity negotiation *and* class identity transformation. If we assume that household workers are active agents, and that social difference is truly constructed in concrete contexts, rather than simply reflected in them, we cannot assume that domestic service cannot provide a context for transformation as well as reproduction. Given our more complex contemporary notions of the dialectic among person, practice, agency, and structure (cf. Bourdieu 1977, 1984; Giddens 1979), it is no longer tenable to hold that people move through structures without transforming them, as well as themselves, in the process. Through their occasional assertion over privileged spheres of practice (even against their employers' wishes) and through their attempts to seek social mobility (even through exploitative institutions of domestic service) servants are revealed to be engaged in a struggle to re-create themselves, the world around them, and their place in it.

Acknowledgments

This essay is based on fieldwork conducted from 1991 to 1993 with the support of a Fulbright-Hays Doctoral Dissertation Research Abroad Fellowship and a Junior

Research Fellowship from the American Institute of Indian Studies. I am grateful to K. M. P. Marlia for her assistance during my research and to the editors of this volume for their comments.

NOTES

1. Some of the major works that focus primarily on gender include Bunster and Chaney (1985) and Chaney and García Castro (1989) in Latin America and Watson (1991) in Hong Kong. Those that focus particularly on race include Preston-Whyte (1976) and Weinrich (1976). Those looking in particular at race and gender include Cock (1980) in South Africa, and Rollins (1985) and Tucker (1989) in the United States. Those that look particularly at ethnicity include Armstrong (1990), Cooke (1990), and Glenn (1986). A number of works also focus particularly on the intersection of gender, race, or ethnicity and class (Gaitskell et al. 1984; Glenn 1986; Hansen 1989, 1990).

2. I was not able to live directly in the railway colony, as housing there is intended only for railway employees, but lived nearby (I did employ a servant, but she had no relation to the railway colony). On a general level, the different nature of sociability among the officers' families and the servants' families, itself a feature of differences in social class, shaped the outcome of the study, as I found my interactions were always more formal and distant in the bungalow than in the outhouse. These differences shaped my research in that I used more formal methods of study (interviewing and questionnaires) among the officers' families, whereas among the servants' families I was able to participate more in daily activities and informal discussions that went beyond what could be learned through such more formal means.

3. The total take-home pay of bungalow peons ranged from 1,500 to 1,800 rupees a month (approximately equivalent to US$50–60 at the exchange rate when I conducted fieldwork).

4. Approximately equivalent to US$1.65 at the exchange rate when I conducted the study. A bungalow peon's total monthly earnings paid to him by the Railways (Rs 1500–1800) may range from 13 to 23 percent of his officer's earnings (Rs 7,800–13,000). An outhouse maid's monthly wage of Rs 50 paid to her privately by the bungalow family may thus range from .4 to 1.2 percent of an officer's monthly earnings, and some outhouse maids do not earn even this comparatively infinitesimal amount.

5. One Tamil dictionary gives the meanings of *vacati* as means, amenity, or facility (Subramanian 1992, 892).

6. On the way in which communication problems may be construed by employers as signs of the incompetence of servants and their childlike qualities, see Kidder (this volume).

7. Families who have moved around a lot due to transfers in the railways, and whose children have been educated in English-medium schools, especially may be inclined to use English in the home, particularly since the children may not even know their parents' native tongue well.

8. This context is different then, from the one described by Gumperz (1971,1982, 39), in which sweepers in a north Indian village "spend most of their waking hours either listening or talking to speakers of the majority dialects" but "would no more imitate the speech of their employers than they would adopt their employers' style of clothing" for to do so would risk retaliation by the dominant upper castes. Such would appear to be one sign of the greater fluidity of caste distinction in the bureaucratic village of the railway colony in comparison with villages with long, ongoing, hereditary interrelations between groups.

9. *Aloo paratha* is a buttery and flaky flatbread stuffed with potato filling.

10. All personal names used are pseudonyms.

11. Narasimha Rao was then the prime minister of India.

References

Appadurai, Arjun

1988   How to Make a National Cuisine: Cookbooks in Contemporary India. *Comparative Studies in Society and History* 30: 3–24.

Armstrong, M. Jocelyn

1990   Female Household Workers in Industrializing Malaysia. In Roger Sanjek and Shellee Colen, eds., *At Work in Homes: Household Workers in World Perspective*, 146–63. American Ethnological Society Monograph Series, No. 3. Washington, DC: American Anthropological Association.

Bourdieu, Pierre

1977   *Outline of a Theory of Practice*. Trans. Richard Nice. Cambridge: Cambridge University Press.

1984   *Distinction: A Social Critique of the Judgement of Taste*. Cambridge: Cambridge University Press.

Breman, Jan

1979   The Market for Non-Agrarian Labour: The Formal Versus Informal Sector. In S. Devadas Pillai and Christiaan Baks, eds., *Winners and Losers: Styles of Development in an Indian Region*, 122–66. Bombay: Popular Prakashan.

Bunster, Ximena, and Elsa M. Chaney

1985   *Sellers and Servants: Working Women in Lima, Peru*. New York: Praeger.

Chaney, Elsa M., and Mary García Castro, eds.

1989 *Muchachas No More: Household Workers in Latin America and the Caribbean.* Philadelphia: Temple University Press.

Cock, Jacklyn

1980 *Maids and Madams: A Study in the Politics of Exploitation.* Johannesburg: Ravan Press.

Cooke, M. T.

1990 Household Workers in Nyishang, Nepal. In Roger Sanjek and Shellee Colen, eds., *At Work in Homes: Household Workers in World Perspective,* 63–73. American Ethnological Society Monograph Series, No. 3. Washington, DC: American Anthropological Association.

Dickey, Sara

1993 *Cinema and the Urban Poor in South India.* Cambridge: Cambridge University Press.

Dumont, Louis

1970 *Homo Hierarchicus.* Chicago: University of Chicago Press.

Gaitskell, Deborah, Judy Kimble, Moira Maconachie, and Elaine Unterhalter

1984 Class, Race and Gender: Domestic Workers in South Africa. *Review of African Political Economy* 27/28:86–106.

Giddens, Anthony

1979 *Central Problems in Social Theory: Action, Structure and Contradiction in Social Analysis.* Berkeley: University of California Press.

Glenn, Evelyn Nakano

1986 *Issei, Nisei, War Bride: Three Generations of Japanese American Women in Domestic Service.* Philadelphia: Temple University Press.

Goffman, Erving

1959 *The Presentation of Self in Everday Life.* Garden City, NY: Doubleday.

Gumperz, John

1971 Dialect Differences and Social Stratification in a North Indian Village. In *Language in Social Groups,* 25–47. Stanford: Stanford University Press.

1982 *Discourse Strategies.* Cambridge: Cambridge University Press.

Hansen, Karen Tranberg

1989 *Distant Companions: Servants and Employers in Zambia, 1900–1985.* Ithaca: Cornell University Press.

1990 Part of the Household Inventory: Men Servants in Zambia. In Roger Sanjek and Shellee Colen, eds., *At Work in Homes: Household Workers in World*

Perspective, 89–118. American Ethnological Society Monograph Series, No. 3. Washington, DC: American Anthropological Association.

Holmström, Mark

1985 *Industry and Inequality: The Social Anthropology of Indian Labour*. Cambridge: Cambridge University Press.

Lave, Jean

1988 *Cognition in Practice: Mind, Mathematics and Culture in Everyday Life*. Cambridge: Cambridge University Press.

1993 The Practice of Learning. In Seth Chaiklin and Jean Lave, eds., *Understanding Practice: Perspectives on Activity and Context*, 3–32. Cambridge: Cambridge University Press.

Preston-Whyte, Eleanor

1976 Race Attitudes and Behaviour: The Case of Domestic Employment in White South African Homes. *African Studies* 35:71–89.

Rollins, Judith

1985 *Between Women: Domestics and Their Employers*. Philadelphia: Temple University Press.

Subramanian, Pavoorchatram Rajagopal, ed.

1992 *Kriyavin Tarkalat Tamil Akarati: Tamil-Tamil-Ankilam*. Madras: Kriya Publishers.

Tolen, Rachel

1996 Between Bungalow and Outhouse: Class Practice and Domestic Service in a Madras Railway Colony. Ph.D. diss., Department of Anthropology, University of Pennsylvania.

Tucker, Susan

1989 *Telling Memories Among Southern Women: Domestic Workers and their Employers in the Segregated South*. Baton Rouge: Louisiana State University Press.

Watson, Rubie S.

1991 Wives, Concubines and Maids: Servitude and Kinship in the Hong Kong Region, 1900–1940. In Rubie S. Watson and Patricia Buckley Ebrey, eds., *Marriage and Inequality in Chinese Society*, 231–55. Berkeley: University of California Press.

Weinrich, Anna K. H.

1976 *Mucheke: Race, Status and Politics in a Rhodesian Community*. New York: Holmes & Meier Publishers.

SERVICE OR SERVITUDE?

The Domestication of Household Labor in Nepal

This essay argues that identities, whether for servants or their masters, are not permanent entities but rather dynamic and multiple evaluations occasioned by the intersection of the subjective motivations of the actors and the objective limits bounding the master-servant relationship. While the underlying power dimension between masters and servants remains structurally stable, the expression and meaning of this relationship can take multiple forms both in contestation and complicity. The notion of identity presupposes a degree of individual agency such that identity construction is not totally determined by structural location alone. At the same time, however, the "construction of identities cannot be discussed in the abstract, separately, from power relations" (Kondo 1990, 43). Thus, within these outer boundaries set by individual creativity and larger structural forces, the task remains to illuminate the complexity of these relations and the identities they give rise to in their historical and ethnographic specificity. Indeed, it is these indeterminate discursive zones that sustain multiple meanings, identities, and subject positions in the master-servant relation. I pursue this line of argument by focusing on the practices of kinship and schooling relating to domestic service in Nepal. For this task, it has been necessary to connect the specifics of the master-servant relationship to broader political and economic processes in society. Such an approach not only illuminates the dynamics of the domestic terrain at a microlevel but also points to the larger processes that impinge on and inform the local discourse and responses, thereby making anthropology "fully accountable to its historical and political-economy implications" (Marcus and Fischer 1986, 86).

This study is based on ethnographic material collected during an eight-month stay in a lower-middle-class neighborhood in Kathmandu city during 1991–92, when I became acquainted with more than a dozen young servants working in the area, and from comparative work in rural western Nepal with sixteen servant-employing households in 1993–94. I spent a total of seven months in Dhading, Bardiya, and Banke districts. The sixteen families had a total of twelve boys and seven girls working for them (three families had two servants each). The age of these servants ranged between nine and seventeen, and five out of the fourteen individuals I came to know in Kathmandu were girls. My observation in rural villages not only provided a comparative insight to the situation in Kathmandu but also revealed the linkages of rural-urban labor recruitment. Through my own initiative and sometimes with the help of these *kamgarnes* (a euphemism for servants; literal translation from Nepali would be "one who works"), I also came to know many of their *maliks* or *sahus* (terms that denote owner, merchant, or moneylender) and some of the parents/guardians of these servants as well. Moreover, two of these servant-employing families were old acquaintances and proved very helpful in the research. At the same time, my understanding of the issue has also been informed and influenced by observing the servants in my parents' home as well as other friends and acquaintances in general. Although all the maliks in particular were initially hesitant and somewhat suspicious of my intentions, most of them became much more receptive and open to my interest in the servants once I convinced them that mine was not a unionizing effort or an attempt to pass moral judgment on their lower-middle-class situation.[1] Upon the express demands of some of the respondents, however, I have used pseudonyms in the text. Given the sensitive nature of my inquiry, I was later surprised by the degree of openness with which they discussed many aspects of their relationships during numerous visits to their homes. Indeed, some of the most revealing moments came on the rare occasions when all the parties—the maliks, their kamgarnes, the parents of the servants, and the anthropologist—were present.

I have used the term malik or sahu because it is the term servants use most frequently to refer to their "employers." The potency of the term malik is quite telling; within the household kin relations, for example, it is used by wives to refer to their husbands and indicates total loyalty and fidelity in an asymmetrical relationship. In contrast, even the lowest peon in a contractual wage relationship will refer to his office boss as *hakim*, not malik. In a recent seminal work on domestic workers it has been proposed that "employing households" should be referred to as "employers" rather than by "other local terms of address or reference" (Colen and Sanjek 1990, 4). Although this is definitely appropriate for regulated contractual relationships, it would at least be misleading, if not unjust, to those kamgarnes who are not "employed" but "kept" (rakheko) without a regular or regulated wage. None of the servants I came to know who were working for a fixed salary received more than Rs 100 a month, and the majority of them worked for no regular wage.[2] A daily wage laborer in Nepal currently receives anywhere between Rs 25 and Rs 40 per day, whereas the monthly salary of a peon, the lowest government employee, has been set at Rs 1,200 per month. The minimum wage that has been fixed for daily laborers (although not always enforced) does not apply to domestic servants. The cost of living for low-income groups is quite dear and rising each year. Rice, one of the staple diets for most people, costs Rs 10 to Rs 12 per kilogram for the cheapest variety, and an adult person requires at least 15 kilograms of it for a month's supply. Since the present study draws attention to those young domestics who have not even attained the threshold of the wage relation, the failure to maintain the important conceptual and historical distinction between malik and employer risks a serious misreading of the situation. Rather than assuming that all servants necessarily receive a "wage" in the standard sense, it is useful to use the term *compensation* or *remuneration* to refer to all those things (e.g., food, living space, clothing, gifts, patronage) received by the servant where there are no fixed wages. According to Marx, capital appropriates not the laborer as a person but his labor "by means of exchange" in wages (1989, 99). But the domestic, by the liminal zone he or she occupies, is appropriated in labor as well as in person. Engels notes in *Origin of the Family* that slavery, serfdom, and wage labor are the three historic forms of servitude (quoted in Hobsbawm 1989, 51). Where does a kamgarne, who neither receives the wage labor of a "free day-laborer" nor meets the obligations of a serf, stand? The apparent contradiction becomes even more obvious when many of the maliks, while themselves engaged in contractual wage and salary employment, maintain nonwage relations with their domestics. The kamgarnes therefore must be understood as not only standing at the margins of "home," kinship, and other belongings but also as occupying the interstices of various historical forms of relations that are sedimented and juxtaposed concurrently.

Similarly, Colen and Sanjek's (1990, 1) suggestion that "we choose the term 'household worker' because it better describes the situation of workers in homes than such stigmatized terms as 'servant,' 'domestics,' or 'domestic servants' . . . as an inclusive term to cover the many types of work in homes" has the unintentional effect of glossing over the lived experience of the servants themselves. More important, the conditions and motivations of both masters and servants across the globe are diverse; the relatively better regulated domestic labor market of Europe or North America cannot be put in the same basket as Nepal or India where domestic labor for the most part rests upon ambiguous oral arrangements with practically little or no state regulation. In place of contractual bonds between a "worker" and an "employer," Nepal's domestic ideology is operationalized in an idiom of servitude and loyalty from the kamgarne in exchange for the benevolent patronage of the malik with strong feudal overtones.

I have been theoretically eclectic in the analytic framework that follows. Bourdieu's formulations on the "theory of practice" have proved incisive in understanding the everyday practices of domination and power involved in the master-servant relationship. Here, the central concept of "habitus" seeks to account for any "practices and representations" representing the conjunction of both subjective motivations and objective limitations in order to dissolve traditional epistemological dichotomies between rules and behaviors (Bourdieu 1977, 72–73). In pursuing the main theme of this essay—fluidity and ambiguities in identity—Bourdieu's notion of "misrecognition" whereby "interested relationship is transmuted into a disinterested, gratuitous relationship" and "overt domination into misrecognized 'socially recognized' domination" (1977, 192) is central to understanding patron-client self-consciousness. For examining the issue of discipline, domination, and consent to domination—so central in a master-servant relation—the ideas of Foucault (1984) and Gramsci (1992) are also illuminating. In terms of ethnographic writings on domestic labor, recent works by Gill (1994), Sanjek and Colen (1990), and Mehta (1960) have influenced my own orientation to the problem in Nepal by imparting a comparative perspective from a host of sociocultural settings. Finally, with the assumption that present identity negotiations cannot be fully explicated without due appreciation of structural forces (Bourdieu 1977), it has been necessary to turn to critical writings on class and dependency in Nepal (Blaikie, Cameron, and Seddon 1977; Mishra 1987; Seddon 1987).

AMBIGUITIES AND EUPHEMISMS

One striking experience of doing ethnographic work among servants is the degree of ambiguity in which the whole master-servant relation is cast. Not only are the basic terms and conditions of the servant's work—such as hours, tasks, leave, and payment—left unspecified, even the identity of the servant is indeterminate so that it can be actualized according to the contingent needs and powers of the "two parties at a particular time, and on the degree of integration and ethical integrity of the arbitrating group" (Bourdieu 1977, 192). I created many an awkward situation in middle-class living rooms in Kathmandu by inquiring about the person serving us tea. Hosts' use of woolly adjectives and superlatives, such as "oh, he is our 'hero' here" or, "she is very much our own family member," was intended to reassure the person in question of his or her fragile position more than to answer the inquisitive anthropologist. The deployment of such hyperbole is meant to shore up the delicately maintained mystifications from the immanent rupture posed by the specifying query. But once the servants were out of earshot, hosts would hasten to clarify that the person was only a kamgarne, lest the person be mistaken for a family member.

Whether due to public courtesy, duplicity, or political concession, public morality in most places in Nepal now makes it poor taste to use the term *nokar* (servant), except perhaps when a servant is deemed to require a dressing-down. Instead, the less-offensive and more-status-ambiguous kamgarne is preferred, by both masters and servants alike. As a noun, nokar is explicit about the subordinate and servile disposition in relation to the master. On the other hand, the term kamgarne, generated from the verb *kaam garnu* (to work), is free of intrinsic asymmetrical coding. Since everyone does some kaam, or work, kamgarne has just enough ambiguity that the relation may be linguistically as well as socially "misrecognized." Bourdieu states that if "elementary forms" of domination, as between masters and servants, are to be sustained, the relationships "must be disguised and transfigured lest they destroy themselves by revealing their true nature; in a word, they must be *euphemized*" (1977, 191 emphasis in original)—hence the need to mask such offensive relational representations, if not the actual practices, by condescending paternalistic or maternalistic euphemisms.

Servants are culturally and politically perceived as inferiors because both the work and station of the domestics are historically associated with certain aspects of slavery and indentured labor. According to certain Hindu texts, the Sudras as the lowest segment on the caste rung were "ordained to live by serving the people of higher varna" (Mehta 1960, 8). The traditional caste hierarchy is composed of Brahmins at the top of the ritual pyramid, followed by Kshetriyas and Vaishyas in the middle, and Sudras at the bottom. Not only has Hinduism been a formative influence on Nepali society; the country has also witnessed institutionalized slavery and indentured labor as well. Even if the modern civil code in Nepal has legally ended caste disabilities, the stigma associated with menial service work, especially domestic chores performed for others, still persists. The devaluation of domestics' status is further compounded when in most cultures servants are employed to perform the tasks that are in themselves inferior functions in the gendered division of household labor.

Contrary to caste expectations, one does also frequently come across Brahmin servants working for non-Brahmin maliks. Since caste status and class positions do not always go together in society, Brahmins may also be forced to take employment not compatible with their ritual functions due to economic constraints. Indeed there is social and ritual (caste) prestige involved in having a Brahmin kamgarne, especially as a cook. According to caste commensality rules in Nepal, people cannot take foods cooked by a person who is of lower caste than they are. In this context, a person who has a Brahmin cook enjoys the privilege of being able to offer hospitality to anyone. Besides the well-known functions of Brahmins as priests, scholars, and astrologers, a lesser-known role is that of a *bhhanche Bahun* (literally, a "kitchen Brahmin"). This is not a recent development either—feudal and aristocratic families have traditionally employed Brahmins in their kitchens since they could afford to spare their womenfolk from the kitchen chores. Brahmin cooks have enjoyed a superior position among other servants due to their caste rank and have usually abstained from washing and cleaning duties.

TIES OF DEPENDENCIES

The situation of the domestics in Nepal cannot be fully appreciated without understanding the rural hinterland, where poverty and marginalization produce conditions that sustain a steady supply of domestics destined to work within Nepal, the surrounding region, and even overseas. Although over 90 percent of the economically active population is engaged in agriculture-related occupations, Nepal has one of the lowest per-hectare agricultural productivity ratios in South Asia due to the combined effects of lack of agricultural modernization, inadequate irrigation facilities, and ecological degradation. Agriculture is mostly of the subsistence type in tiny peasant holdings, and the per-hectare yield for rice, maize, barley, and millet has actually declined over the last two decades (Unicef 1987, 31).

These complex technological and ecological constraints are further aggravated by the skewed distribution of resources: the top 10 percent of the households take away 47 percent of the total annual income in the country while the poorest 40 percent are left with just 9 percent of the income. Similarly, over 50 percent of all holdings are less than 0.5 hectare in size and thus insufficient to feed an average-sized family of six for twelve months (Unicef 1987, 16, 18). According to government statistics, 42.5 percent of the population falls below the officially defined poverty line assessed at $500 income per household per year (Unicef 1987, 16). A more recent World Bank report estimates that over 70 percent of the population may fall below the poverty line (Unicef 1992, 1).

A comprehensive multidisciplinary study of the Nepalese political economy concludes that the relations of exploitation and dependency in Nepal are manifest in both class and regional asymmetries (Blaikie et al. 1977). Seen from this perspective, Kathmandu, the national center, commands the surplus of capital and labor from the rural hinterland. This process is replicated at a deeper level between the Indian metropolis and Nepalese periphery. As a "near-full-fledged" dominion of the "Indian state and the Indian mercantile bourgeoisie," Nepal is a monopoly market for Indian goods and a controlled labor reserve for India's production as well as defense requirements (Mishra 1987, 125).

At the regional level, progressive "development of underdevelopment" and dependency, manifest in the cycle of indebtedness, poverty, high fertility rate, land fragmentation, and alienation, force a large mass of landless and marginal peasant households to augment their meager subsistence by working as porters, agricultural laborers, construction workers, and domestic servants both inside and outside the country. Due to the combined effects of the high annual population growth rate of 2.10 percent (Central Bureau of Statistics [CBS] 1995, 2), shrinking landholdings, and declining productivity, there is both serious unemployment and underemployment in rural areas. The prospects for nonagricultural employment is minimal due to the complex set of historical, regional, and economic variables that inhibit industrial growth in the country. In summary, the acute poverty and dependency of the nation is "exacerbated by being the periphery of a periphery" (Cameron 1994, 75). The 1981 census recorded 402,977 persons who had migrated outside the country, mostly to India, to find laboring and service work (CBS 1991, 16). A major employment avenue for the men from the hills, made notorious by the misnomer "Gurkha," has been to join the armies and paramilitary forces of various countries. Children and women do not lag far behind in following the menfolk in escaping the grinding poverty back at home. According to one estimate, more than 18,000 Nepalese children are working as servants in the Indian capital of Delhi alone (Banskota 1991, 10). Although the Nepalese census does not present servants as a separate labor category (reflecting the official silence on the issue), a nongovernmental agency estimates that as many as 45,000 children may be working as kamgarnes in Kathmandu Valley alone (Child Workers in Nepal [CWIN] 1988, 83). As Mishra notes, the motivation, direction, and volume of such migration underscore the rural-urban and regional inequalities and the supremacy of capital over labor (1987, 128).

RECRUITING NETWORKS

To make ends meet, marginal households are often forced to borrow both cash and foodgrains from better-off neighbors and moneylenders under varying terms. Since the loan secured, usually at usurious rates, is for basic living expenses rather than for productive investment, such crisis borrowings eventually lead to alienation of land and other assets. As the levels of debt and poverty rise many marginal households place some of their members, usually children, to work in the home of the patron, both as a surety on the loan or in lieu of the interest on the loan. These responses to acute marginalization and poverty have been common in Nepal since at least the nineteenth century (Regmi 1978, 132). As Seddon, Westwood, and Blaikie argue, such exploitation and dependence

> reproduce a local labor force in condition of servility and dependence at a bare subsistence level. In the context of multiple relationships between rich and poor, employer and employee, creditor and debtor, the struggle is a silent one of negotiation and manipulation in which the cards are stacked against the weaker party. (1980, 142)

For a growing number of peasants and the landless, even these local patron-client arrangements are inadequate to keep them afloat, even at the bare minimum level. These people must move to distant towns and urban areas for employment and subsistence, thus creating a steady supply of unskilled labor that includes domestic service. Much of the recruiting for servants is done through informal networks of kinship and patron-client ties that link urban areas to the rural hinterland. Intermediaries, who have active connections in both urban and rural areas, play a role here. These intermediaries are not usually paid directly by either side. Instead, they accumulate *goon* (favor) from both sides, which can be later translated into connections, jobs, patronage, or other benefits from having acquired a good servant for a well-placed family in Kathmandu. Such recruitment practices also lend semblance of social legitimacy to these labor arrangements, since everyone concerned—masters, intermediaries, parents/guardians, and the individual domestics—is party to the agreement, even though choice for some may be more limited.

Recruitment through informal networks of patron-client ties has a strong labor disciplining effect: the servant is careful not to offend the master lest he or she tarnish the good name of the intermediaries or parents who were "signatories," as it were, to the deal. These patron-client ties, asymmetrical and exploitative as they may be, are important survival resources for the poor. After all, they do "ensure the survival at the minimum level" (Seddon et al. 1980, 142).

SCHOOL, WORK, AND HOME

The larger inequality inscribed on regional geography is again replicated in the control and discipline inside the domestic sphere. Nepali maliks have an overwhelming preference for domestics from rural areas. Rural villagers are seen to be more *sojho*, a concept that incorporates characteristics of honesty, loyalty, meekness, and obedience. While these are positively valued qualities in a servant (since they aid in the appropriation of labor and the production of symbolic capital), the urban middle-class stereotyping of rural folks as ignorant, dirty, and *asabhya* (uncivilized) simultaneously provides urbanity with a civilizing role and further adds a cultural dimension and rationale for the servant's subordination. It is not only the masters who assert their cultural superiority by deriding and attempting to alter the devalued dialect or hygiene of the rural kamgarne *keta* (boy) or *keti* (girl); many servants and their parents recognize and desire urban middle-class distinctions. A few parents who had their children working in Kathmandu told me that apart from the material necessity, they hoped that after living in an urban home their children will get some "civilization," which connotes a number of attributes, including learning urban high Nepali speech and "talking well," acquiring a refinement of habits, and understanding the ways of the world. A few parents even asked the masters to be "strict" in inculcating good habits (*ramro bani*) while acknowledging their own inability to socialize and discipline. In such cases, the master-servant relation simultaneously embodies a master-disciple or parent-child undertone as well. This is consistent with Gramsci's (1992, 56) insight that intellectual and cultural resources are also necessary if the subordinate class is to be complicit in its own domination.

While looking for domestics, most families in Kathmandu seemed most averse to hiring children who had spent some amount of time in the city. By living independently in urban areas these youths have been proletarianized in some respects. Such individuals are considered too irreverent to suit middle-class domesticity. The age and gender of the kamgarne also play a role in concerns about control and subjugation. Most employers prefer to have young children, and especially girls, in their houses. As I have argued elsewhere, the advantages of such a choice are clear:

> First, the young child can be physically controlled more thoroughly; there is no fear of insubordination to threaten the master's power. Secondly, small servants occupy less space to sleep, need less amount of clothing and eat much less. Of course they need to be paid very little as well. (Shah 1993, 174)

People arriving from the hinterland, especially children, cannot easily find an independent place to stay and work, so a position of a servant, however unpleasant, at least provides the security of shelter and food. The demand side of the equation is not lost upon the maliks. Asked if the master-servant relation is exploitative, a housewife who had two domestics in her home answered in the negative, saying: "We give them what we can afford, besides we don't force them to come here. If they don't like, they can always leave." But some see the vulnerability of the young servants as well as their own limitations. "I wish things were different for these children," said the malik of a servant named Rupa, adding: "What can a single person do? Besides, we can't do without a help in the house now, we have been used to it." Finding it necessary to rationalize the arrangement both personally and publicly, masters will often point out that their servants get a better deal now than the one they had back home. Regular and better meals, clothing, and opportunities to learn better ways and earn some money on the side are some of the positive benefits cited by many employers, all for a relatively light workload compared with the heavy agricultural work in the rural areas. As Rupa's mother, who had two young daughters in service, saw the situation: "At least the [servant] children get to eat and go to school," and at the same time, it is two fewer mouths to feed for her impoverished family living a day's bus ride north of Kathmandu. The following case study presents the case of Rupa, whom I first noticed in 1991 at the neighborhood grocery store. I believe Rupa's case accurately exemplifies the trajectory of those children who have been sent to Kathmandu not only to alleviate the burden at home but also with the expectation that they will get education and training at the same time.

As one enters the brown three-storied house through the metal door one usually sees a little girl diligently scrubbing a pile of dirty dishes. The cement landing with a water tap under the staircase is where Rupa Sharma, the kamgarne girl, does most of her work: cleaning dishes, washing clothes, and filling and ferrying water jars to the kitchen on the third floor. The eleven-year-old girl has been working for this family for the past year, although it is not the first family she has worked for. Rupa was brought to work in Kathmandu in 1988 by her maternal grandmother, who herself had been working for Rupa's mistress's sister for more than a decade. Asked why she had to come to the city, Rupa replies shyly that "there wasn't enough to eat at home." After separating from his father and two brothers, Rupa's father ended up with less than one hectare of dry (*pakho*) and irrigated (*khet*) land from the ancestral patrimony. The family tills this small holding, but it is insufficient to feed their four daughters and one son. When I met the father on one of his visits to Rupa, he told me that the crops hardly last seven months. During the agricultural off-season he tries to supplement his income by doing odd jobs in the city while Rupa's second sister works for another relative of Rupa's master in another town. This is how kinship ties funnel the kamgarnes from a particular village and family into the patron's kinship network over the generations. The other two younger daughters help their parents and tend the few heads of cattle and goats; the son is still too young to help.

Rupa has a busy schedule. She must get up by six in the morning to meet the van that delivers the milk in the neighborhood store. She then wakes up the master's family with steaming cups of "bed tea." Rupa usually makes a second trip to the bazaar to purchase fresh vegetables, rice, and other groceries for the kitchen. She helps the mistress with the cooking to enable the malik to be at work by 10 A.M. Another of Rupa's tasks is to ensure a continuous supply of boiled drinking water for the family. Taps frequently go dry in Kathmandu, and it is Rupa who has to carry water in pitchers from the neighborhood taps that may still be trickling. It would be unbecoming for the maliks to be seen carrying loads in public. On weekends she has to help with the laundry. After the family has eaten the morning meal, another bout commences with the dishes in the scullery for Rupa, after which she finally gets to eat her rice and soup. This kamgarne then puts on her faded blue frock and, grabbing her bag, rushes off to school, which is ten minutes away.

Attending school is the payment for her labor. When negotiations were made, Rupa's mother requested that the girl be sent to school in return for her work. Her meals, clothes, and schooling are what Rupa earns from her labor. She is now enrolled in first grade, and although primary education is officially "free," the government school still charges Rs 250 annually for registration and other miscellaneous fees. Additionally, the maliks spend about Rs 20 monthly on copies, pencils, and other expenses. The primary reason her parents decided to send her to work in Kathmandu was simple economics—it would mean one less mouth to feed and would cover the school expenses they could not afford.

Rupa, who looks rather small for her eleven years, is quite intelligent. Her teacher says she works hard, but she failed her math exam. She tries to fit in her homework and study sessions when there is a relative lull and when she can find a quiet corner in the rather cramped three-room apartment. But her study is often cut short when any of the family members asks her to bring a glass of water, make tea, rush to the market, or do errands in the neighborhood. When she gets back from school around 3:30 in the afternoon, she is often hungry and tired. After a brief rest during which she may try to do her homework, she has to begin the evening round again, perhaps by going to the market. When the malik and his two daughters return home from work and school, snacks must be prepared and served. When there are guests, the workload increases proportionately.

The girl helps with the cooking by cleaning and cutting the vegetables, readying the kitchen, and preparing some simple food. The mistress still does most of the cooking, but she expects to "let Rupa do all this once I have taught her how." Rupa has to serve the food when the family members want to eat in their own rooms or while watching TV. When everyone has eaten, Rupa eats alone and then cleans the dishes and scrubs the kitchen. By this time it is past 10 P.M. and she is exhausted by her day's work. However, she may not be able to go to bed if the family is still watching TV or talking in the living room. When everyone retires to their beds, Rupa pulls out the bedding from under the sofa and spreads it on the floor beneath the TV cabinet to sleep. Some nights, when she is not too tired, she tries to do her schoolwork before sleeping.

There is no leave or "overtime" payment for Rupa. Her parents come to visit her every once in a while, and she goes home with them for a couple of days during *dashain* or *tihar* (the major Nepali religious and public festivals that fall during September and October). Every now and then, Rupa shows signs of homesickness, but if asked, she quickly says that nothing is wrong. When I revisited this family in 1995, Rupa was still working there and was then in grade four, a remarkable achievement by itself. She had become much more confident in her ways and serious about her schooling and said that the mistress now allowed her more time for schoolwork. Rupa had developed some urbane tastes—she enjoys movies and modern pop music now. The mistress, on the other hand, complained that Rupa spends too much time watching TV.

A good number of kamgarne children like Rupa in Kathmandu now attend school when they are not needed at home. This certainly opens up a new window of opportunity for the domestics, but it also involves a great challenge. Juggling daily between disparate domains of identity—as a servant and a student—can be stressful. This tension was most evidently manifest in the case of Chakra, a fourteen-year-old boy working for a merchant's family. While Chakra interacted with his seventh-grade classmates on a more egalitarian footing, employing *tah* or *timi* forms of address during the school hours, he immediately shifted to an obsequious mode once he entered the malik's gate after school. Nepali language has several honorific forms of address to represent the social hierarchy between the speakers. A person of lower status would use *tapain* or *hazur* to address his superiors in social status, kinship relation, age, or class. While his master's children, in grades nine and six, relaxed and got about their homework, Chakra had to serve them refreshments and snacks. Later, while the children studied under a private tutor, Chakra was busy in the kitchen.

Sometimes on weekends, the malik's elder son agreed to help the servant with English homework, a favor Chakra would repay by washing the son's dirty sneakers. How would the two classes interact in the same classroom? That awkward encounter is postponed thanks to the private "English-medium boarding schools" now available for the middle classes. In the morning, when Chakra and his malik's children come out of their gate, they take different routes—emblematic of the different stations and life courses they will follow: Chakra walks to the dilapidated state school while the others wait for the bus that will take them to one of the premier schools in Kathmandu. Referring to a government school in a predominantly upscale suburb, one commentator characterized it as a "kamgarnes' school" because many of the children working in the neighborhood were enrolled there while their masters' children went to private schools elsewhere. Even in these schools, the identity conflict is far from over. A twelve-year-old domestic was acutely aware that "even the teachers speak to us differently." Lale, an orphan boy who studied up to grade five, quit school because he felt "ashamed of his servant status among his classmates" even though his employer had told him to continue.

For Maya, there was a different reason for leaving school. The fourth daughter of landless parents, she had been working for a small landholding family since she was seven. When she was fourteen, she abruptly quit and went back to her rural home because, as she put it, "people in the neighborhood and school were ridiculing and denigrating her for being a servant." Sometimes even her siblings, who often worked as daily laborers, teased her, even though she frequently brought gifts and clothing for them. It appeared that while derisive remarks about her servant position had been leveled at her since she started working, she became sensitive to these taunts once she crossed into adolescence. Second, most girls in Maya's socioeconomic background get married early; all of Maya's sisters had married or eloped by the age of fourteen. Maya's continuing her work and studies at this age meant she was out of the marriage market; hence, the rebuke in the form of ridicule from within her own social milieu and potential suitors.

Maya's dilemma revealed the tension between the peasant values of her family and the middle-class aspirations to which she had been introduced. After staying away for three months, during which she said she did much soul searching, Maya returned to the malik's house; this time she resolved not to pay any attention to the comments because the "schooling was much more important." Moreover, she said that the family treated her like "their own daughter." Her only complaint was that her middle-class employers sometimes engaged in too much pretension and formality, a sharp contrast from her own peasant background.

Theoretically the educational opportunity could work as a ladder for these children to rise out of their dead-end positions. Institutional and social obstacles, however, are still stacked high. Exhausted by work before and after school, these students can hardly find the energy, time, or encouragement to study at "home." It is significant that adolescent servants began to be sent to schools in greater numbers at a particular historical juncture. Since the early 1980s the state, on the one hand, made primary education free, while, on the other, also liberalized the education sector for private investment. As part of the structural adjustment program, the government reduced its supervision of and contributions to state schools and handed them over to resource-strapped local "management committees" under the new policy of decentralization and "people's participation." It is no coincidence that with the flight of the middle-class students, most state schools have been plagued by declining standards and morale. All these structural and personal factors contribute to frequent failures in exams and a high dropout rate for the servant-students. The outcome is a classic self-fulfilling prophecy, with everyone convinced that kamgarnes were not meant to study in the first place.

Similarly, even if schooling more often than not ends in failure, it nevertheless provides a strong justificatory basis for the employers. Rather than occasionally being made to feel defensive about keeping underpaid servants, employers now have recourse to the high moral ground of "providing educational opportunities to the disadvantaged." The sanctifying power of education in Nepali society can rub off on both sides—while servants are elevated to the status of students their masters can perceive themselves in the role of disinterested contributors to development. In short, the modern discourse of development and education provides another layer in the euphemized master-servant relation.

SURPLUS: SYMBOLIC AND ECONOMIC

Though the supply of domestic labor for the major part results from under-lying economic forces, there is considerable variation in the actual experi-ence of servants once domestics enter their masters' homes. Since nothing is contractually specified there is much ambiguity about the exact position of the servant within the domestic geography and hierarchy. The bottom line—as Barth has noted for Pakistan's Swat Pathans—is that by accepting work for remuneration, a person renounces "his autonomy; he is acting at the command of another person, and is therefore inferior to that person" (Barth 1965, 49). Mauss makes a similar point that acceptance of gifts, espe-cially in the absence of equivalent reciprocity, places the recipient in an inferior position to the giver (1990, 65). Since the domestic's remuneration mostly takes the form of gifts, presents, or tips (bakshish) instead of a con-tractual wage, such modes of payment necessarily relegate the kamgarnes to a subordinate position where they have to be obliging and servile to their masters beyond what is required in contractual wage relations. Thus a per-son unable to fend off a patron's or a creditor's commands will speak resignedly: "I have eaten his salt, how can I say no?" This, I posit, is the basic structural character of the relationship. Still, this underlying imperative is not the final closure, and the details of the "autonomy" and "inferiority" for the servant still have to be worked out inside the malik's home in its speci-ficity. It is precisely this fluid, flexible arena that can be molded according to the respective power and interest of the agents to create a particular niche for the servant within the domestic habitus.

It is notable that the initial part of the servant's stay is variously described as the *talim lagaune* (to train) or *sadhaune* (a term used in breaking or taming a young bull to take the yoke). Needless to say, such training for instilling a particular "disposition" in the servant includes much more than just teaching how to shop in the market, use electric appliances, or cook a new cuisine. It has also to do with ingraining a new regime of etiquette, lin-guistic practices, urban hygiene, hierarchy, discipline, and efficiency. The form is just as important as the function—what the nokar, or servant, does cannot be separated from how he or she performs it (Rollins 1990).

The training is essential if the nokar is to become the key anchor in middle-class ideals of respectability. Many maliks will openly admit that their kamgarnes are "shouldering their respectability" (*izzat*). Having a ser-vant is a status indicator, since one of the visible markers of success and upward mobility in Nepal is to be relieved of manual chores (Bista 1992, 132), especially of the domestic kind. This is not only an urban phenomenon in Nepal: among the Manangi businessmen, their success in international business ventures can be demonstrated by the number of servants they can employ in their mountain villages (Cooke 1990, 67). Where caste, class, and gender biases stigmatize any type of manual labor, especially domestic chores, not employing a servant would negate one's status claims. A retired civil servant remarked succinctly: "A nokar is now rather like an ornament to show people, even though we do most of the work." The paranoia of keeping up appearances is indicated by the frequency of jokes about the fellow who introduced one of his relatives as the kamgarne to impress his guests.

If the display of conspicuous labor is paramount to some, other masters emphasize the utilitarian rather than the symbolic gains of keeping servants. A hotel employee in Kathmandu said that it would have been impossible to continue her job after marriage if it had not been for the servant in her family. In fact, a couple of times I heard her half-seriously tell her kamgarne boy, "You are my *annadata*" (bread giver). Apart from cooking and cleaning, the boy looked after the two preschool children during the day. While his employer reported spending approximately Rs 750 per month on his upkeep (room, board, clothing, and irregular spending money), she herself received Rs 2,700 monthly salary. Commenting on the Indian situation, Everett and Savera have argued that the "informal sector" (which includes domestic service) subsidizes the higher profits of the formal sector economy by lowering the "reproduction costs of labor" (1994, 9–10). By taking over the less rewarding domestic responsibilities, servants make it possible for others to engage in formal sector wage employment careers. The surplus value of such arrangements becomes clear when we see that in the industrial city of Kolhapur, in India, women earning Rs 1,001 to Rs 2,000 a month from their salaries are able to keep servants whom they pay less than an average of Rs 100 (Joshi 1995, 142).[3]

It is within these conjunctures that it is possible to see the complex relationships among class, gender, and domestic labor. The daughters-in-law (*buhari*) in Nepal are expected, as in the past, to shoulder the responsibilities for cooking, cleaning, and serving. For educated middle-class women to advance in the modern sector, some of their traditional tasks must be transferred to others, because most middle-class families in Nepal cannot yet afford labor- and time-saving devices like washing machines, cooking ranges, refrigerators, and other household gadgets. Servants, then, play a crucial (albeit unrecognized) role in economically and culturally subsidizing the advancement of women from another class. A few women I interviewed in salaried jobs admitted that they would not have been able to work without a kamgarne, and they would not have been able to afford one without working, either. It is in these contexts that we see the "precarious dependencies" (Gill 1994) emerging between the servants and their mistresses—asymmetrical no doubt, but dependencies nonetheless.

EMBODIED DISCIPLINES

Connerton analyzes the ways in which the body becomes the medium of social memory. The French revolutionaries sought to erase the social hierarchy inscribed in bodily postures and clothing during the old regime, because they knew that "habits of bodily deportment" are also "habits of servitude" among the servile groups (1989, 10). Similarly, Foucault's understanding is that body as embodiment of labor becomes a "useful force only if it is both a productive body and a subjected body" (1984, 173). As I suggested earlier, not only do the servants enable their employers to gain economically, but they enhance their "symbolic capital" as well by performing their task according to hegemonic practices that substantiate and elaborate on class and cultural distinctions. The body becomes a key arena for the symbolic elaboration of these distinctions. The servants are conditioned to adopt docile and diffident body postures: never to look into the eyes directly, not to stand arrogantly upright or to talk back. Particularly characteristic is the *kapal kanyaunu* (scratching the back of the head) posture the subordinate assumes when requesting home leave, money, or an excuse on some account. Even though the request may be outrageous, the malik will be disarmed since the vigorous scratching of the head indicates that it comes from submission and not as a right from outside the operative ideology of patron-client ties. When the nokar is perceived as not doing the bidding or not being as servile as desired, a telling bodily reprimand is issued: "You have accumulated much fat in your buttocks since you came into our home, why should you obey us now?"

The servant's symbolic elevation of the master's status also occurs linguistically. The servant is taught to address the master's family, even those much younger than the servant, with the honorific *tapain* or *hazur* while expecting to be called by the lowly *tah*. For the servant, the boundary between polite behavior and servility can be stretched to the limit. The humility required of the nokar no doubt imparts a sense of efficacy and potency to the master, since there are not many public interactions where another person could be called tah without provoking some kind of unpleasant retort. The temptation for class distinction is strong enough that many "progressive" and educated families imitate aristocratic practices and require servants to address them in the courtly language even if they do not practice the same among themselves. These apparently contradictory practices and values become comprehensible if we take Bourdieu's (1994, 66 emphasis in original) insight that linguistic exchanges are not only instruments of communication but "also *signs of wealth*, intended to be evaluated and appreciated, and *signs of authority*, intended to be believed and obeyed."

In *Phenomenology of Spirit*, Hegel dwells extensively on the nature of the master-slave relation—a relation between a dominant, independent Self and the dependent Other in which the self-consciousness emerges from the asymmetry of their relationship. The master's consciousness of Self materializes only through the mediation and recognition by the Other's dependent consciousness (Kainz 1994, 59). The witnessing and acknowledgment conveyed by the subordinate's recognition provide the material and cognitive plane on which the "independent consciousness" of the master can be manifest. The irony is that the master's Self can be independent only on the condition of its dependence on its minions. In her study of domestic service in Boston, Rollins argues that the presence of an "inferior" being in the house provides a validation for the "employer's lifestyle, her class and racial privilege, her entire social world" (1990, 78). The insistence on display of propriety, submission, and deference is so important for some people, especially in upper-class homes, that people will indulge laziness in nokars but not anything that resembles self-respect, which tends to be interpreted as insolence or outright affront to the personal integrity of the Self. One such housewife reported firing a hardworking servant of six years when she found him sitting on the living room sofa on several occasions. To her, this was both a physical and symbolic threat to her selfhood and domestic order. The etiquette of this household required that the kamgarnes not sit on chairs or anything else when the family was present as a symbolic mark of recognition due to their masters. "Servants must be kept in *thik thaun* (right place). What use are they if they forget their position?" she questioned. By faithfully inhabiting the given social space, the servants assure the masters of their life-world. This is a reversal in dependency that attests to the somewhat precarious basis of superior-inferior consciousness in master-servant relationships.

KIN FOR CONTROL

In rural areas, servants are more likely to be incorporated into the domestic sphere in fictive kinship terms, especially if the class and caste differentials between the employer and the employed are not significant. In a social milieu where it is common courtesy to address each other in kinship terms even when not actually related in agnatic or affinal ties, the nokar may refer to all or some members of the household as uncle, aunt, brother, sister, or some other relationship. In urban areas, on the other hand, middle-class notions of propriety do not usually allow servants to be integrated in kin terms (thereby undermining other distinctions), so an ephemeral domestic-familial rhetoric is deployed. A nokar will often be reminded that he or she is a "member of the family" without specifying the kinship position, or a "person of the home," in order to inculcate a sense of loyalty and diligence. Some masters may also teach their young children to address the servants as *dai* (elder brother) or *didi* (elder sister). But this is an asymmetrical usage, since the kamgarne is not free to reciprocate in appropriate kinship terms and address the children as *bhai* (younger brother) or *bahini* (younger sister). If the malik's children have been gracious enough to use a sibling term, the unspoken yet enforced rule of courtesy enjoins the subordinate to respect the distinction and not presume equality by calling them brothers or sisters in turn.

Borneman posits that "belonging" as a "cultural identity" is dependent on "familial, social, and political membership or expressed in analytical terms: kinship, nationness, and citizenship" (1992, 10). Taking this notion of belonging as a point of departure, the partial terms of kinship, however tenuous and fictitious, are one of the few elements the young servants can hang on to for a sense of identity and meaning in a strange home. Meena, twelve, had worked for her mistress, whom she called didi, since she was about eight. However, she did not address the husband as bhinaju, the kinship relation for an elder sister's husband. Didi meant a lot to Meena, and she often told other kamgarnes in the neighborhood that she wouldn't leave this place even if someone offered more money. While there was no doubt that Meena and her didi were closer than most mistresses and maids, it seemed likely that the girl was using the partial kinship foothold given to her to create her identity as something different from other servants—she asserted that she was not a nokar. The use of a kinship term added with the fact that she was receiving no regular wages buttressed her claim that she was not working for money but fulfilling a familial obligation. On this ground Meena sought to validate her "self," often to the annoyance of other servants in the area. In another case, Lale received *tika* from his mistress during the annual festival of tihar, the celebration of the brother-sister relationship.[4] Despite the ritual sacrament due from a sister, he was "taught" not to address the woman as didi, but her toddlers were often encouraged to address Lale as *mama* (mother's brother). At sixteen, Lale had no illusion about his position in that household: "After all, I am a nokar. They will like me as long as I work well," he said. Lale was a confessed supporter of one of the communist factions and would often speak of the "exploitation of the poor workers and peasants" by the rich, including his employers, when he was visiting me in my room. When it is suspected that a particular kin relation is not *afnai* (one's own), meaning "real" rather than constructed, people often refer to it as *goru beecheko nata*, literally a "relation emerging from the sale of a bull"—in other words, a marriage of convenience at best and a farce at the worst. But there is also an antidote to this "essentialist" notion of kinship in the folk repertoire that seeks to validate those relations not emerging strictly from affinal or agnatic ties. When I inquired of Lale what he felt of the tihar tika, he replied with a clever Nepali aphorism that translates as "having even a blind maternal uncle is better than none," scoring a brilliant pun in the process. Not only was the tika better than no tika, but it was better to be a mama to the kids than a lowly Lale. Even though he recognizes the limits of his inclusion, the annual ritual does remind this orphan boy who has been working in this home for the past seven years "that he is in a family every now and then." A strong tension is evident here—a desire to belong and be part of the familial unit while realizing the impossibility of full incorporation.

It is hard to ascertain to what extent kinship and familial ideology is fully internalized or cynically performed, but it certainly provides one element in the "disposition" whereby the servant can negotiate the domestic terrain. Again it is useful to refer to Bourdieu's distinction between "official kinship" and "practical kinship" whose "boundaries and definitions are as many and as varied as its users and the occasions on which it is used" (1977, 34). Broadening and nuancing the understanding of kinship, Bourdieu argues that in contrast to formal kinship, the nonofficial connections can be "private, kept in an implicit, even hidden state" and instrumentally created to satisfy practical interests (1977, 35).

Though Marx did not fully explicate the kinship-economy relationship, he did point out that the "ties of blood . . . [are] the first condition of the appropriation of the objective conditions of life" (1989, 68) on which Neo-Marxist anthropologists have offered various interpretations. Godelier for one posits that in primitive and peasant societies kinship relations are also "relations of production" and "elements of infrastructure" (1977, 172). P. Rey on the other hand has taken a rather extreme position in stating that kinship is "merely a light veil which hides . . . the process by which the dominant class brings the producers under its control" (Rey as quoted in Seddon 1978, 38). In Bourdieu's refinement, not only does practical kinship wither away when there is no practical purpose left, but it can also conveniently be "disowned" if the need arises (Bourdieu 1977, 34). Such practical motivations become discernible when usually it is the families from the lower socioeconomic echelon who cannot fork out attractive salaries for their domestics who are more willing to negotiate the servant's identity in terms of practical kinship. Indeed, wealthy, aristocratic masters actively discourage any kinship linkages from the servant; the emphasis is on distinction and difference. Both Meena's and Lale's employers were financially unable or unwilling to provide a regular wage. What was missing in terms of a good pay was compensated by the efforts made to incorporate the servants in practical kinship—made all the more convincing by the familial rhetoric and symbolic rituals.

RESISTANCE AND TRANSITIONS

Given the impossibility of economic advancement, most kamgarnes by late adolescence are ready to break out of the arrangement in which they grew up. Masters acknowledge that these adult servants are difficult to control and satisfy since now they may want to be paid a regular and higher salary, remuneration that the maliks cannot or will not give since other younger children—less demanding and more docile—are readily available to take the older servant's place. Second, the emerging sexuality of the servants, whether male or female, may now be perceived as potentially disruptive to the domestic order. The adult aspirations of a nokar are not as easy to accommodate and subordinate within the malik's home. But the break is often not an abrupt one. Many domestics now move out from their master's homes and find wage labor, or the maliks themselves may connect them to a peon job in government or private companies. Indeed, many children enter unpaid domestic service with the hope that the maliks will get them a *jagir* (salaried job) once they come of age. Because of the patron-client networks that oil the political-bureaucratic machinery, this is one of the only ways that the rural marginalized can enter even the lowest rung of institutional employment in Nepal. Hari's experience will help to illuminate one of the "successful" transitions from domestic service.

Hari Thapa worked for a government official for eight years. When he was seventeen, the malik, using his connections, found Hari a job as a chef's helper in a hotel. Hari then married another kamgarne and started a family. The old malik let them stay in one of the rooms in the attic in return for which Hari collected the monthly rent from the other tenants, paid the electricity and water bills, and transferred the balance to the master who now lived in another town. Asked why he quit working for the old malik, Hari replied matter-of-factly: "I could not stay with him forever, I had to start earning for myself one day." He did not consider the work for the old master as real work—work started when he began receiving regular wages for fixed hours.

There is often tension in the contradictory ideologies the young servants are exposed to. To promote a work ethic and remove caste biases, the state in Nepal tries to sanctify and legitimate "work" through the media, textbooks, and political rhetoric. Such ideology may be reinterpreted and redeployed by masters to motivate the nokars to perform their unpleasant tasks diligently. The domestics are often reminded that in modern times (*adhunik jamana*) no job is "big or small" (meaning ritually pure or polluting functions in terms of caste considerations). Work, as the injunction usually goes—not caste or other traditional "superstitions"—is important. Thus, straddling the intersection of various discourses, people tend to selectively employ aspects of kinship, modernization, or leftist rhetoric to engage the labor and the identity of their subordinates. Masters too draw from the same fluidity to "craft" their self-identities as benevolent patrons, civilizers, mentors, or the facilitators of modern education.

But when their "lived experience" tells them that they are perceived, treated, and paid differently from other workers, the servants question and contest the exhortations. The servants' responses may range from resistance to coping and complicity. When conditions are too disagreeable, the servants can "vote with their feet," or they can put up a variety of "primitive resistance," such as foot-dragging, going slow, pilfering, sulking, and nonresponsiveness, without openly challenging the dominant ideology (Scott 1985). Ridiculing their superiors by gossiping, especially in the neighborhood, is also a frequent mode of resistance. Such agency for the most part is directed toward coping, rather than transformation of their situation: "The overall impact on the structure of power of this nibbling away is not very appreciable. But it is one of the few means available to a subordinate class to clothe the practice of resistance with the safe disguise of outward compliance" (Scott 1985, 283).

A common response among these servants is the acceptance of their fate (karma), or the doings of the past life for their present condition. "It was written to be like that," they say, pointing characteristically to their forehead in a sign of resignation to the immutable lifeline supposed to be inscribed there. For others, like Madan, a fourteen-year-old boy working in a rural Bardiya village, the present position of being a servant is a temporary expediency—like "feeding one's belly." He does not think he will remain a nokar much longer, since his employer, an elected official, has promised him a janitorial job in one of the public companies. Similarly, Maya and Meena really do not see themselves as kamgarnes; the former likes to identify herself as a student working for her upkeep while the latter attempts to validate herself via kin incorporation. Even though working and living under similar structural relations, the kamgarnes manage to evolve remarkably varied self-perceptions and self-representations.

The ability to create and legitimate interested relations in euphemized forms is an exercise in superior power. Like the masters who can patronizingly mask the identity of their nokars as "our own family member" one instant and seconds later define it as "only a kamgarne" when the servant is absent from the room, the power of euphemization lies in the ability to take the initiative in making interested relations "misrecognizable" for the precise reason that they can again be objectified in strategic contexts. The deliberate obfuscation of relations and identities allows the agents to inscribe and deinscribe representations according to their powers to legitimate such interpretation. Euphemism allows the deferment of specificity on the one hand and functions as a face-saving device in identity contests by providing a range of possible interpretations on the other. Elaborating on Marx's writing on ideology and mythology, Godelier alerts us to the intentionality of the interested agents in creating "illusory representations of economic and social ties" (1977, 182). The ideologies of *ghar* (home) and *parivar* (family) are often invoked as the entities entitled to the servant's labor and loyalty. Maliks will often reprimand their servants by invoking the code of familial loyalty: "We had thought of you as [our] own [family] person, but we see that a nokar must never be indulged." By threatening to expose the carefully crafted illusion, the master maintains the upper hand in defining the terms of the relation. For such illusions to work, the servants also have to cooperate. This "collective misrecognition" goes on because "nothing suits the khammes [Kabylia term for client or servant] better than to play his part in an interested fiction which offers him an honorable representation of his condition" (Bourdieu 1977, 196), however fragile and susceptible to arbitrary redefinition the negotiated identity may be.

FUTURE PROSPECTS

The economic and social aspects of servants' existence cannot be divorced from the political silence maintained by the state on this issue. In many countries, servants are among the last to be recognized as a part of the labor force and thereby provided with some form of legal protection. The silence of the state on such an issue has been matched by a bypassing of the domestic laborers by workers' movements and trade unionists in most places. Servants are considered to be either too polluted by the nature of their work or too reactionary by their servitude to be included in the ranks of traditional labor movements (Gill 1994, 143; Martens and Mitter 1994, 26; Schenk-Sandbergen 1988, 57).

But such oversight, besides perpetuating class prejudices, overlooks the constraining conditions under which servants live. Unlike the general laboring classes, domestics are much more isolated and under direct surveillance by their employers. Gordon notes, for example, that because South

African domestics "work in isolation, there are few available venues for meetings, [and] it is difficult for them to organize" (1985, xxvi). In those countries where the servants have been able to organize to some extent, small but significant advances have been won regarding basic wages, benefits, leave, and living conditions. Often political parties (India), trade unions (Namibia), church groups (Brazil), or the feminist movement (Mexico) have provided the impetus for this unionizing effort (Everett and Savera 1994; Martens and Mitter 1994). In Nepal, no such agency or movement has so far displayed any initiative for domestic labor.

The unprotected state of the domestic laborer is also indicative of the reactive nature of the state: it will provide recognition to those segments of class interests that can effectively mobilize, as if making virtue out of necessity. This is precisely why the state's proactive presence is necessary in providing the basic minimum protection (such as minimum pay, minimum working age, working hours, and regular leave) to this large yet vulnerable sector that is unlikely to articulate its voice in the near future. The fact that Nepalese politics, which places a premium on high-profile populist issues, has not yet turned the kamgarnes into a vote constituency points to a deeper class alignment. Since members of the middle and lower-middle classes from which the political and social leadership arises also enjoy the comfort provided by the nokars, even acknowledging the servants' issue itself would bring a serious rupture between the elites' professed progressive ideology and their objective status as labor and symbolic appropriators. In taking up the cudgels for the servants, the elites would expose themselves as a party to the problem. The shift from being agents of reform to objects of reform would indeed precipitate a crisis in identity and loss of legitimacy for political leaders of all hues, left and right. This perhaps partially accounts for the complete silence on the problem of domestic laborers in the aftermath of 1990 political democratization when so many trade, occupation, and ethnic organizations, often under the tutelage of one or the other political party, were registered and recognized by the state. In its "misrecognition" of the ideology that refuses to accept that the employer's home may be the servant's workplace deserving normal labor regulation, perhaps the society indulges in a moral economy that Bourdieu (1977, 173) aptly describes as "collective bad faith."

CONCLUSION

In meditating on the issue of domestic labor, the present study suggests that the "master-servant" relation is a binary analytic model intersected by the ethnographic distinctions of class, caste, ethnicity, gender, and age. By combining political economy and ethnographic approaches, the domestic servant serves as a prism to illustrate how regional and national asymmetries and dependencies are replicated and reworked within middle-class homes along class and gender formations. While the preconditions for domestic labor are necessitated by the economy of poverty and marginalization in rural areas, each individual relation of domestic labor and identity is unique in the sense that it emerges out of the immediacy of personal contest and negotiation within the intimacy of the domestic space. Whereas the structural locations of master and servant are determined by class positions, the actual lived experience of the people involved in these relationships is quite varied. In the absence of a regularized contractual employer-employee relationship, the servant's status within the household tends to be socially and culturally indeterminate, especially in its official representation. As I have tried to argue, such ambiguity is conducive to euphemization and mystification of identities, both for the maliks and their kamgarnes. I further argue that because of their greater access to symbolic and cultural resources, the maliks generally enjoy greater control over strategic euphemization and exposure of these identities, processes that are crucial in maintaining hegemonic domination.

In this essay, I have also examined kinship and schooling as the crucial cultural and social capital in the recruitment, discipline, and domestication of kamgarnes. Through partial and selective inclusionary and exclusionary kinship usage and domestic ideology, the masters attempt to instill loyalty and diligence in their servants while disabling full incorporation. Even though the maliks enjoy the initiative in deploying kinship as a domesticating ideology, however, their hegemony is never complete. The servants also engage in a variety of ways to resist, negotiate, or call for fulfillment of kinship obligations from their masters. As precariously liminal figures, many of the child servants take recourse to these kinship idioms—fictive and partial as they are—for a sense of self and identity in their place of work. However partial and tenuous the inclusionary practices may be, they nevertheless afford some space from which to make reciprocal claims of kinship obligations from the masters. Sending the young servants to school during their free time is another social practice that complements the moral and civilizing image of the masters. Although schooling provides a small opening for a few kamgarnes, for most it proves too costly psychologically and physically to sustain double identities and workloads. Yet while education often fails in its stated goals for these children, it nevertheless enhances the maliks' moral claims as benefactors of the disadvantaged, claims that can readily be used to preempt occasional charges of exploitation. Finally, I have also argued that kinship usage and schooling for these domestic servants are intellectual and cultural assets that help to engender the servants' complicity in their own servitude.

Paying attention to the use of fictive kinship in domestic labor provides a useful vantage point from which to examine the kinship system not only as a set of ideal relationships grounded in ties of descent and marriage, but also as a source for utilitarian strategizing, something akin to Bourdieu's "practical relationships" or "practical kinship" (1977, 39). Similarly the study of domestic servants provides a unique vantage point for examining the changing gendered division of labor and the possibilities for urban middle-class women's participation in wage labor outside the home. These are important processes through which the changing capitalist labor force is reproduced (Moore 1988, 42). Since much of the unpaid domestic labor is being undertaken by peasant children, it is freeing many educated urban women to participate in the paid labor market. The fact that servants, both male and female, are doing domestic work that was culturally prescribed for women allows us to review the nature versus culture model and closely parallels feminist theorizing that the private is political (Ortner 1974; Rogers 1978; Rosaldo 1974; Strathern 1984; Yanagisako 1979).

In an ethnography of domestic service, it is necessary to emphasize the hegemonic nature of its operation in all its complexity. Oftentimes the issue of domestic service is rendered invisible as a subject of study or oversimplified into a closed narrative of exploitation and oppression. By no means does the present study claim to tell the whole story. At best it is a "partial truth" (Clifford 1986) attendant to all the tensions and ambivalences inherent in a work done from the subject position of a middle-class academic whose sympathies lie across the class line with the kamgarnes. There are, at the same time, enforced silences as well—what do you say to the frequently asked query from your research participants that literally takes one's breath away: "What will happen to me after you do this writing?" Doing ethnography in the intimate domestic space is simultaneously subtle and politically charged. Cleavages of class and gender, ethnicity and culture, become all the more sharp and vivid. Such an ethnographic site offers new methodological challenge where conventional notions of objectivity, distance, and engagement acquire new meanings and urgency.

ACKNOWLEDGMENTS

I am indebted to Profs. Arthur Kleinman, Sally Falk Moore, and Bruce Owens at Harvard Anthropology Department and my colleague Kathleen Gallagher for reading, commenting, and critiquing earlier drafts of this paper. I express my deep appreciation to the editors of the present volume for keeping me focused on the central theme of identity and challenging me to clarify my ideas. I am also thankful to the anonymous press reviewers for their valuable comments and insights. Although this essay has gained immensely from these various insights, needless to say I am solely responsible for any shortcomings.

NOTES

1. Mehta speaks of similar difficulty in gaining the trust and cooperation for his study on servants in Bombay (1960, 45).

2. The bank rate for one U.S. dollar was approximately fifty-three Nepali rupees in 1996.

3. In 1996, one U.S. dollar equaled approximately thirty-four Indian rupees.

4. Tika is a ritual offering given on the forehead on auspicious occasions as a holy blessing. Depending on the particular ceremony, the color of the holy paste may be crimson, red, yellow, blue, or white.

REFERENCES

Banskota, Amrita
1991   Bal Majdoor Samasya: Samadhan Kahile Hola? *Madhuparka* 25 (4): 7–11.

Barth, Fredrik
1965   *Political Leadership Among Swat Pathans*. London: The Athlone Press.

Bista, Dor Bahadur
1992   *Fatalism and Development: Nepal's Struggle for Modernization*. Calcutta: Orient Longman.

Blaikie, Piers, John Cameron, and David Seddon
1977   *Center, Periphery and Access in West Central Nepal: Approaches to Social and Spatial Relations of Inequality*. Norwich: University of East Anglia.

Borneman, John
1992   *Belonging in the Two Berlins: Kin, State and Nation*. Cambridge: Cambridge University Press.

Bourdieu, Pierre
1977   *Outline of a Theory of Practice*. Cambridge: Cambridge University Press.
1994   *Language and Symbolic Power*. Cambridge, MA: Harvard University Press.

Cameron, John
1994   Nepal's Development Thinking: Twenty Years on in Theory and Practice. *The Economic Journal of Nepal* 17 (2): 71–84.

Central Bureau of Statistics (CBS)
1991   *Statistical Year Book.* Kathmandu: Central Bureau of Statistics.
1995   *Population Monograph of Nepal, 1995.* Kathmandu: Central Bureau of Statistics.

Child Workers in Nepal (CWIN)
1988   *Working Children in South Asia: Realities and Challenges.* Workshop Proceedings. Kathmandu: Child Workers in Nepal.

Clifford, James
1986   Introduction: Partial Truths. In James Clifford and George E. Marcus, eds., *Writing Culture: The Poetics and Politics of Ethnography*, 1–26. Berkeley: University of California Press.

Colen, Shellee, and Roger Sanjek
1990   At Work in Homes I: Orientations. In Roger Sanjek and Shellee Colen, eds., *At Work in Homes: Household Workers in World Perspective*, 1–13. American Ethnological Society Monograph Series, No. 3. Washington, DC: American Anthropological Association.

Connerton, Paul
1989   *How Societies Remember.* Cambridge: Cambridge University Press.

Cooke, M.T.
1990   Household Workers in Nyishang, Nepal. In Roger Sanjek and Shellee Colen, eds., *At Work in Homes: Household Workers in World Perspective*, 63–73. American Ethnological Society Monograph Series, No. 3. Washington DC: American Anthropological Association.

Everett, Jana, and Mira Savera
1994   *Women and Organizations in the Informal Sector.* Bombay: Himalaya Publishing House.

Foucault, Michel
1984   The Body of the Condemned. In Paul Rabinow, ed., *The Foucault Reader*, 170–78. New York: Pantheon Books.

Gill, Lesley
1994   *Precarious Dependencies: Gender, Class, and Domestic Service in Bolivia.* New York: Columbia University Press.

Godelier, Maurice
1977   *Perspectives in Marxist Anthropology.* Cambridge: Cambridge University Press.

Gordon, Suzanne

1985 A Talent for Tomorrow: Life Stories of South African Servants. Johannesburg: Ravan Press.

Gramsci, Antonio

1992 Prison Notebooks. New York: International Publishers.

Hobsbawm, Eric J.

1989 Introduction. In Karl Marx, Pre-Capitalist Economic Formations, 9–66. New York: International Publishers.

Joshi, Savita S.

1995 Women Workers at the Grassroots Level: A Sociological Study. New Delhi: Ashish Publishing House.

Kainz, Howard P.

1994 Hegel's Phenomenology of Spirit. [Selections translated and annotated] University Park: Penn State University Press.

Kondo, Dorinne K.

1990 Crafting Selves: Power, Gender and Discourses of Identities in a Japanese Workplace. Chicago: University of Chicago Press.

Marcus, George E., and Michael M. J. Fischer

1986 Anthropology as Cultural Critique: An Experimental Moment in the Human Sciences. Chicago: University of Chicago Press.

Martens, Margaret, and Swasti Mitter, eds.

1994 Women in Trade Unions: Organizing the Unorganized. Geneva: International Labor Office.

Marx, Karl

1989 Pre-Capitalist Economic Formations. New York: International Publishers.

Mauss, Marcel

1990 The Gift. London: W. W. Norton.

Mehta, Aban B.

1960 The Domestic Servant Class. Bombay: Popular Book Depot.

Mishra, Chaitanya

1987 Development and Underdevelopment: A Preliminary Sociological Perspective. Tribhuvan University Department of Sociology/Anthropology Occasional Papers in Sociology and Anthropology 1:109–37.

Moore, Henrietta L.

1988 Feminism and Anthropology. Minneapolis: University of Minnesota Press.

Ortner, Sherry

1974   Is Female to Male as Nature Is to Culture? In Michelle Zimbalist Rosaldo and
       Louise Lamphere, eds., *Woman, Culture, and Society*, 67–87. Stanford: Stanford
       University Press.

Regmi, Mahesh Chandra

1978   *Land Tenure and Taxation in Nepal*. Kathmandu: Ratna Pustak Bhandar.

Rogers, Susan Carol

1978   Women's Place: A Critical Review of Anthropological Theory. *Comparative
       Studies in Society and History* 20:123–62.

Rollins, Judith

1990   Ideology and Servitude. In Roger Sanjek and Shellee Colen, eds., *At Work in
       Homes: Household Workers in World Perspective*, 74–88. American Ethnological
       Society Monograph Series, No. 3. Washington, DC: American Anthropologi-
       cal Association.

Rosaldo, Michelle Zimbalist

1974   Woman, Culture, and Society: A Theoretical Overview. In Michelle Zim-
       balist Rosaldo and Louise Lamphere, eds., *Woman, Culture, and Society*, 17–42.
       Stanford: Stanford University Press.

Schenk-Sandbergen, Loes

1988   *Poverty and Survival: Kudumbi Female Domestic Servants and Their Households
       in Alleppey (Kerala)*. New Delhi: Manohar.

Scott, James C.

1985   *Weapons of the Weak: Everyday Forms of Peasant Resistance*. New Haven: Yale
       University Press.

Seddon, David

1978   *Relations of Production: Marxist Approaches to Economic Anthropology*. Lon-
       don: Frank Class.
1987   *Nepal: A State of Poverty*. New Delhi: Vikas Publishing House.

Seddon, David, Sally Westwood, and Piers Blaikie

1980   *Nepal: A State of Poverty: The Political Economy of Population Growth and
       Social Deprivation*. Norwich: University of East Anglia.

Shah, Saubhagya

1993   Case Studies on Domestic Servants: Reflections on Rural Poverty. *Tribhuvan
       University Department of Sociology/Anthropology Occasional Papers in Sociology
       and Anthropology* 3:158–77.

Strathern, Marilyn

1984   Domesticity and the Denigration of Women. In Denise O'Brien and Sharon W. Tiffany, eds., *Rethinking Women's Roles: Perspectives from the Pacific*, 13–31. Berkeley: University of California Press.

Unicef

1987   *Children and Women of Nepal: A Situation Analysis*. Kathmandu: Unicef.

1992   *Children and Women of Nepal. Country Report*. Kathmandu: Unicef.

Yanagisako, Sylvia Junko

1979   Family and Household: The Analysis of Domestic Groups. *Annual Review of Anthropology* 8:161–205.

ALWAYS HOME, NEVER HOME
Visayan "Helpers" and Identities

M'en voici réduite à porter le deuil de ma bonne. À la sortie du cimetière, tous les domestiques du quartier défilaient devant moi comme si j'eusse été de la famille. J'ai si souvent prétendu qu'elle faisait partie de la famille. La morte aura poussé jusqu'au bout la plaisanterie. Oh! Madame. . .[1]   *(Jean Genet, Les Bonnes, 1947, 105)*

Jean Genet is not known to have written in order to appease, but to disturb. The characters in his vitriolic play, *The Maids*, denude the founding hypocrisies of a certain type of social inequality. To a large extent, the literary triumph of that play resides in its author's ability to bare the subtle and complex ways in which his "maids" are defined from within as well as from without, in which masters and servants are inextricably entangled, and in which each one's multiple identities result from a constantly renewed negotiation. Among these fictive maids as well as among the Philippine "helpers" whom I intend to bring into focus in this essay, everything is not entirely settled from the onset, but remains somehow fluid and viscous, since agency still has to contend with structure. The present-day reflection on agency has emerged as a welcome correction to the logical excesses of a structuralism sans subject. It would be a great pity to repeat the same mistake in reverse, epistemologically to make a great leap backward, and to focus on agency exclusively as if actors were, as if by miracle, rid of any social, historical, or cultural constraint. Such dialectical interconnection between agency and structure serves here as the epistemological premise to the present interpretation.

The point of my reflection here is to document, in a specific ethnographic context, the identity negotiations that may occur at close range between persons who, in this process, at once reinforce and subvert the hierarchical distinctions of rank, class, or gender that lie at the very core of their social existence. For all practical purposes, such identity negotiations may be the only satisfying form of resistance for most "helpers." For most "employers," the same identity negotiations may be the simplest and most gratifying way of justifying the status quo and thus of validating their social dominance.

■　■　■

Perhaps I should start by introducing my "self" and my circumstances, by stating from the onset what may seem all too obvious: that I am a Westerner, that I am a male, and that I am no longer young. Even if not struck by a triple preemptive blindness to the sociocultural horizon at which I intend to gaze, I wear three sets of distorting lenses, in the absence of any one of which I would see nothing at all. First, being a Southeast Asianist did not make me—instantly or otherwise—either a Visayan person, or a Filipino, or even a Southeast Asian. Second, being male shut me off irremediably from a certain level of female interaction. And, third, the accumulation of years turned out to be, as expected, a dubious attribute when it came to connecting with and relating to an activity that mostly (but not exclusively) concerned and affected young adults in their late teens and early twenties to mid-twenties. In addition, I should also admit to having had, at least in the original thrust of my fieldwork, no intention or interest in focusing on domestic workers in and from the central Philippines.

This is not necessarily the place to ponder why anthropologists have paid so little attention (at least until fairly recently) to the topic of domesticity in general and to the issue of domestic workers in particular.[2] I am sure that there are better historical than theoretical reasons for this state of affairs. Within an anthropology almost exclusively devoted to exotic "others," there may not have been a great deal of space left for so ordinary, so plain, and so banal an activity as domestic work. Manifestly, things have changed.

Only serendipity and the vicissitudes of different ethnographic fieldwork experiences brought my attention to domestic workers. Off and on since the summer of 1979 I have been engaged in several periods of field-work activity throughout what is known administratively as Region VII in the Philippines.[3] I have thus lived in or visited the province of Negros Oriental and the province-islands of Bohol, Cebu, and Siquijor. Through such stays and travels, it would have been almost impossible for me not to notice the pervasiveness of the issue of "domestic helpers."

I use quotation marks when using the phrase "domestic workers" or "domestic helpers," because I find these interchangeable expressions, at least whenever used in Philippine English, to be more problematic than transparent. I have seen both phrases written (rather than heard pronounced) on advertisement placards posted in a variety of settings, from newspaper want ads to the opaque doors of more or less legitimate recruiting agencies. At one level, the phrase "domestic workers" presents itself as objective and neutral, as respectable as well as respectful, even more so since the English text introduces the illusory glamour of the highly prestigious international language rather than the low-grade vernacular (i.e., Cebuano or Visayan), completely bypassing the national language (i.e., Tagalog or Pilipino). In the perhaps slightly more translucent expression "domestic helper," the lengthening modification that the adjective *domestic* introduces seems to attenuate (and consequently obfuscate) the lowliness of the status evoked and connotated by the term "helper." In either case, a "domestic worker" (like a "domestic helper") is nothing more than a glorified "helper."

But in the Philippines in general and in the Visayas[4] in particular, the word *helper* has become an interesting term that functions as an oxymoron because the signifier and the meaning of the word clash. With gentle vagueness, the form "helper" is borrowed from English, a language over which different classes have varying degrees of command. Ironically, the English etymology of this linguistic form most escapes the people whom the word denotes. The expression presents itself as a euphemism, a model of periphrastic indirectness that efficiently dims the bleak social reality of the occupation. The meaning of the word *helper* is quite precise indeed; it designates social subordinates, latter-day maids or servants, who command little or no respect as they hang, powerless and expendable, at or near the bottom of the social ladder. The word belongs to the domain of orality; it is more readily uttered than written, more likely to be heard than read. Ultimately, instead of remaining merely descriptive, the word *helper* has acquired derogatory connotations, a fact that eludes in large measure "domestic workers" who operate overseas and who may return in the future, flagging under the weight of *balikbayan*[5] boxes that index their hard-earned success.

Nobody who has received even the least education or who has the slightest ambition would want to be considered a "helper," with the proletarian orientation and miserable location such a word conjures. Under its mask of neutrality, the phrase "domestic workers" hides quite a different reality, of which the fundamental disempowerment and exploitative character dawns only too late on those who fall for it. Under the tag "domestic workers" or "domestic helpers," English-speaking, often overqualified, poor, and entrepreneurial young Filipinas are willingly shipped overseas, sent to work "abroad," and confined to menial, underpaid tasks for which they are overworked and often despised.

No matter how illusory this might seem to an outsider, from their own viewpoint these "domestic workers" have, by virtue of going "abroad," put their foot on the first step of the social ladder. They may be "domestic workers" but they have also joined the ranks of another category of more prestigious people, that of the "Overseas Contract Workers," better known as "OCWs." False consciousness, actively promoted by local employment agencies, gives these outbound "domestic workers" a largely illusory solace, to see the world, to escape the nearby poverty they know so intimately, and to receive the opportunity to make it in the vast outside world. At least this is what came out insistently and repeatedly in interviews I conducted in 1992–93 with young Boholano women who failed to realistically evaluate their chance of success and failure in planning to go abroad.

I have had at least two brief encounters with such overseas "domestic workers." The first one, in 1980, was indirect and it was meant to be humorous, which of course does not mean that it was insignificant. Upon disembarking from a long bus ride in Cebu City, a group of men politely and jovially invited my wife and me to sign in as "domestic helpers" to go to "Saudi," which greatly amused the surrounding crowd. The humor of the joke derived from its reversal of roles and identities. Being *Amerikano* (i.e., Westerners), we were perceived immediately as more likely employers of domestic workers than as potential "domestic helpers" ourselves. Accordingly, we behaved predictably in not seizing the offered employment opportunity and walked away under general laughter. This practical joke was made at our expense, and yet it put us in our proper place without being terribly offensive.

The second encounter, however, in 1983, was direct as well as depressing in its immediacy. On my way to the Philippines, I had the opportunity to stop in Hong Kong where I was strolling leisurely, when I stumbled upon an impressive conglomeration of young Filipinas on the north coast of the island of Hong Kong. It was a Sunday afternoon, and this was Causeway Bay. There were hundreds of Filipinas taking advantage of their half-day of freedom, gathered by linguistic affinity and nostalgically evoking their respective faraway islands. It was not just the number of assembled women at that other end of the recruitment line that impressed me, but what became so apparent after only a few casual conversations in a mix of Cebuano and English. All these women, despite their training as nurses, teachers, or whatever, were all "domestic workers." Visibly uprooted socially and culturally from their archipelago, they clung with despairing energy to their past and an illusion of respectability in their pitiful line of employment.[6]

My point here is only to introduce what I consider to be a necessary distinction in the archcategory of domestic workers between two types: the "domestic workers" (or "domestic helpers") whom I have just evoked and placed between quotation marks on the one hand and, on the other hand, those who are referred to in Philippine English simply as "helpers" without any qualification. Surely, both are domestic workers in the larger sense and may end up accomplishing quite similar tasks in equally exploitative and alienating settings. "Domestic" or not, both, after all, perform house cleaning in homes that are not theirs. And yet the political contexts in which they operate differ.

"Domestic workers" who remit foreign currency to relatives in the Philippines are caught in the logic of postcolonialism. They find themselves in a slightly different predicament from plain "helpers" who are to a large extent uneducated, monolingual workers, often (but not necessarily) coming from a rural background. For the most part, "helpers" are females, although there are also male "helpers" who perform unskilled manual labor most often outside the home of their employers. "Helpers" employed in the national labor market meet a fate that is strongly determined by class relationships within their own society. Ultimately, this may be seen as a case of internal colonialism; and what separates this type of human exploitation from any other form of colonialism might very well be, on a grander historical scale, a moot point. But, in the context of the Philippine nation-state in which labor has been and remains the principal export and the foremost source of hard currency, Philippine nationals who bring in hard currencies from foreign lands can be expected to have a different status from unorganized "helpers" who have the hardly enviable political clout of a *lumpen-proletariat*.

In the consciousness of many Filipinos, such a contrast looms large. For instance, during my last visit, the story of a Philippine "domestic worker" on the verge of being executed in the Middle East for murder, was the focus of considerable attention in the written press and reportedly prompted feverish diplomatic activity.[7] In contrast, at about the same time, the murder of a Visayan "helper" at her place of employment was rapidly hushed up by the press. Given such contrasts, I find it useful to maintain a distinction between "domestic workers" to which the Philippine government cannot avoid paying some (albeit scanty) attention and plain "helpers" who have to fend for themselves without any representation. In other words, "helpers" are poorer, less visible, and more vulnerable than "domestic workers." Basically, "helpers" are unglorified "domestic workers (with and without quotation marks)." The gap that separates "helpers" and "domestic workers" is a matter of political economy, but it seems compounded by deeply rooted historical and cultural considerations to which I now turn.

The term itself, *helper,* has acquired a supplement of semantic extension in crossing the Pacific Ocean. By the early 1980s, the word belonged (as it still does today) to the active vocabulary of every locutor in the Visayas, regardless of linguistic orientation and linguistic competence. Whether the conversations were in Philippine English, Cebuano or *mixmix, helper* was a shared vocabulary word. *Mixmix* results from recurrent code-switching. Code-switching occurs within a given conversation, and often within a given sentence, between Cebuano and English. *Mixmix* is to Cebuano what Taglish is to Tagalog. Code-switching is not a haphazard phenomenon, but a highly structured event. In *mixmix,* locutors will use English expressions instead of their Cebuano equivalents that are deemed to refer to a now disappearing "deep Cebuano" or "deep Visayan," the linguistic forms of which cannot be actively recalled, because they are forgotten or perceived as archaic, old-fashioned, poetic, or contrived.[8] As might be expected, in *mixmix,* nobody would use anything but the English form "helper."

Perhaps more surprisingly, monolingual speakers of Cebuano also use the word *helper* exclusively, as yet another borrowing from American English. Any Cebuano speaker would feel grammatically comfortable stating *"ako man ang* helper *nila"* (I am their "helper"). However, this seems to be a relatively recent usage, as may be inferred from the absence of an entry for *hilpir* (helper) in Wolff's (1972) dictionary in which one can otherwise find such exotic gems as *hilt sintir* (public health clinic) or *himan* (he-man, masculine) or even *hilikuptir* (helicopter). The three latter borrowings had been integrated into the Cebuano language prior to 1972, since they are cited in Wolff's corpus. Had the Cebuanized word *hilpir* been current by that time, it would not have escaped the fastidious attention of this distinguished lexicographer who placed so much emphasis on the recording of Cebuanized words of American provenance.

Not only has the word *helper* presumably been introduced in Cebuano since then, and with considerable success, but it has even had time to pervert the seeming intentionality that hid behind such a borrowing. According to several Boholano informants, observations in the early 1990s, at first *helper* was meant to be an innovative, unisex, descriptive referent, deprived of any derogatory connotations. Rapidly but not unexpectedly, the word has regained its discriminatory indexicality, so that today, the word *helper* conveys the same load of social stigma as the words that it was originally meant to replace.

Such displaced words appear in Wolff's (1972) dictionary under the slightly disconcerting entries for *buy* (that Wolff translates as "male servant") and *mid* (that Wolff translates as "female household help"), which can be retransliterated respectively as "boy" and "maid." They had become popular in the 1960s under the predominant linguistic influence of American English, and the tenacious neocolonial cultural hegemony of the United States in which a compliant Philippine bourgeoisie reveled. Rather than indexing a social class context, the expressions *ang buy* as well as *ang mid* had an inescapable (neo)colonial overtone, consonant with what occurred at that time in other settings the world over. In addition, these words had been readily adopted and smoothly integrated into Cebuano, which could produce elaborate derivations on such roots. Consider, for instance, *"gapaboy ba siya sa ila?"* ("have they hired him as a boy?") or *"nagpamaid siya sa amo"* ("she was our maid").

Although such words have now completely fallen into disuse, the irony is that they had replaced a previous set of gendered expressions that are still cited in Wolff's dictionary and borrowed from Spanish *muchacho* and *muchacha*. Even more in Cebuano than in Tagalog, part of the vocabulary derives from Spanish, and the linguistic influence of the latter language persisted long after the collapse of the Spanish colonial regime and the Spanish-American War of 1898. The two Cebuano phrases, *ang mutsatsu* and *ang mutsatsa*, had flourished mainly at the very beginning of the twentieth century, after the so-called pacification of the Philippines by the United States. But these Cebuano expressions, despite their persistence, ultimately fell victim to the fact that the meaning of words erode with time. In short, beyond being perceived as derogatory, these terms became oldfashioned. Indeed, by the 1960s, to have a "boy" and/or a "maid" was altogether more "with it" than having a *mutsatsu* and/or *mutsatsa*.

Although these words had become Cebuanized under Spanish influence, and even though the Spanish colonists had brought with them an altogether different notion of salaried or alienated labor, the Spaniards did not have to introduce either the notion of domestic service or the concept of servant. In Cebuano, the verb *batun* means "to take care of," "to attend to," or "to help in raising." The verb extends to a larger than expected semantic domain, being applicable to the raising involved in animal husbandry as well as in child rearing. And indeed the nominalization *ang binatnan* refers not only to an animal that is raised for someone else but also to a foster child. Similarly, the nominalization *ang binatunan* refers not only to a person who helps in raising animals for another but also to someone who helps raise children. This is not a free service. Although arrangements tend to vary, if, for instance, I help you raise your piglets, you can expect me to feel entitled to keep half of the litter for myself. In fostering a child, I am also entitled to some kind of economic compensation, whether monetary or simply the child's labor. Fostering, whether of animals or of children, is thus accomplished by someone who helps out in order to be supported. This places the fosterer in a subordinate position in relation to the parents/owners, a point of importance to which I shall return.

According to the very few of my Boholano informants who showed any active interest in their historical past, there once was a Cebuano expression, *ang binatunan*, which connoted a servant, someone who would be a "helper" today. Displaced by the corresponding English borrowing, the phrase is now relegated to the sublime linguistic world of "deep Cebuano." In other words, a serious skidding in the actual meaning of *batun* seems to have occurred. The Cebuano verb emphasizes the "help in raising" instead of the physical separation that the English notion of "fostering" implies.

Although one can expect to hear the word *helper* more frequently from the mouths of English speakers, the semantic connotations of the word *helper* are quite different in standard English and in Philippine English. The transformation that the passage from one dialect to the other entailed resulted from the existence of another Cebuano verb *tabang* (to help). From such a root, there is indeed a nominalization but it refers to a "helper" of a completely different kind, since the *ang mananabang* designates the "mid-wife."[9] This is a socially respected position that is hardly on a par with that of a modest "helper." Similarly, the verbal derivation *magtinabangay*, which can be translated as "to help each other," implies a relationship of mutual respect and equivalent status between the people involved. However, that is the exception. In contrast, the verb *tabang* tends to carry negative connotations. The nominalization *ang katabang* certainly refers to "someone who helps," a "helper" in the contemporary sense of the term. In daily parlance, however, the Philippine English term "helper" is preferred, perhaps because of the attenuating indirectness that the English borrowing allows in designating an activity that is ultimately deprecated.

The problem is that the connotations of *tabang* in Cebuano and of "to help" in "standard English" are not only different but opposite. In standard English, I "help" someone financially because I am better off than him/her, technically because I am better equipped, politically because I am senior, more powerful, and so on. In other words, the helped person is a supplicant while the helper is in a position of strength; the helped one has an obligation toward the helper. But, in Philippine English, it seems to be the reverse.

The meaning of "to help" is closely aligned with that of the Cebuano *tabang*. As Sally Ness notes, the Philippine English term

> carries with it connotations of dependency and/or junior status [. . .] [T]o "help" with something or to "help" someone is to identify oneself as *less than* the one helped [. . .] To "help" is to [. . .] have no agency or to take no initiative of one's own, but, rather, to follow the orders and instructions of the one being "helped." "Helping" reflects, not on the one asking for help as needy, but rather on the one helping as being without other source of occupation or status. To be available to "help" and to become a full time "helper" is therefore not simply an objective decision to seek additional income. In becoming a "helper," [one] also accept[s] and assume[s] subordinate social positions and interpersonal identities. (Ness 1994, 5–6)

At least in this sense, the very tag of "helper" reinforces the low status of its bearers. While the tag may be relatively recent, the relationship to which it refers is not, as my prodding into semantic history indicates. In this context and elsewhere, words wear out and need to be replaced from time to time to adjust to ever-changing moods and sensitivities.

One wonders whether "helpers" are not, in fact, the contemporary heirs to the tradition of subordination that finds its roots prior to the sixteenth-century arrival of the Spaniards. In this earlier era, the networks of small autonomous Visayan communities were organized in a three-tiered social system, with a *datu* (chief) at the top followed by a number of *timawa* (personal followers or freemen). The third tier of the system was occupied by the *ulipun* (usually translated as slaves), of which there were many different categories that varied from mere indenture to a more constraining bondage. In his now classic study of *Slavery in the Spanish Philippines*, William Henry Scott (1991, 12–16) remarks on the complex varieties of relationships that belong to that category of people. At one point, he casually mentions the case of a "famous Boholano sea-raider [who] was buried in a boat with a full complement of slave oarsmen" (Scott 1991, 16). This seems to be an extreme case, as Scott notes that the *ulipun* system struck the Spaniards most for "the lightness of its demands" (1991, 13).

What appears to be an invariant in the Visayan and for that matter in the larger Philippine social system from pre-Hispanic to post–Martial Law times is the irreducible demands of its social hierarchy. Today as in the past, people of the Visayas find themselves occupying different ranks in their society. If anything, social class assignment seems more rigid—and more so as one descends the social ladder—than the inescapable and often arbitrarily determined rank of pre-Hispanic times.

Heirs perhaps to the tradition of indentured labor that pre-Hispanic *ulipun* embodied, modern-day "helpers" find themselves per force on the lowest steps of the same ladder. Now ensconced in a decidedly capitalistic mode of production, dispossessed "helpers" perform the epitome of exploited and alienated labor. And yet, although this view of "helpers" as inheritors of a deep historical tradition of servile, indentured, and dispossessed work may be accurate, it also neglects the rather formidable paradoxes that permeate the Philippines in general and the Visayas in particular. "Helpers" appear as a striking embodiment of such paradoxes.

Space and geography separate "helpers" from "domestic workers" who most often simply operate as maids (by whichever name) in a capitalistic mode of production in which salary and labor appear to cancel each other out. Time and history separate "helpers" from *ulipun* whose servitude was predetermined and obligatory, given that it was their assigned, often inherited, social status that designated them as *ulipun*. And so, focusing on Visayan "helpers" who live "now" (*karon*) at the end of the twentieth century and "here" (*dinhi*) in the central Philippines, two paradoxes emerge almost at once. On the one hand, "helpers" are not just salaried employees but are involved in much more complex social relationships with their employers' families. In other words, a "helper" who shares meals and lodging with her employer, who raises that family's children, and who receives only meager financial compensation, if any at all, generally derives from her position a supplement of social relationship—I am tempted to call it "intimacy"—from the household for whom she works.

Surely, her employer is her *agalon* (master or mistress), but very often her performance of menial tasks for a minimal monetary reward is compensated by what the "helper" perceives as an attractive opportunity. Quite frequently, the "helper" is not a mere "helper" but what is known in Philippine English as a "working student" (commonly abbreviated as a "working") whom her boss allows to study in school in exchange for her household work. The arrangements vary, but generally her boss (i.e., her *agalon*) can be expected to foot the bill for practically every expense incurred. Specifically, this includes school expenses such as tuition, uniform, supplies, and so on. The boss can also be expected to provide for food and lodging, sometimes even for transportation (especially if the school is deemed to be beyond walking distance), in return for mostly unspecified (and in practice full-time) domestic services at home. Usually, the "working" receives no salary at all, but it is not unusual for her to be granted some pocket money.

Furthermore, it would be unusual today to see someone stay forever as a "helper" with a family. Employers may lament that fact and complain that "helpers" are not what they used to be, as "helpers" do not consider their positions as permanent. The contrast between the *agalon*'s and the "helper's" perceptions does not simply result from their respective positions in a hierarchized social relationship but from the profound asymmetry that reflects the different perspectives from which each apprehends their mutual relationship. For the *agalon*, stability is crucial, as it guarantees the permanence of an altogether satisfying social order. The *agalon* complains about contemporary "helpers'" defection because of a static view of social relations in which a "helper" is a "helper," and always will be so. In other words, by reassurance or by convenience, the social hierarchy here is frozen. In the view from above, to help is a permanent situation, a career as it were, even though pathetic.

"Helpers," in contrast, insist on the temporary character of their position. Some women intend to sell their labor for no more than a few months. Even if the necessity to help lasts for years, there is always the hope (maybe just the dream) on the part of "helpers" that someday, somehow, something unexpectedly happy will occur and propel them out of poverty forever. At this level of abstraction, most "helpers" disengage themselves from their actual circumstances, preferring to consider their work as transient, marking time prior to their eventual marriages. Understandably, they prefer to stress their own potential for social mobility. In the view from below, to work as a "helper" is a process and the social system is always in flux.

Both viewpoints are illusory in seemingly bracketing out reality in opposite ways. The masters, militantly antihistorical, overstress the permanence of the present social order while the "helpers," confident in hypothetical changes to come, overstress the fluidity of their situation. In their opposite perceptions of history, the *agalon* and the "helpers" are united under the cloak of a strictly economic relationship, and a binding social relationship is often established, as a "helper" is always in the process of joining the clientele of her boss qua potential patron.

This latter feature brings me to the second paradox of "helpers," as their occupation often results from their own (whether individual or familial, albeit narrowly limited) socioeconomic strategy. For a young woman raised in an impoverished, rural *barangay* (the equivalent of a village), working as a "helper" for a bourgeois family in town is often perceived as an economic, social, and even political opportunity that may open the road to a better future than what can be anticipated in her *barangay* of origin. Informants explicitly spell out this opportunistic rationale. Moreover, because of the novelty and attraction that towns and cities offer, many young women look forward to "tours of duty" as "helpers." Not only does it appear as a first step in the right direction, but it is also a chance to satisfy their curiosity and their appetite for a more urban and urbane way of living. In addition to being pushed away by economic hardship at home, it is through their own free will and confidence in their choice and future that many young women leave their *barangay* for the unglamorous glitter of a "helper's" life. In the rural environment of Siquijor, I witnessed many women who left home to become "helpers" and whose homesickness (*kamingaw*) brought them back a few weeks or months later, although they declared themselves happy to have seen the surrounding world. After a few of these back and forth trips, many of the women settled in an urban environment and bonded with bourgeois families as "helpers" until their eventual marriages.

In most of these cases, long-term bonding of a "helper" to her *agalon's* family is explicitly determined by the transformation of the "helper" into the *yaya* (nursemaid) of a child, whereby the "helper" gains further entry into the domestic life of the family for whom she works. The personal bond between a child and her or his *yaya* is long-lasting if not permanent. It follows that a "helper" who becomes a *yaya* reinforces her social insertion in the family of her *agalon*. In this process, while remaining a lowly "helper," the *yaya* increases her intimacy with her *agalon's* family as well as what perhaps I should call "complicity" with the child she helps raise. In other words, a *yaya* is an elevated "helper" who commands some respect (and affection) in the household of her employer.

Whether a mere and lowly "helper," or a more familiar and respected *yaya*, any "helper" has achieved a liminal status as she has escaped from the authority of her family of orientation without having yet joined her family of procreation.[10] In this betwixt-and-between status, she also maintains herself as associated with the family for which she works, neither completely part of it, nor ever (as long as she remains a "helper" for that family) separate from it. This neatly reflected the extreme ambiguity I encountered when I attempted to conduct a census. "Helpers" were claimed as residents of a specific household either by their parents, their employers, by both or by neither. In no way was this clarified by the use that informants made of the word *sakup* to signify that a person belonged or did not belong to a specific household. As a noun, *sakup* (accentuated on the first syllable)[11] can designate "the members of a group" (i.e., "those who are included"), as well as "the helpers." The term ultimately connotes the notion of "inside," of "that which belongs." With good faith, both a "helper's" parents and her employers could claim that she belonged to their respective households. Different people, whether a "helper" herself, her parents, or her employers, gave answers that reflected both the actual duration and anticipated future of the "helper's" activities. Somehow in transit, at an unstable moment of their own life cycle, the "helper" finds herself astride families, between her family of orientation from which she has already physically (but neither emotionally nor ritually) separated and another one, her employer's family, to which she belongs and does not belong, and in which she can only mimic and anticipate her own reproductive future. Living most of the time in the *sakup* (enclosure) of her master's house, the helper is always expected to be home (i.e., present as well as feeling at home) in a location to which she only marginally belongs.

In observing the highly constrained lives of "helpers," it is difficult not to remark on yet another paradox, which traverses the entire social life of the Visayas and perhaps that of the Philippine Lowland Christians, in general. I am referring here to the coexistence on the one hand of a rigid social hierarchy that has maintained itself from pre-Hispanic times to the present and on the other hand of a contradictory streak of equality that, as I believe I have illustrated, allows "helpers" to gain intimacy, confidence, and relative respect within the families of their employers. Ultimately, such a dialectic between hierarchy and equality may help undermine the authority of parents, employers, as well as potential spouses, by encouraging a female "helper" to identify with none, one, or more of the social units to which she is entitled to claim membership. In this interplay, at once confusing and fertile, all happens as if despite the constraints that weigh her down at the bottom of the social heap. A "helper" still has some measure of autonomy, some margin of maneuverability, some relevant freedom of choice, that allows her to escape servitude, to live. And yet, social order weighs on her with all its might. Even with a pleasant and respectful *agalon*, even in the intimacy of her mistress, even in the affection of the children she helped and helps raise, a female "helper" has little chance to escape from her condition and from her performance of alienated work. What she retains are identity choices, a perpetual and perpetually renewed negotiation of her ever-changing identities. As Solange, a character in Jean Genet's play *The Maids* says: "C'est facile d'être bonne, et souriante, et douce. Quand on est belle et riche! Mais être bonne quand on est une bonne!" (Genet 1994, 41).[12]

Acknowledgments

An earlier version of this paper was presented at the symposium "Home and Hegemony: Domestic Service and Identity Politics in Asia" organized by Kathleen M. Adams and Sara A. Dickey at the 93rd annual meeting of the American Anthropological Association in 1994. Initial field research in the Philippines was made possible in 1979 by a Summer Grant from the Graduate School Research Fund of the University of Washington (Seattle). In 1980–81 and again in 1992–93, I received a Fulbright-Hayes Research Fellowship administered by the Philippine-American

Education Foundation (Manila). While in the Philippines at different times I was affiliated with the Department of Sociology and Anthropology, Siliman University (Dumaguete City), with the Cebuano Studies Center, University of San Carlos (Cebu City), and with the Office of Research, Divine Word College (Tagbilaran City). Ethnohistorical research in the archives of Spain, the Vatican, and the Philippines was supported in 1982–83 by grants from the Social Science Research Council and from the Spanish-American Friendship Treaty. I received a leave of absence with pay from the University of Washington in 1982–83 and from George Mason University in 1992–93. I was also able to make brief visits to the Philippines in the summers of 1983 and 1986 to attend conferences organized by the Joint Committee on Southeast Asia of the Social Science Research Council. To all these institutions, I express my gratitude. Finally, I wish to thank Kathleen M. Adams, Jon W. Anderson, Jane M. Atkinson, Phyllis P. Chock, Nicole Constable, E. Valentine Daniel, Sara A. Dickey, Elinor Dumont, Joel C. Kuipers, Sally A. Ness, and Vicente L. Rafael for their critical comments. The usual disclaimers apply.

Notes

1. "Here I'm reduced to wearing mourning for my maid. When I left the cemetery, all the neighborhood domestics marched past me as if I belonged to the family. So often did I pretend she was part of the family. Dead, she'll have carried the joke to the extreme. Oh! Madam. . . ." [my translation]

2. Historians were first on the scene, as it were (e.g., Fairchilds 1984; Graham 1988; Katzman 1978; Maza 1983). Among anthropologists, Karen Hansen (1989, 1992) stands out as an authentic pioneer.

3. See Dumont (1991, 1992, 1993, 1995).

4. The Visayas, located between Luzon in the north and Mindanao in the south, constitute the central part of the Philippine archipelago.

5. A *balikbayan* is literally a "returnee to the country." The term, borrowing from Tagalog, is made up of *balik* (to come back), and of *bayan* (country, nation, homeland). Commonly used throughout the Philippines, the word *balikbayan* does not usually refer to travelers merely coming back from a short trip abroad, but to emigrants returning home at the expiration of their contract, or more generally to Filipinos and Filipinas who have spent most of their life abroad and move back to resettle, retire, and presumably, to die at home in the Philippines. It would take an exceptional *balikbayan* to travel light. Philippine Airlines in particular used to provide heavy cardboard boxes, with the word *balikbayan* clearly printed in big letters, to accommodate the often poorly packed, bulky personal belongings, and excess luggage of such homebound passengers.

6. For a particularly cogent approach to Filipina maids exiled in Hong Kong, consult Nicole Constable's chapter in the present volume as well as her previous publications (1994, 1996).

7. More recently, the revolting execution of a Filipina in Singapore drew the attention of the international press. Not only did it generate demonstrations in Metro Manila against the city-state, but a significant part of Philippine public opinion denounced the lack of efficiency and resolve with which, upon learning that the woman was to be executed, the Philippine diplomats stations in Singapore had intervened.

8. "Deep Cebuano" is reputed to be less contaminated by English or even Spanish borrowings than the commonly spoken contemporary Cebuano. While reputed to still be spoken by rural, ancient, monolingual locuters in some remote villages, nowadays it is confined to the refined vocabulary of poets and of people sensitive to the nuances of their native language as well as to the political implications of this linguistic erosion. It was my unfortunate experience to discover that, with few exceptions, younger native speakers of Cebuano may have some command of English but may neither use nor understand, even less translate, any linguistic text that they quickly tag as "deep Cebuano."

9. For readers unfamiliar with Austronesian languages, Cebuano verbal derivations may be difficult to grasp. The issue is complex and I can do no better than referring readers to Wolff's precise treatment of verbal derivations in Cebuano:

> "[I]nflectional affixes are added to roots [. . .] but also to derived bases [. . .] [P]roductive affixes [. . .] are added to roots to form bases which in turn may have inflectional affixes added to them [. . .] When the active inflectional affixes are added to verb bases which contain some form of these derivative prefixes, they undergo morphophonemic alternations." (Wolff 1972, I, xvi)

Readers may feel grateful that I, not being a linguist, do not develop these technicalities further.

10. See Murdock (1965 [1945], 13).

11. Not to be confused with *sakup* (accentuated on the second syllable), which is an altogether different word, meaning as a noun "catch," or "capture."

12. "It's easy to be nice, and smiling, and sweet. When you're pretty and rich! But to be nice when you're a maid!" [my translation]

REFERENCES

Constable, Nicole
1994 *Christian Souls and Chinese Spirits: A Hakka Community in Hong Kong.* Berkeley: University of California Press.

Constable, Nicole, ed.

1996   *Guest People: Hakka Identity in China and Abroad*. Seattle: University of Washington Press.

Dumont, Jean-Paul

1991   Language and Learning in a Visayan Community. In Charles F. Keyes, ed., *Reshaping Local Worlds: Formal Education and Cultural Change in Rural Southeast Asia*, 70–88. New Haven, CT: Yale University Southeast Asia Studies, Monograph No. 36.

1992   *Visayan Vignettes: Ethnographic Traces of a Philippine Island*. Chicago: University of Chicago Press; and Quezon City: Ateneo de Manila University Press.

1993   The Visayan Male Barkada: Manly Behavior and Male Identity on a Philippine Island. *Philippine Studies* 41:401–36.

1995   Matrons, Maids, and Mistresses: Philippine Domestic Encounters. *Philippine Quarterly of Culture and Society* 22 (3): 174–91.

Fairchilds, Cissie

1984   *Domestic Enemies: Servants and Their Masters in Old Regime France*. Baltimore: Johns Hopkins University Press.

Genet, Jean

1994 [1947]   *Les Bonnes*. Paris: Marc Barbezat-L'Arbalète.

Graham, Sandra L.

1988   *House and Street: The Domestic World of Servants and Masters in Nineteenth-Century Rio de Janeiro*. Cambridge and New York: Cambridge University Press.

Hansen, Karen T.

1989   *Distant Companions: Servants and Employers in Zambia, 1900–1985*. Ithaca: Cornell University Press.

Hansen, Karen T., ed.

1992   *African Encounters with Domesticity*. New Brunswick: Rutgers University Press.

Katzman, David M.

1978   *Seven Days a Week: Women and Domestic Service in Industrializing America*. New York: Oxford University Press.

Maza, Sarah C.

1983   *Servants and Masters in Eighteenth-Century France: The Uses of Loyalty*. Princeton: Princeton University Press.

Murdock, George Peter

1965 [1949]   *Social Structure*. New York: The Free Press.

Ness, Sally A.
1994   Embodiments of Philippine Domesticity. Unpublished manuscript.

Scott, William Henry
1991   *Slavery in the Spanish Philippines*. Manila: De La Salle University Press.

Wolff, John U.
1972   *A Dictionary of Cebuano Visayan*. Ithaca: Cornell University, Southeast Asia Program.

G. G. Weix

INSIDE THE HOME
AND OUTSIDE THE FAMILY
The Domestic Estrangement of Javanese Servants

"Pariyem's Confession," a narrative poem by the Indonesian writer
Linus Suryadi, has been praised for capturing the subjective experience of a
Javanese maid working for a contemporary middle-class family.[1] Popular as a
fictional account of servitude in urban Indonesian homes, the poem reveals
what an Indonesian man of letters imagines the social reality of female
domestics to be, including his fantasy of the perfect servant and her eroticized rape by the adult son in the household.[2] The tenor of Pariyem's character's voice rings partly true to the experience of servants in Central Java
because Suryadi contrasts external and internal (Indonesian: *lahirnya dan
batin*) aspects of the maid's relationship to her employers. Such a contrast
often characterizes expression of self and social identity in Javanese culture
(Geertz 1960, 232). Outwardly, Pariyem describes how differences in social
rank distance her from the family because she is "only the maid." Inwardly,
though, her voice weaves a rhetorical connection to the family as the son's
unacknowledged mistress, or so Suryadi portrays her thoughts.

Yes, yes, I am Pariyem
Mary Magdalena Pariyem, my full name
"Iyem" what I'm called everyday
from Wonosari, Southern Mountain

As a servant to [the aristocratic family of] Cokro Sentono
who live at Suryamentaraman Yogyakarta . . . outwardly only a servant
but in my heart I'm a daughter-in-law . . . outwardly only a servant
but in my heart I'm a new [kind of] mistress.[3]

In the preceding stanza Suryadi resolves dissonance between external appearances of social hierarchy—differences in social rank and class—and inward experiences of hidden affinity by personalizing domestic service in Indonesia. To imply that a servant feels herself to be part of her employer's family softens intractable power differences that would otherwise subordinate her by age, gender, and rank (cf. Hart 1986). Pariyem is young, female, and of rural origin; she is also uneducated and describes herself as naive. These characteristics would ordinarily disadvantage her, but the poet contrives to show them as charming, giving her life story an alternate coherence. Ultimately her "confession" resolves the dilemma of secret sexual abuse through her identification with the family who employs her. Rather than question this identification and the contrast between outward and inward experience so common to Javanese expressions of self and social identity, Suryadi simply creates a literary fantasy of a maid who overcomes differences of social rank "in her heart."

Interpreting servants' perceptions of their relationships to their employers in ethnography can be equally problematic. In the 1980s I did fieldwork in a north coast Javanese town, where I analyzed women's wage work in cigarette factories owned by local Muslim elite. In my research I asked how class shaped rural women's perception of their livelihoods; for more than a year I visited factories on the edge of town where I could observe and participate in hand-rolled cigarette production while interviewing workers. When the factories closed in the afternoons I would visit the home of one firm owner who was also my host, a wealthy, entrepreneurial woman whom I will call Bu Haji. In contrast to the blunt, loud talk of factory workers about hours and pay rates, my conversations with Bu Haji's household staff and servants were markedly more reserved. As they described their life experiences to me, household staff spoke mostly about the quality of relationships with employers during their service in the homes of Javanese elite.

Bu Haji also spoke about their servitude; however, she generally drew on the metaphor of adoption; household staff "followed the family" (*ikut keluarga*) and were "adopted, or taken up" (*anak angkat, diangkat*) by the well-off. She expected servants to perform many daily tasks—cooking, cleaning, errands, and transportation—as well as to provide companionship or child care throughout the day. Yet ultimately it was not the quality of

their service, but these idioms of familial order and adoption that characterized her version of servants' tenure and place in the household.[4]

These idioms of fictive kinship for labor relations and domestic service
in particular deserve attention and comparative analysis. Whether in literary works or as moral metaphors in labor policy statements in which workers and employers are encouraged to resolve disputes "in the family way"
(*secara kekeluarga*), claims to familial relations reflect foremost the
employer's interests (Robison 1986). Critically examining these idioms of
fictive kinship begs the question of the power relations involved, particularly in domestic contexts. Recall, for instance, Suryadi's poem, which presents Pariyem's rape and sexual abuse as a kind of illicit love affair. Even in
the worst of circumstances, the poem suggests, Javanese wage earners adopt
the language of the powerful to consider their employers "like kin."

James Scott's analysis of discourse and power in Malay societies assumes
the opposite: that two rhetorical strategies exist. The language of fictive kinship in everyday life dissimilates the exploitative social practices of the
"haves" toward the "have nots" in rural communities (Scott 1976, 45). When
peasants speak of fictional kin ties, they enact a lost "moral economy" to make
claims on the well-off; privately they may gossip or deride the terms (Scott
1985, 282–84). Although Scott revives a class analysis of social differences
between rural and urban Malays that could be applied to servants and their
employers as well, his analysis tends to reduce culturally particular forms of
expression to transparent forms of propaganda. Whatever its faults, "Pariyem's
Confession" does yield some clues to a culturally textured analysis of domestic
servants' lives and an ethnographic portrait of Javanese servitude.

Suryadi's poem suggests that rural Javanese separate social hierarchy
and emotional affinity as outer and inner facets of their social identity as
servants. Contrary to his poem, I would argue that this distinction is not
always a harmonious one. Servitude can become a kind of social paradox.
Although servants are subordinate to their employers and may even identify
with those of higher rank, recent research suggests that rural Javanese also
value personal autonomy and strive to become more autonomous over time
(Hefner 1990, 154–57). This can be seen when servants and household staff
and their employers claim different conceptions of kinship. Employers like
Bu Haji draw heavily upon paternal and maternal roles, as if to extend the
debts of parental care to their social dependents. In this view servants are
socialized much as children are—to be loyal and to show gratitude to those
who hire them.

In contrast, servants in their conversations with me emphasized that
their relationships with Bu Haji were predicated on exchange. They talked

frequently about what their employers had given them. Therein lies the crucial difference between the literary representation of Pariyem, who says she "feels like a daughter-in-law," and servants whom I interviewed in north Javanese households. Social and emotional ties between servants and employers are predicated upon gifts, not secret liaisons. Ironically, the gift binds one closer to an employer even as it provides more opportunity for personal autonomy and estranges one from the familial order.

This essay explores how servants in Java perceive their social identity as a paradox: the more servants are drawn into a rhetoric of familial ties, the more they remain distinct from their employer's family. Servants, especially those who work in elite families' homes, cultivate this paradox as a kind of domestic estrangement. They express the paradox as a split subjectivity common in Javanese cultural terms, of "external and internal" experience. On the one hand, they are temporary members and ideologically engaged in a familial order. On the other hand, a constant series of gifts, mundane and substantial, place them outside the kindred group. Temporary residence brings them into constant contact with a family, yet they are never among its members. The result is to simulate familial ties as expansive, yet also to draw their boundaries to exclude these social dependents. Employers claim paternalizing responsibility for their servants' well-being. Yet if we listen carefully, servants make a different set of claims concerning their employers' generosity evident in prior gift giving. Both draw on idioms of fictive kinship, but only servants emphasize the role of gifts in marking distinctions in social status as well as in creating close ties of dependence and obligation.

These two sets of rhetorical strategies represent the different positions from which servants and employers articulate their relationship. My neighbor Mbak Ari often described Bu Haji as "like [her] mother-in-law" because Bu Haji and her husband had contributed so much to Ari and Budi's wedding expenses, as well as to the expenses of raising two sons. Her discourse on social identity highlighted for me those moments when Bu Haji had bestowed gifts. She felt "like a daughter-in-law" (Javanese: *kaya mantu*) and to prove it, she displayed the gold jewelry given at *Lebaran*, the motorcycle provided for daily transportation, or the school uniforms for her sons. However, Bu Haji never told me she felt "like a mother-in-law." Rather, Ari and her husband could be trusted because they followed her family's firm, P. T. Langit (*ikut Langit*).

Not surprisingly, servants and staff still speak of social dependence in terms of diffuse moral obligation for what they have received from their employers (Mauss 1967). Gifts that cross the boundaries of kin and nonkin relationships can create the possibility of "feeling like kin" (Le Goff 1980). However, they do not dissolve those boundaries. They simply signify that a young servant or staff person is "close" (*dekat*) to their employer. Ironically, continuous in-kind contributions also allow for increased personal autonomy over time, in that they allow the servant increased opportunity to save wages and to engage in other networks of exchange. In some cases, a servant or staff person can eventually withdraw from service and live independently (*mandiri*), although this is rare. The point is that enduring social differences between servants and employers are marked by gifts. Moreover, gift giving both demonstrates the effort and becomes the occasion to overcome those differences.

JAVANESE SERVITUDE: A SKETCH OF CONTEMPORARY CONDITIONS

To show how these processes of domestic engagement and estrangement unfold in people's lives, first let me elaborate on domestic work in Java and on what servants and staff meant by "following" or being "close to their employers." To summarize contemporary conditions of service in Javanese households in the New Order era (1966 to 1998): domestic help is ubiquitous in middle-class and elite homes in Java (Hill 1994, 149).[5] Very wealthy families employ many servants and staff of all ages, both male and female.[6] In this section, I focus on the practices in Bu Haji's household over time. My data are drawn from observations of servant and staff interactions with their employer in her home over the course of two years, and from my travels with some of them to their natal villages at holidays.

The social dynamics between employer and servants could be seen in the interactions of a single Indonesian woman and her maid. The advantage of studying the situations of staff in an elite home like Bu Haji's household is that gift giving is more frequent, explicit, and a relatively public event, and, therefore, more accessible to observation and discussion.

Bu Haji employed no less than forty men, women, boys, and girls as servants and staff in her household. Some were live-in servants; some were day staff who went home to their own residences in the evening.[7] She joked that Indonesian servants were superior to American household appliances. One day she showed me a crew of young boys and girls who did laundry by hand in a tiled room with hoses, drains, and drying racks. "You don't have any [servants] like these in the U.S., do you?" she would ask me. "There, everyone uses machines," and she would gesture at the electric dryer imported from Germany that was used during the rainy season.

The most common pattern of domestic service in urban households is when the senior woman of the household hires a servant from a village, one who is young, female, and has some primary school education.[8] The servant (*pembantu* or "helper") then works for several years before her own marriage doing laundry, cleaning, shopping for fresh produce each day, and preparing and cooking food. Upon marriage or after the birth of her first child, she returns to her own residence in the village and shifts to home-based piece-rate work for income. Another unmarried girl from a rural area is then engaged to take her place in the household. This pattern characterized many homes in urban neighborhoods where I did fieldwork. Middle-class families engage only one or two servants on a regular basis and prefer to hire labor crews for extraordinary occasions. For example, a woman might arrange for caterers to help prepare the food for a communal ritual (*slametan*), or she might hire carpenters and other craftsmen to do temporary renovations in the courtyard. In either case the caterers or craftsmen and laborers might live temporarily in the house compound and be paid after the event or completion of the project. In contrast, ordinary servants are paid according to variable schedules and idiosyncratic conventions.

Hiring servants is still a contractual relationship; they can be paid wages once a week, once a month, or once a year. Yet despite this social fact, Bu Haji and other elite women I knew described servitude as a diffuse process over time in which employees "follow the family" (*ikut keluarga*) and are "taken up" (*diangkat*) or are looked after as social dependents (*anak angkat*), who then become the responsibility of the senior woman of the household.[9] Servants can be quite young when they begin work as domestic staff in Javanese homes. Bu Haji's sister-in-law, Bu Ris, engaged a boy who was only seven years old to accompany her own son to religious lessons to learn to read the Koran.[10] The boy also helped the older servants around the house. When Bu Haji asked if the boy "followed" his grandmother (who was employed in the home as well) Bu Ris replied, "No, he follows me" (Javanese: *ndak, melu aku*).

Individuals of both sexes and all ages can be "taken up" in the role of social dependent; they can be supported indefinitely. Their employers provide room and board, uniforms, and pay the cost of primary, secondary, and religious education in addition to annual wages. Children seven years or older would attend primary and secondary school in the morning hours and do household tasks the rest of the day. In larger households such as Bu Haji's, long-term service would not end when a servant marries. Servants sometimes establish their own residence nearby and enter their employer's household each day, frequently staying overnight. However, those who cannot afford their own residence may rent a room from their employer, or they may continue as an adult to reside in the employers' household.

Servants sustain very little private life while employed in an elite home. They may have a cubicle or closet in which to store personal belongings and clothes; if they attend school, they are given school uniforms and books. At Bu Haji's house the rear hallway contained a row of cabinets where all servants kept their clothing and a few personal items. Little or no pocket money is provided or expected, although some servants manage to take an occasional trip to market while on errands for their employer. Soap, shampoo, towels, and thongs as well as uniforms and meals are provided for them if they do not attend school; some younger servants may spend weeks within the house compound. At night the young boys who worked at Bu Haji's slept in various locations around the house: either in one of two rooms with bunk beds reserved as sleeping quarters, or on the floor in odd corners of the house sprawled over one another on sleeping mats or the small couches. Like village boys who do the neighborhood watch, the young male servants in Bu Haji's home preferred to sit up talking and to nap at other times.

Household tasks are allocated according to a sexual division of labor. Male servants are typically the chauffeurs for various modes of transport—motorcycle, bicycle or car—and they guard residences. Female servants shop for produce and prepare cooked food exclusively. Both male and female servants do laundry, child care, and cleaning, although it is more common for girls and women to be engaged in such household tasks. Older women may supervise younger workers of both sexes. They also have the responsibility to care for their employer's children, watching over (*menjaga*) or accompanying (*ngancani*) their employers' sons and daughters throughout the day. These roles of companion can involve younger servants who escort, assist, and entertain their employer's children as they grow older.

In both middle-class and elite households I have observed, servants are recruited through labor brokers who visit rural villages several hours away. Usually new servants are solicited immediately after the Fasting Month and Muslim holiday, *Idul Fitri*, which is also the Javanese New Year (*Lebaran*). Servants are expected to reside with their employers for a year following the holiday, during that year they are given room and board, clothing, as well as medical treatment when needed. Wages are paid annually just before the next Lebaran. Since wages are paid just before the holiday, typically the money is presented with other in-kind gifts. In Bu Haji's household every staff person was given cloth for new clothes, a bolt of *batik* cloth, cigarettes (for the men), and jewelry (for the women).

Servants may be with a household for a few months, for a year, or for decades. The tenure of their service is determined anew each Lebaran. If a servant's performance throughout the year is unsatisfactory, wages will be paid perfunctorily, and he or she is not engaged for service the following year. Just before the holiday, Bu Haji would sit on the steps with the servants around her; she would joke with them to "come back next year." There appears to be some degree of choice in servants' decision to return to service after the holiday. Younger servants were escorted home by van to safeguard their travel while they were carrying their annual wages and bonus, since it was such a large amount of cash. It was difficult to discover the range for payment of annual wages, but the younger servants told me they earned Rp 30,000 a month plus a bonus (then, roughly $20 a month, or $240 a year). The bonus usually equaled a month's salary. Unmarried servants gave their entire annual wages to their parents. Married servants and older staff saved their wages in a variety of ways: as gold jewelry, or in a bank account. They rarely traveled on the holidays and preferred to rest or to visit neighbors and relatives close by. Younger servants anticipated their visits home as a time when they could "sleep late and eat a lot."

In short, while Javanese servants live in the household of their employer they are subordinate to their employers in rank. However, if employers describe their relationship in paternalistic terms as looking after younger servants in particular, the annual negotiation of service at Lebaran marks a servant's status outside the family. Because servants leave their employer's homes at Lebaran to rejoin their natal families, their status as strangers resurfaces at least once a year. That moment of distinguishing separate lives and loyalties is marked by gifts from employer to servant, including payment of wages.

The Sociolinguistic Context of Servitude

A crucial aspect of servitude is linguistic deference (Romero 1992, 113–17). Since all negotiation of social identity in Javanese society is predicated on speech levels spoken in everyday interactions, it is worth asking how servants speak, are spoken to, and are spoken about in a Javanese household. The term *pembantu*, literally, "helper," denotes a general status of temporary servitude in a household; although a wealthy woman may speak of her "staff" (*staf*), "employees" (*karyawan*), or "entourage" (literally "those who follow me" [*yang ikut saya*]). In traditional Javanese settings distant relatives often worked as temporary servants. To speak of servants as "taken up" (*diangkat*) implies a similar relational process of inflecting domestic relations with familial roles. However, unrelated servants are not adopted; rather, their engagement in service invokes a constant negotiation of social and emotional position in the household.

Familial hierarchy frames the daily negotiation of status in a Javanese home. Javanese-speaking servants answer to their name with the personal pronoun, "*dalem,*" in the formal high Javanese register that is inflected with honorifics spoken to a social superior. Much as Javanese children are socialized to show respect and varying degrees of shame and fear toward strangers and those of higher rank, servants, who are often still quite young when they begin to work in elite households, are expected to be quiet, deferential in their speech and gesture, and quick to follow instructions (Geertz 1961, 110–16). They speak softly in melodious tones of high Javanese, in contrast to the rough crackle of low Javanese spoken by family members. Among themselves, servants speak in low Javanese with minimal code-switching to mark differences in status (with the exception of age).

Servants describe themselves as "following" and also as "near, or far" from their employers. They elaborate this social distance by referring to acts of exchange, citing previously given gifts to validate their place in the household. As younger servants find themselves drawn close to (or distanced from) the household throughout the years, they emphasize that despite their low status in ordinary interaction, at particular moments they are treated "like a son" or "like a daughter-in-law" because of what they have been given. Eventually, many household staff no longer consider themselves "servants," preferring to elaborate how long they had been employed and in what capacity, as evidence that they have overcome the generic role of servant.

THE LOGIC OF THE GIFT

"More than words, perhaps, gifts might win loyalty and affection" (Leupp 1992, 77). Gifts in any social context are culturally invested with meaning (Medick and Sabean 1986). In her comparative study of U.S. domestic service, Judith Rollins is critical of the practice of gift giving from employers to domestics since she encountered primarily the gifts of old clothes in lieu of wages (Rollins 1985, 189–91; also see Romero 1992, 109).

> Thus the pervasiveness of gift-giving in domestic service . . . like the many forms of deference demanded and the other manifestations of maternalism serves to reify the differences between the women: be they in terms of class, race, or human worth. (Rollins 1985, 193)

Romero is equally skeptical of the power of gift, since under capitalism, ". . . employer's gifts or promises of a reward for employee's loyalty are not the same as the obligation a master had to care for his servants" (Romero 1992, 120). The employee's involvement in the interpersonal relationship with an employer is a gamble. In the Javanese case, I am interested in the role of gifts to demarcate and to cross the boundaries between kin and stranger in the household, rather than their extrinsic value as a substitute for contractual payment.

Domestic servitude includes not only a series of material exchanges but also deferred expectations. In Java in particular, to defer, or to set aside self-interest, pervades the structuring capacity in Javanese society (Geertz 1961, 110–14; Jay 1969, 65–67). Deferral, as a stage of the gift, allows for an ongoing relationship between urban employer and rural servant. The irony in servitude in elite homes is that expectation of gifts is itself deferred and set aside throughout the year. The moments of exchange at Lebaran constitute social relations of the household retrospectively, differentiating servants among themselves as those who "received a lot" and those who "received little." Servants' experiences vary according to age, sex, and personal history. However, most servants in a large Javanese household try to remain sincere and unattached (*ikhlas*), which they characterize as the attribute of a good Muslim. In a sense, they await Lebaran and the New Year to see the degree to which their service has been accepted and valued.

Throughout the year more mundane moments of exchange between employers and their servant-staff help to determine the emotional texture of these annual domestic rituals. An unstable alternation between prestation and its absence makes the rhythm of domestic life inherently tenuous for servants. When mundane gifts are bestowed unexpectedly, they are taken as signs of social identity under negotiation; they mark the fundamental difference between family members and strangers. For example, Saya Shiraishi (1986) notes that when someone in a Javanese family finds something missing, money from one's pocket, for instance, one is more likely to say that someone in the family has "borrowed" the sum than to imply the accusation of theft. Only strangers can steal; family members borrow. The gift (or its shadow of negative reciprocity, theft) should only circulate outside the home (Shiraishi 1986, 91). To declare money missing within the household draws attention to strangers living at home. Conversely, to encounter the gift in one's household marks the boundary between family and stranger, in an attempt to transform the latter into the former.

Such gifts recall an older set of exchanges with individuals who were taken in or adopted and who gained debts of loyalty (*utang budi*). The current rhetoric and gestures of gift in elite homes contradict this older sense of exchanges and familial order in crucial ways, which I outline later. In-kind gifts that circulate between social superiors and their dependents now mimic kin relations, thus making the difference between family and stranger ironically more distinct. Servants in Java traverse domestic space by straddling the boundaries of modern elites' homes in personalistic and increasingly tenuous ways.

One can see this especially in the forms of personalized debt (*utang budi*) and sacrifice that are rhetorically deployed by individual servants and firm owners in other contexts, such as at prayer meetings, if only to underscore their passing. One servant mentioned that she felt it was a personal sacrifice (*dadi korban*) when she was asked to work the day after Lebaran even though she had planned a trip with her friends. Another staff woman asked me if I understood the Islamic concept of Judgment Day (*Hari Yang Terakhir*) to explain how and why she was able to work for her employer without promise of compensation for overtime. In general, though, few servants spoke of debts of loyalty, except those who had faced serious illnesses and for whom their employers had paid their medical bills.

Presentations in the New Order era reveal what is increasingly at stake in contemporary domestic labor relations. This is not to say servants aren't evaluated for their work. Two boys told me that "a good servant" was quiet, quick, and easy to teach tasks. They knew that they met this standard if asked to come back for another year of service after Lebaran. If not, the bonus and clothes given at the end of the year also served as advance notice. By displacing contractual payment into the form of gift at a religious holiday, servitude is transformed into an annual relationship between employee and employer. This explains partly why servants are often idle throughout the day, yet clearly compelled to stay within the confines of the home in which they are employed. Evaluation is not based entirely on their service, but on their willingness to occupy the house and to wait for the opportunity to be of service.

Gifts to servants, expected or otherwise, also shape the emotional texture of servitude. Ari described herself as "close to Bu Haji" because Ari's husband had been taken care of by Bu Haji's brothers since he was a small child. Budi was orphaned when he was very young and then raised by an uncle and two older brothers. He was adopted by Bu Haji's father when he was still in secondary school and taken as a companion and schoolmate for Bu Haji's younger brother until he went to college. As an adult Budi began working as a staff manager for Bu Haji at her two factories and several retail stores in town. When Ari married Budi, she became a member of Bu Haji's household staff. For seven years she managed the stock for the retail store and helped to buy and to prepare gifts for interhousehold exchanges.

When discussing interhousehold exchanges, Ari often sat low on the floor next to Bu Haji and chatted about the contributions to neighbors who were planning life-cycle ceremonies. When Ari helped wrap gifts for families celebrating circumcisions, births, and weddings, other household staff and store clerks would sit on the floor and assist her. Bu Haji would instruct Ari on wrapping the life-cycle gifts while she was approving the design of signs to be hung in her retail bookstore. The conversation would swing back and forth between bookkeeping and accounting for the store and reciting the names of kin of various recipients of the gifts being wrapped. In these instances Ari clearly identifies with Bu Haji as she receives instructions, prepares gifts, and serves guests, since she says she is participating in those exchanges without having to give a gift herself. Not quite giver, not quite recipient, she nonetheless participates in the traditional exchanges between households in a satisfying way; and once she told me she enjoyed the process because she was keenly aware of what had been given and to whom.

As Ari told me when I first arrived, "At Lebaran, just watch. Ibu gives all her staff clothing and jewelry as well as bonuses." This narrative of generosity obligates Ari and her husband to attend to Ibu and her family whenever necessary. Residing in an old factory complex that Bu Haji bought in West Kudus to house her staff, Ari follows a strict schedule each day going to Bu Haji's house in East Kudus. She and her husband are available for errands or assistance whenever Bu Haji, her husband, or children need them. They also respond in the evening when telephoned. Ari said she visits Bu Haji's home even on her day off in case something comes up. Her own kitchen is too quiet, simply a place to do repetitive tasks such as cleaning rice, weeding the courtyard, and ironing. Ari refuses to take a servant herself, because she told me it would imply a higher status for herself than the neighbors in the compound. At Bu Haji's home when Ari "visits" (Javanese: *dolan wae*) she is alert to opportunities to supervise in the kitchen or to help with unexpected guests.

Domestic engagement defines servants and household staff as part of the family, yet always as temporary visitors. Since Ari and Budi resided on the other side of town, they were only a short ride or telephone call away. They could bring a change of clothes and stay overnight if needed, although Ari rarely chose to sleep at her employer's home, preferring instead to demonstrate her endurance by going without sleep for the length of ritual preparations. She also distinguished between Bu Haji's house, where she was on call, and her own kitchen, where she could wear casual clothing, eat, or sleep. She and Budi frequently were called to Bu Haji's home to run an errand, to buy snacks in the evening, or to assist with her children. As a lodger in the same housing complex and the resident anthropologist, I was called to assist the children with their schoolwork and to translate invitations or messages into English. At one point when Bu Haji was paying her staff at the close of the holidays she gave me a sum of Rp 25,000 in an envelope. She laughingly included me in her distribution of payments to the domestic staff, saying, "Even you get an envelope, some spending money."

These various exchanges between Bu Haji, Ari, and I during fieldwork made me more sensitive to the ways wages can appear as a commercial transaction between families and their servants. To analyze domestic service as

wage labor intermeshed with a local gift economy does not remove dimensions of economic exploitation from these exchanges, but it does shift analysis from utilitarian explanations of exchange as a means to further social goals
toward a cultural appreciation of the ways the "goods" are given, and how
they can constitute the value of service, connectedness, and emotional ties.

If servitude in Java constitutes certain in-kind exchanges and ambivalent
emotional ties, it does not ensure employee's comfort and economic security.
My two roommates, Fatimah and Mari, worked for Bu Haji and were said to
"follow P. T. Langit" (the name of Bu Haji's company). They were given
room and board in addition to their weekly salary. When they were moved
into a new room adjacent to mine, they were presented with a single double
bed that was too short for them and where they sat in disappointment for
several hours. Mari said softly that she did not look forward to sleeping with
cramped legs. I argued we should inform Bu Haji and request a new bed,
which neither of them "dared to do." They preferred to sleep on mats on the
floor and hope that eventually they would be given a new bed. Mari was particularly rueful that such discomfort was their lot but pointed out that gifts
cannot be questioned. Thus, in-kind gifts are a primary site for servants to
experience the tenuousness of their employment and the uncertainty of
future relations.

However, the logic of the gift remains compelling for servants and other
domestic employers in Javanese households because it subsumes more contractual aspects of employment. Staff did not speak of their wages to define
their tenure and security in their position. Instead, they mentioned the
range and degree of in-kind gifts: medicine and payment of expenses for an
operation, school fees and uniform costs for one's children, a particular piece
of jewelry, or a bolt of batik cloth. Food, clothing, and means of transport
(usually motorcycles or bicycles) or lodging can enhance also a servant's
ability to fulfill expected tasks and increase personal autonomy by increasing
his or her ability to save wages. Gifts include commodities and symbols of
leisure and privilege: sports equipment, such as tennis rackets; gold jewelry;
makeup; and cigarettes in bulk were treasured. Again, these gifts cannot be
explained entirely through utilitarian motives—an employer seeking to
strengthen the ties of loyalty, for instance—although servants and staff
attribute them to the proper, even skillful role of the elite couple in securing
good staff. "She knows how to give the right things," they would say about
Bu Haji, who managed staff for a large household, two factories, and several
stores.

Rather, such luxury gifts indicate the means by which servants can both
emulate and identify with their employers and live like them. James Siegel
points out that even weekly wages paid to workers in factories can be subor-

dinated to the logic of the gift; that is, an offer of money is domesticated through a return of appropriate signs of deference by subordinates to those of higher rank (Siegel 1986, 176–77). In household service, both wages and in-kind gifts to domestic employees hold multiple values as objects of consumption and as signs of exchange to signify domestic labor relations, if not the value of domestic labor itself. Because it is often elite Javanese women, and not their husbands, who pay their staff annual cash wages in an envelope and who present the gifts at Lebaran, domestic labor relations are manifest as these annual exchanges marked by the gender of the giver (Sullivan 1994, 116, 136–38; also see Brenner 1998, 112).

Before they leave for their natal villages, servants and household and office staff who are "taken up" by Bu Haji are given cloth, cigarettes, and jewelry, as well as a cash bonus for the holiday following the fasting month. An entire afternoon is occupied with the payment process; office managers and domestic staff stand in lines down the hall awaiting their turn to approach Bu Haji and her husband seated at a table in the main room. Each staff person nods and ducks as they approach the table; Bu Haji gives them a bundle of wrapped cloth, cigarettes, and an envelope with their annual wages and bonus while her husband records their payment and shakes hands with the employee. Returning to the line, younger servants look embarrassed as people tease them on what they received, or furtively compare what they were paid. One scuffle between two young cooks was resolved when the gatekeeper's wife admonished the two girls to "shake hands like Muslims." She asked, "What kind of people are you, Buddhists?" The restrained moral tenor of the day alternated with emotional excitement as younger servants look forward to their week with their families.

As staff who are closest to Bu Haji's family, Budi and Ari received more elaborate bundles at Lebaran, which one year included furniture and a TV as well as several boxes of filter cigarettes from the firm—which they repackaged and gave to Budi's uncles and their children. Budi and Ari were expected to chauffeur Bu Haji and her children on the morning of Idul Fitri to the public ceremony where everyone prays together (*sholat*). Ari told me this act alone demonstrated how close she is to her employer. She also pointed out that one cannot follow more than one employer or, as in the case of the neighbor who tried to cultivate too many ties of patronage, one becomes "confused" (*bingung*).[11]

The moral obligation for employers who engage very young servants is to provide for their religious and moral education, at least until marriage. In servants' narratives, their parents tell them as children to obey their employers as they would their parents. Elite couples (and even families of modest means) readily admit this responsibility to educate young servants and to protect single female servants from situations of public flirtation, which they claim has dire consequences. Pedicab drivers told me they would sometimes use public phones to call young women working as servants in elite homes, to hear their "sweet voices" even if they could only catch a glimpse of the women over the high walls. However, this moral guardianship is not simply a case of transposing or exaggerating parental authority onto an employer, but an estrangement of social relations once servitude ends. For once servants do marry, they may return to their village and rarely see the employers again. For example, my neighbors retained a teenage girl for three years, and they were always cautious of her reputation and her health. Once she returned to a small fishing village near Jepara, married, and had a child, they rarely heard news of her except at Lebaran, when they would send her some money. On my last visit, they told me that she was uncharacteristically thin.

SETTING FAMILY AND FIRM APART

In this essay, I have argued that servitude in Java thus implies both engagement and an estrangement from a familial order and paternal relations. Whereas discourse defines servants as "part of the family," social practices position servants as subjects both within and without the modern Javanese home. Servants are subjects whose interests are deferred to familial authority rather than to contractual relationships as employees. Domestic service thus assumes a relationship of dependence on the family, but more important, access to the household as a place where staff share personalistic ties to their employer.

These ties contrast sharply with the more tenuous and unpredictable and low-status conditions of contracted wage labor (Wolf 1992). "Those who work" in factories are set apart from "those who follow" a firm. The symbolic gestures marking "those who follow" as within the domain of household relations include the bestowal of an array of token gifts. Staff are given uniforms that set them apart visually; they also are sponsored for schooling, religious education, and various forms of training. Many factory workers I knew hoped that their younger siblings or children would be "taken up" by the family who owned the firm. Particularly when firm owners reside next to the workers, the contradictions of economic pressure and rising expectations in rural communities are muted if the elite household is privileged as a particular kind of domestic space in which kinlike social relationships are initiated, altered, and maintained. Even when candidates interview for official positions in a firm's office, they are frequently inter-viewed by the couple in their living room in the early morning or in the late afternoon hours. In this way the domestic domain mediates contractual employment within and outside the home.

To be accepted as domestic staff maintains an important fiction about money: that following an elite family can shield social dependents from the uncertainties of market exchange. Although the familial mode of relations assures staff of more generalized support and access to credit than a wage, it is nevertheless contingent upon the market and the financial success of the firm. If a firm goes bankrupt, or merges through acquisition with another firm, expectations of support become meaningless. Staff and some servants hope that their children also will be "taken up" by the owners of the firm, or by the next generation, so that "they won't have to think about money." To be taken up by a family of higher rank removes one temporarily from market exchange and local networks and labor obligations among neigh-bors and kin.

If gifts and presentations of money, cloth, and in-kind support redefine familial order, New Order capitalism also allows the gift to be supplemented, that is, to add to an already sufficient exchange an additional, but inessen-tial gesture. To supplement the gift displaces reciprocity and expectations of return. A gift evokes a return that is refused, thereby confirming the gift as a gift. Where an exchange threatens to erupt into reciprocity, a hidden demand for the return, the logic of the gift is threatened, or distorted from a personalistic exchange to a more interested transaction (Derrida 1992, 170–73).

This disruption in gift logic arises when the loyalty of servants, staff, and employees is strained occasionally; for example, if their status outside of the employer's home takes precedence. One young staff member, who was designated as the companion of Bu Haji's teenage daughter, failed to return to Bu Haji's household the week after Lebaran. Instead she remained with her family in a village near Solo for an additional week. When she returned, she clearly expected to be chastised and possibly to be dismissed for her inconsideration. When I saw her seated in the antechamber waiting for an audience with Bu Haji, the young person told me she regretted her actions, but she couldn't bring herself to leave her mother after only a few days. Only her fear and respect for Bu Haji made her return to ask forgiveness and even-tually to be reinstated.

The other inkling of disruption lies in the arbitrary assignment of tasks servants are expected to perform. When Bu Haji renovated the warehouse in the factory complex where her employees and I resided, she asked Ari to stay home and to prepare the workers' snacks. Ari was clearly unhappy to be told to leave her position managing inventory at the store to stay home in the courtyard to serve drinks to the staff and workers. "How is it," I asked her one day near my departure, "that you 'follow someone' if the assignment of tasks is so arbitrary?" She explained, "Of course, if a person can, she tries to rely on herself (*mandiri*). But most people can't, so we have to depend on someone else." The task assignment was temporary, but like the insufficient bed or the ambiguity of returning after Lebaran, it suggested an estrangement borne in silence.

Thus, in New Order Indonesia, domestic labor relations both nostalgize ties between rural servants and staff, even as they replace older rhetorical forms of loyalty with new practices of exchange, alienation, and domesticity. One cannot say what forms of fiction will emerge to represent these practices. Nah, the servant next door who came from Jepara, once borrowed my copy of Pramoedya Ananta Toer's novel, *The Girl from the Coast*. Between daily household tasks she read the first chapter. The next day I asked her what she thought of the story of a village girl who is taken into service as a mistress to an aristocrat in nineteenth-century Java. "It's wonderful," she said. "The girl gets married and receives so many marvelous gifts of clothing and jewelry."

NOTES

1. Suryadi A. G., Linus (1980). *The Inner Life of a Javanese Woman*. Jakarta: Sinar Harapan Press. Published in Indonesia with Javanese words and phrases throughout the text, the poem has an extensive Javanese glossary.

2. Cf. Leupp (1992, 72–73) who refers to ideal master-servant relations as "celebrated in fiction" during the Tokagawa period in Japan.

3. Ya, ya Pariyem saya
   Maria Magdalena Pariyem lengkapnya
   "Iyem" panggilan sehariharinya
   dari Wonosari Gunung Kidul
   Sebagai babu nDoro Kanjeng Cokro Sentono
   de nDalem Suryamentaraman Ngayogyakarta . . .Tata lahirnya, saya hanya babu
   Tapi batinya, saya putri mantu . . .Tata lahirnya, saya hanya babu
   Tapi batinya selir baru.

4. Adoption in Javanese kinship is a variable term; Hildred Geertz (1961) prefers to state that people "borrow" children, since strict relinquishment of rights, known as *pupon*, is rare. The term used here, *angkat*, means literally "to fit"; however,

it has become a common idiom for either adoption or clientage in the current era (Weix 1990).

5. For discussion of the New Order era in Indonesia, see Robison 1986 and Hill 1994. It was a period characterized by President Suharto's rule, increasing international aid, loans, and capital investment.

6. Rollins (1985, 21) suggests that domestic service is associated with women throughout the world; clearly Indonesia does not support this contention.

7. The issue of a historical transformation of live-in to day work is relevant here. Based on my observations, both patterns are in practice in contemporary Indonesian homes (cf. Hansen 1991, 48).

8. This confirms the global pattern described by Judith Rollins: "The typical female domestic is a young migrant from a poor, non-urban area who engages in live-in domestic service until marriage or a more desirable employment opportunity presents itself" (1985, 55). Also see Leupp (1992, 57–61) who refers to "the feminization of servitude" as a historical process, since 50 to 70 percent of urban servants in early nineteenth-century Japanese households were female because it posed advantageous employment for rural migrants.

9. Cf. "Ibuism" Djajdiningrat-Niewenhuis 1987. This process is called "maternalism" in the literature on domestics in the United States, where personalized relationships are one avenue for exploitation (cf. Rollins 1985, 156–73; Romero 1992). Rollins, in particular, does not equate maternalism with paternalism or feudal master-servant relations since, she argues, domestic service is an extension of, or a surrogate for, the woman of the house. However, her analysis makes an unwarranted association between housework and women (cf. Hansen 1991, 52).

10. Leupp (1992, 57–61) notes that for the Tokagawa period, Japanese elites engaged foster-siblings for their children, and the age structure for servants was from the age of nine or ten through the early 1920s. Children typically did not receive wages, although some might accompany the employers' children. "The two children might even become lifelong companions although particularly in wealthy families, a fundamental status distinction between them would be observed."

11. "Service, in theory, was based on loyalty—loyalty to one's master and to his household as a sacred entity" (Leup 1992, 41).

REFERENCES

Brenner, Suzanne
1998   *The Domestication of Desire: Women, Wealth and Modernity in Java.* Princeton: Princeton University Press.

Derrida, Jacques
1992   Given Time: The Time of the King. *Critical Inquiry* 12:161–87.

Djajdiningrat-Nieuwenhuis

1987   Ibuism and Priyayization: Path to Power? In Elsbeth Locher-Scholten and
         Anke Niehof, eds., *Indonesian Women in Focus: Past and Present Notions*, 43–51.
         Dordrecht Holland: Foris Publications.

Geertz, Clifford

1960   *The Religion of Java*. Glencoe: The Free Press.

Geertz, Hildred

1961   *The Javanese Family: A Study in Kinship and Socialization*. Glencoe: The Free
         Press.

Hansen, Karen

1991   Domestic Service: What's in It for Anthropology? *Reviews in Anthropology*
         16:47–62.

Hart, Gillian

1986   *Power, Labor and Livelihood: Processes of Change in Rural Java*. Berkeley: Uni-
         versity of California Press.

Hefner, Robert

1990   *The Political Economy of Mountain Java*. Berkeley: University of California
         Press.

Hill, Hal, ed.

1994   *Indonesia's New Order: The Dynamics of Socio-Economic Transformation*. Ho-
         nolulu: University of Hawaii Press.

Jay, Robert

1969   *Javanese Villagers: Social Relations in Rural Mojokuto*. Cambridge: MIT Press.

Le Goff, Jacques

1980   The Symbolic Ritual of Vassalage. In Arthur Goldhammer, trans., *Time, Work,
         and Culture in the Middle Ages*, 237–87. Chicago: University of Chicago Press.

Leupp, Gary P.

1992   *Servants, Shophands, and Laborers in the Cities of Tokagawa Japan*. Princeton:
         Princeton University Press.

Mauss, Marcel

1967   *The Gift: Forms and Functions of Exchange in Archaic Societies*. London: W. W.
         Norton.

Medick, Hans, and David W. Sabean, eds.

1986   *Interest and Emotion: Essays on the Study of Family and Kinship*. Cambridge:
         Cambridge University Press.

Robison, Richard

1986   *Indonesia: The Rise of Capital.* Asian Studies Association of Australia. Canberra ACT: Southeast Asian Publications Series No. 13.

Rollins, Judith

1985   *Between Women: Domestics and Their Employers.* Philadelphia: Temple University Press.

Romero, Mary

1992   *Maid in the U.S.A.* New York: Routledge Press.

Scott, James

1976   *The Moral Economy of the Peasant: Rebellion and Subsistence in Southeast Asia.* New Haven: Yale University Press.

1985   *The Weapons of the Weak: Everyday Forms of Peasant Resistance.* New Haven: Yale University Press.

Shiraishi, Saya

1986   Silahkan Masuk, Silahkan Duduk: Reflections on a Sitting Room in Java. *Indonesia* 41:89–130.

Siegel, James

1986   *Solo in the New Order: Language and Hierarchy in an Indonesian City.* Princeton: Princeton University Press.

Sullivan, Norma

1994   *Masters and Managers: A Study of Gender Relations in Urban Java.* St. Leonards, NSW (Australia): Allen and Unwin.

Suryadi, Linus

1980   *Pengakuan Pariyem: Dunia Batin Seorang Wanita Jawa.* Jakarta: Sinar Harapan Press.

Weix, G. G.

1990   Following the Family/Firm: Patronage and Piecework in a Kudus Cigarette Factory. Ph.D. diss., Cornell University.

Wolf, Diane

1992   *Factory Daughters: Gender, Household Dynamics and Rural Industrialization in Java.* Berkeley: University of California Press.

NEGOTIATED IDENTITIES

Humor, Kinship Rhetoric, and Mythologies
of Servitude in South Sulawesi, Indonesia

It was early morning in the rural Toraja household that was my field base in 1984–85. Although the front room of the solid stone house was quiet, the kitchen and laundry area at the rear bustled with activity. Sisa, the soft-spoken fourteen-year-old female "helper,"[1] squatted on the kitchen floor assiduously scrubbing laundry as various members of the household hurried through to brush their teeth by the kitchen well or to hunt for mislaid schoolbooks. At the far end of the room, Ekson (the fifteen-year-old male helper) crouched by the hearth tending to the smoked water buffalo meat while fending off teasing speculations about his romantic interests from two of his employers' teenaged sons and their uncle. The jesting grew more ribald when Ne' Lele, the family's elderly female servant, joined in the exchange and turned the focus to the bachelor uncle. Playing on the uncle's fame for his attentiveness to his fifteen fighting roosters, Ne' Lele gestured to the rooster tucked under the uncle's sarong and cackled, "This uncle is so devoted to his rooster wives, he has no interest in real women! See how he strokes his cock with such tenderness and love. . . ." Her risqué taunt prompted shrieks and laughter. Emi (the boss's adult unmarried daughter) and I stood chuckling at the fringes of this scene when attention shifted toward us. Hobbling in our direction, Ne' Lele demanded to know if we were headed to the market in town. We nodded cautiously, and Ne' Lele teasingly suggested that while we were there we should shop for some men for the three of us and if we couldn't find any, then we should "bring back lots of bananas." Again the kitchen shook with raucous laughter, as Emi and I bashfully fled to the well.

As I came to appreciate during my two years of fieldwork in Tana Toraja Regency (South Sulawesi, Indonesia), bawdy humor holds a prominent place in the discourse of many Toraja household workers. It soon became apparent that, for my Toraja friends, such humor did more than simply alleviate the boredom of long tedious workdays. Beyond offering momentary levity, such teasing and jesting facilitated fleeting inversions of authority as well as exploratory realignments of identities. In a sense, Ne' Lele's earthy teasing of Emi and me entailed a subtle erasure of the unequal status and power relations among us, while underscoring our shared gender/sexual identities as well as our shared roles as unattached women.

This essay makes the argument that humor[2] plays a role in negotiating, reaffirming, and at times challenging asymmetrical household relations. Alford and Alford (1981, 151) and Mitchell (1992, 6) have both recently noted that humor is relatively underemphasized in ethnographic studies by anthropologists.[3] This is all the more true of research on the lives of household workers, where the topic of humor is extremely rare (mentioned only in passing, at best). By spotlighting the role of humor in identity politics, it is not my intention to overshadow or trivialize the real struggles of household workers. I do believe, however, that through closely focusing on everyday humor-laden interactions, we can come to a richer understanding of the ways in which household relations between people with unequal access to power are navigated.

Recently, Karen Hansen (1991, 61), Sanjek and Colen (1990, 178), and others have called for more actor-centered examinations of the lived experiences of household workers. In short, rather than conveying the results of large-scale surveys, this essay embraces a microapproach and focuses on closely examining interactions between workers and bosses in several South Sulawesi homes employing household workers. As Diane Wolf has suggested in her study of Javanese factory workers, "It is important to look closely at processes of interaction to see how 'bargaining' or 'negotiating' is actually enacted . . . we need to throw open the doors of the household more broadly, to capture the textures of household dynamics and to allow for a greater range of possible intra-household relations" (Wolf 1992, 22). While Wolf was using the term "negotiation" to refer to economics and decision-making processes, her comments are equally apt for those seeking a more nuanced appreciation of processes of *identity* negotiation.

At this point, some terminological clarification is in order. As outlined in the introduction, my use of the expression "identity negotiation" emerges from recent reformulations of concepts such as "ethnicity," "person," "class," and so forth by Nagata (1981), Clifford (1988), Linnekin (1990), White (1991), and others. These writers share a conception of identity as "an ongoing process, politically contested and historically unfinished" (Clifford 1988, 9). I use the term "negotiation," in turn, to refer to the social processes whereby such identities are articulated, asserted, challenged, suppressed, realigned, and co-opted in both verbal and nonverbal acts and exchanges.

My goal in this essay is to use humor as an avenue to expand our understanding of the ways in which household workers and employers negotiate their interdependent yet unequal identities. Since the 1980s researchers writing about household workers have begun to focus on the dynamics of institutionalized household hierarchies. For instance, Jacklyn Cock (1980, 103) depicted the muted "rituals of rebellion" embraced by household workers in attempts to assert autonomous identities. Judith Rollins (1985, 6), in turn, stressed how interpersonal relations in the household "have the power to generate and perpetuate . . . ideas of inequality" and explored some of the "rituals of deference" and forms of maternalism embodied in the domestic-employer relationship. Likewise, Gill (1994) has extended arguments made by Gramsci (1971), Scott (1985, 1990), and others, to illustrate how interactions between employers and servants not only entail accommodation to dominance but also conflict, reinterpretation, and even resistance. Building on these works, I suggest that humorous exchanges are overlooked as sites of identity negotiation and that microexaminations of playful, expressive interactions can offer us new perspectives on these processes.

Specifically, this essay focuses on Toraja domestic work to illuminate the ways in which historically embedded rank and ethnic hierarchies are transformed, negotiated, and perpetuated in contemporary South Sulawesi. The bulk of the essay examines Toraja workers employed in Toraja households in their homeland, where domestic service is entwined with legacies of rank inequality (and reinforced by poverty and remote village origins). At the end of the essay, the focus shifts to the Bugis- and Makassarese-dominated provincial capital of Ujung Pandang, where I briefly discuss Toraja domestic workers employed by affluent and middle-class Bugis families. In this urban setting, the employee-employer relationship is colored by ancient histories of ethnic dominance and by rural-urban hierarchies. In both arenas, I attend to the strategic role of humor in negotiating these asymmetrical relationships. As some of this humor hinges on mythologies of servitude and kinship rhetoric, these themes are also addressed.

An observation on the current state of research on household workers in Indonesia is appropriate at this juncture. Although there is a small but growing body of journalistic and academic literature on overseas Indonesian workers (cf. Anonymous 1994; Cremer 1988; Robinson 1991; Suardiman 1987), research on contemporary domestic workers in Indonesia has been scant (Ajik 1982; Anonymous 1985; Ayyub 1990; Robinson 1991).[4] This essay, then, also makes a contribution to the underrepresented literature on household workers (or "helpers") in Indonesia. The discussion in the pages that follow is rooted in journal and field note observations from several years of field research (1984–85, and 1988, 1989, 1995) on the closely related topic of rank and ethnic change. During this period I lived in an elite Toraja household in the Sulawesi highlands, a household that was also home to between two and four domestic helpers (at various points in time). In addition, I spent several months in urban Ujung Pandang, as the guest of Bugis families that employed Toraja helpers. In the course of this close-range exposure to these households, I was privy to numerous conversations and interactions with both helpers and their employers. Moreover, it is worth underscoring that as a foreign researcher and guest in these households, I was intimately embroiled in these unequal relations between "helpers" and bosses and my identity was very much "in play" in the humor of both household workers and bosses. For these reasons, I include myself in a number of the vignettes that follow.

LEGACIES OF HIERARCHY: THE ETHNOGRAPHIC SETTING

In a nation of 185 million people, the Sa'dan Toraja are a small minority group, numbering approximately 350,000. They are marginalized by island geography, religion, and a diffuse power structure. The Toraja's closest neighbors are the lowland Islamicized Makassarese and Bugis peoples, the dominant ethnic groups of the region. In contrast to the highly developed kingdoms of these neighboring peoples, the Toraja never united into a centralized political kingdom. In the past, these swidden and wet-rice agriculturalists lived in scattered mountaintop settlements, maintaining social ties through an elaborate system of ritual exchanges (Nooy-Palm et al. 1979). It was only with the arrival of the Dutch colonial forces in 1906 that the Sa'dan Toraja were first united under a single political authority.

Dutch annexation of the highlands also brought Christianization, which further set the Torajas apart from their Muslim neighbors.[5] Although conversion was initially slow, it gathered tremendous momentum in the 1950s and 1960s. Today, over 80 percent of the Sa'dan Toraja are Christians, and the Church is central to the lives and identities of many highlanders. As over 90 percent of Indonesia's inhabitants describe themselves as Muslims, Torajas are particularly self-conscious of their identity as a Christian minority group. For Toraja domestics employed in Muslim Bugis households in Ujung Pandang, religious differences are a resounding theme in narratives of identity.

Social stratification is a key theme in the Toraja highlands. Toraja society is hierarchically organized on the basis of descent, wealth, age, and occupation. In precolonial times, there were essentially three social strata: the aristocracy (*puang* or *to parengngne'*), commoners (*to buda, to sama*), and slaves (*to kaunan*).[6] Status was determined by birth, although financial success or failure allowed some individuals to permeate the barriers of rank. Slavery is illegal in modern Indonesia and the topic of rank is sensitive, but some aristocratic Torajas continue to use the term "slave," albeit in covert whispers. More commonly, elite Torajas use euphemisms based on the rhetoric of kinship, referring to those of low birth as their "grandchildren" (*ampo*) or their "children" (*pia'-pia'*). The selection of kinship idioms for these relations is significant, as these terms simultaneously embody notions of reciprocal familial concerns (filial duty and parental obligations) and parent-child inequality.[7] Another expression for dependents commonly heard in the Kesu region where I worked is "people from behind" (*to boko*), an allusion to the fact that slaves traditionally lived behind the nobles.

Today, particularly in rural villages in the Toraja highlands, relations between helpers and bosses continue to be colored by rank inequities. Often, older "people from behind" continue to work in the households of Toraja nobles in exchange for room and board, as well as periodic gifts of betel nut, clove cigarettes, sarongs, or cash. Younger helpers are often from lower ranks, as well; however, they expect modest wages in exchange for their labor (Rp 30,000/$20 per month in 1995, and room and board). It should be noted that rank inequities are less likely to be paramount in Toraja towns, and villages adjacent to these towns. In these towns, one tends to find actual kinship relations between "masters" and their helpers. Household helpers are more frequently teenaged kin (often nieces and nephews) from distant villages who wish to continue their junior and senior high school educations but cannot afford the costs of the daily commute from their rural homes. In exchange for room, board, and occasionally school fees, these youths are expected to clean house, cook, wash laundry, and baby-sit for their urban relations. Often these rural youths are taken in by their urban kin as "adopted children," and, although their chores may be heavier, they enjoy many of the same privileges and amenities as the biological children in the household. Thus, in both urban and rural settings, the rhetoric of kinship (real or fictive) and familial hierarchy is an important dimension of the employer-helper relationship.[8] However, unlike the rural setting, the hierarchies in the town context tend to be rural-urban rather than rank-based.

Since the 1960s, land shortages and limited local economic opportunities in the highlands have prompted many Torajas to seek wage labor away from the homeland (Volkman 1985). Although Torajas of all ranks and classes move to urban centers in Indonesia, the majority of Toraja migrants are commoners and descendants of slaves hoping to gain an economic foothold in cities like Ujung Pandang. While male migrants to Ujung Pandang tend to outnumber females (Nooy-Palm et al. 1979),[9] nevertheless, many migrants are young single women from relatively impoverished, remote areas of Tana Toraja (especially Kecamatan Mengkendek and Bonggakaradeng). These women find employment as household workers, shop clerks, and hotel workers and remit portions of their wages to family members back home.

NARRATIVES OF INTERWOVEN IDENTITIES: MYTHOLOGIES OF SERVITUDE AND ESCAPE FROM SERVITUDE

Before we can proceed to explore the ways in which humor is used by helpers and "masters" alike in order to negotiate asymmetrical household relations, we need to better appreciate how embedded notions of hierarchy permeate these relations. Specifically, we need to appreciate the ways in which these legacies emerge in everyday narratives. In this section I explore the ways in which nobles draw on mythologies of rank and servitude to affirm household hierarchies. I also discuss how lower-rank helpers draw on another set of mythologies involving a slave trickster to highlight positive images of their group as clever and resourceful. Through examining these narratives we can better understand the pronounced hierarchical circumstances that serve as a backdrop to the humorous interactions between rural Toraja nobles and their helpers.

Ne' Duma and his wife, Indo Rampo, Torajas of aristocratic descent, reside in a village a few kilometers from a major Toraja town. In 1985 their household consisted of five of their children (aged nine to twenty-eight) as well as two female servants, one elderly and one in her midteens. The family also retained a young male servant who tended to their water buffaloes and chopped firewood. In addition, young boys and girls from neighboring low-ranking families with traditional ties of servitude were frequently called upon by the family to perform various tasks.

On one of my first evenings in this household, Ne' Duma and Indo Rampo each introduced me to the entwined legacies of rank and domestic service in contemporary Tana Toraja. As we sat on velveteen chairs watching *The Brady Bunch* on the flickering generator-run television, Indo Rampo leaned over to me and gestured to the cluster of young boys solemnly gazing at the television through the front door (which was deliberately left ajar). Lowering her voice, Indo Rampo whispered, "The ones there are descendants of slaves: they are good children, obedient and quiet . . . and they are good about helping around the house." At the time I was startled by her use of the term "slaves" (she used the Indonesian term, *hamba*). When I commented that I had thought slavery was outlawed in Indonesia, Indo Rampo nodded and observed that the language of Indonesian independence was creating a good deal of confusion. In her words,

> True, we're not supposed to use the word *slave* anymore, but this doesn't change their birth.[10] These days descendants of slaves . . . think "freedom" with [Indonesian] independence means "freedom for slaves"—but actually, it only means "freedom from the Dutch." They aren't free because they were bought by our ancestors. . . . It's the same as if an ancestor bought a tree, then his descendants would have claim to its branches, leaves, twigs, flowers, and fruit. The original slave is the trunk, and his children and grandchildren are the leaves and flowers: they all belong to the descendants of that noble who owned the trunk. That's our tradition.

I sat quietly reflecting on my host's comment. I liked Indo Rampo and was grateful for the warmth with which she welcomed me into her household, yet I also felt discomfort at being a part of a feudally structured home. My thoughts were interrupted by Indo Rampo's daughter Emi, who asked me if my house in the United States was like that of the *Brady Bunch*, replete with a servant and machines to wash the floors and dishes. When I answered that I had none of these things, she and the others in the room (including the two female helpers) looked at me with disbelief. I explained that in the United States only the rich employed servants and, as an ordinary person, I did all of my own chores. They all laughed with what seemed to be disbelief. Then, after a pause, Ne' Duma reflected, "But isn't your last name Adams? And wasn't there once a president called Adams?" When I acknowledged that this was correct, he grinned and declared, "Then you are being modest—you are not an ordinary person—you are an aristocrat!" I tried to counter that Adams was a very common name in the United States, but his daughter and the adolescent female helper who shared our bedroom had launched into teasing me about how I probably had a fleet of helpers at home and had undoubtably never scrubbed a shirt or floor in my life.[11] My protests only met with more disbelieving giggles.

While the humor in this exchange escaped me at the time, it was clear that Ne' Duma was either consciously or unconsciously renegotiating the "common" identity I had publicly asserted. As a long-term guest in the household, it seemed important that I be outfitted with a noble identity and aligned with the family.[12] That the helper joined in this enterprise, teasing me about my presumed lack of basic experience in the female realm of daily domestic tasks was also noteworthy. Through teasing and jest, all of the members of the household were constructing a place for me in the household hierarchy.

Shortly after dinner that evening, Ne' Duma resumed my introduction to the themes of rank identity that color domestic service in contemporary Tana Toraja. As the two helpers were clearing away the dinner plates, Ne' Duma announced that we would begin my "lessons." Excusing myself to fetch my list of carefully compiled questions, I returned to find Ne' Duma absorbedly drawing in my notebook. Pushing aside my questions, he gestured to his drawing and announced, "This is where we start. Get out your tape recorder, this is what's important." There in my notebook, he had sketched an elaborate kinship chart stretching back some twenty-five generations to the ancestors who were said to have descended on a locally prominent mountain peak. For the next two hours, Ne' Duma recounted with verve the deeds of his deified ancestors. Included in his narrative was an account of the origin of the first slaves. His tale of the genesis of slaves is recounted as follows:

> The Old Lord [known as Puang Matua] had six children who emerged from the leaves of a tree growing in the cinders of his bellows. One of these children, Pande Nunu, behaved in the way that slaves do: he ate his brothers' leftovers and married a woman from Illin who wore a clay bracelet and a metal anklet [adornments associated with slaves]. At the time of the first *merok* feast, people asked Pande Nunu's sons, Dattu Bakka' and Pong Malaleong, to chop bamboo roasting sticks and to plant palm fronds in the ground for shade. They balked and grumbled that they should not be treated like water buffaloes working the fields. . . . But the other members of the community . . . [pointed out] that although their lordly father [Pande Nunu] had indeed sprung from Puang Matua's forge, Pande Nunu chose his own destiny when he wed the woman with the clay bracelet. Still, the two brothers balked.
>
> Competitions were held to resolve the conflict, but although the brothers repeatedly lost to their adversaries, they stubbornly refused to

acknowledge defeat. Things were finally settled with a cockfight [the traditional means of conveying divine judgment]. The brothers lost, bowed their bodies and thereafter were treated like water buffaloes. As no woman was willing to wed these brothers, Puang Matua [the Old Lord] molded them a wife of clay, named Potto Kalembang. Then Puang Matua captured the Prince of Wind in a voluminous net and coaxed him to breathe life into the clay woman. Thus began the division of nobles and slaves.[13]

Ne' Duma's first formal "lesson" clearly embodied not only an affirmation of his family's noble status but also a reminder of the dialectical importance of lower-ranking groups to the construction of his claims of preeminence. That is, it requires at least two groups to construct rank, class, and other identities (Wilmsen 1996). In a sense, through this narrative account of the origins of nobles and slaves, Ne' Duma was introducing me to his own identity as well as reaffirming the household order.

Lower-ranking helpers in the Toraja highlands have their own contrasting mythic narratives. Many of these narratives stress the exploits of the trickster slave Dodeng, who acquired riches and high status by outsmarting his noble "masters." These narratives are recounted in various settings, but I most frequently heard them at funeral rituals. Perhaps this is not surprising, as helpers' subservient status is most publicly on display in the context of funeral rituals. Funerals are frequent and crowd-drawing events in Toraja culture, lasting anywhere from twenty-four hours to ten or more days. Prominent families generally attend funerals on a regular basis, bringing with them an entourage of helpers. Not only do these helpers perform a variety of tasks at these rituals (They prepare snacks for the family, lay out bedding, fetch water, and generally keep the family's funeral quarters tidy.), but their presence also serves as a visual display of the family's high status. As Errington (1989) notes, establishing power in indigenous Indonesian societies is about show and display. For an elite family, traveling with a large entourage of servants is an important way to display power. In this sense, the public presence of servants affirms and constructs the powerful identities of the aristocrats they serve.

Upon arriving at a large Toraja funeral, families and their servants are publicly escorted by the hosts to a guest reception pavilion. In this formal, very visible procession, family elders take the lead, and at the tail end of the procession are the low-ranking helpers toting provisions. Eventually the family is led to its own bamboo pavilion where they will reside for the course of the funeral. Here helpers are generally relegated to the fringes: most of their time is spent at the rear of the pavilion, working and chatting. Not surprisingly, then, it is in this context where hierarchy is so visibly on display that Toraja helpers shared humor-laden tales of the clever slave Dodeng. I was introduced to one of the most popular Dodeng stories at the first funeral I attended. In the relaxed evening hours of the funeral, a teenaged male helper and several of his friends took great relish in recounting the following legend to me.

> Dodeng was a slave of a young noble named Parengan. Parengan was in love with Lebonna. The lovers made a pact that if one should die, the other would immediately commit suicide so that their bones could comingle together in one grave forever. One day Lebonna fell ill and died. But Parengan forgot his promise. Some months later, his slave Dodeng was sent to gather palm wine berries near the burial cliffs. There Dodeng heard Lebonna's spirit call to him, begging that he remind his master of their pact. Dodeng returned home and urged his master to hasten to the palm grove to taste the fresh palm wine. His master went to the cliffside grove and there heard the voice of his long-dead love. Recalling his promise, he was filled with shame and remorse and killed himself on the spot.
>
> Parengan's family held a great funeral and buried him in the familial burial cliff, unaware of his promise to Lebonna. But Parengan's spirit would not remain in the grave; instead, it roamed the village. Assuming that the water buffalo sacrifices made at Parengan's funeral had not been sufficient, the family sacrificed a prize water buffalo and tried assorted other remedies, all to no avail. Eventually, Parengan's family grew desperate, at which point Dodeng (who had remained silent) declared that he had the solution. The family announced that if he could rid them of Parengan's spirit, he would be rewarded with both his freedom and all of Parengan's wealth. Dodeng had them rebury Parengan's body in Lebonna's grave, which solved the problem. And so, clever Dodeng gained not only his freedom, but great wealth.

In recounting stories of Dodeng's exploits, these low-ranking helpers both collaborated with and contested nobles' construction of their identities. While Dodeng fulfills certain aspects of the imagery of the dutiful, subservient slave, he ultimately leaves this identity behind. In celebrating Dodeng as a hero, these helpers could be said to be making a muted statement about their unwillingness simply to accept their legacy of low birth. Moreover, the constructions of noble and slave identity in this story are noteworthy: the nobles in this tale are not only out of touch with what is going on around them, but helpless. It is only the low-ranking servant Dodeng who is fully aware and capable of delivering them from their predicament. In essence, Dodeng cleverly preys on the nobles' ignorance, winning both freedom and fortune. On several occasions when low-ranking helpers told me stories of Dodeng, they noted with amusement that several tourist businesses owned by descendants of slaves had been named for Dodeng. Clearly, the image of a contemporary Dodeng manipulating the new wealthy powers (tourists) for his own ends resonated with my friends.

Having delineated some of the ways in which themes of rank, and narratives pertaining to rank identities permeate relations between noble employers and their helpers, we can now turn to address the theme of humor and identity negotiation more directly.

HUMOR AND THE RHETORIC OF KINSHIP: STRATEGIES FOR NEGOTIATING SUBSERVIENT IDENTITIES

Given that Toraja funerals and other ceremonial events not only entail extraordinary public displays of rank but also bring together larger groups of helpers (offering settings that are notorious for banter and flirtations), it is not surprising that many of my cases of humor and identity negotiation occurred at ritual gatherings. In this section I explore three cases in which humor served not only to amuse but also to challenge, reaffirm, or breech the asymmetrical relations between bosses and their helpers. The first case occurred at a 1987 funeral for an aristocratic Toraja. The second and third cases transpired in rural Toraja households.

Case One: Humor and Husband-Hunting at a Toraja Funeral

The 1987 funeral for an elite Toraja had been hailed as one of the grandest funerals of the decade, with elaborate pageantry and thousands of local and foreign guests. It was a relatively slow morning on the third day of the funeral, and my aristocratic Toraja host (also a single woman in her late twenties) and I, assisted by her two female helpers, were cutting cloth for the funeral when our attention was called to a gigantic Bugis man who had just arrived at the funeral grounds. According to rumor, he was a bachelor and one of the wealthiest men on the island. His appearance was quite remarkable: he sported enormous military greens with raggedly cut sleeves (revealing a tattooed arm), mirrored sunglasses, numerous gold chains, rings, and large diamonds. Even for Toraja eyes, which were well accustomed to eccentric-looking tourists, this Bugis millionaire was quite an alien manifestation. As one awestruck child whispered, "He is like the clowns on TV." Jestfully, my Toraja female host turned to me and chided, "Ah, there's a husband for you! Go talk to him!" Her lively middle-aged female helper (who had been engaged in an animated conversation with us before the Bugis bachelor's arrival) interjected, "Ah, but you are *both* single—good candidates for him. . . .You can *both* go talk to him, and we can make wagers on who he will select as his mate!" The others in the room burst into laughter. In rebuttal, my host proposed that her helper take him on as her second husband, as she would "fit"[14] better with him. Then she playfully urged the helper to go serve him coffee, noting with a grin that she was offering her the perfect pretext for flirting with the Bugis millionaire. The teasing and laughter about who would make the best bride for this Bugis guest continued weeks after he departed.

Beyond enlivening a task-filled morning, this humor played on juxtapositions of identities. My elite Toraja host initiated the jest by underscoring the status I shared with the colorful Bugis bachelor, as an older, unmarried, and somewhat comically marginal non-Toraja. Her married helper, in turn, was able momentarily to secure an advantaged position for herself: In essence, the helper's humor moved her boss into the same category of bizarre aliens, by emphasizing her boss's and my shared identities as single women well past what Torajas consider the ideal age for marrying. However, the helper had not counted on her boss's teasing rebuttal, which drew on yet another set of hierarchical identities. Playing on the stereotype of lower-ranking people as sexually promiscuous and underscoring her helper's duty to serve guests, the boss regained her supremacy in the teasing. In this case of playful jest (which was clearly pleasurable to all involved), we find fleeting reversals of authority and hierarchy, as well as momentary inversions of unequal status, evocative of Geertz's classic article on deep play (Geertz 1973). Of course, in highlighting how the humor played on realigning various identity hierarchies (non-Toraja/Toraja, single woman/married woman, noble boss/ low-ranking helper, etc.), I do not intend to overshadow the fact that the teasing also embodied an erasure of these distinctions, as we were all women sharing laughter about the potential drawing powers of a foreign man.

Case Two: Body Humor and an Alien Being

Shortly after I arrived in Ne' Duma's household, Erma, the teenaged helper, momentarily shifted the household hierarchy by making me the focus of her teasing. In this instance, Erma cleverly drew on body humor highlighting imagined racial differences to forge a bond between herself and her employer's twenty-eight-year-old daughter. The three of us had been chatting by candlelight in our shared bedroom late one night, when Erma turned and whispered to her employer's daughter, prompting a burst of giggles. At my persistent prodding, they eventually shared the reason for their laughter; apparently Erma had whispered her speculations about the color of my menstrual blood. Given my white skin, she had mused that my menstrual blood was likely to be white as well. Their continued giggles and their swats on each others' thighs underscored the bond that Erma's humor had created between them: they were the same and I was jestfully deemed the "other." In this case, rank distinctions had temporarily evaporated, as Erma's bodily humor had diverted attention to imagined racial distinctions.

Case Three: Earthy Humor and Commanding Performances

The elderly female servant in Ne' Duma's household introduced at the beginning of this essay (Ne' Lele) was particularly skillful at using her las-civious sense of humor to negotiate the asymmetrical relationships that formed the fabric of her life. Ne' Lele was a slight, hunched-over, grey-haired woman in her seventies who had worked for Ne' Duma's family for years. She spent the better part of her days gathering greens for the pigs, washing pots, tending to the livestock, and arranging rice bundles to dry in the sun. When not busy with these tasks, she sat chewing betel nut and caressing the household kittens in her small, dimly lit room that doubled as a storage closet. When her employer's teenaged children (and this anthro-pologist) ventured into the kitchen, however, Ne' Lele would burst into earthy banter. Hobbling to the center of the kitchen, she would swat at the genitals of females in her path, asking with hearty chuckles, "What's this?" The young men, in turn, were pestered about the size of their "bananas." Her mischief always provoked fleeing shrieks and eruptions of laughter. Watch-ing Ne' Lele, it was clear that in those moments she was in control, and the tables were turned. Rather than being sent scurrying by her elite employers, she was the one sending them scurrying: through humor she was able momentarily to take command.

Ne' Lele's age allowed her to get away with these antics. When the female head of the household, Indo Rampo, happened upon such scenes, she would chuckle from the sidelines and comment, "Old people are funny. . . ." When Ne' Lele's humor trespassed certain lines, however, her employers used the same strategy of humor to reaffirm the boundaries and return her to her proper place. On one rare occasion, when Ne' Lele turned her lascivious teasing on her male boss (Ne' Duma), he responded by gesturing to her and declaring, "This is my grandchild." Although ostensibly a comical move (as Ne' Lele was approximately ten years older than him), the boss's comment served as a reminder of hereditary status distinctions. For, as noted earlier, in contemporary Tana Toraja, elites frequently employ the rhetoric of kinship to refer to slaves, calling them their "grandchildren" or "children." While Ne' Duma's comment prompted chuckles, Ne' Lele was reminded of her place in the home hierarchy and promptly abandoned her banter.

The differing sources of humor used in this interaction merit consideration. It strikes me as significant that servants' humor often tends to be about sexuality and the body (The younger female servants in many of the rural households I knew often teased their bosses' daughters about romance, sex, breast size, etc.), whereas the aristocratic bosses' humor more frequently concerns kinship. In jesting about anatomy and sex, servants such as Ne' Lele highlight shared aspects of human identity. In short, they level the distinctions of rank. Not surprisingly, the Toraja bosses I knew rarely jested with their helpers on this earthy level. Instead, they tended to select the hierarchical theme of kinship as the source of their humor.

Generally, in such encounters, nobles' invocation of the metaphor of kinship quickly silences servants' jesting challenges to the hierarchical household order. However, there are instances in which it is the helpers themselves who invoke and embrace the idiom of kinship. For example, following Ne' Duma's death, the town of Rantepao was abuzz with rumors about how many water buffaloes were to be slaughtered at his ritual. During this period, I occasionally overheard Ne' Duma's servants declare to Rantepao acquaintances that Ne' Duma had been their "grandfather." Such embrasures of the kinship idiom invariably won these helpers momentary attention and a certain degree of authority in the gossip about the funeral preparations. Sometimes the rewards for embracing the euphemism of kinship can be even more dramatic. For instance, Bigalke (personal communication 1992; also cited in Volkman 1985, 138) has recounted how a former Toraja slave was able to secure an attractive position at a nickel mine in Central Sulawesi by claiming that he was a "child" of a high Toraja noble. By manipulating the Toraja paternalistic rhetoric of kinship between nobles and their retainers, this man was able to impress someone too removed from Toraja to appreciate the multiple nuances of their use of the term "child."

HUMOR AND TORAJA HELPERS
IN UJUNG PANDANG

Having explored rural Toraja helpers' use of jest to negotiate the rank hierarchies of the household, at this point I offer a preliminary discussion of the extent to which humor figures into helper-boss relations in a markedly different setting. Lured by the possibilities of making a better income and escaping the ensnaring legacies of low rank in the homeland, some Toraja women and men migrate to the Bugis-Makassarese port city of Ujung Pandang. Some of these economic migrants find employment as domestic helpers in Toraja, Bugis, Makassarese, and Chinese homes where, in 1995, they earned an average of US$23 per month, as well as room and board. Although, for cultural and linguistic reasons, the vast majority of Toraja domestic workers with whom I spoke in Ujung Pandang expressed a marked preference for working for Toraja families, not all of them were able to secure such positions. In a pattern similar to that found in towns in the Toraja highlands, Toraja families in Ujung Pandang tend to take in younger highland kin wishing to pursue their education in the provincial capital. These student migrants take on the functions of "helpers" in their urban relatives' homes in exchange for housing and assistance with tuition. Thus, as the work opportunities in Toraja households are limited, many of the lower-ranking economic migrants from the highlands are obliged to seek employment in the homes of affluent and middle-class Chinese and Bugis families.

According to Toraja informants, Chinese families are particularly inclined to hire Christian Torajas who, unlike Muslim Bugis and Makassarese helpers, have no reservations about preparing pork-based meals. Moreover, I was told that Toraja helpers were reputed to be less prone to dragging their families into disputes with their employers. Ujung Pandang Chinese and Torajas with whom I spoke noted that the Bugis cultural emphasis on family honor meant that employers who disciplined their Bugis female helpers could find themselves facing dramatic confrontations with the young woman's kin. These informants reasoned that this was a less likely outcome with Toraja employees (although one might argue that it is not cultural factors but rather the distant origins of these Toraja employees that make it impossible for their families to confront the employers over perceived injustices).

For the Torajas I interviewed, the least desirable situation for household workers was in the homes of Muslim Bugis and Makassarese families. For Toraja migrants who find themselves in such situations, the employee-servant relationship has multiple dimensions of inequality: ancient histories of Bugis-Makassarese ethnic dominance, rural-urban hierarchies, as well as class and religious distinctions. Perhaps because these multiple hierarchies tend to make for more formal, distanced relations between Bugis-Makassarese employers and their Toraja helpers (who tend not to work in these homes for long periods of time), humor does not appear to be as pervasive a theme in these urban household relations. Even in these more formal, multiply-hierarchical circumstances, however, there are occasions when humor plays a role in identity negotiation. The following example suggests that a further exploration of these themes in urban, multiethnic settings is merited.

An affluent Bugis family I knew employed three household workers: two of these workers, a Makassarese chauffeur in his early forties and a Bugis cook in her sixties, were long-term, live-out employees. To help assist the cook with dishwashing, laundry, cleaning, and child care, the family had hired a live-in teenaged Toraja helper. The girl's status in this household was multiply disadvantaged: not only was she lowest in the household employee hierarchy, but she was not Bugis, not Muslim, and not urban. As a rural, impoverished Christian worker in an urban Muslim household and as the only member of the household who did not speak Bugis, this Toraja girl was teased incessantly by her employers, their teenaged children, and occasionally even the chauffeur.

Almost daily, when family members sat on the back veranda eating afternoon sweets and chatting in Bugis, they would periodically turn to this Toraja helper and ask if she understood them, sometimes prodding her to guess at the topic of their conversation. Her responses always prompted eruptions of laughter. While the family considered their banter with this servant as humorous teasing, there was often more ridicule than humor in these interactions. The flow and content of the banter was markedly different from the more relaxed tone of the humor between Toraja servants and nobles in the homeland. In contrast to the cases in the Toraja highlands, in this urban situation, the Bugis employers were more frequently the instigators of these teasing sessions (which perhaps suggests their own discomfort with the presence of this Toraja servant in their household).

Whenever I visited, however, this Toraja servant found she had an opportunity to momentarily invert her customary outsider status. Each time we spoke in Bahasa Toraja together, she would gleefully giggle, "Now we can talk behind *their* backs!" When her employers' curiosity was piqued and they pressed to know what we were saying, she would throw me a quick, triumphant look, and then reassume the demeanor of the bashful young helper, retreating to the kitchen, while I fumbled for an answer. Through these playful exchanges, then, this Toraja helper contested her employer's everyday characterization of her as slow and linguistically impeded: in her Toraja conversations with me, she was not only displaying her linguistic talents to this Bugis family, but asserting that, in some areas, at least, she knew more than they.

CONCLUSION: HUMOR AND IDENTITY NEGOTIATION

In this essay I have argued that humor plays a much-overlooked role in negotiating asymmetrical household relations. In examining body humor, teasing about romance, play with kinship idioms, and linguistic exclusion games in Ujung Pandang, we can see not only articulated constructions of servant and employer identities but also attempts to negotiate, reaffirm, and, at times, even challenge the asymmetrical relations in the household. Through looking closely at helpers' use of humor, we can come to appreciate that these individuals are hardly passive adherents to their subservient status. Through humor and competing narratives of identity, servants find oblique ways to realign their identities, momentarily erasing rank and other boundaries between themselves and their employers.

Bakhtin observed that "laughter places everything in cheerfully irreverent quotation marks" (cited in Goldstein 1990, 16). As Goldstein suggested, it seems that "quotation marks also provoke thought by functioning as question marks. They make cultural categories available for examination by saying, in effect, these are not 'natural' categories" (1990, 16). Although Goldstein is discussing Iranian theater in Israel, I believe her observations are useful for our consideration of humor's role in negotiating asymmetrical relations in the household. In the cases examined in this essay, helpers' identity-negotiating humor appears to "work" by drawing a variety of alternative identities into the worker-boss equation. In essence, by introducing and playing with an array of new categories of identity (single/married, Toraja/ non-Toraja, etc.), household workers pose question marks around the hierarchical worker-boss identity couplet that forms the fabric of their daily lives.

In the sense that servants use humor to assert new identities based on new sets of boundaries and even to obliquely challenge their employers' attempts to domesticate them, humor may be viewed as a "weapon of the weak" (Scott 1985, 1990). Ironically, however, humor is a strategy that can be co-opted, for employers also draw on humor to reaffirm their positions of authority. In considering humor as a means for renegotiating hierarchical worker-boss relations, it pays to note that the "weapons of the weak" also tend to be weak weapons. For the most part, other than momentarily boosting self-esteem, these strategies do not permanently rescue servants from their daily oppressions.

Acknowledgments

An earlier version of this paper was originally presented in the panel "Home and Hegemony: Domestic Service and Identity Negotiation in Asia" (organized by Kathleen Adams and Sara Dickey) at the 1994 American Anthropological Association annual meeting in Atlanta. I am particularly grateful to Jane Atkinson, Sara Dickey, Richard Scaglion, and Judith Wittner for their thoughtful comments on earlier versions of this essay. I also wish to thank Karl Heider for his valiant efforts to provide me with difficult-to-locate material needed for this essay.

NOTES

1. Similar to the case in the Philippines described by Jean-Paul Dumont (this volume), the Indonesian term for household workers embraced by both employers and workers is *pembantu*, which translates as "one who helps" or "helper." This is also the term most frequently used by Torajas. Although in discussing the theoretical literature I tend to use the term "household worker" for the reasons underlined by Sanjek and Colen (1990, 1), for ethnographic accuracy I prefer to use the gloss "helper," which I believe embodies more of the sense of "connectedness" (and asymmetry) frequently found in Indonesian household worker-employer relations (also see Weix, this volume).

2. Following Martin (1987, 173), Mitchell (1992, 4), and others, I use the term *humor* as a gloss for all that is comical, amusing, or funny.

3. Some notable exceptions include Basso 1979, Bricker 1973, Hill 1943, Mitchell 1992, Peacock 1968, and Radin 1956.

4. Kathryn Robinson (1988) briefly addresses domestic servants in expatriate households as part of a larger study of the political economy of development in a mining town of Soroako, Sulawesi.

5. See Bigalke (1981) for a delineation of the historical role of the Dutch Reformed Church in fortifying Toraja ethnic consciousness.

6. I follow the convention established by Nooy-Palm et al. (1979, 44) and others and translate *to kaunan* as "slave."

7. As many Torajas told me, "Before one thinks of oneself, one must think of one's parents. One's first duty is to one's parents."

8. Recent writings by Robinson (1991, 18) and Weix (this volume) suggest that such familial assumptions not usually associated with wage work are a common theme in Indonesian domestic work.

9. Volkman (1985, 137) reports that in the Sesean region of Tana Toraja where she worked, the ratio of male to female migrants was about equal. In the three valley communities I surveyed in 1985, there were somewhat more male than female out-migrants.

10. Indeed, several Toraja aristocrats stressed to me that it was simply the term "slave" (*kaunan*) that was illegal, not the concept. As some said, "Today, we can't say 'This is my slave' anymore, so instead we say 'This is my grandchild.'" For a more detailed discussion of the contemporary problematics of rank in Tana Toraja, see Adams 1997.

11. It is noteworthy that the adult daughter (Emi) also did these household tasks. In fact, the female helpers who developed close emotional ties with Emi often teased her about her "expert sweeping." In a sense, this teasing affirmed their common ground and bridged the estrangement of rank differences.

12. It is perhaps noteworthy here that indigenous ideas about contamination and pollution are linked to one's rank status. In noble households, special eating utensils were reserved for the elite—the use of these bowls by individuals of lower rank was thought to be polluting. In the household in which I resided, helpers generally used a separate set of older metal plates rather than the ceramic plates used by the family. Moreover, they ate from a separate rice bowl, which was avoided by most of the noble family members (particularly the older family members). When Indo Rampo once caught me serving myself from the helpers' rice bowl, she was clearly aghast and shooed me into the living room to serve myself from the family's rice container.

13. For another fuller poetic account of this myth, see van der Veen's (1965, 105–43) translation of the buffalo litany recited at the *merok* feast.

14. The notion that partners should "fit" (*cocok / cog-cog*) with one another is pervasive in Indonesia. This notion also carries over to expectations that helpers and bosses should "fit" one another. As Robinson has noted, "an employer and an employee should *cog-cog* (be harmonious) and women will leave rather than suffer an unhappy relationship" (Robinson 1991, 45).

REFERENCES

Adams, Kathleen M.

1997 Constructing and Contesting Chiefly Authority in Contemporary Tana Toraja, Indonesia. In Geoffrey White and Lamont Lindstrom, eds., *Chiefs Today: Traditional Pacific Leadership and the Post-Colonial State*, 264–75. Stanford: Stanford University Press.

Ajik, Soeharti

1982 *Kondisi Kerja Pembantu Rumah Tangga di Suatu Pemukiman Elite di Surabaya*. Surabaya: Pusat Latihan Penilitian, Universitas Airlangga.

Alford, Finnegan, and Richard Alford

1981 A Holo-Cultural Study of Humor. *Ethos* 9:149–64.

Anonymous

1985 *Penelitian dan Pengembangan Pengaruh Ekonomi Terhadap Ketahanan Kerja Pembantu Rumah Tangga di Surabaya*. Jakarta: Lumbago Ilmu Pengetahuan Indonesia.

1994   *Nowhere to Turn To: A Case Study on the Indonesian Migrant Workers in Hong Kong*. Hong Kong: Asian Migrant Centre.

Ayyub, M. Rusli
1990   *Laporan Penelitian Kedudukan Pembantu Rumah Tangga dalam Upaya Memberi Hukum: Suatu Studi di Kota Administratif Palu*. Palu: Balai Penelitian Universitas Tadulako.

Basso, Keith
1979   *Portraits of "the Whiteman": Linguistic Play and Cultural Symbols Among the Western Apache*. Cambridge: Cambridge University Press.

Bigalke, Terrace
1981   A Social History of Tana Toraja: 1870–1965. Ph.D. diss., University of Wisconsin, Madison.

Bricker, Victoria Reifler
1973   *Ritual Humor in Highland Chiapas*. Austin: University of Texas Press.

Clifford, James
1988   *The Predicament of Culture: Twentieth Century Ethnography, Literature and Art*. Cambridge: Harvard University Press.

Cock, Jacklyn
1980   *Maids and Madams: A Study in the Politics of Exploitation*. Johannesburg: Ravan Press.

Cremer, Georg
1988   Development of Indonesian Migrants in the Middle East: Present Situation and Prospects. *Bulletin of Indonesian Economic Studies* 24 (3): 73–86.

Errington, Shelly
1989   *Meaning and Power in a Southeast Asian Realm*. Princeton: Princeton University Press.

Geertz, Clifford
1973   Deep Play: Notes on the Balinese Cockfight. In *The Interpretation of Cultures*, 412–53. New York: Basic Books.

Gill, Lesley
1994   *Precarious Dependencies: Gender, Class and Domestic Service in Bolivia*. New York: Columbia University Press.

Goldstein, Judith
1990   An Innocent Abroad: How Mulla Daoud Was Lost and Found in Lebanon, or the Politics of Ethnic Theater in a Nation at War. In Richard G. Fox, ed.,

Nationalist Ideologies and the Production of National Cultures, 15–31. Washington, DC: American Anthropological Association.

Gramsci, Antonio
1971   *Selections from the Prison Notebooks*. New York: International Publishers.

Hansen, Karen Tranberg
1991   Domestic Service. What's in It for Anthropology? *Reviews in Anthropology* 16:47–62.

Hill, Willard W.
1943   *Navaho Humor. General Series in Anthropology* 9. Menasha, WI: George Banta Publishing.

Linnekin, Jocelyn
1990   The Politics of Culture in the Pacific. In Jocelyn Linnekin and Lin Poyer, eds., *Cultural Identity and Ethnicity in the Pacific*, 149–73. Honolulu: University of Hawaii Press.

Martin, Mike W.
1987   Humor and Aesthetic Enjoyment of Incongruities. In John Morreall, ed., *The Philosophy of Laughter and Humor*, 139–55. Albany: State University of New York Press.

Mitchell, William E.
1992   *Clowning as Critical Practice: Performance Humor in the South Pacific*. Pittsburgh: University of Pittsburgh Press.

Nagata, Judith
1981   In Defense of Ethnic Boundaries: The Changing Myths and Charters of Malay Identity. In Charles F. Keyes, ed., *Ethnic Change*, 81–116. Seattle: University of Washington Press.

Nooy-Palm, Hetty, et al.
1979   *The Sa'dan Toraja in Ujung Pandang (Sulawesi, Indonesia): A Migration Study*. Amsterdam: Koninklijk Instituut voor de Tropen and Ujung Pandang: Universitas Hasanuddin.

Peacock, James
1968   *Rites of Modernization: Symbolic and Social Aspects of Indonesian Proletarian Drama*. Chicago: University of Chicago Press.

Radin, Paul
1956   *The Trickster: A Study in American Indian Mythology*. New York: Greenwood Press.

Robinson, Kathryn G.

1988   *Stepchildren of Progress: The Political Economy of Development in an Indonesian Mining Town.* Albany: State University of New York Press.

1991   Housemaids: The Effects of Gender and Culture on the Internal and International Migration of Indonesian Women. In Gillian Bottomley, Marie De Lepervanche, and Jeannie Martin, eds., *Intersexions: Gender/Class/Culture/Ethnicity,* 33–51. Sydney: Allen and Unwin.

Rollins, Judith

1985   *Between Women: Domestics and Their Employers.* Philadelphia: Temple University Press.

Sanjek, Roger, and Shellee Colen, eds.

1990   *At Work in Homes: Household Workers in World Perspective.* American Ethnological Society Monograph Series, No. 3. Washington, DC: American Anthropological Association.

Scott, James C.

1985   *Weapons of the Weak: Everyday Forms of Peasant Resistance.* New Haven: Yale University Press.

1990   *Domination and the Arts of Resistance: Hidden Transcripts.* New Haven: Yale University Press.

van der Veen, H.

1965   *The Merok Feast of the Sa'dan Toraja's.* Gravenhage, Netherlands: Martinus Nijhoff.

Volkman, Toby

1985   *Feasts of Honor: Ritual and Change in the Toraja Highlands.* Urbana: University of Illinois Press.

White, Geoffrey

1991   *Identity Through History: Living Stories in a Solomon Island Society.* Cambridge: Cambridge University Press.

Wilmsen, Edwin N.

1996   Introduction: Premises of Power in Ethnic Politics. In Edwin N. Wilmsen and Patrick McAllister, eds., *The Politics of Difference: Ethnic Premises in a World of Power,* 1–23. Chicago: University of Chicago Press.

Wolf, Diane

1992   *Factory Daughters: Gender, Household Dynamics and Rural Industrialization in Java.* Berkeley: University of California Press.

MICHELE RUTH GAMBURD

NURTURE FOR SALE
Sri Lankan Housemaids and the Work of Mothering

Current economic hardship and a dearth of employment opportunities in the rural Sri Lankan village of Polwatta[1] have driven women overseas to earn money as live-in domestic servants in the Middle East. With one in four of the adult women in the village employed abroad, and with three-quarters of these migrants leaving behind small children, local images of mothers, wives, and families have undergone subtle yet wide-ranging changes over the past fifteen years. As migrant women take on the formerly masculine role of breadwinner, they fragment the bundle of family responsibilities previously thought of as "mothering," redistributing parts of the role to a number of different people, both male and female. As the ways for women to love and care for their husbands and children are transformed, the social valuations of the worth and meaning of each option come under negotiation and reconfiguration. Evolving roles and behaviors conflict with existing values, ideals, and habits of family life, both challenging and rein-forcing more established thinking about motherhood, gender hierarchies, personal identity, and women's work.

Self-identity depends largely on context, theorists of identity and agency argue (Hall 1988, 1990). People define themselves with respect to the people, places, situations, social standings, and activities that surround and embrace them. It stands to reason that changing social and economic

contexts carry with them changing senses of self. Increasing integration in
the global economy has drastically rearranged local labor patterns in rural
Sri Lanka over the past fifteen years, bringing about a concomitant shift in
patterns of thought and behavior in the village of Polwatta. I look at social
structure as both shaping and shaped by the everyday practices of ordinary
people (Bourdieu 1977; Ortner 1984, 1989). Starting with the assumption
that most modern social systems entail a certain degree of hierarchy, I look
at how people create and transform systems of power and inequality.
Williams defines hegemony as "a lived system of meanings and values"
(1977, 110), which "has continually to be renewed, recreated, defended,
and modified. It is also continually resisted, limited, altered, and challenged"
(1977, 112). I argue that the production of meaning, or the construction of
reality, is a major dimension of political power. In this essay I examine how
the new economic opportunities open to women in the village relate to the
shifting systems of meaning and identity in Polwatta.

The transnational migration of labor prompts shifts in power relations
not only on the international level but also in the migrants' own households. Exciting new work focuses on the mutually reinforcing identities of
household workers and their employers (see Constable 1997; Gill 1994;
Rollins 1990; and many authors in this volume). I document the microprocesses of social change, examining alterations in images of appropriate roles
and behaviors for women, and shifting relations of authority between
women, their families, their villages, and their employers. I focus on female
migration as part of the larger pattern of social change in a rural village in
Sri Lanka, tracing how women's employment as domestic servants changes
meanings of "the domestic" in the homes they leave behind. The title *Home
and Hegemony* chosen by this volume's editors beautifully encompasses
power relations in two "homes," in both of which migrant women work,
live, love, and struggle for power and authority. In this essay I examine how
migration influences women's identities as workers and mothers.

GENERAL BACKGROUND ON POLWATTA
AND MIGRATION

Drawing on extensive interviews conducted during eighteen months of village fieldwork in 1992–94, this paper explores migration from the rural village of Polwatta, a community of about fifty families on the southwest coast
of Sri Lanka. The population of the administrative unit containing Polwatta
and four other villages nearly doubled in twenty-five years, from roughly 500
in 1969 (G. Gamburd 1972, 68) to roughly 1,000 in 1994, creating concomitant chronic under- and unemployment in the village area.[2] While

land pressure and high unemployment on the coast were long-term problems dating from at least the colonial period (Risseeuw 1991, 15), the problem had grown dramatically with the population explosion in recent years. Older means of subsistence could no longer support the village. Corresponding to the first major jump in oil prices, the mass migration of labor from Sri Lanka to the Middle East started in 1976. Due to the increase in wealth from prices kept high through the operation of the Organization of Petroleum Exporting Countries (OPEC),[3] the oil-producing countries in the Gulf required masons and carpenters to work on construction projects, and many Sri Lankan men, including several from the Polwatta area, went abroad to work in these capacities. Five to ten years later the construction jobs for male laborers tapered off, while the demand for domestic servants, which arose in the early 1980s, continued to grow.

In 1993, a total out-migration of roughly 500,000 people represented almost 3 percent of the national population of 18 million. Estimating 400,000 women abroad out of a female population of 9 million people means that 4.5 percent, or one in twenty-two, of Sri Lankan women worked abroad in 1994.[4] Further considerations of age, family affluence, and caste circumscribe the migrant population, raising percentages of migrants in particular communities, such as the relatively poor area around Polwatta. In 1994, I found that in Polwatta's administrative unit, over a quarter of the households (48 out of 161) had or had had a member working abroad; approximately a sixth of the people over eighteen (61 out of 462) were or had been abroad. Unlike most international migrant flows (Hansen 1991; Van der Veer 1995), the vast majority of village migrants were married women, and about a quarter of the women over eighteen in the village area (55 out of approximately 225) had experience overseas. Clearly this migration represented the largest single change in local, social, and economic orientation in the recent past.

Housing accommodations for village families demonstrate Polwatta's relative poverty—the driving force behind labor migration. Many families made do with single-room clay houses[5] topped with tin sheets, tar sheets, or woven coconut-frond mats. In contrast, wealthier households in the neighboring village lived on acre or half-acre land plots in large cement or brick houses with tile roofs. The majority of Polwatta villagers could not afford toilets, using neighboring cinnamon gardens instead. Wells with good drinking water supported many besides their owners, and only a limited few could afford electricity.

From the village perspective, migration to the Middle East provided an opportunity to make vast sums of money in a short period of time. Often the explicitly stated goal for female migration was to achieve a certain standard of physical comfort in housing, such as buying land, constructing a better house, getting electricity, and building a well and a toilet. Realizing that they could barely make ends meet financially, younger, lower-income couples in Polwatta often decided to send the woman abroad. If the couple had several children, saving for a piece of land or a new house often proved impossible on the man's wages.[6] Working as housemaids in the Middle East, female migrants earned more than a male day-laborer's salary for performing the same "women's work" they did without wages at home. Households often planned for the man to continue working in Sri Lanka, supporting and looking after the children with the help of a female relative, while the woman worked abroad on a series of two-year contracts. Between 1992 and 1994, Polwatta sported many new houses in varying degrees of completion. Construction progressed in fits and starts, as funds became available.

Poorer village families had little or no savings to rely on in times of need; far from carrying cash reserves, many or most owed large debts to moneylenders. These debts included money borrowed to pay a job agent to find a woman a job abroad, as well as funds borrowed for consumption and emergencies at other times. Moneylenders' standard rate of interest was 100 percent interest over ten months, or 20 percent of the principal per month for ten months. With a job for a housemaid costing on average Sri Lanka Rs 13,000/ (approximately US$260 at 1994 exchange rates), prospective housemaids often agreed to repay a moneylender Rs 26,000/ or even Rs 30,000/ (US$520 or 600) in exchange for the cash to pay the job agent. Housemaids earned between US$60 and $100 per month (plus room, board, and gifts), and common village wisdom suggested that housemaids on their two-year contract abroad often worked eight to twelve months to pay back the moneylender before beginning to accumulate money for their own purposes. Many families showed little external profit from the migration for the first several years, because the lion's share of the woman's wages went to pay off debts.

Although many couples initially planned to rely on the husband's wages to support the family in Sri Lanka, husbands often stopped working early in their wives' stay abroad. The dearth of good jobs, the disagreeable nature of the occasional day-labor available, and child-care responsibilities at home, combined with the promise of lavish remittances from abroad, tempted many men to stop searching for work. Those families relying on women's remittances for daily consumption and for emergency funds often found it difficult or impossible to stretch the money to pay off debts and save for larger plans (see also Ariyawansa 1986; Brochmann 1987). In some families, serious arguments started over who should control the money and how it should be spent. Their households grown dependent on their continued remittances, many women found themselves with no choice but to return to the Middle East repeatedly.[7] Their continued physical absence greatly diminished their control over the money they sent home (see Gamburd 1995b).

The growing presence of migrant women in the labor force has changed the profile of Sri Lanka's working class. Over 90 percent of the Sri Lankan women who travel abroad to work in the Middle East find jobs as housemaids (Sri Lankan Bureau of Foreign Employment [SLBFE] 1997). Assessing the class identity of Sri Lanka's migrant housemaids proves difficult and, at best, context-specific. Women who do menial service jobs for what their Arabic employers deem a pittance often remit wages equivalent to local middle-class salaries in Sri Lanka. By cleaning toilets abroad, some women save enough money to construct toilets for their own houses in Sri Lanka, a sure sign of upward mobility and social respectability in the village. Working class (or lower) in the Middle East, successful Sri Lankan housemaids garner a grudging respect in their native villages. Migration and the wealth it brings hold the potential to upset local relations of class, caste, and gender. In their struggle for position in the newly fluid social hierarchy, migrant women and their families re-create and reconfigure those very hierarchies.

Gendered patterns of migration made class differences visible at the local level. Only the poorer families in the village sent women abroad;[8] richer families sent men if they sent any family members at all. Jobs for men cost two or three times as much as jobs for women, and poor families without capital assets often found they could not borrow enough money to pay for a man's job abroad. Even if they found a moneylender willing to risk fronting them so much money, few dared to go so deeply into debt. The benefits of sending a man to the Middle East nevertheless filled many local families with longing; men's wages were often three to six times more than women's wages abroad, so the families who could muster up the financing often profited greatly from the job after several months.[9] While families where women went abroad often found themselves relying on the women's wages for daily consumption, families with men working abroad (usually but not always those high-caste families already rich by local estimation) often had enough money not only for consumption but also for savings, construction, and investment.

Migration in many ways widened the gap between the rich and the poor in the Polwatta area, with the rich sending men to lucrative jobs, the poor sending women as housemaids, and the moneylenders creaming off the lion's share of women's profits. At the same time, migration gave job opportunities to women, to lower-caste individuals, and to poor people in an economic environment where having any job at all was both a rarity and a necessity. Migration offered the (in many but not all cases largely illusory) opportunity of financial advancement to those who would otherwise have had no such source of income. New job opportunities in the Persian Gulf thus created possibilities for individual and family advancement, but the system favored those who already had significant economic assets. Work abroad both challenged and reinforced patterns of gender and class relations in the village.

FAMILY AND MOTHERHOOD IN SOUTH ASIA

Identity depends in many ways on culturally constructed categories. While individuals conform to a greater or lesser degree to social classifications and accompanying behavior roles, even those who challenge nearly all of the aspects of a category's defining characteristics do so with an awareness of the dominant discourse. Given that the majority of Polwatta migrants left small children behind, migration inevitably had a large effect on family roles. In this section I explore how the changing context of women's work led them to challenge existing stereotypes surrounding "motherhood."

The importance of the family had long been held as a defining character- istic of South Asia, with the woman as wife and mother taken as central to the family. Sri Lankan and Indian history, mythology, and literature contained multiple examples of submissive, self-sacrificing, modest women and benevo- lent goddesses bringing honor to their families and harmony to the cosmos. Similarly, examples abounded of evil women and malevolent goddesses who challenged the authority of their fathers and husbands, aggressively asserting their sexuality and openly wielding power, thus bringing disaster to their fam- ilies and chaos to the cosmos. Authoritative images portrayed the "good" woman as one who was sexually restrained and submitted her will to the "civ- ilizing" will of her father, husband, or son (Wadley 1995). Traditional images provided few examples of how women could hold legitimate power outside the family and house. Sri Lankan scholar Sirima Kiribamune argues that because it was inauspicious for a woman not to be married, there was no approval in middle-class Sri Lankan families for women who wanted a career instead of a family (1992, xli). Whatever the more nuanced realities in particular families, these images still acted as a model in Polwatta.

In Polwatta, men and women alike often considered the behaviors sur- rounding motherhood and family work a straightforward expression of women's biological nature. Culturally constructed gender roles took on the authority of biological necessity. The anthropological literature character- izes South Asian villagers as eager to have children, because offspring, especially sons, were seen as social insurance for a couple's old age. A wife's power increased with the birth of her children, culminating when her own sons brought wives into the household. Women's fulfillment of their "natural roles" in home activities—birth, child care, housework, and food preparation—left paid labor as a secondary, ancillary activity (Jacobson 1995, 60). In Polwatta, many villagers, even my perceptive research associate, discounted housework as "work" and felt that housewives "did nothing" for a living. Official Sri Lankan statistics, which ignored or erased the economic contributions of "housewives" or "unpaid family workers," reflected these same assumptions (see Kiribamune 1992, xxvi). Many surveys disregarded housework, women's efforts in the informal economy, contract work, or casual labor, terming women who performed a variety of different work as it became available "unemployed" (Marecek 1992, 207). Similarly, surveys on migration (e.g., Korale 1989) struggled to decide if a woman who left the "workforce" in Saudi Arabia to return home to her duties as a "housewife" in Sri Lanka should be termed "unemployed" merely because she looked after her own family instead of someone else's. Migrant domestic labor highlighted these conceptual dissonances in the taken-for-granted categories of "work" and "home," challenging the "naturalness" of mothering and the power structures that surrounded it.

Doing research on women's work not only revealed the idealized images of wives and mothers, it also revealed how important these images were to the identity of those who held them. I found in Polwatta that girls were taught to work and stay close to home, while boys roamed and played freely. Many poor, working-class women who could not afford to follow ideal restrictions on women's mobility traveled widely and socialized freely. However, they too prized the same middle-class ideal that respectable women should not (by definition) venture freely into the public sphere. Though women's work was clearly highly valuable in the village, the pervading ideology branded a family where women worked outside the home as low status, which contributed to the masking of women's work as "work." For instance, a wealthy and influential woman who ran a flourishing trade in coconut fiber products in the Polwatta area insisted modestly that her husband, also present at the time, supported their family, while she stayed at home and had no job. Kiribamune argues: "Upward social mobility [is] associated with the confinement of women to the household and the economic dependence on a male bread-winner" (1992, xxxi). I found in Polwatta that if a woman sought work outside the home, it indicated that her husband could not earn enough to support his family, thus challenging his ability to fulfill his role as breadwinner. By leaving their homes to work abroad, migrant women lost a measure of honor, a blemish offset but not erased by financial success. Women's ideal roles as wives and mothers left no space for their work outside the home; migrant mothers seemed simultaneously to try to conform to ideal images in their self-portrayals, and to battle the ideological restraints on their employment.

With the cognitive dissonance surrounding women's roles and personal identities, women became more critically aware of the gender hierarchies, class differences, and international relations of power in which they were situated. Domestic service in conjunction with international migration pulled women out of their own households. Family work that had once been a woman's universally accepted "sacred calling" intrinsic to her identity as wife and mother was now performed for strangers who commodified her labor power, paying her a salary in international currency. New consciousness of class and gender roles allowed and encouraged the critical reevaluation of these hegemonic structures of power, inequality, and dominance.

THE FRAGMENTATION OF MOTHERHOOD

The migration of domestic servants fragmented the bundle of duties and responsibilities traditionally thought of as "motherhood." Three sets of parents (Arabic employers, Sri Lankan nannies of Arabic children, and Sri Lankan caretakers of migrants' children) and three sets of children (Arabic children, Sri Lankan migrants' children, and Sri Lankan caretakers' children) shared in each other's affection and labor. Many of the Polwatta migrants mentioned that both "the Madam" and "the Boss"[10] of their Arabic families worked outside the home. Domestic servants, who aided other women in managing the overlap between office and home, often felt themselves to be taking over many aspects of the role of wife and mother vacated by their Madams. As housemaids lived and worked in West Asia, ties of affection began to bind them to their employers and especially to the children of their employers, for whom they often "cared" in more than one sense of the word (see also Colen 1990). Neither family nor strangers, the housemaids gradually became familiar with new customs, foods, places, languages, and people. As they integrated into the household of their employers, so too the new habits and patterns of those left in the village flowed to soften the starkness of their absence from their own homes and families. As the years passed, their children missed them less and less, growing fonder of their more immediate caretakers, the men and women who looked after them on a daily basis. Just as housemaids grew emotionally attached to their charges abroad, their own children back in Sri Lanka came to love the caregivers at home.

Between the employer's family, the migrant's family, and the families who stepped in to care for the migrant's household, there was a continual redistribution of jobs, roles, labor, love, and money in the reproduction of children, families, and laborers. The dynamics of social change encompassed not only economics but also, and perhaps more significantly, local and international patterns of love and affection.

Relations of domestic service were in many ways much more complicated than other relations between middle- and upper-class employers and their working-class employees. Servants worked (and often lived) in the houses of their employers, becoming deeply and personally integrated into the intimacies of their private lives. Employers created and maintained a social space between themselves and their servants, at the same time demanding loyalty and diligence from the women caring for their children. Elaborate etiquette regulating dress codes, forms of address, restrictions on sociability, and demarcations of accessible and inaccessible space served to distinguish household worker from family member (see also Gill 1994; Hansen 1989). James Scott (1990) argues that household workers often lived a dual life, enacting one set of behaviors and voicing one set of ideas in the company of their employers, another in private with their own families and peers. My research suggests that the personal and often isolated nature of domestic service highlighted the subjective uniqueness of each work experience, creating an ambiguous situation where personal ties mitigated active protest against exploitation and worked against a consciousness of class solidarity with other servants. Barriers of class, often compounded with those of race, ethnicity, or nationality, separated master from servant, but at the same time, housemaids and their charges developed physical and emotional intimacies that challenged the maintenance of clear-cut cultural and personal boundaries between master and servant. I explore the tension between the maid's perpetual marginality and her de facto centrality in the following case study.

MOMMY'S BOOBY: LAKSHMI

Housemaids' duties varied from family to family, often including housecleaning, laundry, ironing, shopping, cooking, car washing, light gardening, and child care. Of all of these intimate functions, child care proved the hardest to classify purely as "work." Although migrant women set out to nurture their charges (for money), while providing material benefits to their own offspring (for love) (see also Colen 1990, 101), the bounds of duty and affection were quickly blurred.

Lakshmi, a migrant from the Polwatta area, told the following story of working for British expatriates in Bahrain. Pregnant, the Madam returned to England to have her child. When she came back to Bahrain, the Madam handed Lakshmi the new infant, saying, "This isn't my baby but yours." Lakshmi expressed a real and lasting love for the baby boy. She was the one to bathe him, and she said, "It was my heart that was sad if the baby cried." Although his mother told her not to spoil the youngest baby by coming every time he cried, or he would never give her any time to work, Lakshmi found it very hard to obey this order. Since both the Madam and the Boss were very busy, Lakshmi did everything for the child, even remembering what medicines needed to be given and when. She said that she was more mother to the boy than his own mother; he did not call her by her name but called her "Mommy" instead.

Lakshmi recalled that during the years that the baby's mother was breast-feeding him, he would reach down Lakshmi's shirt as well. The baby would touch her side (she was fat then, she says, and her flesh hung out of her short blouses) and say, "Mommy's booby." The love and desire in the gesture emphasize the physical connection between the housemaid and her charge. Lakshmi said she felt quite embarrassed when this happened in front of the Boss. Although the housemaid in many ways acted as the children's mother, she did not act as the Boss's sexual partner. Not yet familiar with hierarchy and difference, the baby by word and gesture assumed the woman he loved to be a part of his family in every way.

Intimate ties between domestic servants and the families for whom they worked were not restricted only to affection between nannies and the children for whom they cared. Their involvement in their employers' lives gave housemaids a great deal of power in interpersonal household dynamics. Despite their economic and social subordination, household workers' knowledge of the people for whom they worked gave them informal but effective leverage in disputes, as the following story shows.

While working for another British couple Lakshmi found herself caught between husband and wife. In this household Lakshmi did not get along with the Madam and talked mostly with the Boss. One night there was a business party, which the Madam did not want her husband to attend. She said if he was going, he had to take the children, too. He asked Lakshmi if she would baby-sit for two hours, and she agreed. The Madam then stormed off and locked herself in the master bedroom, so that her husband, who was still in his work clothes, could not shower or change. Lakshmi told him that there were clean towels in the children's bathroom, and also soap and shampoo. He asked if she had any clean shirts in the laundry, and she ironed him

one. Soon after the Boss left for the party, his wife came out of the bedroom
to ask if he had gone. She said that she would take care of the children and
sent Lakshmi to her quarters.

Lakshmi related the preceding story as background for a longer story
concerning an injury, to explain the Madam's lack of sympathy with Lakshmi's
request for time off. Several days after her employers' quarrel, on her day off,
Lakshmi injured her arm while picking fruit from a tree in a park. Gradually
stiffening over the afternoon and evening, her arm became extremely painful
by the next morning. Lakshmi came to work intending to tell the Boss about
her troubles. She set up the family's breakfast one-handed. Carrying his
shoes, the Boss came to breakfast, hurrying to make a flight out of the country. Lakshmi polished his footwear while he ate and never had a chance to
discuss her injury. After his departure, Lakshmi explained her predicament to
the Madam, who lectured her, accusing her of maneuvering for an extra day
off. Although the Madam allowed Lakshmi to visit the doctor, she refused to
grant any sick leave despite the sling on Lakshmi's arm. Lakshmi scrubbed
the five bathrooms and looked after the rest of the house single-handed; the
Madam grudgingly allowed her to skip the ironing for several days. Lakshmi
felt sure the Boss would have treated her differently.

Lakshmi told the two stories to point out two paradoxical and contradictory dynamics. First, she emphasized that her knowledge of domestic relations made her a powerful player in her employers' household. Second, she
pointed out the vulnerability of the housemaid to her employers' grudges
and goodwill—just like a family member. Living so intimately with a family,
housemaids like Lakshmi hold a great deal of implicit authority and power
in intrafamily politics through the centrality of their role in the house.
Abroad, the mothering housemaid simultaneously filled three equally paradoxical roles: to the children she was at once a marginal outsider and their
primary caregiver; to the "Boss" she was a foreign woman and the nurturer of
his children; and to the "Madam" she was her replacement and her
employee, her double and her opposite. Her work, mothering the children
and taking care of the house, set her directly in the sphere of the (usually
female) employer, who was at once liberated from household duties and sup-
planted from a powerful position of caregiving and nurturing. Despite her
knowledge and intimacy, however, the housemaid remained economically
and socially subservient to her employers. No matter how central the housemaid's labor became, and in spite of close bonds with her employers, the
maid, always slightly apart, encountered discrimination and antagonism as
well as intimacy and love in the house of her employers. Although housemaids' stories did not reveal discourses as clearly separate as Scott's "public"

and "hidden" transcripts (1990), still, out of these contrasting identities of marginal insider and intimate outsider came a growing critical awareness of gender hierarchies, class differences, and the international relations of power in which they were embedded.

LONG-DISTANCE MOTHERING

Interpersonal dynamics just as complex as those arising in the Middle East surrounded the absence of mothers from their Sri Lankan homes. Critics of migration often extolled "the mother," in the process nostalgically idealizing a "traditional family" of yesteryear. Many critics felt that the migration of mothers had bad effects on their children, leaving them malnourished, neglected, unruly, and truant from school. With a large portion of the adult women absent from the village, migration affected not only the migrants' children but also the children of local women assuming extra child-care duties. Critics noted the possibility of eldest daughters leaving school early to take care of the family, with early pregnancies and marriages resulting. They predicted a higher divorce rate among couples, a proliferation of extramarital affairs, misuse of money, drug addiction, gambling, and other social ills due to the absence of one spouse (Gunatilleke 1992; Gunatilleke and Perera 1987; Korale 1983, 24; Schampers and Eelans 1986). But while some scholars blamed migration for the breakdown of family life, often the troubles that made marriages in Polwatta disintegrate (e.g., economic hardship, wife beating, alcoholism, sexual coercion and abuse, infidelity, and desertion, to name but a few) formed part of the reason the migrant chose to leave the country in the first place. The impact of migration on women's roles and personal identity must take as its basis both an accurate understanding of ideals and stereotypes, as well as a realistic understanding of village family life.

Gameela Samarasinghe (1989), a Sri Lankan psychologist, looked at the social-psychological costs of female migration, noting that Sri Lankan mothers rarely left extremely young children, especially those under one year of age. Nevertheless, she found that in 1987 mothers of some 40,000 children under the age of five were working in the Middle East (1989, 15). The primary caregivers with whom the migrants left their children unanimously felt that they were fulfilling all the functions that a mother would perform, and the majority of them claimed they were more loved by the children than the biological mother (1989, 34). Samarasinghe found children's health and emotional well-being not noticeably impaired, especially after they adjusted to the situation, but she did note a possible neglect of children's schooling (1989, 39). In a longer-term study, Dias and Weerakoon-

Gunawardene (1991) found that the longer the migrant mother stayed away from home, the more difficult the situation became for the children, and the greater the incidence of child neglect and delinquency.

While some neighbors, newspaper reporters, and scholars condemned migrant mothers for "heartlessly abandoning" their children in pursuit of money, the migrants portrayed their work abroad as undertaken on behalf of the material well-being of those very children. They did not divide working for wages from child care and family. Sirima Kiribamune writes of non-migrant Sri Lankan women:

> When women work solely to support their families, it is extremely difficult to differentiate the roles of mother, home-maker and income-earner. For them earning an income is the means to keep the home fires burning, to make the children a little more comfortable and to give them the material needs or that little extra for which the husband's income alone is not sufficient. (1992, xliii)

In poor families where husbands, when present, worked intermittently as unskilled casual laborers, migrant women also sought employment not only to supplement their husband's salaries, but also as the sole breadwinners providing material benefits for their families. In this section I examine shifting self-perceptions of two Polwatta mothers who left their children to earn money abroad. Pride in accomplishment and frustration in failure stemmed from their sense of financial obligation and responsibility as wives and mothers. The emotions attached to these new facets of female identity complement and compete with older images of the South Asian mother as the source of all nurturing and the absolute center of family life. In her work in Brazil, Nancy Scheper-Hughes shows that many of our commonsense conceptions of "mother-love" are culturally learned instead of biologically given (Scheper-Hughes 1992, 15). Similarly, as economic necessity and a scarcity of local jobs for both men and women forced women to seek employment abroad, shifting roles and identities highlight the constructed and contextual nature of motherhood and "mother-love" in Sri Lanka. Through their actions, village migrants broadened the spectrum of acceptable ways for women to "love" their children and care for their families.

"HE WON'T LET ME GO ANYWHERE": KAMALA

The new economic opportunity to work abroad in the Middle East brought the role of female breadwinner into direct conflict with the role of wife and mother caring for a family and performing the household chores. Despite changing economic and social circumstances, women still faced stern criticism for not fulfilling the traditional expectations of motherhood and marriage (also see Risseeuw 1991, 266–67).

Kamala spent three years working in the United Arab Emirates (UAE). Her two sons were eleven months old and two years old when she went abroad, and neither son recognized her when she returned. While she was gone her mother and husband shared the care of her boys. Kamala's relationship with her husband had deteriorated rapidly after her return from the Middle East. They quarreled frequently about control over the money she had remitted, most of which her husband seemed unable to account for. Village rumor suggested he had "lent" most of it to his lover, a lower-caste woman who lived across the street. Kamala had hoped her husband would use her remittances to buy land and build a house, or purchase the house they had rented for the past six years, but he had not done so. He also refused to let Kamala give her parents gifts or compensate her mother for looking after her children, a slight that they took very personally, severing all relations with their daughter. Feeling the goals of her migration had not been accomplished, Kamala wanted to return to the UAE. Gesturing with her head toward the front yard, where her husband tended their small vegetable garden, Kamala said quietly, "He won't let me go anywhere." Alienated from her natal family, dispossessed of her money, and at odds with her controlling husband, Kamala had attempted suicide several months before our interview.

Kamala found herself caught between her hopes for what she could have accomplished for her sons, husband, and parents with the money she earned abroad, and the stark reality of her loss of three years' time and wages. Her self-image as a daughter, mother, and wife in more traditional terms suffered, because her migration placed her at odds with her parents, deprived her of three years of her sons' childhood, and allowed her husband to start an affair with another woman in her absence. With her family relations in shambles and her new plans unfulfilled, Kamala found neither her old identity nor her new one tenable. Much of the burden of her success in Polwatta's world of uncertain transitions rested in Kamala's husband's hands. Whereas older social structures, ritual forms, and gender roles all worked to support the "traditional" wife and mother, migrant women striving to create a new social identity of working mother, world traveler, and breadwinner ventured into dangerous, uncharted territory. The liminality of domestic work abroad promised the possibility of renewal and new beginnings in Sri Lanka, but in Kamala's case a failed transition left her in what she felt was an unbearable situation. Her attempted suicide publicly proclaimed her despair to the community.[11]

"BUT LOOK WHAT'S HAPPENED TO THE BOYS!":
ON THE "NEGLECT" OF PRIYANTHI'S CHILDREN

While Kamala's household failed to prosper from her migration, other families, such as Priyanthi's, accumulated considerable material wealth through the remittances of housemaids. Some villagers accused both Kamala and Priyanthi of abandoning their children to work abroad. Others, both migrants and caregivers, felt that the arrangements made for the children, which often involved extended kinship networks, proved adequate and minimized disruption. Although migrants did worry about leaving their children behind, they argued that they were going abroad primarily to benefit the children by providing them with money for food, clothing, and school fees, a new and better house, and better prospects for the future. Priyanthi, a Polwatta migrant whose earnings abroad had substantially improved her family's material well-being, encountered mixed reactions to her decision to spend ten years working abroad. Although many admired her industry, at the same time they judged her an inadequate mother.

Before Priyanthi returned from her fifth two-year trip to the Middle East, I interviewed her husband, Ariyapala. His sons were all at school, and he had just woken up after working the night shift at the hospital where he had been an attendant for fifteen years. Although Ariyapala held a good job by village standards,[12] in 1982 he and his wife had agreed that they needed extra income to make ends meet. They decided to send Priyanthi to the Middle East to work. Their youngest son was a year and a half old when she left, and he cried and did not recognize her when she came home two years later. Life in the village had been difficult without Priyanthi's presence. While she was away, Ariyapala said that he and his father looked after the boys.

Later on the day of our interview with Ariyapala, during a conversation in my research associate's kitchen, my associate remarked that Ariyapala and Priyanthi might be able to start a business with the money she brought back from abroad. My associate's wife, overhearing this, commented, "She's good at making money, but look at what's happened to the boys!" Village gossip, perhaps fueled by jealousy of Priyanthi's material prosperity, condemned Priyanthi for "abandoning" her sons, saying they had all "run wild" in her absence.[13] My research associate's wife remarked disapprovingly that the sons did not always eat their meals at their own house, especially when their father was drunk, but wandered widely. In the local idiom, eating from tea shops and spending time away from home indicated a lack of coherence in family life—a clear condemnation of their absent mother, who was faulted for valuing money too much, and her family too little.

I spoke with Priyanthi several months later, four days after she returned from her fifth trip abroad. Confronted with this criticism, Priyanthi made it very clear that she had gone abroad to earn money not for herself but for her children. Countering accusations that she had abandoned her boys, Priyanthi said that she only went overseas so that she could "bring up her children," or improve their lot in life. Priyanthi emphasized how difficult her work had been, stating that it was better to *beg* in Sri Lanka than to work abroad. Priyanthi saved her salary for large endeavors and sent little home for daily consumption, because her husband was earning money for the family. Upon returning home in 1983 after her first trip abroad, Priyanthi said she bought their house and land from a lower-caste family who were leaving the area. The house, a large tile-roofed building with seven rooms, was one of the most impressive structures in Polwatta. After subsequent trips, she purchased furniture, constructed a well and a toilet, wired the house for electricity, and put cement on the floor in the front of the house. These accomplishments were concrete and lasting symbols of what she had done for the sake of her family.

Priyanthi placed herself as the active agent in the household, taking responsibility for the family's material well-being. She did not dwell on emotional issues of her sons' development, saying merely that their father earned enough to feed them, and that their father and grandfather should certainly have been able to look after them adequately. She felt that her shift toward material mothering should have been accompanied by a concomitant shift toward competent psychological fathering and grandfathering. Priyanthi felt her first priority was to provide material necessities for her children, and she adamantly refused responsibility for any domestic problems that occurred during her migration.

MONEY MATTERS

Both Priyanthi and Kamala struggled with their husbands over the use of the money they had earned abroad. Older gendered patterns of money management in the village worked against the migrant women's efforts to control the wealth they brought to their families. These same patterns worked against an easy transition from housewife to breadwinner.

If a man provided the bulk of the household income, most village couples assumed that ideally the husband would bring about two-thirds of his wages to his wife, who managed the household accounts with that money. The remainder of his salary he kept for his own (social) needs, such as cigarettes and alcohol. However, housewives with working husbands often lamented that the men gave them too little and still left them with the responsibility for putting food on the table. Women could try to get more money from men by concealing any money they did have, by ridiculing their husbands in public for being poor providers, or by refusing to cook for, speak with, or have sex with their husbands (see also Risseeuw 1991). Even if a woman contributed to the family income or became the family's sole bread-winner, her husband remained, at least in people's perception (including his own and his wife's), the main decision maker and the head of the family. Women's wages usually went directly for family use, and women who spent even small sums of money (much less than the one-third allowed working men) for their own individual pleasure confronted public condemnation of their "selfishness." Unemployed husbands, however, felt it within their rights to demand money for their social activities. Returned migrants regu-larly confronted complex negotiations over the distribution and use of their savings—negotiations with direct significance for the larger issues of village gender roles, individual rights, and family responsibilities.

Priyanthi's husband, Ariyapala, drank heavily throughout my stay in the village. My research associate confidently expected Priyanthi to "take Ariyapala by the ear" when she returned from the Middle East, collecting his monthly salary and putting it toward household expenses instead of toward drink. In village opinion, the wife should control household spend-ing, and Priyanthi's absence was held partially responsible for Ariyapala's behavior. When I interviewed Priyanthi shortly after her return from the Middle East, she seemed ready to reassume responsibility for her household. Of Ariyapala, she noted affectionately that he spent everything he had at once, saying, "Today he is like a White man (spending lavishly), tomorrow like a beggar (with no money left)." Every time she returned home from abroad, she found the house stripped of the additions she had acquired for it during her last vacation. "This time even the kitchen knives are gone," she lamented. Dreaming aloud of what she could have accomplished, Priyanthi said that she would have had a special "American" (luxurious) house and a car if she had found generous places to work in the Middle East, and if she had had a good husband. By her promises to restore order to the family finances, Priyanthi implicitly accepted her responsibility as a wife to control her husband's spending. At the same time, her unusually open vocal expres-sion of her displeasure with her husband indexed her disapproval of the state of their household as she had found it on her return.

Polwatta women have a series of criteria for what constitutes "a good man": he does not drink, waste money, or beat his wife. Young women learn these criteria, and they also learn that they should never appear to object to a husband lacking in these good qualities (see also Risseeuw 1991). Women often hesitated to challenge the gender hierarchy directly, fearing what others might say about their breach of tradition (see Kiribamune 1992, xix). Rather than openly voicing their feelings or publicly rebelling against unjust treatment, many women instead learned how to manage their husbands through endurance, manipulation, and deception. Even in cases of alcoholism and abuse, women rarely left their husbands, because they saw no viable alternatives to married life. In contrast to these existing patterns, returned migrants, more vocal than many other women, occasionally criticized their husbands openly, blaming them for the irresponsible behavior that drained away the family's wealth. Kamala's suicide attempt and Priyanthi's public disapproval of Ariyapala indexed these two returnees' attempts to hold their husbands to a higher standard of behavior. But despite her disappointment in her husband, neither woman publicly considered separation. These two women served as object lessons for other local women who, in conversation, often referred to the family and financial situations of returned migrants. Made more independent and vocal by their migration, Kamala and Priyanthi challenged some of the existing gender roles, while accepting and reinforcing others.

WOMEN'S WORK

Negotiations over acceptable images of women's work encompassed not only women's work abroad but also their duties and responsibilities in the homes they departed. As migrant women left their families, their absence created a vacuum to be filled by others. Only rarely were caregivers officially paid for their labors. While migrants struggled with their new identities of domestic workers and breadwinners, those who filled their shoes at home also faced complex transformations.

Despite the number of unemployed husbands in the village, only one or two families of the sixty or so I interviewed admitted openly that men had taken over any child-care chores. The gendered division of labor in the village clearly marked mothering and housework as female. Most men's sense of masculinity would be threatened by doing household chores and caring for young children. Dutch anthropologist Carla Risseeuw writes of a rural Sri Lankan village near Polwatta:

> Men cannot "stoop down" in the widest sense, without experiencing severe emotional stress. . . . The principle that he is "higher" than a woman, and more specifically his wife, permeates the actions, thoughts and emotions of both men and women. . . . Handling dirt, faeces, cleaning toilets, being impure, doing repetitive, relatively less prestigious work,

which often lacks the status of work as such or "prestige" of the proximity of danger, is the female expression of the principle of gender hierarchy. (Risseeuw 1991, 271)

To a large extent both men and women in Polwatta accept this division as just and judge themselves and others according to it. Most migrants say that they are leaving their offspring in the care of their mother or mother-in-law, but in my daily interactions in the village, I noted more male participation than people generally reported. In Priyanthi's household, her husband and his father looked after her four sons while she was abroad. Men and their families glossed over men's housework to preserve men's masculine image. Since Priyanthi's husband, Ariyapala, held a well-paying job at the hospital, he was in part sheltered from village ridicule for taking on his wife's chores. When questioned, Ariyapala pragmatically, though somewhat defensively, accepted the logic of his domestic duties. As more men take over what are generally considered women's chores in the place of their migrant wives, older concepts of gender roles and family responsibilities slowly change.

A GRANDMOTHER'S NURSERY: CAROLINE

Relations between migrant mothers and their children's caregivers are often fraught with tensions, revealing strains in the fragmentation of motherhood and difficulties in the commodification of nurture. Kamala's migration was facilitated by her mother, Caroline. Herself a mother of ten children, some of whom still lived at home, Caroline looked after a house full of grandchildren while her daughters and daughters-in-law worked in the Middle East. Caroline's crippled sister and her mother also lived with the family, helping Caroline with coconut fiber rope-making and child care. Her husband, who worked in another part of the country, returned home twice a month for the weekend. Caroline said that she prayed continually for good health, so that she could continue to look after her many grandchildren.

While Kamala was working in the UAE Caroline looked after her two boys, sending them back to their father in the evenings after dinner. Relations between Caroline and her son-in-law were strained at best. Caroline mentioned that although she fed her grandsons while Kamala was away, their father rarely reimbursed her for the cost of their food. Once, when Kamala had sent Caroline some money from the Middle East, Kamala's husband had gotten violently angry, and the quarrel had ended, as many serious village fights did, at the police station. Kamala had sent neither money nor letters to her parents after that time. With tears in her eyes, Caroline said that Kamala had behaved very ungratefully. Although Caroline had looked after Kamala's sons for three years, Kamala had sent no money, given her no thanks, and had not even come to visit Caroline in the hospital when she was recovering from an operation. Hurt by Kamala's behavior, Caroline and her husband had not visited Kamala in the hospital following her suicide attempt. Caroline's reaction to her daughter's "ingratitude" showed a nascent awareness of the changing value of women's work. Although migration brought about some professionalization of mothering as women worked abroad for wages, the general image that women took care of children naturally and gladly remained. But while Caroline loved her grandchildren, she also said that child care was costly and time-consuming labor. Aware of her pivotal role in facilitating the migrations of her daughters and daughters-in-law, Caroline articulated her sense of injustice, saying that her labor should be reciprocated with both love and money.

CONCLUSIONS

When women took the half-step from housewife to migrant housemaid, village images of women changed both figuratively and literally. In the midst of one interview, a father sent his son to fetch a large, framed picture of one of his daughters, taken in a Jordanian studio, posed with a backdrop of Grecian columns. Before the burgeoning of the migration of labor to the Middle East, nearly all the large studio photographs found in village houses depicted couples on their wedding day, with smaller snapshots capturing the wedding ceremony and celebrations. In 1994, most migrants' houses contained a photo album, often filled with scenes from overseas: housemaids in black veils and long dresses, smiling Arabic children, city streets, and desert landscapes. Sent from abroad to make the strange familiar, these pictures occupied the same physical space as marriage photos in village houses. Larger posed portraits from the Middle East emphasized a woman's work instead of her marriage, picturing her as an individual in service, not half of a couple.

In this essay I have focused on the fragmentation of motherhood as women sold their nurturing skills abroad, leaving their own children in the care of others. When village women migrated from Sri Lanka to the Middle East, they acted in opposition to a series of stereotypes for the behavior of good mothers and wives. In the Middle East the biological mother was freed from child care for more profitable work by the foreign maid; in Sri Lanka, mothers left the husbands and children to whom their lives ideally should have been dedicated, moving into the public sphere, selling their labor as a commodity on the international market, and earning valuable foreign exchange for their country.

Migration fragmented the duties of the "mother" both at home and abroad, with three sets of women providing very different types of care to three sets of children. Changes surrounding migration challenged personal relations and personal identities in the village, particularly altering what it meant to "love" your children. Polwatta women who looked after children (their own or another woman's) showed their love in well-worn ways, but many, like Caroline, had a growing awareness of the potential monetary value of their work. Pathbreaking migrant mothers such as Priyanthi and Kamala who left their children behind strove to forge new roles and identities to encompass their work abroad. Having become breadwinners to secure a good life for their offspring, they pragmatically dismissed charges of greed and heartlessness for failing simultaneously to fulfill a more nurturing role. Housemaids such as Lakshmi often expressed the impression that they had come to be more "mothering" than the biological mother of the children for whom they cared. With few role models and ever-changing personal circumstances, each migrant woman continually renegotiated her emergent identity in her family. Through their actions, village migrants broadened the spectrum of acceptable ways for women to "love" their two sets of children and care for their two families.

Changing images of motherhood suggested changes for fathers as well. While ideal roles lagged behind village practices, more men, especially younger fathers whose wives were in the Middle East, found themselves at least partially responsible for taking care of their children. Men's participation in household chores seems gradually to be challenging gendered conceptions of housework. Although most of the caregivers were female relatives, men also contributed to household tasks in new and traditionally "motherly" ways. Female labor migration also spurred changing images of family responsibility. While older traditions of female subservience shielded men from criticism, Priyanthi's outspoken condemnation of her husband's irresponsibility, and Kamala's anguished suicide attempt showed (albeit in drastically different ways) that migrant mothers had begun to demand radical adjustments in the roles and behaviors of their husbands. These cases also illustrated the anger, frustration, and pain accompanying shifts in hegemonic structures of domination and resistance.

The fragmentation of motherhood challenges not only family relations in Polwatta but also the carefully constructed separations between employers and employees in West Asia. While migrant women often came to love the children they cared for, as domestic servants they never entered fully into the family life of their employers. Kept at a social and physical distance, housemaids occupied a shifting territory between intimate strangers and marginal insiders where dynamics of employer and employee intermeshed with more subtle and more personal power plays. Nevertheless, however tenuous, domestic workers' sense of belonging in the households where they worked gave them some basis on which to challenge the class hierarchy of the international division of labor. As growing numbers of housemaids migrate abroad and share their experiences with others, despite the isolation of their work, they may begin to share a working-class awareness of domestic service, both at home and abroad, as "work." Even though change comes slowly, women's new economic opportunities clearly lead to challenges of existing village hierarchies and gender roles and may lead to increasing confidence in the international arena as well.

ACKNOWLEDGMENTS

I would like to thank the editors of this volume as well as my colleagues Sharon Carstens and Lisa Gezon for their helpful suggestions in revising this piece. Many of the insights herein are theirs; the flaws are my own. This research was made possible in part by USA National Science Foundation Dissertation Research Award grant number DBS 9207143.

NOTES

1. The name "Polwatta" means "Coconut Garden" in Sinhala. To preserve the privacy of the people involved, I have used pseudonyms for both the village and its inhabitants.

2. Sri Lanka's population has nearly doubled in the fifty years since the eradication of malaria after World War II. The census of 1963 put the national population at 10,625,000 (Yalman 1967, 13), while the 1981 census counted 14,848,364 people (Rand McNally 1987, 253). A census in 1994 estimated the current population at around 18.5 million people.

3. More than three-quarters of the Sri Lankan migrants work in Saudi Arabia, Kuwait, and the United Arab Emirates (UAE) (see Sri Lankan Bureau of Foreign Employment [SLBFE] 1993b).

4. My figures in this section come from interviews with Dr. Mananwatte (1993) of the Ministry of Employment and Vocational Training, and Mr. Ruhunage (1993) of the SLBFE, as well as information in Herath 1993; Sri Lankan Bureau of Foreign Employment [SLBFE] 1993a, 1993b; and Wansekara 1993.

5. "Clay" houses were constructed of wattle (wood and twig framework) covered with daub (a special mixture of mud, lime, and straw).

6. The average family size of migrants was higher than the average size of families in the general population, leading Sri Lankan researchers to conclude that a main reason for migration is improvement of the family's economic status (Dias and Weerakoon-Gunawardene 1991, 48; Samarasinghe 1989).

7. In 1994 some women had worked for more than ten years abroad.

8. See the discussion of gender roles below for an explanation of this bias.

9. In 1993, women working as housemaids generally earned US$60–100 a month, or Sri Lankan Rs 3000/–5000/. Salaries for men varied, but approached US$300–500, or Rs 15,000/–25,000/. This made a female migrant's salary roughly equivalent to what a male clerical worker or security guard (lower-middle-class jobs) might earn locally and makes a male migrant's salary very desirable indeed. By comparison, in a day-labor job such as those available to many of the female migrants' husbands, a man might make Sri Lankan Rs 125/ a day, or Rs 3750/ a month in the unlikely event that he found steady work.

10. Housemaids regularly refer to their female employer as "the Madam" or "Madam," and their male employer as "the Boss" or "Boss." Here I have adopted the English terminology they used.

11. The implications of suicide as a form of social protest are explored further in Gamburd 1995a.

12. Over the course of one month, Ariyapala usually worked fifty-two hours overtime, for which he received Rs 430/ (US$8.60) extra a month. With that bonus, he earned Rs 3,700/ month (US$75)—roughly what a schoolteacher or security guard would earn. See note 9 for comparable wages in other fields.

13. Inquiring later, I discovered that although neighbors found Priyanthi's sons undisciplined, even the older two boys, whom neighbors judged the most reckless, had studied well beyond the neighborhood average, and their "disreputable" interests in fashion and foreign tourists were not unusual among their peers. Priyanthi's youngest son, whom I knew the best, seemed a cheerful, intelligent, level-headed fourteen-year-old.

References

Ariyawansa, D. M.

1986   Report of the Survey on Change in Economic and Social Status of Expatriate Labour for Unskilled Occuaptions. Unpublished manuscript. Economics Department, University of Kelaniya, Sri Lanka.

Bourdieu, Pierre

1977   Outline of a Theory of Practice. Cambridge: Cambridge University Press.

Brochmann, Grete

1987 *Escape Route to Dependency? Female Migration from Sri Lanka to the Middle East.* Oslo: International Peace Research Institute.

Colen, Shellee

1990 Housekeeping for the Green Card: West Indian Household Workers, the State, and Stratified Reproduction in New York. In Roger Sanjek and Shellee Colen, eds., *At Work in Homes: Household Workers in World Perspective*, 89–118. American Ethnological Society Monograph Series, No. 3. Washington, DC: American Anthropological Association.

Constable, Nicole

1997 *Maid to Order in Hong Kong.* Ithaca: Cornell University Press.

Dias, Malsiri, and Nedra Weerakoon-Gunawardene

1991 Female Labour Migration to Singapore and Hong Kong: A Profile of the Sri Lankan Housemaids. Unpublished ms. Colombo, Sri Lanka: Center for Women's Research.

Gamburd, Geraldine E.

1972 The Seven Grandparents: Locality and Lineality in Sinhalese Kinship and Caste. Ph.D. diss., Columbia University. Ann Arbor, MI: UMI.

Gamburd, Michele

1995a Housemaids at Home and Abroad: Labor Migration and Social Transformations in a Sri Lankan Village. Ph.D. diss., University of Michigan. Ann Arbor, MI: UMI.

1995b Sri Lanka's "Army of Housemaids": Control of Remittances and Gender Transformations. *Anthropologica* 37:49–88.

Gill, Lesley

1994 *Precarious Dependencies: Gender, Class and Domestic Service in Bolivia.* New York: Columbia University Press.

Gunatilleke, Godfrey

1992 Sri Lanka. In Godfrey Gunatilleke, ed., *The Impact of Labour Migration on Households: A Comparative Study in Seven Asian Countries*, 227–63. Tokyo: United Nations University Press.

Gunatilleke, Godfrey, and P. D. A. Perera

1987 The Asian Migration to Arab Countries. Unpublished ms. Colombo, Sri Lanka: Marga Institute (Sri Lanka Centre for Development Studies) Document M933.

Hall, Stuart

1988 "Minimal Selves," in *Identity: The Real Me, ICA Document 6*, 44–46. London: Institute for Contemporary Arts.

1990 Cultural Identity and Diaspora. In Jonathan Rutherford, ed., *Identity: Community, Culture, Difference*, 222–37. London: Lawrence and Wishart.

Hansen, Karen Tranberg

1989 *Distant Companions: Servants and Employers in Zambia, 1900–1985*. Ithaca: Cornell University Press.

1991 Domestic Service: What's in It for Anthropology? *Reviews in Anthropology* 16:47–62.

Herath, K. M. K. P.

1993 Monthly Statistics on Labour Migration: October 1993. Unpublished ms. Colombo, Sri Lanka: Sri Lankan Bureau of Foreign Employment.

Jacobson, Doranne

1995 The Women of North and Central India: Goddesses and Wives. In Doranne Jacobson and Susan S. Wadley, eds., *Women in India: Two Perspectives*, 15–110. Columbia, MO: South Asia Publications.

Kiribamune, Sirima

1992 Reconciliation of Roles. In Sirima Kiribamune, ed., *Women, Work and Family in Sri Lanka*, xi–lix. International Centre for Ethnic Studies Series: 3. New Delhi: Navrang.

Korale, R. B. M.

1983 *Migration for Employment to the Middle East: Its Demographic and Socioeconomic Effects in Sri Lanka*. Colombo, Sri Lanka: Ministry of Plan Implementation.

1989 Reintegration of the Sri Lankan Returned Migrant. Paper presented at the National Seminar on Sri Lankan Migrant Labour. Sri Lanka: Marga Library.

Mananwatte, Sarath

1993 Personal interviews. December 10, 1993 and December 17, 1993.

Marecek, Jeanne

1992 Through American Eyes. Women, Work and Family Life: Old Myths, New Realities. In Sirima Kiribamune, ed., *Reconciliation of Roles: Women, Work and Family in Sri Lanka*, 264–91. International Centre for Ethnic Studies Series: 3. New Delhi: Navrang.

Ortner, Sherry

1984   Theory in Anthropology Since the Sixties. *Comparative Studies in Society and History* 26:126–66.

1989   *High Religion: A Cultural and Political History of Sherpa Buddhism*. Princeton: Princeton University Press.

Rand McNally

1987   *Universal World Atlas*. Chicago: Rand McNally.

Risseeuw, Carla

1991   *Gender Transformation, Power and Resistance Among Women in Sri Lanka: The Fish Don't Talk about the Water*. Manohar: New Delhi.

Rollins, Judith

1990   Ideology and Servitude. In Roger Sanjek and Shellee Colen, eds., *At Work in Homes: Household Workers in World Perspectives*, 74–88. American Ethnological Society Monograph Series, No. 3. Washington, DC: American Anthropological Association.

Ruhunage, L. K.

Personal interview. December 13, 1993.

Samarasinghe, Gameela

1989   *The Psycho-Social Implications of Middle East Migration on the Family Left Behind*. Colombo, Sri Lanka: Centre for Women's Research (CENWOR).

Scheper-Hughes, Nancy

1992   *Death Without Weeping: The Violence of Everyday Life in Brazil*. Berkeley: University of California Press.

Schampers, Toon, and Frank Eelans

1986   The Effect of Migration on the Well-Being of Sri Lankan Children Left Behind. Unpublished ms. Colombo, Sri Lanka: Marga Institute Document M899.

Scott, James

1990   *Domination and the Arts of Resistance: Hidden Transcripts*. New Haven: Yale University Press.

Sri Lankan Bureau of Foreign Employment (SLBFE)

1993a   *Employment of Sri Lankans in Foreign Countries*. Colombo: Sri Lankan Bureau of Foreign Employment.

1993b   *Migration for Foreign Employment and It's (sic) Recent Trends: A Report Based on the Airport Survey, Stage III 'B', January to December 1992.* Colombo: Sri Lankan Bureau of Foreign Employment.

1997   *Statistical Handbook of Foreign Employment 1997.* Colombo: SLBFE.

Van der Veer, Peter, ed.

1995   *Nation and Migration: The Politics of Space in the South Asian Diaspora.* Philadelphia: University of Pennsylvania Press.

Wadley, Susan S.

1995   Women and the Hindu Tradition. In Doranne Jacobson and Susan S. Wadley, eds., *Women in India: Two Perspectives*, 111–36. Columbia, MO: South Asia Publications.

Wansekara, W. M. V.

1993   *Migration Statistics of Sri Lanka, 1985–1992: Country-wise Report.* Colombo, Sri Lanka: Sri Lankan Bureau of Foreign Employment.

Williams, Raymond

1977   *Marxism and Literature.* Oxford: Oxford University Press.

Yalman, Nur

1967   *Under the Bo Tree.* Berkeley: University of California Press.

Louise H. Kidder

DEPENDENTS IN THE MASTER'S HOUSE
When Rock Dulls Scissors

... the dominant person isn't always the least dependent one.   (*Albert Memmi, Dependence, 1984, 8*)

ROCK, PAPER, SCISSORS

The children's game in which two players simultaneously toss their hands to signal rock, paper, or scissors is played in several languages and cultures. The winner is the person whose choice can "cover" or "dull" or "cut" the other person's. The relationships among the elements do not follow the linear logic that says if A is greater than B and B is greater than C, then A must be greater than C. If the relationships were linear, rock would always win, but the rules state that scissors cut paper, paper covers rock, and rock dulls scissors. The hierarchy shifts with the context and forms a circle; the relationships loop around.

Other images with circular properties appear in some M. C. Escher drawings. In one picture you can follow a staircase with your finger and think you are going down the steps only to find out that the "bottom" is at the same level where you began, back at the "top." I use these examples not to say that winning or being on top is only a game or illusion but to describe relationships that are nonlinear. In Escher's world what goes "down" comes back "up" and in Rock, Paper, Scissors, each element can damage the other.

The relationships between Western expatriates in India and the people they employ as servants also do not lie simply on an axis of domination and subjection. It has taken me a long time to see this and not fear I would minimize the injustice or injuries of colonial privilege by saying so (cf. Kidder 1996). The problems in the "master's" house involve more than domination and subjection, because the hierarchy is not simply linear. The servant's knowledge and the master's ignorance, the servant's mastery and the master's dependence, complicate the picture and contradict colonial assumptions of worth.

There is no single meaning attached to employing servants that applies to all times and places. And there is no unitary relationship between servants and employers. In eighteenth-century France, for instance, aristocratic families employed "man-servants" not only to provide services but also to be symbols of conspicuous consumption (Maza 1983). Men's wages were twice women's, so the more men a family had on display as doormen, valets, pages, cooks, and butlers the more status the family gained. The relationship between masters and their man-servants was "a triangular relationship involving masters, servants, and the public" (Hansen 1991, 48). Expatriates' relationships with servants in India have other meanings because they are in a different context. Expatriates in India today depend on servants not for a public display of status but for private assistance. Being dependent on servants—to purchase groceries, prepare meals, turn on hot water heaters, drive and repair cars, and translate Indian languages and cultures—is a problem that expatriates discuss among themselves. Foreign currencies make Westerners economically dominant, but for daily living they are very dependent on Indian "help."

I experienced the paradoxical relationship of being simultaneously dominant and dependent in 1964 when I had just received my B.A. degree in psychology and went to teach English in a women's college in south India. My outsider status had two edges. As a Westerner I always had access to dollars in a country where such foreign currency could not be bought. My income was modest by American standards (less than $100 per month), but it placed me on a par with Indian professors, and my housing allowance was generous. Two of us (my husband and I) rented an apartment that would house an Indian family of six. And for a very small sum my husband and I hired a man and woman to serve us as cook, laundress, water carrier, grocery buyer, and translaters for transactions we could not understand. We were economically dominant and personally dependent on two people we hardly knew.

In 1970 we returned to India and I decided to study how expatriates (primarily Americans and smaller numbers of Britishers, Germans, Scandinavians, and other Europeans) learned to live in India, with and without Indian servants. This essay explores aspects of relationships between expatriates and their servants that I have hitherto ignored.

The British colonization of India until 1947 and the subsequent economic domination by North America and Europe create the context for research even today. Colonialism has a long half-life and white Westerners who land in India still assume privileges of the "masters" who preceded them (cf. Kidder 1996). Caste and class within Indian society also shape the roles of Indian "masters" and "servants," so these are not uniquely colonial inventions (cf. Dickey 1995). What distinguishes the relationships of expatriate masters and Indian servants, however, is the expatriates' outsider status and postcolonial privilege. Expatriates have far more purchasing power and far less knowledge and skill for living in India than they would back home. This imbalance between living skills and purchasing power creates special problems in the expatriate's house. The hierarchy of domination and subordination is based on expatriates' money and privilege, but the master's nearly total dependence on servants disrupts the linear order. Who has control shifts with the context, and the relationships loop around to form a circle.

Loops occur in other relations of domination and subordination where two parties alternate being dependent on one another. Jean Baker Miller examines patterns of domination and subordination between husbands and wives and writes that "subordinates . . . know much more about the dominants than vice versa . . . and often know more about the dominants than they know about themselves" (1976, 10–11). Knowing more about oneself and the other is an adaptive survival strategy for someone who is subordinate, and it can also be used to subvert the hierarchy. Joy Charlton (1983) writes about how secretaries have access to information and acquire discretionary powers that rival those of their bosses but never appear in their job descriptions. And in Japanese there is a term for men who are "petty tyrants" because they berate and belittle their wives in public but obey them in private. If many relations of domination and subordination have a built-in paradox whereby the dominant person depends on the subordinate, what is unique about expatriate masters and domestic servants is that the nonlinearity is at times very pronounced. The loop is large when expatriates try to protect their health and well-being. The question of who is in control can be hard to answer.

COMPATRIOT EMPLOYERS AND DOMESTIC WORKERS

Among Indian employers of domestic servants there is little ambiguity about who is in control. Indian employers and domestic workers have more nearly linear relationships (Dickey 1995). The servants who help cook or clean house do not know any more about Indian culture than their Indian employers. They do not serve as translators or interpreters for their employers. And anything servants say or write in their own language, if overheard or seen, can be understood by their Indian employers. The employers rely on their servants for labor but not for superior knowledge of the society and culture in which they live. Indian employers feel vulnerable to transgressions of class lines, and they worry about servants carrying dirt or disease into the home and stealing the family's valuables or secrets (Dickey 1995). But they do not depend on their servants to be the cultural mediators, interpreters, or experts on daily life. The hierarchy is linear and rarely reversible.

Relationships in the United States between domestic workers and employers are similarly linear and nonreversible (Rollins 1985). The white women whom Judith Rollins observed expected domestic workers to make a show of being inferior. The employers hired servants to perform jobs the employers would not perform rather than jobs they *could not* perform. The domestic workers' unequal status was a job requisite. Employers expected the women they hired to act as though they also believed themselves to be inferior to confirm the hierarchy. Shellee Colen (1989) interviewed West Indian domestic workers in New York City who described similar demands. Women who had been teachers and nurses in the West Indies discovered they had to act "maidish" to please their employers in New York (Colen 1989, 175). The penalties for not enacting a lowly status could mean loss of their jobs and their green cards because many domestic workers' immigration status depended on their sponsors.

Women from Sri Lanka working as domestic servants in Saudi Arabia are in double (or triple) jeopardy. As outsiders in their employers' land, they depend on their employers for visas. Many women arrive with large debts owed to an entrepreneur who provided transportation and found them jobs. Some women endure physical and sexual abuse to maintain their jobs and immigration status (cf. documentary film, *Birds of Passage*). These women are caught in the snare of indentured servitude (see also Gamburd, this volume).

EXPATRIATES AND ASYMMETRICAL DEPENDENCIES

The Westerners I interviewed were ill-equipped and inept in varying degrees at managing the practical necessities of living in India. They were outsiders,

and their domestic workers knew much more than they about the social customs and practical details. Before 1947 we would have called them coloniz-
ers (Memmi 1967); in this postcolonial time I call them expatriates. They
included missionaries, foreign aid workers, foreign government officials,
businesspeople, Peace Corps volunteers, students, and researchers.

Relationships between the expatriate employers and Indian servants
they employed were asymmetrical in several ways:

- Expatriates had money.
- Indian servants had skills and knowledge for daily living.
- Expatriates depended on servants for food, water, hygiene.
- Servants depended on expatriates for a livelihood.
- The expatriate was the boss but was helpless in an Indian kitchen or
  marketplace.
- The servant was the subordinate but was more competent in the
  house and the marketplace.

Servants had a "homeland" advantage working in their own culture and
language. Even unschooled servants knew much more about living in India
than did their employers. They could speak, most could read, and many
could write the local language better than their employers. And they knew
all about the mundane matters that Indian nationals take for granted: how to
shop for household provisions, where to buy meat and produce, how to cook
in an Indian-style kitchen, from whom to order fresh milk, where to pay
electric bills, how to supervise repair work, when to give alms, how to dis-
pose of trash. These are a few of the hundreds of details foreigners found
bewildering and frustrating. But, for a very small price, the foreigner could
purchase the skills and knowledge of a servant to solve all these problems.

WHEN SERVANTS SEEM LIKE CHILDREN

Expatriates' relationships with servants was the topic of so many conversations that some expatriates complained about their friends who did nothing
but "talk about servant problems" (Kidder 1996). Rather than acknowledge
their own dependence, however, expatriates often complained about servants acting like children.

In a conversation about servants, one expatriate told about a fight
between two servants who were a married couple. The expatriate family
threatened to fire their cook because he had fought with his wife who also
served in the house. Complaining about these adults fighting and threatening to fire one of them put the focus on the two unruly servants fighting like
children. And like children they should be punished. However, had the

expatriates followed through with their threat, *they* would have suffered, too—they would lose the services of the person who provided food, water, and general maintenance of their kitchen. Describing the servants fighting like two children belies the expatriates' nearly childlike dependence.

In another expatriate's story a servant was described as childlike in his judgments and sentiments:

> D [expatriate man]: Well, we've sometimes wondered about Pimo.[1] I mean, we have to explain everything to him. You know, when we left the other day I told him not to let anyone into the house. And if anyone comes to look at the tape recorder, tell them to come back later when we're home. But I thought later, my god, I didn't tell him not to let any water buffaloes in! Or not to hang Alice [the family's infant daughter] up on the line! He really knew so little when he came to work for us. But then he gets so attached to any family he's working for that it's really complicated.

Indian employers also talk about domestic servants in ways that sound derogatory or paternalistic, but the context and therefore the meaning of their complaints are different (e.g., Dickey 1995). Indian nationals frequently provide lifetime employment to servants who begin working as "boys" or "girls" and continue through adulthood. Indian employers commonly provide medical care for a servant who has worked for the family and also extend care into the servant's old age. A servant who becomes "attached" to an Indian family acts rationally because he or she may have that job for life, or at least for a very long time, whereas a servant who becomes "attached" to an expatriate family is at a loss when that family leaves, until another expatriate family appears looking for domestic help.

"COMMUNICATION" PROBLEMS

"Communication" problems between domestic workers and expatriates are sometimes simply about language but can also be more complex than that. Misunderstandings have several plausible explanations. As a rule, domestic workers employed by expatriates specialize in working for foreign nationals. Indian servants who specialize in expatriates' services gradually learn the language (usually English) and culture of expatriates by working for numerous families in succession. Among their culinary specialties are making stone-ground peanut butter, homemade mayonnaise, cheesecake, chocolate brownies, and many other items that are not part of Indian cuisine. They know which shops and markets sell the foods and utensils needed for expatriates' kitchens. And they become familiar with the brands their employers prefer. Despite their experience in working for Westerners, however, "communication" is still not perfect. Miscommunication can arise about how to do a job or which brand name of an item to purchase. Neither of these is critical to an expatriate's ability to live or eat, but what seems unimportant to a disinterested observer is not trivial to the expatriate who feels thwarted.

> B [EXPATRIATE WOMAN]: I have a terrible communication problem with my cook—you wouldn't believe it. She bought me some cigarettes this morning, but I told her they were the wrong kind. So she just took them back [and didn't return with the right kind]!

The employer might have failed to specify the brand. The shop might not have had that brand. The cook might have misheard the name. And she could have intentionally come back empty-handed on her second try. Hiring other people to do one's work has the potential for "communication" problems built into every interaction, especially if one wants the other person to do it the "right" way. This "remote control" problem can occur between Indian employers and domestic employees, too, and the more control employers want over the outcome, the more vigilant they must be. Among expatriates there are many opportunities for the remote control to fail, particularly when they employ Indian workers to reproduce Western styles. In the following instance an expatriate ordered custom-built furniture and described the difficulty of monitoring the details.

> J [EXPATRIATE WOMAN]: You should have seen [S] trying to get this furniture made—it took over a year! And every day [S] would go down to the place where they made the furniture—they called it a factory! One day she took me along, and I watched her—she had to tell them each move.
> S [EXPATRIATE WOMAN]: I would stand there and tell them—"No, not that piece of veneer. I want this piece."

This telling of the story implies the workers could not be counted on to make good choices; the expatriate employers had to monitor each step if they wanted it done "right."

DO IT YOURSELF

When Indian employers discuss domestic "servant problems," they worry, as do expatriates, about hygiene and honesty. What makes the expatriates' stories different is the relative inability of the expatriate to perform the work him- or herself. Expatriates are more dependent on domestic servants and Indian "help." In the following account from an Indian employer she describes theft as a ground for dismissal, but she does not sound less helpless (Dickey 1995, 6):

> And if she steals, of course, definitely . . . I wouldn't even think twice before firing her. I don't/I'm not scared of doing the house job myself. I mean, I make sure that she knows nobody is indispensable . . . you show them that you can do it yourself.

Few expatriates demonstrated that they could do it themselves. One American woman who worked in her own kitchen was considered remarkable:

J [expatriate woman]: The P's are a wonderful couple. They're really unusual, that's the only word for it. Especially H. She's the only American woman in town that I know of who does all her own cooking . . . and she goes to the market and all, and in addition she teaches every morning at this school.

She's just amazing, especially for [agency] people. Almost all of the other [agency] women I know do practically nothing—they really just sit at home and play solitaire and then complain that there's nothing to do.

Me: Do they get along with H?

J: Oh yes. Everyone just likes and admires H. And there's no bad feelings. Also, H never says to them, "Look, you're a trained nurse, why don't you go out into this village just once a week to do something." She just goes along doing her own things. And she's so unique that people admire her. You know, I think it must be that when you come here you get introduced to a certain group of people and maybe don't break out of that. And it seems that these [agency] women all get into the same circle and the same pattern and do nothing. But somehow H broke out of it. I don't know what it was.

Expatriates' success in maintaining good relations and retaining servants can be the difference between being happy or miserable in India. In field notes I described an expatriate woman as follows:

> She's a very soft-spoken woman, in early thirties, with a sixth grader and a one-year-old.
>   She's very unhappy here—largely due to servant problems and the feeling that you can't trust anyone—this has been her experience. Her cooks have not kept the kitchen clean as she wanted and they've cheated her on money and by taking things.

She says they were very disappointed with their experiences here—her husband gave up his job in the States because they were so sure they'd like it here and would want to stay for four years that he quit because he couldn't take more than two years leave of absence. Now they're going back after two years and he's got to find another job.

She's doing her own cooking now because she still hasn't found another cook. She said on the phone to an American friend:

Maybe they've put me on their black list, because I had a fellow who said he'd come work for me and he was supposed to come yesterday morning but he never showed up. . . .

Even an "old India hand," a missionary who lived in India sixteen years without "servant problems," suddenly faced such problems:

Well, I'm doing my own cooking now. We never had any servant problems all sixteen years until just now. We had the same cook for ten years, but then he decided he didn't want to work in [this city] anymore. He wanted to go back to Madras—he's from there, he's not [from here]. So he started coming in to work drunk. Now I don't mind if he drinks outside, just as long as he comes to work sober, and on time. But one day he was really bad. He got his words all mixed up so I could hardly understand him and he started talking back to me. And then we noticed that some of our things were missing too. So we let him go. Then we've had one cook after another, but they all go after about a week.

My husband lost all of his American nylon shirts! And I've lost some of my wedding silver and personal things like that. And what really made me unhappy was that my daughter Terry bought herself a pure silk saree with some Christmas money she had and that was taken!

So I'm just doing all my own work now. I just have the gardener. But he helps me—he gets the vegetables ready and so I just have to cook them. And he helps me clean up.

Another expatriate woman who hired and fired many servants in succession greeted an Indian woman walking along the road with a "Hello," then turned and said to her son:

Who's that? Is that one of the Mary's we've had? [She then turned to me and added:] I've hired and fired so many cleaners—sweepers—and they keep recognizing me but I can't keep track of them all!

The British company for whom this expatriate's husband worked provided their family with a sixteen-room bungalow that was a source of both comforts and fears:

> I haven't seen much else in India. It still is rather dirty. But we've got a nice place with [this company]. They give us a bungalow, you know. We have [to her son] what was it at the last count . . . sixteen rooms? I keep having nightmares that some morning I'll wake up and there'll be half of India in my courtyard! I mean, we've got enough space for ten persons and half the people here haven't got anywhere to live. Oh well.

She continued, describing additional comforts of the company housing:

> We also have a nice pool. . . . At first we were living on Residency Road. But that was no good for the kids. So we asked for a transfer to [this house]. [Here] they've got lots of playmates all in the compound. And they've got the pool just 15 yards from our house. So they're in the water most of the day!

Her family also had a car provided by the company and previously had a driver who not only chauffeured them but also maintained the car in good working condition. Now, without a driver the expatriate felt she could never be sure of reaching her destination:

> They give us these lousy little Standards here [Indian car]. But it gets me around. We had a driver before and he used to take care of it. But now I'm driving it myself and I never know if I'll get there! Well, what're you going to do?

GENDERED FIELDS

The employers/expatriates who told most of the stories about "servant problems" are women—wives and mothers. They were responsible for their family's meals and therefore responsible for the marketing and cooking performed by servants. The women of the expatriate households were the supervisors whose remote control of servants produced the breakfasts, lunches, and dinners. When family members became ill, however, the responsibility lay with the cook—for failing to boil the water, clean the food, or sterilize kitchen utensils. Some of the foods made for expatriate families are risky preparations—mayonnaise, stone-ground peanut butter, and raw salads—and even under the watchful eye of an expatriate the raw eggs, peanuts, and salad greens can carry disease. An American woman who traced her husband's illness to the mayonnaise blamed the cook:

> We discovered that we were poisoning [my husband] right in our own kitchen . . . . he was eating sandwiches and I wasn't—and it must have been the mayonnaise that [the cook] was making—I don't know if it was a batch of bad eggs or what, but that was doing it—he was getting poisoned in our own house! (Kidder 1996)

The expatriate supervisors are usually women, but the cooks who work for Westerners are usually men (e.g., named Anthony or Andrew or Joseph or Jodi or Raj or Swamy). This gender reversal adds one more loop to the alchemy of dominance and subordination intertwined with dependence.

THE EQUITY QUESTIONS

Expatriates can afford to pay salaries to servants that far exceed the salaries Indian employers might pay. The differential not only "spoils" servants by an Indian employer's standards but also foregrounds the difference between expatriates' wealth and what their Indian friends have. Sometimes the difference between the purchasing power of Western expatriates and their Indian colleagues is so large that it threatens their presumably shared status. Expatriates who can pay domestic servants a salary close to civil servants' salaries compress the difference between working-class and middle-class Indians. And an act of "generosity" by a Western employer of domestic servants foregrounds the contrast between expatriates and Indian nationals. Ironically a simple act of "kindness" adds insult to the injuries of colonialism.

In social psychological research on social justice, a relationship between two people can appear "equitable" even if their rewards or outcomes are unequal. This form of equity is measured as the ratio of one person's "inputs" and "outcomes" in comparison with another person's inputs and outcomes (e.g., Lerner and Lerner 1981). By this formulation, the relationship between a person with a high level of skill who earns a high salary and a person with a low level of skill who earns a low salary is equitable provided their skill levels are proportionate to their income levels. What we see in the relationship between Western employers and Indian domestic workers is that "masters'" and "servants'" *skills for living in India* are *inversely* related to their salaries. Their lives describe not a null relationship but a negative correlation between *having skills for living* and *making a living* in India. Obviously other inputs account for the difference. We could add education and knowledge of English and familiarity with science and technology as key components of the expatriates' inputs, but these are also skills and inputs that their Indian colleagues possess. An important ingredient for expatriates is simply being a Westerner. This is a significant "input" because the exchange rates for Western currency and the postcolonial legacy allow a person of modest means by North American or European standards to enjoy substantial privileges in India. The key ingredient is an accident of birth—having been born in countries that profited from colonial rule.

The "equity" of these relationships is distorted by the history of colonialism and its contemporary remnants just as interracial relationships in the United States are distorted by the history of slavery and lingering racism. Ralph Ellison (1947) wrote about these twists and tensions in the *Invisible Man* as his narrator mused about the responsibilities that lay with one old man in the basement of a paint factory:

> I wondered how an apparently uneducated old man could gain such a responsible job. He certainly didn't sound like an engineer; yet he alone was on duty . . . was the only one who knew the location of all of the water mains. (1947, 209)

When the narrator discovers how the paint is made he says, "But I thought the paint was made upstairs . . .," and Lucius Brocway explains:

> Naw, they just mixes in the color, make it look pretty. Right down here is where the real paint is made. Without what I do they couldn't do nothing, they be making bricks without straw. An' not only do I make up the base, I fixes the varnishes and lots of the oils too . . .
>
> A whole lots of folks wonders about that without gitting anywhere. But as I was saying, cain't a single doggone drop of paint move out of the factory lessen it comes through Lucius Brocway's hands." (Ellison 1947, 210)

Ellison's narrator discovered that the person in the basement could make or break the fortunes of the company by adding the right or wrong bases to the paint. His position was pivotal, but his status and compensation were minimal compared with the people who worked upstairs. The people upstairs reconciled the inequalities by "adding value" to their personal merits—by being white in a culture that has a history of white-skin privilege.

Relationships of domination and subordination are particularly vulnerable to subversion when the dominant person is dependent on the subordinate. The possibility of subversion makes the relationships nonlinear and unstable. Even simple errors or accidents—of omission or commission—disrupt the hierarchy. When an Indian cook puts untreated water in a Westerner's drink, the threat is invisible but the outcome is clear and predictable. When Ellison's Invisible Man mixed the paint, he could have brought down the company's fortunes.

CONCLUSIONS

I began this essay being wary of examining how masters were simultaneously dominant and dependent in the servants' land, fearing this analysis would sound like a pardon for colonial relations. Albert Memmi describes his initial reluctance to examine this:

> I had a tendency to try . . . to reduce everything to dominance and subjection. . . . I was painting a picture of oppression in order to condemn and combat it. Perhaps I had the impression, in spite of myself, that if I had introduced a third element into the opposition between dominance and subjection, I would have attenuated the responsibility of those who are dominant. I am quite willing to admit today that . . . I was full of passion, humiliation, resentment against injustice, and impatient hope for changes in the course of things and in my own life. (Memmi 1984, 7).

Examining how dependence interacts with domination and how together they shape colonial relationships seems as necessary as it is risky. Saying the hierarchies are nonlinear does not make them benign. They are oddly complex, as when scissors cuts paper, paper covers rock, and rock dulls scissors.

Notes

1. Names of persons referred to in the fieldwork have been changed to provide anonymity.

References

Charlton, Joy
1983   Secretaries and Bosses: The Social Organization of Office Work. Ph.D. diss., Northwestern University, Evanston, Illinois.

Colen, Shellee
1989   Just a Little Respect: West Indian Domestic Workers in New York City. In
       Elsa M. Chaney and Maria García Castro, eds., *Muchachas No More: Household
       Workers in Latin America and the Caribbean*, 171–94. Philadelphia: Temple Uni-
       versity Press.

Dickey, Sara
1995   Perilous Partnerships: Domestic Service, Household Boundaries and the
       Instability of Class in Urban South India. Paper presented at the Conference on
       South Asia, Madison, Wisconsin.

Ellison, Ralph
1947   *Invisible Man*. New York: Random House (1972 Vintage Edition).

Hansen, Karen Tranberg
1991   Domestic Service. What's in It for Anthropology? *Reviews in Anthropology*
       16:47–64.

Kidder, Louise H.
1996   Colonial Remnants: Assumptions of Privilege. In Michelle Fine, Lois Weis,
       Linda C. Powell, and L. Mun Wong, eds., *Off-White: Theorizing Whiteness*,
       158–156. New York: Routledge Press.

Lerner, Melvin J., and Sally C. Lerner, eds.
1981   *The Justice Motive in Social Behavior: Adapting to Times of Scarcity and Change*.
       New York: Plenum.

Maza, Sara C.
1983   *Servants and Masters in Eighteenth-Century France: The Uses of Loyalty*.
       Princeton: Princeton University Press.

Memmi, Albert
1967   *The Colonizer and the Colonized*. Boston: Beacon Press.
1984   *Dependence: A Sketch for a Portrait of the Dependent*. Boston: Beacon Press.

Miller, Jean Baker
1976   *Toward a New Psychology of Women*. Boston: Beacon Press.

Rollins, Judith
1985   *Between Women: Domestics and Their Employers*. Philadelphia: Temple Uni-
       versity Press.

DOLLS, T-BIRDS, AND IDEAL WORKERS

The Negotiation of Filipino Identity in Hong Kong

A FILIPINO PARTY

In June 1996, while on a short visit to Hong Kong, I was invited by some old friends to attend a party one Sunday afternoon at the office of the Mission for Filipino Migrant Workers, a nonprofit organization run by Filipinos that caters primarily to the needs of domestic workers in Hong Kong.[1] The party, held in a small air-conditioned room next to St. John's Cathedral, was to celebrate the success of the Philippine Independence Day celebration that was held in Central District the previous week, and to thank the domestic worker volunteers who had helped plan, organize, and raise funds for it. In addition to myself, and six or seven regular staff members and domestic worker volunteers at the mission, the party was attended by another ten or so Filipina domestic workers. As the afternoon progressed and we had gorged ourselves on various Filipino delicacies, impromptu performances began, and one by one people were urged to sing.

Fourteen women and one man took turns singing in a variety of Filipino dialects on an imaginary stage between the desks and office chairs. Some songs had recognizable English counterparts, but most were popular Philippine folk songs. Those sung in regional dialects drew peals of laughter as everyone tried to translate the lyrics into Tagalog, the national language of the Philippines. Two women sang a verse they had learned in grade school about a mountainous group of peoples in the Philippines. Along with the woman standing next to me, they explained to everyone that this one was a derogatory song, revealing their newly discovered concern for respecting cultural diversity. Bella, the domestic worker standing beside me, explained that these dialects were as "foreign" to most of them as they were to me, since the women all came from different regions of the Philippines. Among the performers was Maria, a woman in her late forties. She hammed it up as she danced suggestively and crooned a Spanish love song. The audience howled with admiration for her flirtatious act and romantic singing voice and begged for an encore. Only later did I fully appreciate the poignancy of her high-spirited performance when I learned that Maria's husband had recently died of cancer back in the Philippines. As the story was recounted to me, when Maria requested a few days' leave from her work to attend the funeral in the Philippines, her employer told her that it would "not be convenient at that time." Maria is said to have answered—with the wit and sarcasm that quickly becomes incorporated into domestic worker humorous folklore—"Ma'am, I wish you'd told me that earlier. I would have told him not to die so soon."

As I watched the performances, Bella commented in amazement that among the fifteen people performing, ten different Philippine languages were represented. One good thing about the mission, she continued, "is that it crosscuts and successfully overcomes many of the Philippine regional divisions. In the Philippines there was the colonial divide and rule, you know? There are great differences in language and culture. . . . But here in Hong Kong we are *Filipino* migrant workers, not Visayans, Ilocanos, and so on."

NATIONALISM, REGIONALISM, AND CLASS

Although Filipinos in Hong Kong often think of themselves in terms of regional—as opposed to national—identity, Bella's statement stuck in my mind. During earlier periods of research I frequently encountered indications of the regional or linguistic subdivisions within the Filipino community. Different sections of Statue Square, Chater Road, and the Hong Kong Shanghai Bank—the areas of Central District where Filipino domestic workers congregate in the thousands on their Sundays off to eat, chat, read letters, give manicures, and so on—are spatially subdivided into regional and local groups and their informal but regular meeting places (Constable 1997a). Various "circles" or social groups, ranging from dance troops to Bible study groups and charity organizations, often break down along regional and dialect lines and clearly reflect such distinctions in their ties, networks, and links with home.

Class or occupational differences and religious differences can also create divisions within the Hong Kong Filipino community. Although local Hong Kong people often assume that all Filipinos are "helpers," many are not, and the social distinction between those who work as professionals and those who are domestic workers or contract workers can be pronounced. Differences in the class background of Filipina domestic workers also exist. Some come from urban, middle-class, educated backgrounds while others have little education or come from poor rural or urban regions. These distinctions, however, appear to blur and become less significant when women come to Hong Kong and share an occupation that is generally viewed by Hong Kong locals as lowly and demeaning.

As I aim to show in this essay, despite the significant ethnic, regional, linguistic, and class differences among Filipinos in Hong Kong, a sense of "Filipino" national identity is also present. The sense of national identity expressed and exhibited by Filipina domestic workers, however, is not unified, simple, or straightforward. It is highly contested, and therefore raises the issue of the inherent ambiguity of the "imagined community" (Anderson 1983). Unlike the broad-scale, macroconceptions of nationalism analyzed by Gellner (1983), Smith (1986), Hobsbawm (1993), Chatterjee (1986, 1993), and other noted scholars, this essay focuses on discourses of nationalism that are expressed and negotiated on a much smaller scale, in conversations, and in the course of interactions and activities. Filipino identity in Hong Kong, as I aim to show, emerges out of the microprocesses of daily life. Expressions of Filipino identity are aimed at least in part toward, or in response to, a non-Filipino audience that includes employers and other Hong Kong people who have their own, often derogatory, notions about the Philippines and Filipinos. The broader political and economic situation, and the social boundaries between Filipinos and non-Filipinos in Hong Kong have created a unique context in which Filipino identity is expressed and articulated (Barth 1994). One purpose of this essay is to explore an array of ways and circumstances in which Filipina domestic workers express themselves as Filipino—or Filipina—in Hong Kong.

Rather than focus on activities that take place within the private homes where Filipinas work, here I focus primarily on Sunday "free time" activities that are of a far more public nature. Not only does this make methodological sense, since it was far easier to observe and interact with domestic workers outside of their workplaces, but it also allows us to see more clearly the artifice of public and private, home and work, labor and leisure dichotomies.

When a domestic worker exits her employer's home on her day off, she is often still viewed as, and must therefore still negotiate, her domestic worker identity. This essay thus represents, in part, an effort to problematize the distinction between work and leisure and, as Calagione and Nugent recommend, it illustrates the "reciprocal narrative constitution of work and identity, and the way performances and audiences contribute to that process" (1992, 11).

Domestic workers do not articulate a simple or singular nationalist ideal. Sometimes domestic workers "buy into" nationalistic sentiments promoted by employment agencies and Philippine state institutions (which share many of the same interests). Philippine identity is also engendered in particular ways, linked with ideas of what constitutes proper gender roles and images. As reflected in the letters and articles in *Tinig Filipino* described in the following, domestic workers sometimes champion the ideals promoted by agencies and state institutions; in so doing they reinforce and support many of the forms of discipline imposed on workers by employers and the wider Hong Kong public. In other cases, as in the case of the "helper doll" protest described later, domestic workers contest and resist derogatory gender, national, and occupational images expressed by their employers and by Hong Kong people at large, thereby reinforcing the view of themselves as aggressive and demanding. Or, as in the case of the "10/10" celebration, domestic workers may ignore or unwittingly or subtly undermine the images of docile and self-sacrificing workers promoted by the Philippine government and state supporting institutions (Scott 1985, 1990). One point stressed here is that Filipina domestic workers resist simple categorization as either active resistors or passive subjects (Abu-Lughod 1990; Calagione and Nugent 1992). They both buy into and contest the images of Filipinos expressed by employers and other Hong Kong locals and the totalizing nationalist discourse promoted by Philippine employment agencies and state institutions. The question then becomes how and why.

After providing some background to the situation of domestic workers in Hong Kong, three different expressions of Filipino identity are examined: the image of Filipinos voiced and espoused by domestic workers in letters and articles published in the popular magazine *Tinig Filipino*; ideas about Filipinos embodied in a "domestic helper doll" that was manufactured and sold in Hong Kong in the mid-1980s and Filipino reactions to the doll; and the complex array of images promoted and expressed in the "10/10" celebration held in June 1996 in honor of Hong Kong's ten outstanding employers and workers. These examples suggest different productions of Filipino identity, variably intertwined with gender and class identity. Domestic workers accept, promote, or contest and negotiate such images and in so doing often find opportunities for pleasure, pride, and power in Hong Kong, despite the demeaning and difficult work conditions that many experience.

FOREIGN DOMESTIC "HELPERS" IN HONG KONG

Since the 1970s the number of Filipina domestic workers in Hong Kong has increased from just a few hundred to more than 130,000. In 1996, close to 10 percent of Hong Kong households employed domestic workers of some kind, and the number of households employing full-time, live-in domestic workers doubled between 1987 and 1993 (Hong Kong Government, Census and Statistics Department, 1995). Elsewhere I have examined this phenomenal increase in Hong Kong's foreign workers within the broader context of the "world perspective" recommended by Sanjek and Colen (1990; Constable 1997a). Here I will only briefly highlight some of the most important factors.

With rapidly growing unemployment, rising inflation, and lack of foreign currency with which to repay mounting international debts, the Philippine government began vigorously and successfully promoting its migrant workforce in what is called the "labor export policy" in the 1970s. The remittances of these overseas contract workers (OCWs)—which total more than US$6 billion annually—are of vital economic importance to their family members, and also essential to the nation-state and the multitudes of private and government institutions that profit from the international labor trade. Remittances, once required by Philippine law, now depend on a continued sense of familial and national obligation and loyalty among overseas workers, and the creation of what has been called "long-distance nationalism" (Anderson 1992). Thus Filipino men and women who work all over the world are praised by Philippine government officials for their patriotism, hard work, and personal sacrifice and are dubbed the nation's "silent heroes" (*Kabayan* 1996, S-6), "modern heroes" (*Kabayan* 1996, S-4), or "new economic heroes" (Asian Migrant Centre 1992).

In Hong Kong, from the mid-1970s on, there was a growing demand for full time, live-in "domestic helpers" to provide child care, cooking, cleaning, and care of the elderly.[2] English-speaking expatriates were among the first in Hong Kong to hire Filipina domestic workers in the mid-1970s, citing their ability to speak English as a major attraction. By the early 1980s, hiring Filipinas had caught on among the local Chinese population as well. By then Chinese domestic workers were scarce, and the few remaining were considered too "uppity" and well beyond the means of most middle-class households. The Chinese *amahs* who had emigrated to Hong Kong in the 1920s and 1930s from the silk-producing areas of Guangdong to work as maids were getting too old (Sankar 1978a, 1978b; Stockard 1989). *Muijai* (young

Chinese female bondservants) had long been illegal and had disappeared from the scene decades earlier (Jaschok 1988, 1994; R. Watson 1991); and younger Chinese women were far more interested in factory work, which was considered far less degrading than the work of a household servant (cf. Armstrong 1990; Constable 1996; Salaff 1981; Sankar 1978a, 1978b;). Even after factories were shifted to mainland China, and manufacturing jobs began to dry up in Hong Kong during the 1980s and 1990s, Chinese women seemed reluctant to do full-time paid household work. Instead they preferred to stay in their own homes or to work as janitors in shops or offices. Between the degrading reputation of household work and the impossibility of balancing the needs of one's own family with a full-time domestic worker job, few local women were available for such work, and thus the demand for foreign domestic workers continued to increase.

An important factor fueling the demand for foreign workers in Hong Kong in the 1980s was the opening up of service-sector jobs that were considered ideal for previously unemployed but literate and educated middle-class women (Salaff 1981). Banks, hotels, restaurants, shops, communications, and tourism boomed as the economy shifted from one based on production to one based on service, creating numerous managerial and lower-level administrative and clerical positions. Lack of household help contributed to preventing educated or middle-class Chinese women from working outside of their homes. Extended households that depended on grandparents to take up housework and child-care duties had become far less common by the 1980s, especially in urban parts of Hong Kong. People who had older parents or in-laws living with them increasingly believed it was not right to expect them to help. Thus foreign workers became an ideal and viable solution, and middle-class Chinese women who would never have considered working in factories were, I was told, "lured" into the workforce.

The relatively low legal minimum wage for foreign domestic workers in the 1980s made it possible for even lower-middle-class Chinese households to hire them. Chinese women who earned an income only slightly above a domestic worker's wage sometimes preferred to work than to remain at home.[3] Even though the official minimum wage for foreign domestic workers rose to HK$3,500 per month (almost US$500 per month) plus room and board in 1993, a number of domestic workers whom I met worked for what would be considered lower-middle-class Chinese households. Their employers, for example, worked as bank tellers, shop clerks, and newspaper sellers, and they lived in crowded flats that were little more than 500 square feet.[4]

Most foreign domestic workers in Hong Kong are from the Philippines. In 1995 there were more than 130,000 Filipino domestic workers in Hong

Kong—mainly women in their twenties and thirties—and another 23,000 from Thailand, Indonesia, India, and Sri Lanka (personal communication, Immigration Department, Hong Kong Government, June 1996). On average, Filipinas remain in Hong Kong for four years (two contracts), although I met some who had been there for ten or fifteen years. Most workers send money home to support family members and an estimated one in five Filipinos depend on such remittances for their livelihood (Catholic Institute for International Relations 1987). Domestic workers often cite economic need as a major factor in their decision to work overseas, but many are also motivated by other factors such as a desire for travel and adventure, and, as surveys suggest, Filipina domestic workers do not come from the poorest sector of the Philippine population (French 1986a, 1986b).

Throughout the 1980s and early 1990s, private and public criticisms of Filipina domestic workers in Hong Kong became more vocal, yet many Chinese employers continued to view Filipinas as the best candidates for becoming household workers (see Constable 1997b). They were viewed on the one hand as more "Western influenced" and educated than women from other parts of Asia. In the colonial context of Hong Kong, this was a good thing; it meant that they could help tutor children in English and that they knew something of appliances and "modern" ways of thinking. On the other hand, and somewhat paradoxically, they were also viewed as coming from an "inferior" or "backward" part of Asia. They were therefore expected to be in financial need, desperate for work, and grateful for the opportunity to come to Hong Kong. If Filipinas were desperately in need of money, many employers assumed, they would be subordinate, submissive, and dependent workers. Some Hong Kong employers, especially those who were themselves newly middle class and had little previous experience with "servants," seemed to expect foreign domestic workers to be more like the bondservants of old rather than professional nannies or housekeepers (see Constable 1996).

After the initial optimism regarding Filipina workers, by the late 1980s comments from Chinese employers, from employment agents, and from letters sent to Hong Kong newspapers became increasingly bitter and critical. According to some Hong Kong people, Filipinas were too demanding, too vociferous in expressing their complaints, too independent, and not subservient enough. Gradually criticisms of the old Chinese amahs subsided only to be replaced by a nostalgic yearning for the good old days of "superior" Chinese servants (Gaw 1991).

Although the number of Filipinas increased from 105,000 to 127,000 between 1993 and 1996, between late 1995 and early 1996 their numbers dropped by almost 4,000. During the same time period, 1993 to 1996, the

number of Indonesian domestic workers increased from about 10,000 to
16,000 (personal communication, Immigration Department, Hong Kong
Government, June 1996). According to some employment agents, the
choices of workers, not employers, account for this trend. With the
approach of 1997, agents speculated, Filipinas have become increasingly
reluctant to come to Hong Kong, and they are attracted to work in other
parts of the world such as Taiwan and Italy. Some employers, including those
who still hire Filipinas, suggest that Filipinas are "too difficult." The
increased demand for Indonesian domestic workers, I was repeatedly told, is
linked to the fact that they are more "subservient" and "less likely to complain or make demands" on their employers. Indonesian domestic workers
are also reputed to be passive and willing to work for less than the legal minimum wage. A smaller group, without the same support structures, experience, and knowledge of Hong Kong as Filipinos, and with little knowledge
of English or Chinese, Indonesians are believed by many Hong Kong people
to be much less likely than Filipinas to complain or demand their rights (see
Asian Migrant Centre 1994).

The slight decrease in numbers of Filipinas and the ideas about the
increase in numbers of Indonesian domestic workers raise some important
issues. As the number of Filipino workers in Hong Kong increased, they
became more knowledgeable of their legal rights, and many support groups
and resources were established to assist them. Yet as their knowledge and
support structures grew, Filipinas increasingly came to be viewed by
employers as ungrateful, haughty, aggressive, and too demanding. Some
employers went so far as to suggest that foreign domestic workers are sly and
out to "trick" their employers, getting paid to do nothing.[5] In short, it
appears that because Filipinas are not thought to "behave like maids,"
another group that is considered more complacent and less aggressive is
gaining popularity.[6] It is with such a pattern in mind that we consider some
of the contradictory expressions of Filipino identity, and their possible
implications for the Filipino domestic worker community in Hong Kong.

TINIG FILIPINO[7]

Several magazines and newspapers published in Hong Kong claim to cater to
the interests of overseas workers in general and Filipina domestic workers in
particular. Many of them share similar stated objectives. An article published in the newspaper *Kabayan*,[8] explains that like the magazine *Diwaliwan*,[9] it was "conceived primarily to help ease the loneliness and boredom of
our OCWs [overseas contract workers] and through its printed pages,
inform, educate, and influence them to continue practicing a set of values,

so that the international community will have confidence in the Filipino" (*Kabayan* 1996, S-2). The same article cites a Filipina domestic worker in Rome who praises *Diwaliwan* because it "encourages us to always practice devotion to duty coupled with honesty, because, I am not only representing my name, but also my country." *Tinig Filipino*,[10] another popular magazine that caters to the interests of domestic workers in Hong Kong (and more recently also in Italy and the Middle East), has similar goals. Its editor in chief was herself once a domestic worker, and the magazine invites contributions from its readers. Unlike *Kabayan* and *Diwaliwan*, whose publisher is Filipino, based in the Philippines, and reputed to have close ties with Philippine government and overseas employment agencies, *Tinig Filipino*'s publisher is European. The magazine is based in Hong Kong and not thought to be so closely connected with employment or remittance agencies.[11] According to some informants, therefore, *Tinig Filipino* is subject to less self-censorship and can be considered less of a Philippine government "mouthpiece." Nonetheless, a good deal of the content of *Tinig Filipino* is similar to the other two publications: it serves largely to enhance the reputation of Filipinos as ideal overseas workers, thereby contributing to the continued demand for them, and indirectly reinforcing their ability to remit more than US$6 billion annually to the Philippines.

Although but a part of *Tinig Filipino*'s wider content—which includes short stories, jokes, beauty tips, success stories, beauty contests, activities of migrant worker groups, advice columns, and so on—numerous letters and articles submitted by readers attempt to promote greater self-discipline among the domestic worker community in the name of Filipino pride. Domestic workers frequently warn their compatriots that while in Hong Kong they should behave in ways that reflect well on their homeland. It is their responsibility, furthermore, to oppose the negative stereotypes held by local Chinese regarding such things as Filipino drinking, gambling, poverty, backwardness, loose sexual morals, gossiping, loitering, and littering in public places.[12]

In response to criticisms of Filipinos in the local newspapers, domestic worker Aquarius Fe writes in *Tinig Filipino*: "Let us do something . . . to prevent the Hong Kong people from having the negative impression that we Filipinos . . . are dirty and uncooperative which will just be an addendum to the negative labels that we already have . . ." (1990, 32). She also criticizes the public fights she has witnessed in Statue Square:

> Well, sometimes we cannot avoid being mad or angry. . . . However, we can always talk about it peacefully and avoid heated arguments which may lead to fights like those I've mentioned. Remember, we are all foreigners in Hong Kong and we are supposed to act like brothers and sisters. . . . After

all, we are of the same race. We all came here to work and make money
and not enemies, right? (Fe 1990, 33)

In response to local criticisms, domestic workers encourage one another
to exercise greater self-discipline in Statue Square, Chater Gardens, and
other public places. In a letter to the editor of *Tinig Filipino*, Edith Autor
reiterates Fe's points and writes that this is the time and the season

> to prove to Hong Kong community that we Filipinos are people with
> value, honor and dignity. We can start to prove to them right where we
> are: In our places of work—that we are hardworking and honest. In public
> transport—that we do not make too much unnecessary noise. In public
> places—that we do not shout or yell to one another. . . . We do not literally
> "litter" ourselves in the corridors or in the passageways . . . . (1991, 4)

In a letter that could easily have been written by a local Chinese critic,
Filipina domestic worker Vickei Dorde asks her compatriots, "Where are
your manners?" In her letter she describes a variety of disturbing scenarios:
Filipinos drinking in public, making fun of others, not waiting their turn in
lines. She writes:

> You take a bus or a train with a bunch of friends. You are all excited and
> exchanging conversation. You completely forgot that you are in a public
> vehicle and your noise irritates other passengers.
>   Another Sunday scene: A group of friends in search of a certain lady
> who has taken some amount of money from one of them but refuses to pay,
> or looking for someone for a confrontation because she allegedly grabbed
> somebody's boyfriend. Added to this is a heated discussion between two
> ladies who were playing cards earlier. Are we that desperate that we no
> longer show decency in public anymore? (1992, 32)

Women are admonished to behave in more refined "ladylike" ways in the
name of Filipino pride. June Laggawan Sannad expresses disgust at the
behavior of a compatriot on a bus who

> sat with legs up and feet at the window. Just imagine, a lady sitting with
> legs up and feet at the window of a public transportation! Although she
> was wearing jeans, for me it was improper to sit the way she did. . . . Let us
> not be so selfish by behaving in any way we want. . . . Let us bear in mind
> that . . . we do not only carry our own name but the whole name of [all]
> Filipinos and that our misbehavior affects the reputation of the whole

Filipino community. To the lady concerned, I'm sorry but I think we should discipline ourselves next time. (1993, 5)

Local domestic worker and journalist Vady Madamba cautions readers to remember that "avoiding discotheques and pub houses doesn't only keep us from temptation and suspicious eyes but it may earn us—the whole Filipino community—good reputation from our hosts" (1991, 65). Domestic worker Oly Rueda stresses the moral responsibility of domestic workers to their "race" despite their "lowly" position in Hong Kong:

Reading these commentaries [in the Hong Kong newspapers] has urged me to call upon every Filipino helper to belie those criticisms by preserving the epitome of a dainty and demure image as well as indulging in activities geared towards the enrichment of our Philippine culture.

. . . If we still have the . . . feelings of a true Filipino, let us join hands to prove to the whole world that Filipino maids still have moral values though how lowly we are in this foreign land. Let us help the government of our host country in its drive to maintain a clean environment. Let every one of us develop a sense of responsibility by avoiding litter[ing] around. But foremost, let us realize that whatever misbehavior we show in our sojourn is a disgrace and a shame to the whole Filipino race. (1992, 16)

A letter from Evangeline C. Ragus describes her employer's view of the Philippine government and economy:

Hearing all our country's flaws being enumerated by a Chinese made me feel so ashamed. . . . Furthermore, with millions of Filipinos being out of the country, the image of the Philippines and its citizens has worsened. In Hong Kong, other than being 'kung-yans' [gungyahn, servants or literally "workers" in Cantonese] during working hours, the Filipinos are the squatters, litterers, gamblers, hawkers at the Square, etc. (1992, 33).

Ragus also pleads with her fellow Filipinos to behave in ways which will make them, in the words of Carlos P. Romula, "proud to be a Filipino anytime, any place . . ." despite the humble fact that "the immediate past and the present could make you hesitate. (1992, 33)

Filipinos encourage one another to adopt more refined and less coarse and "lower-class" feminine manners and decorum, often in the name of Philippine pride. It is important to note that—in addition to expressing transnationalism—the image of Filipino workers promoted by these letter writers (in a forum that is supposedly subject to little direct Philippine government control) corresponds well with the interests of Hong Kong employers and the Philippine state and bureaucracy that stands to gain by maintaining their popularity and thus their important financial contributions. Meanwhile other competing images are also being manufactured and marketed in Hong Kong. One striking example comes in the form of the domestic helper doll.

THE HELPER DOLL

In 1986, at a time when there were approximately 30,000 Filipina domestic workers in Hong Kong, the "helper doll" was created. Rice Paddy Babies Ltd., a North American–owned toy manufacturing company in Hong Kong, launched the new doll for sale in the colony. The "Filipino domestic helper" doll sold for HK$230 (approximately US$30). These new dolls (their infantile appearance reminiscent of the once best-selling "Cabbage Patch Dolls") reportedly came in male as well as female versions, although the female versions were the ones that were remembered. Each doll wore a black and white uniform, and each carried his or her own miniature "Philippine passport" signed by "Rice Paddy Babies Philippine Consul-General Hong Kong," John Damron, the president of RPB (HK) Ltd. Besides passports, the dolls also carried miniature employment contracts. They were sold in upscale and tourist shopping areas under the promotional banner "Will you sign my contract?" (*South China Morning Post* [SCMP] 1986a, 1986b, 1986c). According to Damron, the company expected the dolls to become especially popular as gifts for children and "friends who have moved away from Hong Kong and can't afford a little help anymore" (*SCMP* 1986c).

Rice Paddy Babies Ltd. did not anticipate the furor that ensued and eventually caused the company to discontinue the manufacture and sale of the dolls. The Filipino community in Hong Kong, including several domestic worker organizations and members of the professional Filipino community, reacted very angrily. The Philippine Consul, Jesus Yabes, questioned the legality of using the name of the Philippine consulate and was quoted in local papers as saying that the dolls were "insulting to Filipino people." The Consul remarked that the dolls are degrading and that "[people] think all Filipinos are domestic helpers which is not true" (*SCMP* 1986b). Others in the Filipino community were also concerned about the racial stereotypes that were being commodified in the form of a Filipino worker doll and about the "wrong ideas" that the dolls' documents and lifetime contract communicated. The miniature contract read, for example, "The Helper shall be employed for a lifetime" and "The Helper shall receive monthly wages as the Employer wishes." Echoing, on the surface, the sentiments of some activist Filipino groups in Hong Kong, Mr. Damron remarked that there was nothing shameful about being a domestic helper. Domestic workers who made similar statements in different contexts resented the fact that Mr. Damron could defend his dolls with such rhetoric. There is a difference, Filipina domestic workers told me, between expressing pride in an occupation that should not be perceived of as shameful, and commodifying and capitalizing on "cute" stereotypes of Filipinos.

The helper doll was not explicitly eroticized, yet still embodied certain popular fantasies about domestic workers. Reminiscent of Chinese bonded child servants of the past, the dolls were described to me as immature in appearance. They were childlike, "cute," and helpless, their identity defined almost entirely by their occupation. The dolls wore a uniform and came with a lifetime contract stating that their wages would be determined by their employers. They were bought, not hired; and they were carefully and strategically packaged for Hong Kong "buyers." The female doll's perpetual immaturity and her identity as a Filipina domestic worker was unambiguous. Although the maker of the doll was an American who had spent close to a decade in Hong Kong, he claimed he was completely unaware that Filipinos might consider the dolls offensive. Yet to the Filipino community in Hong Kong, the dolls were clearly offensive, not only because they essentialized the notion of Filipinos as domestic workers, and because others profited from the image, but because the cute doll represented the ultimate in objectifying domestic workers.

The domestic worker doll could be analyzed in a number of different ways, but for the purpose of this essay, it serves to illustrate certain ideas (or fantasies) about foreign workers, and, more important, it illustrates one issue around which the Filipino community—or at least some members of the community, crosscutting regional, dialect, or class differences—were not willing to simply sit back and passively allow derogatory images of themselves to be produced and marketed. To the wider Hong Kong public who might have been aware of the outrage the helper doll evoked, this boisterous reaction simply confirmed their sense that Filipina domestic workers were unwilling to accept their role as servants and accommodate themselves to their proper position in Hong Kong. Those who protested against the doll fueled the image of Filipinos as politically active, aggressive, defensive, and outraged. This image, to be sure, conflicted and contrasted with the images of polite guests and docile workers expressed by the contributors to *Tinig Filipino*.

THE 10/10 CELEBRATION

The 10/10 celebration of June 1996 involved an even more complex production and interaction of images and intentions. Its stated goal was to honor and entertain overseas contract workers, the "silent heroes" of the Philippines who remit over US$6 billion each year. According to a *Kabayan* article,

> this project is a brainchild of *Diwaliwan* publisher Dante A. Ang to give due recognition to the sacrifices of our OCWs. . . . Mr. Ang believes that our silent heroes need not be silent any longer in the sense that their laudable qualities and exemplary performance need to be recognized not only by the Filipino people but the host countries as well. . . . These 10 awardees may serve as real models to all OCWs around the world and for the younger generation to emulate. . . . These Pinoys do not only represent their names, but their country as well. (*Kabayan* 1996, S-10)

Sanctioned by a number of state institutions, on one level the celebration reflected an attempt to create and reinforce a sense of transnationalism or long-distance nationalism, important in reinforcing overseas workers' sense of personal and economic commitment to the homeland. It was also, simultaneously, a public relations and marketing ploy designed to elevate the reputation and boost the morale of Filipina workers and to encourage the "younger generation" to follow the overseas workers' lead. Yet the audience and participants also shaped and transformed the celebration in ways that were very likely unintended by the organizers.

Bell Publishing Company puts out the newspaper *Kabayan* and the magazine *Diwaliwan*, and, as noted, is reputed to be associated with employment agencies and remittance companies in the Philippines and in Hong Kong. Along with several other Filipino organizations in Hong Kong, Bell organized the 10/10 celebration as an afternoon of entertainment, including musical performances, speeches, and a presentation of awards to honor the ten most outstanding domestic "helpers" and employers in Hong Kong. Cosponsored by the Philippine National Bank, Duty Free Philippines, the Overseas Workers Welfare Administration, an employment agency, a remittance company, and several other organizations, this was the Hong Kong counterpart to a competition honoring ten outstanding employers and overseas workers in Rome the previous year. Although many of the domestic workers who I spoke with had never heard of the competition, and were therefore unaware that they could nominate friends, coworkers, or employers for the award, most had heard about the performance that would draw a number of famous performers from the Philippines, including Eddie Gutierrez, Jennifer Mendoza, and Michelle Ortega.

The program, like the stated objective of *Kabayan* and *Diwaliwan* cited earlier, was intended to promote a positive image of Filipinos. It was also meant to "entertain and honor" the ten outstanding workers and employers.

Yet given the fact that most of the entertainers were from the Philippines and that little attempt was made to use any language other than Tagalog (which the employers did not understand) the event was more for Filipina domestic workers than for Hong Kong employers.[13] Indeed, on that Sunday afternoon, Queen Victoria Stadium was packed with thousands of Filipinas who had paid HK$35 (between four and five U.S. dollars) to attend the event, which lasted almost five hours. The only non-Filipinos in attendance were the ten employers, their family members, a Cantonese rock star, the Chinese security staff for the stadium, and myself. Aside from the stars, the program also included local Hong Kong Filipino dance groups, the local Filipino symphony orchestra, and radio talk show hosts of the "Philippines' Tonight Show." Certain VIPs from the sponsoring organizations also attended. Speeches were made by the consulate general, the head of the Philippines Duty Free Shop, and a message from President Fidel Ramos (about economic growth, the recent creation of thousands of new jobs in the Philippines, and expressing praise for the "economic heroes") was delivered by the executive secretary of the Philippine government. Each of these items in the program received notably lukewarm reception from the audience. Indeed, the stars and radio hosts received ear-piercing screams of excitement and howls of laughter, and the symphony orchestra's selection of a medley including the Beatles' "Hard Day's Night" clearly struck a sensitive chord and earned them a thunder of applause. But the political VIP speeches received very little attention or applause and provided a chance for many women to get up, stretch their legs, and escape quickly to the restrooms.

Like many other Sunday programs that are designed to entertain Filipinas and to "keep them out of trouble" on their day off, the 10/10 celebration was also explicitly designed to popularize and publicize the notion of "outstanding" Filipina workers and Chinese employers.

The morale-boosting and reputation-building aspect of this event was noteworthy, and far more explicit than many other Sunday programs. Yet in many respects it resembled many other concerts, talent shows, and beauty contests often held in Hong Kong that allow domestic workers to express a sense of personhood beyond being "helpers." As Cohen, Wilk, and Stoeltje suggest, such contests "showcase values, concepts, and behavior that exist at the center of a group's sense of itself and exhibit values of morality, gender and place" yet they also expose such values to interpretation and challenge (1996, 2).

The general intent of the organizers, in selecting and presenting the ten outstanding workers, was to promote a positive image of Filipinas who embodied the ideals of Hong Kong employers, an ideal that is in most ways, as mentioned earlier, highly compatible with the political and economic goals and interests of the Philippine state in relation to overseas workers and their remittances. Yet the image was not without its contestations, variable interpretations, and challenges. This was especially evident when, toward the end of the program, after three and a half hours of entertainment, the "10/10" were finally introduced.

Following the rules to the competition that were published in *Kabayan*, outstanding workers could be nominated by other workers or employers, but they could not nominate themselves. Employers were nominated by workers. All nominations had to be made using the forms that were published in *Kabayan*.[14] To qualify, in addition to being required to hold a valid Philippine passport, workers had to

- have no criminal record;
- have been working for two years in his/her present employer [sic];
- have a high regard for his [sic] country including the country in which he/she works;
- have helped a countryman either physically, mentally, socially, or spiritually;
- have a significant accomplishment worth recognizing;
- be regularly sending remittances to the Philippines through recognized Philippine banks with remittance centers in Italy, Hong Kong or other countries;
- whenever he/she comes home, for a vacation or due to a finished contract, he/she must be patronizing the Duty Free Philippines [shop]. (*Kabayan* 1996, S-4)

Outstanding employers had to be

- humane in dealing with the Filipino OCW [overseas contract worker];
- kindhearted in the sense that he/she gives the OCW an opportunity for self-improvement;
- fair, who pays his/her employee on time and at the rate authorized by the law in his/her respective country;
- above all he/she must treat the OCW with respect. (*Kabayan* 1996, S-4)

The board of judges was made up of the editorial board and staff members of *Diwaliwan*. The competition drew more than 300 nominations of workers, and 200 employers. In cases of workers who appeared equally qualified, the "length of service" was the determining factor in their selection (*Kabayan* 1996, S-4).

The employers were introduced first. Nine of the ten were Chinese, many of them in visible or highly respected professions.[15] Their speeches reflected, above all, their appreciation and respect for their "helpers." One of the employers, who accepted the award on behalf of his wife, was the father of a child whose life had been saved by Pascuala Dasta, a domestic worker who, in so doing, had sacrificed her own life. His wife was given the award for her continuing economic support toward Pascuala's family. The audience responded approvingly to one employer who said that "only an outstanding helper can produce an outstanding employer." Although this statement could be interpreted negatively to mean conversely that if an employer is bad, it is the fault of the worker, the audience responded warmly to what they interpreted as a statement of the worker's power in shaping the relationship, the idea that the identity of worker and employer are intertwined, and that it "takes two" to make the relationship work. The overall image of Filipina workers expressed by the employers was very positive and similar to the ideal expressed in articles and letters in *Tinig Filipino:* they are devoted, dedicated, responsible, hardworking, and self-sacrificing. This view, though shared by many, is contrary to that which is expressed by the Employers of Overseas Domestic Helpers Association and critical employers who often view Filipina domestic workers as spoiled, demanding, selfish, and lazy.

After the employers left the stage, the outstanding domestic workers were presented with their awards and invited to make brief speeches and to shake hands with the VIPs (the Philippine Consul General, the Honorable Executive Secretary of the Philippines, and many others). Nine of the ten outstanding workers wore long, sequined, designer evening gowns, and most of them appeared even more formal, glittering, and made up than the "stars" from the Philippines. These women could be said to embody certain ideals of Filipina womanhood: glamorous, sexy, and feminine, yet hardworking and devoted equally to home, family, and nation. Such images are perpetuated in snapshots that are sent home and photographs in Philippine newspapers that inspire more young women to seek work opportunities overseas. But while the glamour and ultrafemininity represented by these women counterbalances the reality of the day-to-day work, drudgery, and boredom experienced by many domestic workers, it also creates a cause for concern among women employers who often much prefer less attractive and more gender-neutral domestic workers without makeup and dressed in baggy T-shirts and blue jeans (see Constable 1999).

The tenth outstanding domestic worker, Conchita, raised even more controversial issues as she marched onto the stage, with her short hair and muscular build, dressed in the traditional Filipino men's formal costume of black trousers and white embroidered shirt. A lesbian ("T-bird" or "thunderbird" in local slang) member of the domestic workers union, well known for her political activism in Hong Kong, Conchita embodied highly contested gender issues. The announcer, revealing her own awkwardness with the situation, stammered with her introduction of Conchita, which began "Mr., ahem, I mean Ms. Conchita. . . ." Conchita was greeted with loud cheers, whistles, and a roar of applause from the audience, including a cluster of women waving placards that read "Workers Union." In contrast to the other nine women who were honored, according to their introductions, largely for their financial contributions to their families and communities back home, and for their dedication to their employers, Conchita did not fit the same image of Filipina womanhood. Conchita's written profile resembled more the brief published descriptions of the finalists in Italy for whom the fourth condition, that they have "helped a countryman," seemed central to their selection. Conchita's nomination seemed to rest largely on her political activism, dedication, and "willingness to help fellow Filipinos" *in Hong Kong* (rather than at home), and her identity also seemed very much tied to Hong Kong.[16] As such, Conchita created a rupture in the "official" image of Filipina womanhood that was being promoted for Hong Kong consumption.[17] Although the judges may have been well aware of Conchita's identity as a T-bird when they selected her, they might have been unaware of the stir she would cause and the enthusiastic reception she would receive from the audience.

Conchita was not the only visible T-bird in the program. When the first dance troupe arrived on stage early in the program, the Filipina sitting next to me volunteered with some curiosity or embarrassment that the "men dancers" were in fact "not men, but T-birds" and asked me if I knew what that meant. In light of a spate of hostile letters to the editor of local newspapers in early 1996, the issue of lesbianism among domestic workers had become far more sensitive than it had been in earlier years. Prompted by a television news program in which one Filipina estimated that a quarter of the domestic workers in Hong Kong were lesbians, Chinese employers became concerned about what, until recently, had been interpreted as simply a "gender-neutral" and sexually unthreatening style of dress among domestic workers (see Constable 1997b). A Chinese employer responded hysterically with the following letter to the local papers and a plea for the Hong Kong Employers of Overseas Domestic Helpers Association to become involved:

> It is time for Hong Kong employers to be alerted to the threat posed to our children by Filipino T-birds or tomboys (as they are called). There are an

alarming number of T-birds. . . . How can we tell our children about bug-
gery? How can we explain the different women the maid brings home?
And how can we reason about the trousers, rolled up sleeves, the hair
cropped like a man, the men's clothes? . . . T-birds will bring to our homes
and our children the danger of venereal and killer diseases. . . . We must
monitor those who defend T-birds. . . . If we don't, I'm afraid, soon Filipino
maids' groups will be demonstrating on the streets for the right to be lesbian and the right to work in our homes forever. (Ching 1996)

Another letter, this time from a Filipina in Hong Kong, expressed similar concerns, but linked the issue to obligations Filipinas have to their
country:

There is a need to address this worrying trend [toward lesbianism]. We owe
it to the community here, our employers, and for the sake of our country to
be able to deal with T-birds. T-birds will lose their jobs, once they are
found out. That is the most troubling consequence. Ways must be found to
help lesbians turn over a new leaf. (Sombrio 1996)

Despite the criticisms expressed by women I spoke with who did not
attend the 10/10 event—"they nominated themselves as outstanding workers!"; "it is just an employment agency's scam to make money"; "people only
attended because of the stars who were present"—this event, like many others, allowed the participants to present themselves in ways that differed
greatly from either Hong Kong locals' images of lowly maids or the Philippine government's and employment agencies' ideas about ideal workers. The
glamour of the event was striking. These workers were serenaded by famous
singers and praised for their dedication to their families, their employers,
and their country by media stars and politicians. The event was an occasion
for the participants to dress to the height of fashion and to express a different sense of personhood than that exhibited six days a week in their employers' homes. The event highlighted the fact that life in Hong Kong not only
is hard work and drudgery but also involves glamour and excitement, a point
that would be stressed in *Diwaliwan* and *Kabayan* in the month to come.

At the same time, one wider message conveyed to Hong Kong employers (if they were even aware of the event at all, since unlike the event in
Rome the previous year, it did not receive attention from the local Hong
Kong papers or television stations) was that Filipinas were not loitering on
the streets, organizing political protests, or making demands for higher
wages. Instead they participated in an event that glorified their contributions, sacrifices, and dedication to their employers, their work, their nation,

and their families back home. Yet to the women who participated and observed, the event provided a variety of images of domestic workers, some of which—notably the image of T-birds—clearly conflicted with the ideals of employers, agents, and government public relations officers.[18]

NEGOTIATING IDENTITY

In this essay I have tried to show how Filipino identity can be expressed and negotiated in the course of interactions, conversations, and day-to-day activities. I have also tried to convey a sense of the complex and contradictory nature of Filipino identity politics in Hong Kong. Discussions of nationalism, as I contended at the beginning of this essay, can benefit from taking into account the micropolitics of daily life. To be Filipino in Hong Kong is not as simple as Bella's statement about overcoming regional divisions implied. Expressions of Filipino identity in Hong Kong reflect different audiences, objectives, and motivations. Filipina domestic workers, moreover, are neither active resistors nor passive subjects (Abu-Lughod 1990; Calagione and Nugent 1992). The party at the mission, the uproar over the helper doll, the 10/10 celebration, and the admonishments that appear in the pages of *Tinig Filipino* each point to the negotiation of Filipino identity that takes place within the public spaces of Hong Kong. These examples begin to suggest how values are performed, showcased, and also challenged (Cohen et al. 1996). We can also begin to see the "narrative constitution of work and identity" (Calagione and Nugent 1992, 11); some of the complicated interweavings of gender, class, and national identities; and the inherent ambiguity of the "imagined community" (Anderson 1983).

The spontaneous protest that emerged over the helper doll crosscut various sectors of the Filipino community. United in their opposition, although perhaps for very different reasons, both Filipino professionals and domestic workers objected to the representation of Filipinos as objectified, immature, helpless dolls that are controlled by their owner-employers. As a result of their seemingly unified protest—from the vantage point of non-Filipinos in Hong Kong—the protesters fueled some of the very images that the Filipino organizers of the 10/10 celebration hoped to counter. The 10/10 celebration should be seen as more than an attempt (by employment and remittance agencies, publishers, government institutions, and others who are linked to the profitable business of overseas contract work) to promote an image of workers that appeals to Hong Kong employers. It was also an attempt to secure the commitment of overseas workers through (long-distance) nationalist means, by promoting and perpetuating an image of Filipina women as devoted to both home (their own and that of their employers) and nation.

As the criteria for nomination of the ten outstanding workers outlined, workers must have a high regard for their country and a commitment to their "countrymen." They must also send remittances through recognized Philippine banks and shop at Duty Free Philippines, thus exhibiting their economic commitment and facilitating the channeling of money back to state institutions.

The audience at the 10/10 celebration opposed, or at least passively resisted, the part they were meant to play in the nationalistic script. While the energy and enthusiasm for the Filipino stars was, as described, unmistakable, the reception of the officials and government representatives was at best lukewarm, and the audience refused to grant them the recognition they desired.[19] The Philippine national anthem, for example, was only barely audible compared with the loud and spontaneous singing of "A Hard Day's Night."

While the organizers of the event shared some of the objectives of the *Tinig Filipino* letter writers who admonish their compatriots and urge them to fit themselves into a respectable mold, the audience and participants in the 10/10 celebration can be said to have expressed some other ideas. They wanted to be entertained and have fun, not to turn the event into a government-sponsored show of nationalism. For a few hours, their focus was more on the possibility of experiencing the pleasure and glamour of life in Hong Kong than on their role and identity as domestic workers and their obligations to home.

Various interest groups—workers, their families in the Philippines, the Philippine government, Hong Kong employers, employment agencies, Filipino professionals in Hong Kong—all share an interest in maintaining the popularity of Filipina workers, and in simultaneously maintaining their continued commitment to home. Yet, paradoxically, as Filipina domestic workers become better equipped to defend their legal rights and learn, for example, how to demand their legal wages and benefits, file grievances against employers who require them to work illegally in a shop or factory, or complain about physical abuse, they come to be labeled as "troublemakers" who risk being replaced by ever more complacent workers. Yet Filipino nationalists of various sorts, ranging from government spokespersons, employment agents, movie stars, and workers themselves insist that, indeed, Filipinos do make ideal workers, and they continue to admonish those who threaten to sully the sacred image. Meanwhile, as Filipinas spend more time in Hong Kong and develop social lives and leisure activities there (and some have already spent more than fifteen years there and only visit the Philippines for a week or two each year) Hong Kong may begin to feel more like home than "home."

ACKNOWLEDGMENTS

The primary examples described in this essay were collected during research con-
ducted in Hong Kong during June and July of 1996. I appreciate the funding I
received from the Hewlett Foundation, International Small Grants Program, and the
Chinese Studies Program of the University Center for International Studies at the
University of Pittsburgh. Earlier research conducted among Filipina domestic workers in the summer and fall of 1993 and summer of 1994 was partially funded by the
Research and Creative Activities Support Fund at Western Michigan University.
This paper was presented at the Anthropology Department Colloquium, University
of Pittsburgh, September 1996. I gratefully acknowledge the careful readings and
suggestions of Joseph Alter, Kathleen Adams, and Sara Dickey.

NOTES

1. Instead of "domestic helper" (or "DH"), the terms that are officially used to
refer to foreign paid household workers in Hong Kong, I use the term "domestic
worker." "Domestic worker" is preferred by many politically active Filipinas, who
consider the term "helper" diminutive and devaluing of their labor.

2. Men are also hired as domestic workers, but women remain by far the largest
group. Men's duties are more likely to involve gardening, driving, and running errands.

3. One Chinese employer who I interviewed in 1996 said she only had
HK$1000 of her own salary remaining if she calculated what she paid the domestic
worker and her room and board each month. Asked if it was worth it, she answered,
"Of course! It is so terribly boring to stay home every day." Other women claimed
that if they could afford not to work, they would.

4. A full-time shop clerk would earn around HK$6,000 per month, not
including room and board.

5. Some of these domestic workers were paid below the minimum wage, sometimes by mutual agreement with the employer. "Poorer" employers, however, were
not the only ones who "underpaid" domestic workers. According to the Hong Kong
government, the median income of households employing full-time live-in domestic
workers in 1993 was HK$35,000 per month (about US$4,500 per month), and the
average household size (not including the domestic worker) was about four (Hong
Kong Government, Census and Statistics Department, 1995, 3).

6. A member of the Employers of Overseas Domestic Helpers Association
who I interviewed expressed her vehement opposition to the current government
initiative suggesting that all full-time workers, including foreign domestic workers,
would receive maternity benefits, including a period of maternity leave with pay,

after a set period of service, if medically required. "They simply want *us* to serve *them!* Just imagine, *I* would have to bring *her* soup in bed!" she said. Some members of the employers association are also beginning to advocate for mainland Chinese women to be allowed to come to work as domestic workers in Hong Kong after 1997.

7. Some parts of this section are a revised version of part of chapter 8, *Maid to Order in Hong Kong,* Cornell University Press (Constable 1997a).

8. *Kabayan* can loosely be translated as "those who share the same homeland." *Bayan* means "country" or "homeland." The prefix and suffix *ka* and *an* can be translated as "ness" and can indicate obligation to a place, or collectiveness.

9. *Diwaliwan* combines the terms *diwa* (spirit or thought), and *aliw* (comfort or console) and can be translated as "consoling thoughts."

10. *Tinig Filipino* means literally "voice of the Filipino" and is often translated as "voice of migrant workers."

11. Dante A. Ang, head of Bell Publishing HK Ltd., which publishes *Diwaliwan* and *Kabayan,* founded the 10/10 competition. He is also the president and managing director of a public relations firm in the Philippines and is described as a "well-travelled media practitioner and businessman" (*Kabayan* 1996, S-4).

12. Foreign domestic workers are frequently criticized by Hong Kong locals, in day-to-day conversations and in the local press, for their behavior in public places, especially in Statue Square and other parts of Central District (see Constable 1997a).

13. Some of the jokes recited by one of the hosts were also popular ones that make fun of the English-speaking ability of local Chinese. Humor was also created in parodies of Cantonese.

14. *Kabayan* is sold in Statue Square and other parts of Central District on Sundays and is also available for purchase at affiliated remittance offices.

15. It seemed curious to me that nine of the ten outstanding employers were Chinese (and one German) since most domestic workers I have spoken with express a preference for Western employers.

16. Her T-bird identity may also be linked in a particular way to her life in Hong Kong. Several domestic workers have told me that women "become" T-birds in Hong Kong and that in the Philippines it is far more difficult to publicly assume or maintain this identity. This topic requires further research.

17. In the Hong Kong competition, in contrast to that in Rome, all of the ten finalists were women domestic workers. The finalists in Rome included other occupations and men.

18. Constable (1997b) discusses Filipina domestic workers' ideas about T-birds and provides a discussion of sexual images of Filipina domestic workers. A quick perusal of *Tinig Filipino* from the first half of 1996 suggests that, unlike in earlier issues, it contains little or no reference to T-birds.

19. The other person whose reception lacked enthusiasm was a Cantonese rock star. Despite his invitation and encouragement, all but a few members of the audience refused to sing along with him.

REFERENCES

Abu-Lughod, Lila
1990   The Romance of Resistance: Tracing Transformations of Power Through Bedouin Women. *American Ethnologist* 17 (1): 41–55.

Anderson, Benedict
1983   *Imagined Communities: Reflections on the Origin and Spread of Nationalism.* London: Verso Press.
1992   *Long-Distance Nationalism. World Capitalism and the Rise of Identity Politics. The Wertheim Lecture, 1992.* Amsterdam: Centre for Asian Studies.

Armstrong, M. Jocelyn
1990   Female Household Workers in Industrializing Malaysia. In Roger Sanjek and Shellee Colen, eds., *At Work in Homes: Household Workers in World Perspective*, 146–63. American Ethnological Society Monograph Series, No. 3. Washington, DC: American Anthropological Association.

Asian Migrant Centre
1992   Philippines: Making the Export of Labor Really Temporary. *Asian Migrant Forum* 6:19–20.
1994   *Nowhere to Turn To: A Case Study on the Indonesian Migrant Workers in Hong Kong Kowloon.* Hong Kong: Asian Migrant Centre.

Autor, Edith
1991   There Is a Season. *Tinig Filipino*, August, p. 4.

Barth, Fredrik
1994   Enduring and Emerging Issues in the Analysis of Ethnicity. In Hans Vermeulen and Cora Govers, eds., *The Anthropology of Ethnicity: Beyond Ethnic Groups and Boundaries*, 11–32. Amsterdam: Het Spinhuis.

Calagione, John, and Daniel Nugent
1992   Workers' Expressions: Beyond Accommodation and Resistance on the Margins of Capitalism. In John Calagione, Doris Francis, and Daniel Nugent, eds., *Workers' Expressions: Beyond Accommodation and Resistance*, 1–11. Albany, NY: State University of New York Press.

Catholic Institute for International Relations
1987   *The Labour Trade: Filipino Migrant Workers Around the World.* London: Catholic Institute for International Relations.

Chatterjee, Partha

1986   *Nationalist Thought and the Colonial World: A Derivative Discourse?* London: Zed Press.

1993   *The Nation and Its Fragments: Colonial and Post-Colonial Histories.* Princeton: Princeton University Press.

Ching, Linda

1996   Motives for Defense of Lesbians Questioned. *Eastern Express Hong Kong*, January 22.

Cohen, Colleen Ballerino, Richard Wilk, and Beverly Stoeltje

1996   *Beauty Queens on the Global Stage: Gender, Contests, and Power.* New York: Routledge.

Constable, Nicole

1996   Jealousy, Chastity and Abuse: Chinese Maids and Filipina Helpers in Hong Kong. *Modern China* 22 (4): 448–79.

1997a   *Maid to Order in Hong Kong: An Ethnography of Filipina Workers.* Ithaca, NY: Cornell University Press.

1997b   Sexuality and Discipline Among Filipina Domestic Workers in Hong Kong. *American Ethnologist* 24 (3): 539–58.

1999   At Home, But Not at Home: Filipina Narratives of Ambivalent Returns. *Cultural Anthropology* 4 (2): 203–28.

Dorde, Vickei

1992   Where Are Your Manners? *Tinig Filipino*, December, 32.

Fe, Aquarius

1990   To Whom It May Concern. *Tinig Filipino*, March, 32–33.

French, Carolyn

1986a   *Filipina Domestic Workers in Hong Kong: A Preliminary Survey.* Chinese University of Hong Kong, Centre for Hong Kong Studies, Occasional Papers No. 11.

1986b   Filipina Domestic Workers in Hong Kong. Ph.D. diss., University of Surrey, England.

Gaw, Kenneth

1991   *Superior Servants: The Legendary Amahs of the Far East.* Singapore: Oxford University Press.

Gellner, Ernest

1983   *Nations and Nationalism.* Oxford: Blackwell.

Hobsbawm, Eric

1993   *Nations and Nationalism Since 1780. Programme, Myth, Reality.* Cambridge: Cambridge University Press.

Hong Kong Government, Department of Census and Statistics
1995   "Domestic Helpers" In *Social Data Collected by the General Household Survey*, 3–11. Hong Kong: Census and Statistics Department, Special Topics Report No. 12.

Jaschok, Maria
1988   *Concubines and Bondservants: The Social History of a Chinese Custom*. Hong Kong: Oxford University Press.

Jaschok, Maria and Suzanne Miers
1994   Women in the Chinese Patriarchal System. In Maria Jaschok and Suzanne Miers, eds., *Women and Chinese Patriarchy: Submission, Servitude and Escape*, 1–24. London: Zed Press.

Kabayan
1996   The "10/10" Story. *Kabayan*, June 24–30, Volume 1, no. 51, S-1–S-16.

Madamba, Vady
1991   Discotheques and Pubhouses: Let Us Avoid Them. *Tinig Filipino*, December, p. 65.

Ragus, Evangeline C.
1992   Inheritor of the Glorious Past? *Tinig Filipino*, December, 33.

Rueda, Oly
1992   Some Food for Thought. *Tinig Filipino*, April, 16.

Salaff, Janet
1981   *Working Daughters of Hong Kong: Filial Piety of Power in the Family*. Cambridge: Cambridge University Press.

Sanjek, Roger, and Shellee Colen
1990   *At Work in Homes: Household Workers in World Perspective*. American Ethnological Society Monograph Series, No. 3. Washington, DC: American Anthropological Association.

Sankar, Andrea
1978a   Female Domestic Service in Hong Kong. In Louise Tilly, Susan Berkowitz Luton, and Andrea Sankar, eds., *Female Servants and Economic Development*, 51–62. Ann Arbor: Michigan Occasional Papers in Women's Studies, No. 1.
1978b   The Evolution of the Sisterhood in Traditional Chinese Society. Ph.D. diss., University of Michigan, Ann Arbor.

Sannad, June Laggawan
1993   Some Disgusting Behavior. *Tinig Filipino*, September, 5.

Scott, James C.

1985 *Weapons of the Weak: Everyday Forms of Peasant Resistance.* New Haven: Yale University Press.

1990 *Domination and the Arts of Resistance: Hidden Transcripts.* New Haven: Yale University Press.

Smith, Anthony

1986 *The Ethnic Origins of Nations.* Oxford: Blackwell.

Sombrio, Rose

1996 Don't Just Cry for the T-birds. *Eastern Express Hong Kong,* January 22.

South China Morning Post

1986a Domestic Dolls Degrade Us, Say Angry Filipinos. *South China Morning Post,* May 18.

1986b Filipino Maid Doll Insulting. *South China Morning Post,* May 24.

1986c Company Refuses to Change Dolls. *South China Morning Post,* June 1.

Stockard, Janice

1989 *Daughters of the Canton Delta: Marriage Patterns and Economic Strategies in South China, 1860–1930.* Hong Kong: Hong Kong University Press.

Watson, Rubie

1991 Wives, Concubines and Maids: Servitude and Kinship in the Hong Kong Region, 1900–1940. In Rubie Watson and Patricia Buckley Ebrey, eds., *Marriage and Inequality in Chinese Society,* 231–55. Berkeley: University of California Press.

GENDER, ISLAM, AND NATIONALITY
Indonesian Domestic Servants in the Middle East

INTRODUCTION

Indonesian workers are increasingly mobile in their quest for paid employment, with Indonesia following the global trend of rapid increase in international labor migration over the last two decades. The new forms of global
migration and the associated growing ethnic diversity of international labor
markets are related to fundamental transformations in economic, social, and
political structures in this postmodern and post-Cold War epoch (Castles
and Miller 1993, 2). Much of this movement is temporary, from countries
with high unemployment to countries characterized by full employment; in
particular the movement of unskilled workers to take up low-skilled work in
countries where nationals have the option to refuse such employment.
Many of the receiving countries are former "third world" nations, experiencing shifts in their relation to the global economy. Much of the movement of labor has been within Southeast Asia (from Indonesia, the Philippines, and Thailand to Brunei, Singapore, and Malaysia), but many
Southeast Asian workers have gone to East Asia (especially Hong Kong)
and to the Middle East. Governments have encouraged the out-migration of
their nationals as a way of generating national income; for example, from
remittances.

The explosion in Indonesian migration overseas exhibits the features of the "new" migration detailed by Castles and Miller (1993, 8): it is characterized by globalization (more and more countries are involved), by acceleration (growth in volume), by differentiation (involving different categories of migrants from the same country), and by a process of "feminization" as women are increasingly involved in all types of migration. However, much of this labor trade is unregulated or even illegal; hence, the workers are liable to exploitation. In a world in which labor has become an export commodity for many of the nations struggling to meet the needs and expectations of their citizens, consideration of individual rights can be pushed aside.

Indonesia's New Order[1] government is what Herbert Feith (1980) has termed a "repressive developmentalist" regime, a regime that has facilitated rapid economic growth, while exercising a "heavy weight of power" that bears down on its citizens (1980, 41). Rapid economic growth has brought significant changes in the national economy, including greater linkages to the global economy; the policies of the New Order (pursued though a series of Five Year Plans) have opened up the country to foreign investment, creating new forms of waged employment, and have been instrumental in opening up the Indonesian labor market to international labor flows.

The Indonesian government's current support for female labor migration stands in marked contrast to the broad thrust of its policies for women, where women's status as citizens is predicated on their difference from men, defined primarily in terms of their roles as wives and mothers (Robinson 1994).[2] Indonesian official gender ideology "naturalizes" a particular form of the patriarchal family as a foundation of the national political system. The political ideology of the family principle/family basis (*azas kekeluargaan*) becomes a way of legitimating the authoritarian system of government. The assumed patriarchal power in the family becomes the model for patriarchal relations in the bureaucracy and government (see Robinson 1994).

The general framework of government policy is outlined every five years in the Guidelines for State Policy (Garis Besar Haluan Negara, or GBHN). Women made an appearance in the guidelines as a special category in 1978, but as "reproducers of the next generation of workers"; that is, in terms that reinforce the emphasis on women's citizenship resting on their difference. It is not until 1993 that women appear as workers in the GBHN. While this may be read as embracing of equal opportunity for women, the shift in language emphasizes not so much women's rights to seek opportunities, but their importance as "human resources" for Indonesia's development. Whereas in earlier discourse their difference as women (their fertility) is the basis for their citizenship, as the citizen is redefined as "human resource" for development, the gender specificity associated with women's domestic roles recedes (Although in fact the basis of their economic participation remains gender specific, women are particularly important in international migration, working as housemaids, or as "nimble-fingered" workers in the rapidly expanding light industrial sector.) (see Robinson 1997).

Domestic service is a significant informal sector occupation for poor third world women. In particular it has served as an occupation for women from rural areas moving into the growing cities of the developing world (see, e.g., Boserup 1970). It is a curious occupation, sharing some of the characteristics of waged (contractual) employment, with overtones of personal relationships. The personalized aspect means that even though at one level, domestic service is the same the world over, at another level it is culturally specific. The forms of interpersonal relations in domestic service are closely linked to gender and family relations that are involved also in the expression of ethnic differences, particularly in multiethnic countries like Indonesia. Family relations in Indonesia, furthermore, become implicated in manifestations of state power because of the government's reliance on the family principle/family basis (*azas kekeluargaan*) as legitimization of its power.

Domestic service is regarded as "unskilled" labor because it requires no formal training. However, women universally are regarded as more suitable than men for this work precisely because skills training is a part of their female socialization. Domestic service operates as part of the informal, or unregulated, sector of the economy. The conditions of work, often in isolation in the employer's home, have great potential for exploitation. Cultural constraints are significant in mitigating this potential: in the Indonesian context, assumptions about the familial nature of the relationship require the exercise of a kind of parental authority on the part of the employer (see later).[3]

Indonesia has the largest Islamic population in the world, and there has always been a steady flow of Indonesians going to the Middle East to make the pilgrimage to Mecca. There has been a long history of Indonesian workers traveling to the Middle East on an unregulated basis; workers were attracted not only by the possibility of higher earnings but also by the hope of having the opportunity to make the pilgrimage to Mecca. The large-scale movement of women workers is a relatively new phenomenon. Whereas aspects of their gender identity provided some protection in their role as housemaids in their home country, Indonesian women have found themselves subjected to sexual harassment and harsh treatment in the Middle East. The new international migration, however, contributes to the formation of complex "ethnoscapes" where people from diverse cultures are thrown together and must negotiate interactions on a daily basis (Appadurai 1990). In the case of domestic servants, this negotiation must take place in the private domain of the employers' homes.

This essay takes up the issue of international labor migration by Indonesian women workers as housemaids to the Middle East, outlining the history of the growth of this labor market, then focusing on the public discourse surrounding their experience. The situation of these women has given rise to a highly contested public debate, in which the government's policies have been subjected to trenchant criticism. This public debate, which engages the ethical, moral, economic, and political issues involved in labor export, has been widely reported in the Indonesian press. The rhetoric of the debate indicates that these Indonesian women have become pawns in the economic strategies of the Indonesian government and in its political relations with Saudi Arabia. This essay examines the newspaper accounts of the debate, focusing on the reports in the Jakarta daily, *Kompas,* which has closely followed the issue. The debates reported in the newspapers draw on a range of discourses: economic rationalism, Islamic and moral issues, and gender relations in the context of state ideology.[4] The final section of the essay investigates recent interventions by feminist groups, which have championed the political rights of these women workers, in ways that challenge the terms of the dominant (and contradictory) state discourses.

Feminist theory has increasingly been concerned to open up the "understanding of women's experience and politics to the plurality of women and their embeddedness not only in gender relations but also in significant relations such as colonialism, race and class" (Stasiulis and Yuval-Davis 1995, 28). Spivak has commented that the

> central gender issue in contemporary capitalism is the position of home-
> workers and outworkers. Caught between the private sphere of gendering
> and the international space of capitalism, they have no access to the pro-
> tection offered by the state public sphere. (quoted in Connolly 1993, 106)

The challenge to feminist theory from postcolonial and class-based critiques has resulted in the understanding that binary frameworks are inadequate to understand gender relations, or the complex intersections of gender differences with class, race, ethnic, religious, and national identities and interests. Global and national restructuring projects in particular throw the inadequacies of binary models into sharp relief, not only in terms of their capacity to explain the complexities of women's everyday lives, but also in terms of their inability to encompass the new models in transnational feminist encounters that respond to the new global forms (Stasiulis and Yuval-Davis

1995, 28–29). In analyzing the debates about Indonesian women working overseas, we see first the complex intersections of shifting ideologies and state practices in regard to gender, second international class divisions reflected in labor migrations and identities based on the "imagined" identities of nationality and common religion, and third the constitution of the oppressive conditions of the work of Indonesian housemaids in the Middle East. Competing binary notions have all been brought into play in the public debate around this instance of "trafficking in women," in part accounting for the lack of fit between the arguments put forward by different protagonists in the debate.

SOUTHEAST ASIAN MIGRATION TO THE MIDDLE EAST

The sudden influx of capital into the oil-producing states after the OPEC oil price increase in 1973 led to a boom in construction and industrial development. However, in the capital-rich oil states

> shortage of labor hindered development plans, particularly in infrastructure and heavy industry. The native populations of the capital-rich states were, on the whole, young and poorly educated. Tradition generally prohibited female participation in the salaried workforce and local customs discouraged manual labor. (Ling 1984, 21; see also Azzam, Nasr, and Lorfing 1985)

Many other Middle Eastern and Asian countries became sources of unskilled and skilled labor to fuel this boom; in Southeast Asia, the Philippines and Thailand were quick to enter this labor market. Indonesia missed out on the initial boom, but by 1983 was organized to enter this market, with the establishment of regulatory provisions under *Angkatan Kerja Antar Negeri* (AKAN), or Labor Movement Between Countries, to handle requests from overseas.

For the Indonesian government, the export of labor was a means of realizing a "comparative advantage" in the global economy: a new export in the form of abundant cheap labor. It was also an "inexpensive and rapid method of alleviating unemployment" (Stahl 1986, 81). By September of 1983, an estimated 47,000 Indonesian nationals were working in Saudi Arabia, and there were hopes that the number would double in the following year (*Berita Buana*, 22 September 1983).[5] Much of the recruitment and export of Indonesian labor was illegal (Stahl 1986, 82). The Indonesian ambassador to Saudi Arabia commented that labor migration would both lead to increased work opportunities for Indonesians and earn valuable foreign exchange.[6] The Indonesian Government's Fourth Five Year Plan

(1984–89) set a target of sending 240,000 migrant workers to various over-seas countries. The Department of Manpower estimated this would bring in more than 1 million U.S. dollars in foreign exchange earnings in the five-year period (*Kompas*, 7 April 1984). This target was exceeded, and was dou-bled to half a million workers in the Fifth Five Year Plan (Hugo 1996, 491).

The Indonesian government's hopes that the Middle East would become a source of jobs for skilled Indonesian workers were not realized. This labor market had already absorbed thousands of male construction workers from countries such as the Philippines, Thailand, and Pakistan. By 1983, the construction boom was ending, and there were few job opportuni-ties for the male Indonesian workers initially recruited. The Indonesian ambassador to Saudi Arabia announced that as the need for construction workers had dried up, Indonesia would endeavor to send skilled personnel for the service sector, such as nurses and skilled maintenance workers (*Kom-pas* 7 April 1984).

There was another side to the boom, however: an increase in demand for household servants. As a new sign of prosperity, families in many oil countries import maids, cooks, gardeners, watchmen, drivers, and house ser-vants, whether their services are really needed or not. This is tantamount to a "demonstration effect" where a family's status is measured by the number of household servants/assistants it employs (Sherbiny 1984, 646).

By 1984, the majority of new Indonesian migrants to the Middle East were women, mostly working as housemaids. A sample of the files of 400 Indonesian migrants to Saudi Arabia in 1984 and 1985 revealed that 78 percent were women, all working as housemaids. Their reported ages were between twenty-five and thirty-four. Of these women, 26 percent had never attended school, while 63 percent had some primary school education. Almost all came from the rural areas of Java. Most had no previous employ-ment experience as housemaids and no relevant training (Cremer 1988, 76). According to another survey of workers recruited through an agency in Yogyakarta, Central Java, about 80 percent of the clients were women, aged twenty-one to thirty, and 60 percent were single. Three-quarters of these women were already working in Indonesia (half of them in urban areas), but they reported that they sought higher wages and more certainty in employment by migrating to the Middle East. The employment niche that opened up for them was related to their female gender. Saudi Arabian households sought women to carry out domestic work, and this was an accepted occupation for Indonesian women. However, their Islamic faith was also important in suiting them to this employment. From the women's point of view, 22 percent reported that an added incentive to work in Saudi Arabia was the opportunity to make the Muslim pilgrimage to Mecca

(Suardiman 1987, 37–38). From the point of view of Saudi employers, Indonesian women were regarded as acceptable as domestic workers because of their Islamic faith. Indonesian authorities expressed an assumption that the women would be safe in the devoutly Muslim atmosphere of Saudi Arabia, but this assumption was not shared by other nations. The Indonesian women were able to move into this niche in the Saudi Arabian economy because some of the countries that had supplied the male construction workers would not allow the recruitment of women as housemaids due to perceived problems in "worker protection" (Cremer 1988, 77). Moreover, other countries supplying male construction workers, such as Pakistan, had limited recruitment to women over age forty-five (Heyzer and Lycklama 1989, 29).

PUBLIC OUTCRY ABOUT WOMEN WORKERS IN SAUDI ARABIA

By 1984, stories were appearing in the Indonesian press alleging irregularities in the process of recruitment of Indonesian workers—reports of aspirants being cheated by recruiting agents or being given false promises about the availability of work or departure dates (e.g., *Kompas*, 7 April 1984). In April 1984, the Indonesian ambassador to Saudi Arabia raised the problem of labor recruiters who behaved improperly. He said such cases caused the government embarrassment (*Kompas*, 7 April 1984). Indonesia was not the first country to experience these problems, however. Ling reported rampant abuse of foreign workers in the Middle East including the practice of sending workers inappropriate to the job. By 1984, both Philippines and Thailand had taken steps to regulate and monitor the activities of recruiting agencies, in response to complaints of such abuse (1984, 35).

While there has been ongoing concern about the activities of labor recruiters and the general working conditions of Indonesians in Saudi Arabia, the biggest public outcry has been over allegations that Indonesian women workers have been badly treated or sexually abused by their Saudi employers. In a 1984 press conference, the Indonesian ambassador denied an Indonesian journalist's suggestion of this. He asserted there had only been a few cases of abuse, out of the thousands of Indonesian women working there. Important in the ambassador's denial was his assurance of the protection afforded by the Islamic character of Saudi Arabian society:

> Islamic tradition and Islamic law is very strong in Saudi Arabia, not like in developed Western nations. Over there, men and women who are not *muhrim* (closely related, so that marriage is prohibited) rarely meet, let

alone "interfere with" (*menganggu*) each other. If this Islamic law is vio-
lated, the punishment is harsh. (*Kompas,* 7 April 1984)

His statement encodes an implicit "occidentalist" reference to the
West, invoked as a place of potential harm to women (see Nader 1989).
This is contrasted with the presumed care for women as a "natural" conse-
quence of strict adherence to Islamic law in Saudi Arabia. In this view, the
Islamic "oriental" societies are assumed to have a commonality that is
opposed to the presumed unity of the West.

The following month, the issue of the treatment of Indonesian domestic workers became the focus of a lengthy and heated public debate in the
Indonesian press. The debate began with reported comments by Dr. Lukman
Harun (the chairman of the Foreign Affairs Department of the Central
Committee of the Islamic organization Muhammadiyah), who had recently
returned from a visit to Saudi Arabia. He expressed concern about the situation of Indonesian workers in Saudi Arabia, claiming that the majority of
workers were not known to the Indonesian embassy. Of an estimated 42,000
Indonesians in Saudi Arabia, only 12,000 were registered at the embassy.
Not only were the recruiting agencies and employers not notifying the
embassy of movements of Indonesian workers, he also claimed that they
worked under difficult conditions, at variance from those promised by
recruiters. Household servants worked long hours without rest, and they
were often moved from one employer to another in an arbitrary fashion
(*Kompas,* 9 May 1984).

Muhammadiyah is the Islamic organization most closely associated with
Islamic renewal through ties to Saudi Arabia, as opposed to the emphasis on
Indonesian traditions by other Islamic organizations such as Nahdatul
Ulama. As a leader in this organization, Lukman Harun agreed with the
view that Saudi law was predicated on strict adherence to Islamic law, and
that it was harsh to wrongdoers. However, as he noted, this did not in itself
offer protection to the women workers, because of the difficulty housemaids
would have in reporting crimes to the police: "They don't know the right
channels for reporting and they don't speak Arabic. It is difficult for them to
report to the Indonesian embassy in Jeddah because they are spread all over
the country. They often had no money and their passports are usually held
by their employer" (*Kompas,* 9 May 1984).

In contrast to the government rhetoric about shared Islamic orientations
making for a harmonious "fit," Lukman Harun's remarks seemed to suggest
that the strict Islamic code in Saudi Arabia in fact created problems for those
women who were abused by their employers. First, they could not leave the
houses without their employers' permission. Moreover, as women they were

not permitted to go about on their own. Harun further commented that if a woman could stand her situation no longer and requested to return home, the employer would demand compensation (for the recruitment costs) that would be beyond her economic means. Many Indonesian nationals living in Saudi Arabia had expressed the view that the government should stop the migration of women to work as servants. Lukman Harun suggested that the government reconsider the decision to recruit women workers for the Middle East, adding that if the government continued this policy they should have stricter selection criteria, take responsibility for ensuring that the women understood the situation in Saudi Arabia, and ensure that potential employers were carefully screened (*Kompas*, 9 May 1984).

Lukman Harun's comments carried weight due to his status as an official of a major Islamic organization. A presumption behind the recruitment of Indonesian women as housemaids was that there was a coherence of interests and social and cultural practices between Indonesia and the Middle East, due to their shared identity as Muslims. Also, labor migration to the Middle East was a logical outcome of the growing volume of Indonesian pilgrims to Saudi Arabia.

Harun's comments are also predicated on Indonesian presumptions about the mutual rights and obligations of domestic servants and their employers, which relate to Indonesian ideas of appropriate gender behavior. In the next section I discuss notions of the appropriate relations between servants and employers.

DOMESTIC SERVICE IN INDONESIA

Paid domestic service has a long history in Indonesia, as a feature of the urban centers. It is not unrelated to forms of unpaid work carried out by many unmarried women in rural communities (see Robinson 1991). As an occupation, domestic service exemplifies contradictory aspects of labor relations in poor regions of the global economy, particularly in the so-called informal sector. Related to wage labor, domestic service involves a contractual sale of labor power. However, other aspects of the relation reflect familial assumptions not usually associated with waged work. There is an enforced intimacy between employer and servant due to the sharing of domestic space. The hierarchical relation between them draws on notions of parental responsibility and filial duty, as well as the contractual obligations of an employer-employee relationship. The familial assumptions are indicative of the origins of this kind of service in village society, where real kinship relations were often involved or the connection was represented in an idiom of kinship (Robinson 1991, 38; also see chapters by Weix and Adams in this volume).

Although servants are formally free, they do not leave the house without permission. This is an aspect of the control of their labor power but also reflects an assumption that they are part of the household and are not free to go out in the world at will. Hence it is also an aspect of the familial assumptions surrounding the relations between servant and employers. Servants expect such concern and protection from their employers (see Robinson 1991). Given the anomalous situation of having young unrelated unmarried women living in the home, assumptions about the protective nature of the relationship are important to safeguarding the reputation of both servant and householder. Women are, to an extent, exchanging one set of oppressive family relations for another. However, they still maintain basic control of their lives. It is, after all, a contractual relationship and they can leave at will (and frequently do).

Evidence suggests that the personalized, familial cast to relations between domestic servants and employers is breaking down, especially in the capital city of Jakarta, where recruitment is now more likely to be through agencies, rather than through networks of kin and fellow villagers (see Robinson 1991). However, these views of the proper character of relations between servants and householders infused the debates over the situation of Indonesian women in the Middle East. The debates are also infused with a paternalism that reflects the significance of familial ideology in the official doctrine of the New Order (see Robinson 1994).

STATE AND ISLAM: INTERVENTIONS IN THE CONFLICT

Lukman Harun's comments were not welcomed by the government and certainly not by the recruiting agencies' organization, the Indonesian Manpower Suppliers' Association (IMSA). The minister for Manpower, Sudomo, responded the day of the publication of Lukman Harun's comments, denying a problem existed. His response set the tone for one of the strategies to defuse the criticism: repeated declarations that the reports of abuse were not well founded. Sudomo warned of the danger of generalizing from particular cases, noting that he had not received any official reports of such cases (Kompas, 10 May 1984). IMSA asserted they knew the whereabouts of all the workers and demanded that Lukman Harun prove his allegations, in particular the claim that 80 percent of these female migrants were suffering abuse. Lukman Harun responded by saying he had no "hard facts" but spoke on the basis of impressions from Indonesians living in Saudi Arabia, who reported to him that many women worked from 6 a.m. to 2 a.m. without rest, and that many suffered ill-treatment, including sexual assault.

Furthermore, he said this view was supported by letters to Saudi newspapers and by reports on German television (*Kompas*, 12 May 1984).

IMSA attempted to deny responsibility for any problems and rebutted the implicit criticism of its members, laying the blame on illegal immigration: there had always been illegal Indonesian migrants to Saudi Arabia and many workers in Saudi Arabia predated the formation of IMSA. The numbers had increased since the oil boom. Workers went on visas to make the Islamic pilgrimage and overstayed (*Kompas*, 15 May 1984). It is noteworthy that there is evidence that recruiting agencies have sent workers on visas for pilgrims, in situations when the government would not authorize them traveling as workers (*Tempo*, 2 June 1984). Of thirty-five recruiting agencies only eight were licensed to send women. IMSA claimed illegal channels accounted for about 15,000 women. IMSA defended the procedures for liaising with the embassy over registration of workers and argued there was sufficient surveillance of their everyday living and working conditions. Although no hard data were available on negative experiences, one IMSA spokesperson ventured that such experiences composed little more than 1 percent, which he deemed good by international standards. Nevertheless, the IMSA undertook to organize a seminar to determine ways in which they could address problems of migrant workers (*Kompas*, 15 May 1984).

That the allegations concerning treatment of women workers were made by a respected spokesperson for organized Islam (with its concern for the protection of women) explains the high-profile public debate and the maneuverings of the government to defuse the issue. Sudomo attempted to downplay the concerns about the failure of the state to protect women working overseas. He commented that apparently the majority of migrant house servants were *janda* (widows/divorcees), as if this made allegations of mistreatment of less concern (even if it were true). He noted that the government required recruiting agencies to monitor the suitability of prospective employers and to provide work contracts to the recruits. He also stated that the recruiting agencies had a responsibility to monitor the situation of the workers in Saudi Arabia (*Kompas*, 10 May 1984). That is, he defended the adequacy of the procedures that the government had put in place.

The conflict took on new dimensions when Lukman Harun was chastised by the minister, Sudomo, and other government officials for potentially harming relations between the two countries. Sudomo later revealed he had been visited by an angry Saudi ambassador who entertained the possibility of a formal protest (*Kompas*, 30 May 1984). This issue continued to overshadow concerns about workers' rights, and the question of the government's responsibilities was absent in this aspect of the dispute.

A member of Parliament, Imam Churman, expressed anxiety that the issue had the potential to "confuse" relations between the two nations and called for them to reach an agreement. However, his view on the political and diplomatic implications differed from that of the minister. In his perspective, the responsibility to protect the workers fell to the two nations. A major cause of the problem was the number of illegal migrants: how was it possible for them to be employed? The Indonesian government had a responsibility to bring the labor recruiters into line if the allegations were true. Imam Churman emphasized an obligation (on the part of both governments) to protect women workers, even though as yet no laws specifically dealt with this. He agreed with Lukman Harun that the policy should be revisited, suggesting it would be better to stop further recruitment while a review took place, and while the problems faced by the women already in Saudi Arabia were ironed out. If women were still to be sent to Saudi Arabia, it was necessary for the process to be more selective, for the embassy to be notified of the identity of the employer, and for the embassy to monitor the process (*Kompas*, 10 May 1984).

Kompas and other newspapers also published personal accounts by migrant workers to the Middle East that validated the allegations, revealing the difficult working conditions, the reneging on provisions of contracts, and instances of sexual harassment (see, e.g., Subardjo 1984). The news magazine *Tempo* had a feature story on the issue, which presented several accounts by women who had suffered sexual abuse. Zaenah, who had left her husband and child behind in Java, was raped by a friend of her employer while she was alone in the house: "I wanted to scream, but to what end? There was no-one to hear. The house was empty, the neighbors far away. Who was I to ask help from?" She became pregnant as a consequence, and her employer sent her home ("with Rp 1,5 million and a big disgrace"), to a husband who then wanted to divorce her (*Tempo*, 2 June 1984). A second Indonesian woman, Rumizah, appeared to have had good luck; her employer was kind to her and often gave her extra money, including funds to make the pilgrimage to Mecca. However, she also "struck disaster" when he began having sex with her. "I didn't protest, I didn't know what to do," she told the reporter. When she was in an advanced state of pregnancy, her employer sacked her and paid for her to return home (*Tempo*, 2 June 1984). To be sure, not all the stories were negative. *Tempo* also interviewed Sofia, who had been well treated and generously recompensed by her employer. "For worldly fortune, I have brought home money, for fortune in the hereafter, I have made the pilgrimage to Mecca" (*Tempo*, 2 June 1984).

Kompas published a number of letters from Indonesians living in Saudi Arabia protesting against the conditions of housemaids (13 May 1984). A young man wrote of his encounter with a distressed woman who had fled her employer, who had exploited and tortured her. A maid wrote to her former employers in Indonesia plaintively asking their help to return to Indonesia, and another correspondent wrote an open letter to Ibu Tien (the late wife of President Suharto), painting a graphic picture of sexual abuse of Indonesian women, who the writer said employers considered "cheap." She asserted their conditions of life were like those described by a Sri Lankan correspondent to the *Arab News*, who alleged that the women were made to suffer by their mistresses, regarded as concubines by the householders, and open to abuse by the children. These allegations echoed reports of abuse and exploitation of Thai and Filipino maids in the Middle East. According to Ling, Philippines investigators found that nearly a third of Filipina maids reported sexual harassment by employers (1984, 34). These accounts present a picture of women who, rather than being protected by the Islamic-based constraints on women in Saudi Arabia, were subject to abuse because they were outside the social sphere within which women are required to be protected. The Indonesian women's Islamic faith provided no protection; they were treated in the same manner as domestic workers from other Asian countries.

Kompas followed up with an editorial endorsing the view that the practice of exporting female labor to Saudi Arabia be reviewed. The editorial urged the government to dispatch a fact-finding team to Saudi Arabia and to use the outcome to ensure better screening and monitoring. The editorial focused on the fact that the workers in question were women, usually uneducated, and inexperienced in the world, implying a particular obligation on the part of the government to offer paternalistic protection. However, the editorial also echoed the government's rhetoric, expressing an anxiety that if the problem was not addressed it could begin to affect relations between the two countries (15 May 1984).

Islam, Gender, Nation

That the issue had significance beyond a secular debate about labor conditions became clear when the Majelis Ulama Indonesia announced that it wished to meet with the minister for Manpower to discuss the issue of sending women workers overseas. The Majelis Ulama, or Council of Religious Scholars, is an organization established under the auspices of the Department of Religious Affairs. This organization makes judgments (*fatwah*) or expresses opinions on issues, as to whether they are in accord with Islamic laws and teachings. Hence, the issue was identified as pertaining not just to the rights of Indonesian women as workers, or as Indonesian citizens, but also pertaining to their membership in the *ummat* Islam (the universal community of Muslims). The Majelis Ulama said that ever since their national workshop, which was prior to the energetic public debate evoked by Luk-man Harun's comments, their organization had been trying to meet with the minister for Manpower to discuss the issues pertaining to overseas Indone-sian women workers. At the workshop, questions had been raised as to whether the "export of female labor" was in accord with Islamic law. Hasan Basri, the chairman of the Majelis Ulama, said that *syarat* (stipulations based on Islamic precepts) covered female labor migration: the woman must go accompanied by her *muhrim* (nonmarriageable close male kin), and her safety needed to be guaranteed on the journey and in her workplace. Fur-thermore, if there is no guarantee of protection of her personal safety in her workplace, then it is forbidden by law (*haram*) to send the woman overseas. On the face of it, he had arrived at a judgment that female labor migration overseas, when women travel as individual workers, was not in accord with Islamic precepts. However, he stopped short of drawing this conclusion, stating that although Majelis Ulama felt it was necessary to make a pro-nouncement on the matter, the reports of negative experiences went "mouth to mouth" and had not been properly researched. For this reason, they had called for the meeting with the Indonesian government that they hoped would clarify the situation. Commenting on IMSA's position, Basri said: "Apparently the formal procedures are fine; it's the practice that we don't yet know about." His reluctance to make forceful pronouncements on the issue seemed to relate, in part, to a discomfort in acknowledging the neg-ative aspects of the women's experience at the hands of fellow Muslims. "These negative things can happen anywhere, not only in Saudi Arabia. And if there are excesses, it doesn't mean all Arabs are bad" (*Kompas*, 17 May 1984).

The head of an Islamic women's organization (Wanita Islam Indonesia) took a stance that emphasized the gender issues over concerns about rela-tions with a fellow Islamic nation. This leader concluded that the migration of women domestic workers should be stopped because it could give a nega-tive impression of Indonesian women to other nations.

> Let's not allow a situation where there is a view, if you want a servant, get
> an Indonesian. In this country the aspirations of Indonesian women can-
> not be made equivalent to a money value, no matter how large. (*Kompas*,
> 17 May 1984)

The head of the organization for the wives of police (Perwari) said the problem had "several aspects." In what was perhaps a veiled criticism of the position taken by Islamic scholars in the debate, she drew a contrast between the prohibition (referred to by Hasan Basri) on women making the pilgrimage to Mecca unless they were with their *muhrim* (close male kin) and women workers not only going without their *muhrim* but being sent into strangers' houses. For her, the important issue was the secular question of women's skills and education; it would be preferable to send skilled workers such as nurses and office workers, as these sorts of women would be less vulnerable to abuse and less subject to negative stereotypes (*Kompas,* 17 May 1984).

The extent to which the debate was leading to conflict between Islamic groups and the government was indicated by President Suharto's intervention. He asked that the discussion between the Majelis Ulama and the minister for Manpower be held quickly and that the issue be resolved *secara kekeluargaan*—"without conflict, in accord with family principles" (*Kompas,* 19 May 1984). Suharto's declaration embodies one of the principles of Indonesian-style democracy espoused by the New Order government, which emphasizes harmony and consensus decision making. Through this ideology, the New Order government asserts that Indonesia has a unique and distinctive political tradition that is organic, not competitive, and hence truly democratic, differentiating Indonesia from other nations. The family trope used in this formulation naturalizes authoritarian power relations, mirroring the purported and idealized patriarchal authority of the father in the household (see Robinson 1994). The president attempted to defuse the issue, emphasizing that one could not argue that all the women had a negative experience.

Sudomo responded by announcing he would meet the Majelis Ulama delegation the following week and that he would put out a statement to "clear the air" (*Kompas,* 19 May 1984). In the days before the meeting, the minister again attacked Lukman Harun in the press, arguing that he had been reckless and risked destroying Indonesia's good relations with Saudi Arabia; further, Sudomo stated that Harun was politically motivated. The minister said his department had sent a team to Saudi Arabia to check the facts, and the allegations were not true. According to the Indonesian ambassador to Saudi Arabia, since 1983 there had only been 221 cases of complaints from Indonesian workers (male and female), and all had been resolved between the embassy and the Saudi government. The complaints related to contracts and nonpayment of wages, rather than work conditions or sexual assault. However, the minister also announced that his department was overhauling the system to implement practices that would lessen "excesses that may occur," in particular by requiring preparatory training and better contracts. He acknowledged that the embassy had a duty to oversee these women's situations and to give them legal advice and assistance. Before they departed, his department advised them of the risks, but these women made their own choices. According to the minister, the women were not forced to go to Saudi Arabia, but they had a strong desire to improve their families' future. As he declared, "We respect their strong desire that is pure and noble" (*Kompas*, 25 May 1984). His comments invoke another trope deriving from the ideological promotion of patriarchal "family principles" as a cornerstone of development ideology: that of the mother sacrificing her own individual interest for that of her family. Sudomo's statement is an acknowledgment of problems, but his emphasis on the women's right to make their own decision, in the light of known risks, would appear to be at variance with the view of the Majelis Ulama concerning the women's right to protection.

The government seemed caught between its economic agendas and the public demands for moral accountability. For example, after a meeting with the president, the head of the Supreme Advisory Board (Dewan Pertimbangan Agung) commented that sending women workers overseas is a good thing, because work opportunities in Indonesia were still limited (*Kompas*, 27 May 1984). His remarks highlighted a conflict between an economic perspective in which women workers are principally an export commodity (although couched in terms of rights to work) and a moral point of view, couched in terms of Islamic values, that places human rights at the center of concern.

On May 30 Lukman Harun wrote to the English language daily, the *Jakarta Post*, refuting allegations that he was politically motivated and clearly and eloquently putting forth his case. He reiterated his concern that the embassy had only 13,453 names in its database, whereas the Ministry for Manpower had issued 47,000 permits. He also rejected the charge he was wrecking relations with Saudi Arabia. "The relations between Indonesia and Saudi Arabia have existed for hundreds of years based on religion. Housemaids are a small problem and is [sic] a new aspect of the Indonesian-Saudi relationship." Furthermore, Lukman Harun underscored that his role in both Muhammadiyah and the Majelis Ulama was precisely concerned with maintaining good relations with other Islamic countries. His motivation was not political but rather grew out of "the desire to provide information and suggestions to the Indonesian government," to protect its standards as well as the "reputation of Indonesian women." He went on to discuss the situation of the housemaids, pointing out that "their status differs greatly from that in Indonesia." The Arabic term used to describe their work (*khadamah*), he claimed, meant "someone who should serve and dutifully follow an employer's will in all matters." Also, the "status and position of women" in Saudi Arabia differed from that in Indonesia; in particular, women in Saudi Arabia were forbidden to go out alone. "Big houses with high fences make it difficult for our housemaids there to communicate with the outside world." According to Lukman Harun, the contracts, which "deal mostly with the workers' obligations and contain nothing of their rights," were signed by the worker and the agency, but not the employer. He suggested that the concern of the labor recruiting agencies to make profits at the expense of their workers was the real threat to relations between the two countries; the government should subject all current "labor suppliers" to greater scrutiny (*Jakarta Post*, 30 May 1984). He had previously written that he was delighted to hear of the proposed meeting between Sudomo and the Majelis Ulama (of which he was also a member), commenting:

> If they speak with a pure heart, with humanitarianism and with regard to the value of Indonesian women, while thinking of good relations between Indonesia and Saudi Arabia, and in a manner that is in accord with Islamic teachings, they will certainly come to the same opinion as myself concerning the problem of women domestic workers in Saudi Arabia. (*Kompas*, 17 May 1984)

The meeting between Sudomo and members of the Majelis Ulama reached a temporary resolution of the problem, in the sense of putting a stop to the public debate. The two parties agreed that it would be difficult to stop the flow of workers because the women were going in search of livelihood. Sudomo argued: "Forbidding them will not solve the problem: the solution is to reduce the excesses." Sudomo reiterated that his department did not force the women to go, that they went of their own accord, having been appraised of the risks involved. The government had to respect their right to seek a livelihood. Speaking for the Majelis Ulama, Hasan Basri pronounced: "It is our duty to protect women, and that is the responsibility of men, as it is written in the Quran." The parties resolved that the supervision and protection offered the women needed to be increased, for example, by increasing the staff at the Indonesian embassy in Saudi Arabia, including raising the number of labor attachés. So the Majelis Ulama agreed that greater government oversight of the female overseas workers would fulfill the Islamic obligation to protect the women (*Kompas*, 30 May 1984).

In terms of deflecting the "hot" issue of the negative implications for relations with another Muslim country, one of the members of the Majelis Ulama delegation commented that the problem of mistreatment of servants was not just a problem in Saudi Arabia but was found everywhere, including Jakarta. Rhetorically invoking Islam, Sudomo criticized people who looked down on servants: "It is a *halal* (permissible according to Islam) occupation" (*Kompas*, 30 May 1984). The parties also agreed that some of the problems stemmed from the low skill levels of the workers recruited. Because of low skill levels in Indonesia (e.g., a shortage of English speakers), Arabs requested low-skilled workers such as housemaids. Both parties agreed more effort was needed to send skilled workers, such as nurses and shop assistants, who would not be so easily exploited (*Kompas*, 30 May 1984).

Sudomo invited the Majelis Ulama to discourage the women from migrating by ensuring they were aware of the negative aspects of the situation, but the Majelis Ulama were reluctant to agree to this, acknowledging that the women were exercising a right to seek work. Hasan Basri commented: "For us the issue is, is it permissible [according to Islamic principles] for women to go and work overseas? We didn't want to express an opinion until we had had this meeting." Both parties agreed it was difficult to have an Indonesian team oversee the conditions of the women, as the Saudi Arabian government might perceive it as interference in domestic politics. Commenting to the press on the outcome of the meeting, the president added it was necessary to examine the laws of the two countries further.

In early June 1984, Sudomo met with Lukman Harun and four other Muhammadiyah leaders. Occurring at the beginning of the fasting month, this was a traditional time when all disputes are to be resolved. The meeting was widely reported by the press, and commentators made note of the friendly joking atmosphere between the parties. Sudomo again referred to the agreement he had recently reached with the Majelis Ulama, that the appropriate solution to the problem was to limit the occasional excesses, by increasing the protection offered to the women. He reiterated that it was difficult to stop the flow of women workers to the Middle East, without infringing on their basic human right to seek a livelihood. The other Muhammadiyah leaders clarified to Sudomo that they supported Lukman Harun in his concern for the fate of domestic workers but apologized for any problems his comments unwittingly caused. Harun did not retreat from his earlier position, providing Sudomo with a recording of interviews with women domestic workers in Saudi Arabia. Sudomo gave some acknowledgment that there was a problem to be settled by providing Muhammadiyah with a "hot line" to report negative cases (*Kompas*, 3 June 1984).

The final scene in the first act of this drama was an editorial in *Kompas* on the same day, which commented that Sudomo acted swiftly to investigate the allegations and that the research showed the situation was "not as bad" as described by Harun. The piece noted a contrite reference to the role of the press in creating the drama and concluded that the matter can be "stopped here" (3 June 1984).

Although the meetings between the minister and the Islamic leaders had arrived at a kind of resolution, the issues raised in the debate show the complexity of the legal and ethical issues that emerge because of international migration. There is no clear legal basis on which the governments can effectively protect their citizens working in another country. Add to this the complexities of cultural values, including gender ideologies and religion. The common element of the Islamic faith and the assumed commonality of interest of members of the *ummat* Islam further clouded the issue. To sum up, the interests of international diplomacy and the economic agendas of the Indonesian government were colliding with presumptions of appropriate forms of paternalistic protection for (Islamic) Indonesian women, and the apparent failure of these Islamic norms to operate across national boundaries, while still within the bounds of the *ummat* Islam.

CONSEQUENCES OF THE CONTROVERSY

The recruiting agencies (through IMSA) argued that the negative reports had caused some female recruits to change their minds (*Kompas*, 16 May 1984). However, other reports indicated that many women were prepared to take their chances, in spite of the negative publicity regarding potential risks. For these women, the assumed potential for high earnings, as a way of improving their own and their families' fortunes, made the risk worth taking.

Sudomo suggested that Indonesian workers overseas form associations to provide each other with mutual support. Referring to the problems faced by housemaids in Saudi Arabia, he suggested that an organization based around cooperatives or savings associations (*arisan*) would be beneficial to their well-being (*Kompas*, 11 June 1984). The *arisan* is a cooperative savings association run like a lottery. Members contribute a set amount each week and then draw lots to win the whole amount, each member having one turn to win. The *arisan* is associated with the notion of *gotong royong* (mutual aid) that is understood as a cornerstone of Indonesian-style democracy. Interestingly, Sudomo seemed to be recommending that the women address their problems by reconstituting a uniquely Indonesian form of sociality in the foreign environment.

Having reached a "resolution," the government attempted to stifle future negative comments on the experiences of Indonesian workers overseas. Sudomo issued a decree that all Indonesian workers recruited overseas had to sign an agreement with the Department of Manpower that they would not reveal to newspapers any problems they experienced. In signing the agreement the workers acknowledged that such revelations could damage relations between the Indonesian government and Saudi Arabia. They had to undertake to resolve their problems first with their employers, seeking further help from the labor agency and the Indonesian embassy. This decree valorized the relations between the Indonesian government and other foreign governments above the rights of their citizens working abroad. In reporting the story, *Kompas* pointed out that the reports to newspapers had occurred precisely because these other avenues had proven unresponsive (10 July 1985).

The government also reported a tightening up of the regulation of the recruiting organizations. In January 1986, *Tempo* reported that Sudomo had revoked some of their licenses as a consequence of their not responding to warnings. Moreover, it was now required that recruiting companies maintain branches or agents in Saudi Arabia, and workers had to be trained before leaving. Finally, the government set a ratio of seven women to three men for Indonesian workers in Saudi Arabia. Sudomo told the newspaper *Suara Karya* that they would not send household servants any longer, only skilled workers (nurses, office workers, and shop assistants). Workers going to Saudi Arabia now had to pass a test in Arabic, administered by the Department of Manpower. By the late 1980s, the government was holding up permits for workers until they had been trained in skills (such as cooking and sewing).

By the mid-1980s, with the drop in oil prices, there was evidence of reductions in migration from Southeast Asia to the Middle East (Russell 1986). Conferences in the Middle East had begun to raise issues of political and social "dangers" associated with non-Arab migration, and terms such as "cultural invasion" were common in the Middle Eastern press (Russell 1986, 692). However, the numbers of Indonesian workers migrating to the Middle East has continued to rise. Sudomo (the minister of Manpower in the early 1980s), commented that it might be preferable to consider sending Indonesian housemaids to Malaysia, rather than Saudi Arabia, because Indonesia and Malaysia shared a common Malay heritage (*Kompas*, 5 June 1984). This comment reflects the style of discourse of the early government statements on the suitability of Saudi Arabia as a destination for workers, due to the commonalties among Islamic nations. Here again, the discourse of suitable destinations for overseas domestic workers is couched in terms of negotiating shared religious and cultural orientations. The market for Indonesian labor has grown in Malaysia and in other Asian destinations (particularly Singapore and Hong Kong). By the early 1990s, newspaper reports began to reflect the increasingly diversified destinations of the women migrants, with stories of the problems they faced in other places, particularly Hong Kong (e.g., *Jakarta Post*, 23 October 1992).

In spite of the proposed changes, Saudi Arabia remained Indonesia's most important destination for legal overseas migration, with the majority of migrant workers being women seeking unskilled work as housemaids. In 1990, *Kompas* ran a further series of articles on the situation of Indonesian women workers in Saudi Arabia. These articles cataloged the same kinds of abuses as had occurred in the late 1980s (Utomo 1990). There were irregularities in the contracts offered, recruits were subjected to excessive demands for payments from the agencies (some of it purportedly to pay for the training imposed by the government), and workers continued to report exploitation, physical and sexual abuse, and difficulties in obtaining redress for their grievances. The consulates and embassy (reported to be receiving about seventy-five complaints from migrant workers per day) had not arrived at a way of defending the rights of their citizens in the foreign country (Hugo 1996; Utomo 1990). *Kompas* interviewed the responsible minister at the time, Cosmas Batubara. When asked about the possible solution to abuse of these women, he discussed the need to develop the kind of "training" they had before leaving Indonesia: they had to understand the local culture. For example, they had to recognize that it was the Saudi custom to eat late at night (rather than complain about long working hours). They had to understand the restrictions on women's movements that were the local custom and, in particular, recognize that if they are called by their employer, they mustn't smile, as he may misinterpret this as a sexual invitation (Utomo 1990, 121). Hence, the problems were thrown back on the women, drawing on the rhetoric of their lack of skills as the cause of the problems.

The number of Indonesian workers overseas has continued to rise, and women working as domestic help still comprise the majority (Hugo 1996; *Kompas*, 1 December 1993). There have been no changes in spite of repeated government statements that it intends to increase the volume of skilled workers, in order to both limit excesses and to increase revenues from remittances (reported by *Kompas* in 1994 as reaching nearly $1 billion in the period 1989–94) (*Kompas*, 24 February 1994). The agencies were blamed by the government for the "excesses" and in early 1994, the government yet again announced measures to tighten up procedures (*Kompas*, 24 February 1994). The minister for Manpower, Abdul Latief, also announced he had signed agreements in Malaysia and Saudi Arabia guaranteeing Indonesian workers the same rights as nationals in those countries (*Kompas*, 24 February 1994).

Government interventions have not defused the issues, and there are still calls for prohibition of women working as housemaids overseas. For example, during the 1997 election campaign, there were calls from the Islamic party (PPP) for the practice of recruiting women to work overseas as servants to be stopped, echoing a call made earlier in the year by the minister for Women's Affairs (a call that has gone unheeded by her cabinet colleagues). Although the economic imperatives of the New Order and the global economy are propelling these women outside of the "protection" of

the family, the ideological cornerstone of the New Order, the call for prohibition reflects the dominant ideological construction of gender relations in
New Order policy, where women have their primary role as subordinate to
male household heads, in the protection of the patriarchal family. The call
to prohibition demands that the state act in terms of the paternalism this
ideology implies.

INTERVENTION BY NONGOVERNMENTAL ORGANIZATIONS

Not all interested parties endorse prohibition as a solution, however. In
1990, a group of human rights and feminist activists established an organization, Solidaritas Perempuan (SP) (which they gloss in English as
Women's Solidarity for Human Rights). This organization is specifically
concerned with promoting the interests of *women migrant workers,* a term
they prefer to the sanitized *Tenaga Kerja Wanita* (TKW), or female labor
force, used in official discourse. In their view, the acronym TKW has
become synonymous with housemaids, whereas women migrant workers also
work in other occupations. Also, the term differentiates women from men,
when they argue all migrants have the same concern, seeking a livelihood
(Triwijarti 1996). In discussing the issues, SP members prefer to use the
more direct class-based language associated with the Old Order government
of the radical nationalist Sukarno. For example, they embrace the term
buruh, or laborer, a term New Order discourse replaced with the Sanskrit
derived *karyawan* (functionary/employee). Also, in naming their organization, they use the more earthy term for women—*perempuan*—as opposed to
the more polite term *(wanita)* used in New Order language. The history of
the development of the organization shows the importance of international
political alliances in countering transnational exploitation of workers. In
1990 an Indonesian human rights activist attended a seminar in Korea on
the issue of "Trafficking in Women" through which she became aware of the
lack of support for the problems faced by female migrant workers. This international meeting revealed twelve cases of ill-treatment of Indonesian
workers that had not been resolved. As a consequence of this, in December
of that year a group of activists established SP as a consortium of nongovernmental organizations (NGOs) concerned with women's rights and
workers' rights, to act as a pressure group to influence government policy in
this area (Triwijarti 1996). Currently SP includes about thirty NGOs who
represent migrants, women, human rights, and student groups to defend
unskilled Indonesian migrant workers (interview with SP activists, Jakarta,
June 1997). SP members see their role as supporting individual workers and

influencing government to improve the regulation of the export of workers. These members have endeavored to increase public awareness and understanding of the problem; for example, through press conferences to publicize their findings or holding workshops in the areas from which migrant workers have been recruited.

Through their support for individuals they have collected a substantial body of information on the characteristics and experiences of women workers, as well as the risks they face. This accumulated knowledge becomes the basis of SP's broad campaigns. They support individual workers in cases of mistreatment, for example, women who have been sent home without fares, working with the Legal Aid Institute (LBH), which provides legal aid. In some cases they have helped bereaved parents seek justice through demanding autopsies of their dead children. They argue that although they have documented thirty cases, there are hundreds of unexplained deaths and disappearances of overseas workers. In 1996 SP waged a campaign about the deaths of migrant workers, documenting about thirty cases in which relatives were given no clear cause of death. In June 1997 they took up the case of Darsih, a woman who died in Bandar Sri Begawan (Brunei). In letters to several Indonesian newspapers they argued that although there have been media reports of scores of women who have died abroad, the real number may be greater. They maintained that the deaths were mainly due to violent actions against the women (torture, sexual harassment, unsafe working conditions and travel accidents). However, many bereaved families have had difficulty in establishing the circumstances surrounding the deaths as the government has not been open. Solidaritas Perempuan has expressed concern about the large numbers of women who have disappeared, lost from contact. The labor recruiting agencies only have contact for the two years duration of the work contract, but SP has identified many lost women, some of them missing for up to seven years. The SP organization has accused the government of being more concerned with the international relations with the countries involved (including Malaysia, Singapore, Brunei, Hong Kong, and Saudi Arabia) (Susilo 1997).

In early 1997, for example, SP held a workshop in one of the rural migrant workers' generating areas, where they asked women and families to recount their experiences. Women spoke of abuse in the training compounds even before departing to Saudi Arabia. A bereaved father recounted receiving his daughter's corpse: officially he was informed that she had committed suicide but the circumstances surrounding her death were never made clear. He accepted it as *takdir* (destiny) but expressed his desire to know what had happened. He explained that he had sent his daughter in order to improve the lives of his family members and now they still had the debt to the moneylender of Rp 600,000. Many bereaved families find themselves in this position, having borrowed money against the hoped-for future earnings of the women.

According to SP, the women and their families are often unwilling to expose the cases: if their daughters are pregnant as a consequence of rape, families might say "they liked each other." They feel the public opening up of these cases places a burden on them (*keberatan*) if it means their female relatives' sexual violation and death are exposed to public scrutiny.

The SP organization has recorded cases of abuse by Department of Manpower (DEPNAKER) officials, who, since the demise of IMSA in the mid-1980s, have a greater role in the regulation of the "traffic." For example, returning migrants are routinely charged Rp 150,000 for transport back to their village, regardless of the actual distance traveled. SP reported a case of a woman forced to pay Rp 400,000 for transport back to Central Java. In SP's view, this is just an excuse to obtain money, an excuse that is justified by the argument that the migrants are village people and hence too stupid to return home safely from Jakarta, when in fact they have been around the world (interview in Jakarta 1997). The women pay a fee to DEPNAKER for protection (*perlindungan*) but receive none. Findings by SP mirror accounts of worker abuse by Department of Manpower officials reported in the newspapers, which have published reports of women returning from Saudi Arabia being forced to make illegal payments to them, including Rp 200,000 or more for transport to their villages (*Jakarta Post*, 12 July 1994; *Kompas*, 20 June 1992).

According to SP, the recruiting agents are only monitored to ensure that they are following the administrative regulations, not for their general performance (such as their treatment of women workers). The sanctions are only for failure to keep to the administrative regulations. Recruiting agents are not held responsible for cases of ill-treatment or death (i.e., for failures of the system that is supposed to protect the women). Only one agent has had his license revoked, according to SP, because of a well-publicized case in which a woman was sold for sex. There seems to be little improvement on the situation of the early 1980s where recruiting agencies were criticized for charging large amounts of money for services that were not effectively delivered. The amounts workers pay up front have increased in response to government regulations requiring the agencies to provide predeparture training. According to SP, the problems are exacerbated by the fact that at the village level the recruiters are often the village headman and his wife; that is, the people charged with ensuring adherence to the law.

The SP organization is critical of the call for prohibition: "They want to stop it, we want to regulate as the women have the right to work (and that must be defended). Even those women who have had bad experiences some-times want to go back." To SP, the issue is one of workers' rights: these women have a right to seek work overseas, and have the right to protection within a legal framework. In SP's view, the Indonesian government has an obligation to provide protection to workers, including workers overseas. For example, SP argues that the government should institute sanctions against labor recruiters who operate outside the legal framework, targeting those recruiters who send illegal migrants or fail to provide the services to the workers in terms of government regulations. The government also should take action against the domestic labor suppliers who are linked to the causes of workers' deaths, or who are involved in the cover-up. The SP organiza-tion has appealed for more government and public assistance to the victims and their families, as well as argued that the Indonesian government should ratify the 1990 International Labor Organization (ILO) convention on migrant workers, which would provide a framework for negotiating with the countries receiving Indonesian workers. This convention, however, has only been ratified by a handful of countries to date, far short of the twenty it needs to become operational.

In April and May 1997, SP was involved with other NGOs campaign-ing against draft labor legislation that the minister put before the Indone-sian parliament. The draft is intended to be umbrella legislation for the fourteen labor regulations between 1887 and 1969 (*Jakarta Post,* 5 March 1997). Groups opposing the new legislation argue that the new laws not only limit the right to strike but also remove provisions concerning rights of women workers, including the right to menstruation leave and the pro-hibition on women workers taking night shifts and heavy work. The protests have also focused on a lack in the legislation, the failure of the draft laws to include clauses providing protection for Indonesian workers overseas, the majority of whom are women. A group protesting outside Par-liament (DPR) on April 8, 1997, requested that the law give protection to women workers overseas who have been raped and sexually abused and who work unregulated hours (up to fifteen to twenty hours per day) (*Republika,* 10 April 1997).

Solidaritas Perempuan rejects the assumption of women's difference that underlies official New Order ideology and that gives credence to public calls to offer women paternalistic protection by prohibiting the interna-tional migration of unskilled female labor. The SP organization sees the underlying reason for the abuse of the women workers as: "We live in times in which it is OK to buy and sell people (*manusia dijual belikan*)." In SP's view, migration is not simply a desperate response to grinding poverty but occurs precisely because of the creation of the international labor market.

Indeed, SP argues, it is not only poor rural women lacking in skills who seek work as housemaids; now one sees educated women (even with degrees) seeking unskilled work overseas.

The government has continued to assert that the problems experienced by the women migrants derive from their low skill levels. Now women have to undergo compulsory training before they can work abroad. The training consists of skills such as sewing, child care, and learning 200 words of Arabic. This training seems principally to serve the function of allowing the government to argue that the workers are "skilled," hence fulfilling the conditions it has set for itself. The training has no effect on the kinds of jobs available to migrant workers. (Apparently the plan to send nurses and other skilled workers was not realized because the educational levels of Indonesian workers were not acceptable to the Saudi employers.) According to SP, these training programs have not been routinely reviewed for their effectiveness. One independent researcher who carried out an evaluation found that the workers felt the training to be of limited utility, having little relation to the jobs they had to perform. Much of the training was in the form of lectures and didactic instruction, and little of it was hands-on training. Anecdotal evidence suggests that some of the violence to the women comes after they have misused modern household appliances (like washing machines and vacuum cleaners). Once the women are alone in the house of the employer they are isolated and powerless. Many do not know how to use the telephone and/or how to telephone Indonesian diplomatic representatives in the foreign country. However, such practical training was not foregrounded in these predeparture seminars.

DISCUSSION

As with rural migrants taking up domestic service in Indonesian cities, the motivation for international migration derives from their class position, but the occupational niches available are gender specific. The forms of exploitation to which migrant women have been subjected, especially sexual abuse, are also gender specific. Public controversy about their employment invoked contradictory constructions of the feminine: a dominant discourse drawing on New Order ideology, and also Indonesian Islam, to argue that women's "difference" necessitated their protection; and a dissident view that demanded the creation of conditions that would allow women to pursue their aims to work, under conditions of equality with other citizens.

Public opinion, as represented in the newspaper stories and letters to the editors, had demanded that the government intervene, by acting in a paternalistic manner (in accord with a perceived Islamic sentiment) to safeguard the well-being of its citizens abroad. Although the Indonesian government usually defines its role in relation to its citizens in a paternalistic manner, in this case it rejected the demand from its citizens to act paternally, to protect women working overseas as servants. In arriving at a position that would satisfy its critics, including a compromise with the arbiters of Islamic principles, the government had to steer a path between demands for the protection of women, demand by the women to seek work abroad, and its own economic agendas. The government was also confronted with the difficulties experienced by national governments in offering protection to their citizens working in other countries. The factor of Islam influenced both the domestic debate about relative rights and responsibilities and the international question, given that the issue revolved around relations between two countries with Islamic populations. It is a dilemma for Indonesia to chastise Saudi Arabia, the heartland of Islam, for an apparent failure to abide by what is held to be a fundamental Islamic precept: specifically, the protection of women. Indeed, it would appear that the strength of the acceptance of this precept of Islam is at the heart of the problem. Indonesian women are not subjected to the same degree of exclusion from public life as is apparently the case in Saudi Arabia (Azzam et al. 1985). While Indonesian and other Asian women were flocking to Saudi Arabia to take up both skilled and unskilled occupations, the Saudi Arabian government was considering ways for Saudi women to participate in the modern workforce without leaving their homes; for example, by working in information technology (Cremer 1987). Some of the newspaper accounts of the problems of the housemaids were accompanied by photographs of urban Arab houses, conveying the impression of secluded family life carried out behind high walls. This image is in marked contrast to the way in which Indonesian family life seems to spill out into the streets, particularly in village settings.

CONCLUSION

The government is apparently caught between its economic agendas and the public demands for moral accountability. There is conflict between an economic perspective in which women workers are principally an export commodity (although couched in terms of their rights to work) and a moral point of view, couched in terms of Islamic values, in particular the need to protect women (that view, in turn, reflects the dominant ideology of gender promoted by the New Order). Economic interests (i.e., women as a valuable human resource) are the basis of the government's failure to regulate properly this "traffic in women." Since 1990 the human rights NGOs have called the government on its rhetoric of the women's rights to work, demanding that it give these women the legal protection they are entitled to as Indonesian citizens. There is a tension in Indonesian government policy between treating women as different in their capabilities and potentialities, and treating them the same as men, in their capacity as workers.

In the context of internal migration, Indonesian women working as domestic servants in Indonesian cities are protected by cultural assumptions that are reproduced in the context of the reality of the woman's capacity to escape an invidious situation. Cultural credos about male responsibility to protect female honor are not adhered to in the case of the Indonesian domestic workers abroad, whereas they do appear to influence the way female servants are treated at home. In the Middle East they are regarded as "other" and outside the protection afforded women of Saudi households. The conditions of their work, isolated in Saudi households and with their contracts and conditions of work mediated by contractors to whom they are indebted, have more the character of indentured labor than the "free" labor that is meant to characterize the (global) capitalist economy.

Spivak confronts the issue of the female subaltern in the nationalist agendas of the postcolonial nation in her analysis of the story of "Doulati the Bountiful," a young tribal woman who is sold into indentured prostitution as a consequence of her father's indebtedness. The story ends with her death from venereal disease, collapsed on the drawing of a map of India, that the local schoolmaster has prepared for Independence Day. Her story is a poignant reminder that the globalising of women's ability to sell their labor "is not an overcoming of the gendered body. The persistent agendas of nationalisms and sexuality are encrypted there in the indifference of super-exploitation" (Spivak 1992, 113). The Indonesian women working in the Middle East have an ambiguous relationship to the Indonesian state. While their citizenship is formally defined in terms of their gendered role in the family, their female gender also fits them for the specific occupational niche as housemaids in the wealthier economy of Saudi Arabia. These women take to Saudi Arabia a habitus[7] that provides them with a different "commonsense understanding of the world," including "what is 'natural' or even imaginable, that is at variance with the commonsense understanding of the world in which they find themselves" (Bottomley 1992, 122). Hence, the Indonesian women are regarded as "other," as "cheap," their practice of commodified labor in the intimate family setting apparently leaving them at risk of sexual harassment, while their status as migrant workers puts them outside of the protection of the state, subjected to unfair work conditions. Their weak position as unskilled female workers forces them to accept in human working conditions. The international deployment of their labor leaves open the question, who will protect them? The domestic servants were ill-treated because of their vulnerable status as unregulated workers in the home, and because they were women.

POSTSCRIPT

Throughout 1998, Indonesia witnessed tumultuous political change, with the resignation of President Suharto on May 21, as a consequence of pressure exerted via demonstrations by activists opposed to the nepotistic and corrupt New Order regime. Women's organizations, including SP, were centrally caught up in the political demonstrations and in the reform movement (*reformasi*) that has continued to pressure for democratization in Indonesia.

A horrific feature of the political unrest preceding Suhato's resignation were the brutal rapes of ethnic Chinese women in Jakarta on May 12 and 13, during several days of rioting in the city. Protests about the rapes, and the manner in which they symbolized the use of women as "an instrument of war," in the words of one activist, have galvanized women's organizations throughout the country. The outcry has been flamed by subsequent revelations of the systematic use of rape as a form of political terror in other parts of the country (in particular, East Timor and Aceh) throughout Suharto's period in power. After the Beijing Conference on Women in 1995, some Indonesian women's organizations had taken up the call for an end to violence against women, a hitherto unarticulated issue in Indonesia. In the wake of the May rapes, and in the political climate of reform, calls to stop violence against women have become some of the main rallying cries of women's organizations, and the focus of many street demonstrations (Robinson 1998).

In this new political climate, there is the beginning of a more public discussion of the violence inflicted on women working overseas. In October 1998, for example, women who had borne babies as a consequence of being raped by their Saudi employers demonstrated outside a labor supply agency, to demand that the government and the labor supply companies undertake to provide financial support for the children. Officials of the Department of Labor now concede that there are problems in guaranteeing the security of women workers in the Middle East.

Nonetheless, it was the effects of the Asian economic crisis on the Indonesian economy that precipitated the dramatic change in political climate. The monetary crisis has had differential effects throughout the archipelago, but some of the rural areas of Java that have provided the majority of migrants to the Middle East have been hard hit. Employment opportunities have dried up as factories and other business enterprises become victims of the economic crisis. The burgeoning light industrial sector in Java had been a site of rapidly increasing female employment prior to the crisis. Hence, the women of rural Java have even greater incentive to seek employment opportunities overseas.

In spite of the vibrant political agitation occurring in Indonesia, little has actually changed. New Order structures and regulations on the whole still remain in place. It remains to be seen if the growing women's presence in politics and the increasingly public use of the rhetoric of human rights has real consequences for Indonesian women who seek to improve their economic situation by pursuing more lucrative employment overseas.

ACKNOWLEDGMENTS

I would like to thank Dr. Chris Manning and Ms. Neng Arniati Hartanto for providing me with much of the material for this chapter.

NOTES

1. The New Order is the term chosen by President Suharto to characterize his regime, which has ruled Indonesia since 1966.

2. Yuval-Davis and Anthias (1989, 7) identify such "maternalist" politics as typical of many forms of "national processes and state practices."

3. This familial quality of domestic service has been noted by a number of writers in different contexts. Having said this, the precise content of the assumptions about familial relations differs in varied historical and social situations (see, e.g., Anderson 1991; Marks 1993).

4. My previous writing on domestic service in Indonesia (Robinson 1986, chapter 9; 1991) provides a framework within which I contextualize these debates. This previous work draws on my fieldwork experience in the mining town of Soroako (South Sulawesi Indonesia 1977–79), where domestic service was a new form of work for women, and also on my experience as a householder employing servants, while working in the South Sulawesi provincial capital (Ujung Pandang) in 1984–85. In addition to getting to know my own servants and their social worlds, my large and relatively empty house became a meeting point for other servants in the neighborhood, who would often discuss their lives with me.

5. This essay relies heavily on reports in Indonesian daily newspapers, in particular *Kompas,* the major Jakarta metropolitan daily, but also *Berita Buana* and the *Jakarta Post* and the news magazine *Tempo.* To avoid confusion, rather than list every citation in the references, I have noted the dates of publication in the text.

6. He claimed that workers were able to send up to 60 percent of their salary as remittances to the home country (*Berita Buana*, 19 August 1983). For a review of the literature on the contribution of remittances to national development, see Russell (1986).

7. In her analysis of the experience of migrants, Bottomley (1992) uses this term, taken from Pierre Bourdieu, meaning here "a way of being, a habitual state" (especially of the body) (1977, 214n).

References

Newspapers and magazines: *Kompas, Berita Buana, Tempo* (dates provided in the text).

Anderson, Patricia
1991   Protection and Oppression: A Case Study of Domestic Service in Jamaica. *Labour, Capital and Society* 24 (1): 10–39.

Appadurai, Arjun
1990   Disjuncture and Difference in the Global Economy. In Mike Featherstone, ed., *Global Culture: Nationalism, Globalization and Modernity*, 295–310. London: Sage.

Azzam, Henry T., Julinda Abu Nasr, and I. Lorfing
1985   An Overview of Arab Women in Population, Employment and Economic Development. In Julinda A. Nasr, Nabil F. Khoury, and Henry T. Azzam, eds., *Women, Employment and Development in the Arab World*, 5–38. Berlin: Mouton.

Boserup, Esther
1970   *Women's Role in Economic Development*. London: Allen and Unwin.

Bottomley, Gillian
1992   *From Another Place: Migration and the Politics of Culture*. Cambridge: Cambridge University Press.

Bourdieu, Pierre
1977   *Outline of a Theory of Practice*. Trans. Richard Nice. Cambridge: Cambridge University Press.

Castles, Stephen, and Mark J. Miller
1993   *The Age of Migration: International Population Movements in the Modern World*. Houndmills, Basingstoke, Hampshire: Macmillan.

Connolly, Clara
1993   Culture or Citizenship? Notes from the Gender and Colonialism Conference, Galway, Ireland, May 1992. *Feminist Review*, no. 44: 104–8.

Cremer, Georg

1987   Nach Dem Ölpreissturz: Folgt Ein Exodus Der Süd-Und Südostasiatischen Migranten aus Nahen Osten? *Internationales Asienforum* 18 (1–2): 69–94.

1988   Development of Indonesian Migrants in the Middle East: Present Situation and Prospects. Bulletin of Indonesian Economic Studies 24 (3): 73–86.

Feith, Herbert

1980   Repressive-Developmentalist Regimes in Asia: Old Strengths, New Vulnerabilities. *Prisma* 19 (1): 39–55.

Heyzer, Noeleen, and Geertje Lycklama à Nijehold

1989   Designing a Policy Research on the Trade in Domestic Helpers. In *Trade in Domestic Helpers: Causes, Mechanisms and Consequences. Selected Papers from the Planning Meeting on International Migration and Women, Quezon City, Philippines November 30–December 5, 1987*, 1–20. Kuala Lumpur: Asian and Pacific Development Center.

Hugo, Graeme

1996   Changing Patterns and Processes of Population Mobility in Indonesia. Paper prepared for Indonesia Update 1996. Canberra: Australian National University.

Ling, L. Huan-Ming

1984   East Asian Migration to the Middle East, Causes, Consequences and Considerations. *International Migration Review* 18 (1): 19–36.

Marks, Carole C.

1993   The Bone and Sinew of the Race: Black Women, Domestic Service and Labor Migration. In Barbara H. Settles, Daniel E. Hanks III, and Marvin B. Sussman, eds., Families on the Move: Migration, Immigration, Emigration, and Mobility. Part One. *Marriage and Family Review* 19, no. 1–2 (Special Issue): 149–73.

Nader, Laura

1989   Orientalism, Occidentalism and the Control of Women. *Cultural Dynamics* 2 (1): 323–55.

Robinson, Kathryn M.

1986   *Stepchildren of Progress: The Political Economy of Development in an Indonesian Mining Town*. Albany: State University of New York Press.

1991   Housemaids: The Effects of Gender and Culture on the Internal and International Migration of Indonesian Women. In Gillian Bottomley, Marie De Lepervanche, and Jeannie Martin, eds., *Intersexions: Gender/Class/Culture/Ethnicity*, 33–51. Sydney: Allen and Unwin.

1994   Indonesian National Identity and the Citizen Mother. *Communal/Plural* 3:65–82.

1997   Islam, Gender and Citizenship: Indonesian Women Workers in the Middle East. Paper presented to the Center for Southeast Asian Studies, University of Wisconsin-Madison, 7 November.

1998   Indonesian Women's Rights, International Feminism and Democratic Change. *Communal/Plural* 6 (2): 205–19.

Russell, Sharon Stanton

1986   Remittances from International Migration: A Review in Perspective. *World Development* 14 (6): 677–96.

Sherbiny, Naiem A.

1984   Expatriate Labor Flows to the Arab Oil Countries in the 1980s. *Middle East Journal* 38 (4): 643–69.

Spivak, Gayatri Chakravorty

1992   Women in Difference: Mahasweta Devi's "Doulati the Bountiful." In Andrew Parker, Mary Russo, Doris Summer, and Patrick Yaeger, eds., *Nationalisms and Sexualities*, 96–121. New York and London: Routledge.

Stahl, Charles W.

1986   Southeast Asian Labor in the Middle East. In Fred Arnold and Nasra M. Shah, eds., *Asian Labor Migration: Pipeline to the Middle East*, 81–124. Boulder, CO: Westview Press.

Stasiulis, Daiva, and Nira Yuval-Davis

1995   *Unsettling Settler Societies: Articulation of Gender, Race, Ethnicity and Class.* London: Sage.

Suardiman, Siti Pardini

1987   Rural Women's Migration to Cities and Overseas: Indonesia. In *Agricultural Change, Rural Women and Organizations: A Policy Dialogue*, 37–40. Organized by Asian and Pacific Development Center All-China Women's Federation. Kuala Lumpur: Asian and Pacific Development Center.

Subardjo, H. N. Bambang

1984   Pengalaman Saya Bekerja di Arab Saudi. *Kompas*, 5 May 1984.

Triwijati, Endah

1996   LSM perempuan transformatif. In Mayling Oey-Gardiner, Mildred Wagemann, Evelyn Suleeman, and Sulastri, eds., *Perempuan Indonesia: Dulu dan Kini*, 354–76. Jakarta: PT Gramedia Pustaka Utama.

Utomo, Y. Priyo, ed.

1990   *Perjalanan Nasib TKI-TKW: Antara Rantai Kemiskinan dan Nasib Perempuan.*
Jakarta: PT Gramedia.

Yuval-Davis, Nira, and Floya Anthias

1989   *Woman, Nation, State.* Houndmills, Basingstoke, Hampshire: Macmillan.

KAREN TRANBERG HANSEN

AMBIGUOUS HEGEMONIES
Identity Politics and Domestic Service

The stories about domestic service and identity in South and South-east Asia so vividly depicted in this volume are part of a larger transhistorical and cross-cultural narrative that by and large shares an excruciating conundrum. At issue is the ambiguous relationship of domestic servants as workers in, but never full-fledged members of, the households of the persons for whom they labor. Reflecting on this book's Asian variations of the domestic service quandary made me recall the first film I ever saw that went to the heart of this matter. The film in question was *La Noire de. . .* [*Black Girl*], produced in 1966 and written and directed by one of Africa's finest creative writers and filmmakers, Ousmane Sembene. The film's stark story of a young African woman brought from Dakar in Senegal to work in a white household in France is a study in disenchantment that ends shockingly in the young maid's suicide. The film is uncannily contemporary and anthropological in its microlevel focus on transnational interaction on the home front where the private becomes public, identities are at war, and French cultural hegemony produces gendered alienation of an extraordinary kind.

There have been other films, of course, documentaries as well as fiction, that have placed race-, class-, and gender-structured inequalities under public scrutiny through the lens of domestic service. In particular, I have used two documentaries effectively to capture the domestic service conundrum when teaching about this subject: *Yes Ma'am* (1982), which depicted both the subservience and professionalization of African-American domestics who work for upper-income white employers in New Orleans; and *Maids and Madams* (1985), which discussed the lives and experiences of African women domestics working in white homes during the apartheid regime in South Africa. There have been several other films in recent years that do not have domestic service as their lead story but nonetheless use the relationship as a backdrop for dealing with some of society's many ills.

What makes *La Noire de. . .* so extraordinary is the sensitivity with which Sembene captures the troublesome relationship between the African maid and the French woman for whom she works. It is the ambiguities inherent in this vexing relationship that recent scholarly work has sought, from different angles to be sure, to engage with as reflected in titles such as *Precarious Dependencies* for Lesley Gill's study of domestic service in Bolivia (1994), and my own work on Zambia, which I entitled *Distant Companions* (Hansen 1989). Responding to the contributions to the present volume, I am tempted to ask whether contemporary domestic service in South and Southeast Asia represents replays of previously performed relationships elsewhere. Are these spectacles in private homes in Asia a dèjá vu? The answer is both yes and no.

Because I am not a regional specialist on Asia, I use this postscript to explore how we might come to understand the vexing nature of domestic service in a very general way. I also offer some specific thoughts inspired by this rich collection of essays. Most of my comments concern hegemony, the concept that the editors invoke in their introduction. There are obvious limits on the degree to which concepts developed with a view to understanding particular issues may be extended to other situations. I suggest that if this concept is to be helpful at all for illuminating how domination and opposition interact in domestic service relationships, we must read hegemony *instrumentally* rather than *symptomatically*. I sketch what such a reading might look like. And I suggest that the problematic of domestic service does not arise where it most obviously is looked for: in the private household. Although the essays here are very particular in their individual approach and specific topic, together they point toward a single unfolding story of domestic service inequalities deeply embedded in the overall processes of state formation and nationalism in South and Southeast Asia.

DOMESTIC SERVICE AS PRIME-TIME POLITICS

Much like in the past, local and global inequities in economic and political terms both give rise to and help constitute contemporary domestic service in a variety of labor forms in the West and the Third World. As we enter the twenty-first century, paid domestic service is on the rise, rather than declining, across the Western and non-Western world. So is its unpaid cousin "kept household help" because of growing inequalities and increasing dependency burdens within households caused by poverty, civil war, natural disaster, and AIDS. It is the popular media that have kept this unfolding story within view, not the social sciences and certainly not anthropology.

Keeping servants offers a way of life that has not disappeared in the late twentieth century. In fact, it is prime-time politics, and it is about much more than domestic work. As Rachel Tolen notes in her essay on Indian servant employment practices in Madras, images of domestic service circulate in the public sphere, reminding us of the contentious political discourse surrounding the conditions of household workers both at home and abroad. "Thousands of foreign women are being held in Britain in conditions of slavery," according to a 1989 news report that commented on the award of £300,00 damages to Laxmi Swami, a maid who had been beaten and imprisoned by two Kuwaiti princesses (*The Independent* 1989). In the United States in 1993, Zoe Baird withdrew her name from consideration as attorney general because of public criticism over her hiring of undocumented immigrants as household help (*Chicago Tribune* 1993). Former Prime Minister Benjamin Netanyahu of Israel and his wife, Sara, learned the power of the modern nanny—not to mention of the press—when their children's caretaker, whom they had dismissed for burning the soup, gave an unflattering description of Mrs. Netanyahu shortly after Mr. Netanyahu assumed office in 1996 (*New York Times* 1996). The sorry headlines include the hanging of Filipina maid Flor Contemplacion in Singapore in 1995 and the appeal of the death sentence of another Filipina maid, Sara Balabagan, in the United Arab Emirates for murdering her elderly employer who had raped her (*Chicago Tribune* 1996a, 1996b). But the considerable number of Asian maids who worked in Kuwait were conspicuous by their absence from news reports in the United States on the Gulf War in 1991. Far away from home and isolated in Islamic Kuwaiti society, what happened to them? Was this silence the only possible result of the confrontation between the scholarly construction of the violent orient (Asad 1973) and the image of the faceless servant?

Cynthia Enloe deserves special recognition for showcasing the transnational dimension of domestic service in her feminist presentation of international politics (1990). When preparing a review about the state of research on domestic service across the disciplines in the late 1980s, I found little scholarly research on the place of domestic service in the new international division of labor (Hansen 1991). And I did not find much available literature on Asia, a complex world of countries that organize servant-keeping practices in their own cultural terms, exhibit contractual labor relations in local and expatriate servant-employing households, and engage in legal and illegal recruitment of local servants for work, especially in the Middle East. Taken together, the contributions to the present volume help to fill in this gap by zeroing in on what has been special about domestic service in Southeast and South Asia as we leave the twentieth century behind us.

In its focus on domestic service in Asia, largely in the late twentieth century, and mainly through the lens of cultural anthropology, the present collection differs from previous anthropological work on this topic in several ways. Most noticeably, several contributors frame their observations in ways that represent the cultural turn in the discipline. This shift has reconfigured the previous era's concerns with class-oriented analyses in the direction of interpretive formulations revolving around issues of identity and subjectivity. It appears as if a familiar narrative, once told in class terms of subordination and agency and now couched in cultural terms of hegemony and identity, still demands attention. Yet the overall political and economic context the contributors to this volume are concerned with differs from earlier transnational and cross-cultural encounters involving this region. This is so because of worldwide production shifts in labor and capital and of developments in communications technology and transportation that are facilitating the movements of people, commodities, and ideas at an unprecedented scale (Appadurai 1990). On a global scale, the growing number of workers for whom another person's home constitutes the principal work site commands attention for several reasons. They have to do with questions not only about local culture, personal identity, and community politics but also with increasing local and worldwide economic and political inequality. I have already suggested that it is these processes that both give rise to and help constitute contemporary domestic service in its variable labor forms.

AMBIGUOUS HEGEMONIES

As a welcome addition to the rather neglected study of domestic service in Asia, the individual contributions to this volume point to larger debates about identity politics across the vast and diverse regions of Asia and elsewhere as well. Along with the explanatory change from class and agency to identity and subjectivity to which I just referred has come a shift in conceptual categories. In effect, the cultural turn engages new concerns with representation, meanings, and memory, among others. Simplistic resistance paradigms are being questioned, as in G. G. Weix's careful qualifications of Scott's "moral economy" and Kathleen Adams's characterization of the "weapons of the weak" as weak weapons. In spite of the power asymmetry inherent in servant-keeping arrangements, the essays in this volume vividly demonstrate that the dilemmas of Asian servants are not everywhere or only the products of their work situation within private households. Because they are also creatures of their own desires, and afflicted by their own cultural terms including local notions of servitude, gender, age, and religion, the workers we get to know here are, in Jean-Paul Dumont's words, both actors and characters in local struggles between different loyalties and social hierarchies.

The editors suggest in their introduction that hegemony offers a good hook for debates about shifts in identity and that domestic service is a well-suited site for examining the negotiation of such shifts. Although the term hegemony is not new to Western political discourse in which it signifies domination of one sort or another, it has been used so broadly to refer to ideological consensus in recent culturally oriented scholarship that it risks losing its explanatory power. In effect, in many invocations of hegemony, the class character of society is hidden from view. Trying to explain the leadership failure of the Piedemonte bourgeoisie, Gramsci understood hegemony as a result of complex forms of struggle between various groups on specific sites in which power became configured in a very particular way. The process that we refer to as hegemony organizes diverse and sometimes conflicting elements as consent about ways of doing things, meanings, and values that are created, maintained, or challenged. This is to say that hegemony is a complex notion that has to do with the uneasy relationship between domination and opposition. Most specifically, hegemony refers to the way in which these elements "hang together" in a relative but never complete unity. And because it is fragile, hegemony must be continuously produced and reproduced.

Although it may appear as an oxymoron to those who translate hegemony as domination, the title of my postscript, ambiguous hegemonies, is meant to highlight this very lack of consensus, the possibility of opposition, and the tolerance of alternative meanings that may make the concept of hegemony of some use in relationship to domestic service. While none of the individual contributors to this volume explicitly apply the concept of hegemony, they nonetheless use the ideas it entails about the uneasy relationship between domination, consent, and resistance to characterize the precarious realities of domestic service lives. And they acknowledge implicitly that whatever else it is, hegemony is not a bipolar process. As Louise Kidder demonstrates in her discussion of Indian servants in expatriate households, it is not a question of either/or, but of both/and. Expatriate employers can only go so far in ordering their Indian servants around because they themselves are so dependent on the living skills of their workers. Rachel Tolen turns to a related paradox in her analysis of how servants in a railway settlement in Madras are empowered with new skills and knowledge even while they are oppressed by their Indian employers.

IN THEIR PLACE?

The essays in this volume are refreshingly particular in what they actually look at, depicting domestic service arrangements that vary from one place to the next. Still, they all are concerned with the conundrum that arises in homes with hired help about what is private and what is not and the meaning of membership of the household. The language of family or kin, described by Saubhagya Shah for Nepal and Kathleen Adams and Jean-Paul Dumont for Indonesia and the Philippines, hides the extraction of labor as does the expectation of gifts by Javanese servants that G. G. Weix describes. And the widespread assumption that women do domestic work, to which Kathryn Robinson refers, naturalizes a gender division of labor that at times puts men to work in private homes, such as in the case of the "bungalow peons" Rachel Tolen introduces us to in Madras.

Depending on the specific context, servants actively reshape the role their employer assigns to them, attempting to use it to their own advantage. Exploiting the very stereotypes that also dominate them, servants remodel hierarchical realities to their own advantage. The young servants Saubhagya Shah describes in Nepal appear to accommodate living with their identity as dependent workers and at the same time exploiting it. A more oppositional strategy is described for some of the Filipina servants Nicole Constable studied in Hong Kong.

Above all, the domestic service arrangements we are introduced to in this volume are not presented as total or complete institutions with disciplinary tools developed by the logic of Goffman or Foucault. The beauty of many of these essays is that they examine the social and cultural relations between servants and other social groups—relations that affect the domestic service situation, making it a microcosm of the surrounding society rather than a total institution that is analyzed in its own discursive terms. From Nicole Constable we learn about associations and organizations that bring together young Filipina domestics in Hong Kong when away from work and from Kathryn Robinson about political institutions that affected the international migration of Indonesian servants to Saudi Arabia, particularly in the 1980s. Michele Gamburd confronts the fragmented lives and duties of Sri Lankan women maids in the Middle East who leave husbands and children behind in order to earn enough money for the upkeep of their households. And Sara Dickey's essay about servant/employer interaction in Madurai, a city in Tamil Nadu, India, introduces us to the class discourse of both groups with an immediacy that speaks directly to local understandings of morality on both sides of the class divide and far beyond the servant-employing household.

Paid domestic work has a long history in South and Southeast Asia, as Sara Dickey and Kathleen Adams point out in their introduction. Individual contributors give evidence of the increasing prevalence of domestic service in the postcolonial period. Their rich descriptions of the shifting micropolitics of identity construction between domestic workers and their employers privilege locally inflected kin, gender, caste, and regional terms in explaining the "how's" and "why's" of domestic work. But the conundrums of the vexing relationship in paid domestic work are not only the results of personal identity politics. As I have stressed throughout, they are also the outcomes of much larger social, economic, and political processes that are increasing the importance of this work in the global political economy. In effect, as the twentieth century approaches its end, paid domestic work has become part of state-society relations and transnational politics that are keeping domestic workers in a place that would surprise the scholars of modernization who characterized their work as obsolete and predicted its decline.

TOMORROW'S SCHOLARSHIP

To explore the complexity of domestic service across the vast expanses of Asia, regional scholars, including anthropologists, might do well to extend the line and nature of their inquiry as well as the kind of sources they examine. For example, many of the contributors point to, but do not fully engage with, the complexity of gender construction in relationship to issues of femininity, masculinity, and youth, which hover just below the surface of the essays by Michele Gamburd, Kathryn Robinson, and Saubhagya Shah but really are present in most of the works. We may also draw inspiration from historians who in their preoccupation with domestic service keep returning to previously studied periods, casting light on them from new angles, mining fresh archives, or turning to historical and regional contexts that have received little prior attention (e.g., Gerard 1994; Hill 1996). And to be sure, after the publication of Gary Leupp's work on urban Tokugawa Japan

(1992), there are interesting new questions to ask about the comparative and historical place of domestic service in relationship to major socioeconomic transformations both in this region and beyond it.

The cultural turn in anthropology opens the door for many potential new sources of knowledge about domestic service, some of which are explored with good effect here. They include the stories that Indian servants and employers in Madurai told Sara Dickey about one another as well as the jokes that Kathleen Adams examines in the Indonesian servant-keeping households where she stayed. Paintings and other images like photographs, advice books, and didactic literature in general, creative literature, newspapers, cartoons, and, as I indicated at the outset, films are among the rich sources we may explore creatively with a view to fleshing out in more detail the shifting contours of the domestic service story in South and Southeast Asia and elsewhere. Swapna Banerjee, for example, turned to Bengali domestic manuals for insights into the construction of the mistress-servant relation in colonial Calcutta (1996). Another recent study examined nineteenth-century American paintings for their representation of domestic servants (O'Leary 1996). What is more, academics must learn to reckon with popular sentiments about sexuality in order not to lose sight of the fact that identity politics of hired help also are fought out through sex, at times violently so.

Last but not least, taking an important inspiration from Cynthia Enloe, future lines of inquiry into the construction and negotiation of domestic service identities must not stop short at representation but be linked to examinations of the local and global social and political realities that play parts in their production. Attempting to shore up their sagging economies, several countries in South and Southeast Asia have made bilateral agreements for the export of women domestic workers (Chin 1998; Heyzer, Nijehold, and Weerakoon 1994). In Singapore, Saudi Arabia, Italy, and North America, foreign domestic workers increasingly perform the household work that no one else would do. Their legal status, for example in Canada, has worsened rather than improved in the last two decades (Bakan and Stasilius 1997). Concerns have already been expressed about the future of Filipina maids in Hong Kong after the British handover of this territory to China in 1997 (*The Independent* 1997). If we are to continue to unravel the vexing questions arising from the global reproduction of paid domestic service within the next century, we need to examine employment practices, labor standards, and legal rulings as well as morality, social responsibility, and identity questions. Although mistreatment and abuse of foreign domestic workers has been reported, their situation at large has received surprisingly little attention by international human rights groups (Gatmaytan 1997). I conclude with the expectation that the global reach and expansion of contemporary domestic service practices will invite renewed research efforts to examine a rather problematic relationship that, perhaps because of its relative intractability as both a public and a very private matter, has not drawn the scholarly and humanitarian attention it deserves.

REFERENCES

Asad, Talal

1973   Two European Images of Non-European Rule. In Talal Asad, ed., *Anthropology and the Colonial Encounter*, 103–18. London: Ithaca Press.

Appadurai, Arjun

1990   Disjuncture and Difference in the Global Cultural Economy. *Public Culture* 22 (2): 1–24.

Bakan, Abigail B., and Daiva Stasilius, eds.

1997   *Not One of the Family: Foreign Domestic Workers in Canada*. Toronto: The University of Toronto Press.

Banerjee, Swapna

1996   Exploring the World of Domestic Manuals: Bengali Middle-Class Women and Servants in Colonial Calcutta. *SAGAR: South Asia Graduate Research Journal* 3 (1): 1–26.

Chicago Tribune

1993   Baird's Ex-Domestics May Face Deportation. January 23, Section 1, p. 10.

1996a   Tackling Abuse of Workers: United Nations Studies Treatment of "Exported" Women. June 9, Section 5, p. 7.

1996b   Indentured Servants: 1,5 Million Women Brave Unknown Risks to Support Their Families. June 23, Section 13, pp. 1, 6, 8.

Chin, Christine B. N.

1988   *In Service and Servitude: Foreign Female Domestic Workers and the Malaysian "Modernity" Project*. New York: Columbia University Press.

Enloe, Cynthia

1990   Just Like One of the Family: Domestic Servants in World Politics. In Cynthia Enloe, *Bananas, Beaches, and Bases: Making Feminist Sense of International Politics*, 117–94. Berkeley: University of California Press.

Gatmaytan, Dan

1997   Death and the Maid: Work, Violence, and the Filipina in the International Labor Market. *Harvard Women's Law Journal* 20:229–61.

Gerard, Jessica

1994   *Country House Life: Family and Servants 1815–1914*. Oxford: Blackwell.

Gill, Lesley

1994   *Precarious Dependencies: Gender, Class, and Domestic Service in Bolivia*. New York: Columbia University Press.

Hansen, Karen Tranberg

1989   *Distant Companions: Servants and Employers in Zambia 1900–1985*. Ithaca: Cornell University Press.

1991   Domestic Service: What's in It for Anthropology? *Reviews in Anthropology* 16 (1): 47–62.

Heyzer, Noeleen, Geertje Lydama à Nijehold, and Nedra Weerakoon, eds.

1994   *The Trade in Domestic Workers: Causes, Mechanisms and Consequences of International Migration*. London: ZED Books Ltd.

Hill, Bridget

1996   *Servants: English Domestics in the Eighteenth Century*. Oxford: Clarendon Press.

The Independent (London)

1989   Foreign Maids Trapped in "Slave Trade." December 12, p. 3.

1997   Chinese Threat to Silence the Sparrows. Hong Kong Handover: Foreign Maids Fear Their Livelihoods Will Be Taken Away. March 28, p. 16.

Leupp, Gary P.

1992   *Servants, Shophands, and Laborers in the Cities of Tokugawa Japan*. Princeton: Princeton University Press.

Maids and Madams

1985   Mira Hamermesh, writer/director. Distributor: Filmakers' Library, New York.

New York Times

1996   The Nanny Track: A Once-Simple World Grown Complicated. September 26, Section F, p. 9.

La Noire de. . .

1966   Ousmane Sembene, writer/producer. Distributor: New Yorker Film, New York.

O'Leary, Elizabeth

1996   *At Beck and Call: The Representation of Domestic Servants in Nineteenth-Century American Painting*. Washington, DC: Smithsonian Institution Press.

Yes Ma'am

1982   Gary Goldman, producer. Distributor: Filmakers' Library, New York.

CONTRIBUTORS

KATHLEEN M. ADAMS is an associate professor of anthropology at Loyola University of Chicago. Her publications include articles in *American Ethnologist, Ethnology, Museum Anthropology, Southeast Asian Journal of Social Science, Cultural Survival Quarterly, Annales of Tourism Research*, and edited volumes.

NICOLE CONSTABLE is an associate professor of anthropology at the University of Pittsburgh. She is the author of *Maid to Order in Hong Kong: Stories of Filipina Workers; Christian Souls and Chinese Spirits* and editor of *Guest People: Hakka Identity in China and Abroad*.

SARA DICKEY is an associate professor of anthropology at Bowdoin College. Her publications include *Cinema and the Urban Poor in South India*, and articles in the *Journal of Asian Studies, American Ethnologist, Wide Angle*, and edited volumes.

JEAN-PAUL DUMONT is the Clarence J. Robinson Professor of Anthropology at George Mason University and author of several books in French and in English, including *The Headman and I: Ambiguity and Ambivalence in the Fieldwork Experience* and *Visayan Vignettes: Ethnographic Traces of a Philippine Island*.

MICHELE RUTH GAMBURD is an assistant professor of anthropology at Portland State University. She is the author of the forthcoming book *The Kitchen Spoon's Handle: Transnationalism and Sri Lanka's Migrant Housemaids*, and of articles in *Anthropologica, Anthropology of Work Review, South Asia*, and Sri Lankan journals.

KAREN TRANBERG HANSEN is a professor in anthropology at Northwestern University. Her publications include *Distant Companions: Servants and Employers in Zambia 1900–1985* and *Keeping House in Lusaka* as well as articles in *American Ethnologist, Review of Anthropology*, and *Public Culture*.

LOUISE H. KIDDER is a professor of psychology and women's studies at Temple University. She has taught in Japan as well as India. Publications include *Research Methods in Social Relations, The Psychology of Intergroup Relations: Conflict and Consciousness*, edited volumes on research methods in social psychology, and articles on intergroup relations and the social psychology of justice. She currently serves on the editorial board of the *Journal of Social Issues*.

KATHRYN ROBINSON is the chair of the Department of Anthropology in the Centre for Asian and Pacific Studies at Australian National University. Her publications include *Stepchildren of Progress*, as well as articles in assorted anthropological journals and edited volumes.

SAUBHAGYA SHAH is a doctoral candidate in anthropology at Harvard University and a lecturer in the Department of Sociology/Anthropology at Tribhuvan University in Kirtipur, Nepal. He has worked as a consulting sociologist for development programs and as a journalist for *The Rising Nepal*. His publications include articles in edited volumes.

RACHEL TOLEN is an anthropologist affiliated with the International Scholarship Program at Indiana University. Her dissertation examined issues of class, culture, lifestyle, and labor through an exploration of relations between the households of officers of the Indian Railways and the servant households that work for them. In addition, she has conducted historical research on the representation and reformation of criminal tribes by missionaries in colonial India, which has been published in *American Ethnologist*.

G. G. WEIX is an associate professor of Anthropology and Director of Women's Studies at the University of Montana. Her publications include the forthcoming book *Strange Gifts, Familiar Debts: Islam and Industry in North Java* and articles in the journals *Indonesia*, *Visual Anthropology*, and *Critique of Anthropology*.

INDEX

Abu-Lughod, Lila, 7, 224, 240
Aceh (Indonesia), 277
Adams, Kathleen M., 10, 11, 14–15,
   174n. 10, 257, 287, 288, 289;
   "Negotiated Identities," 157–78;
   "Negotiating Homes, Hege-
   monies, Identities, and Politics"
   (coauthor), 1–29
Adoption, 138, 142, 144, 152, 161
African-American women, 3–4
Agarwal, Bina, 34
Age, 5, 10, 11, 287; Java, 143, 145;
   Nepal, 93–94, 95–100, 110, 111.
   See also Children
Agriculture, Nepal, 92
Ajik, Soeharti, 160
Alford, Finnegan, 158
Alford, Richard, 158
Alienation: Java, 146; Nepal, 93, 94
Alonso, Ana Maria, 2
Altruism, Madurai (India), 47, 48, 49
"Always Home, Never Home"
   (Dumont), 119–35
Ambiguity, 90–92, 286–90
"Ambiguous Hegemonies" (Hansen),
   283–92
American expatriates, in India, 209
Anderson, Benedict, 223, 225, 240
Anderson, Patricia, 278n. 3
Ang, Dante A., 234, 243n. 11
Angkatan Kerja Antar Negeri (AKAN),
   253
Anthias, Floya, 278n. 2
Anthropology, 5, 11

Appadurai, Arjun, 6, 9–10, 32, 66, 252,
   286
Arab News (newspaper), 261
Ariyawansa, D. M., 182
Armstrong, M. Jocelyn, 6, 20n. 4,
   83n. 1, 226
Asad, Talal, 285
Asia, South and Southeast, 6–7. See
   also specific countries
Asian Migrant Centre, 225, 228
Association of Southeast Asian
   Nations (ASEAN), 6
Atkinson, Paul, 20n. 6
Australia, 4
Autor, Edith, 230
Ayyub, M. Rusli, 160
Azzam, Henry T., 253, 275

Baird, Zoe, 285
Bakan, Abigail B., 290
Bakhtin, 173
Banerjee, Swapna, 290
Banskota, Amrita, 93
Barth, Fredrik, 9, 20n. 5, 101, 223
Basri, Hasan, 262, 263, 265, 266
Basso, Keith, 174n. 3
Beijing Conference on Women, 277
Bell, Susan E., 20n. 6, 36
Bell Publishing Company, 234
Bell Publishing HK Ltd., 243n. 11
Berita Buana (newspaper), 253, 278n. 5,
   279n. 7
Bigalke, Terrace, 170, 174n. 5
Birds of Passage (documentary film), 210

Black Girl (film), 283, 284
Blaikie, Piers, 90, 93, 94
Body, 103, 168–70
Bolivia, 284
Borneman, John, 105
Boserup, Esther, 251
Bossen, Laurel, 56n. 1
Bottomley, Gillian, 276, 279n. 7
Bourdieu, Pierre, 8, 66, 90, 91, 103–4, 106, 109, 110, 112, 180, 279n. 7
Brady Bunch (television show), 6, 163
Brahmans: Madras (India), 37–40, 47–50, 66, 74; Madurai (India), 37, 38; Nepal, 87, 91, 92
Brandewie, Ernest, 6
Brazil, 110, 191
Breman, Jan, 65
Brenner, Suzanne, 150
Bricker, Victoria Reifler, 174n. 3
Britain, 285
British expatriates, in India, 209
Brochmann, Grete, 182
Brown, Michael F., 7
Brunei, 249, 271
Bugis, 160, 167–68, 170, 171–72
Bujra, Janet M., 4, 19n. 1
Bungalow amma, 65; knowledge transfer, 68–77; practice, privileged spheres of, 77–80
Bungalow peons, 64–65, 66, 83nn. 3, 4; knowledge transfer, 68–77; practice, privileged spheres of, 77–80
Bungalow people, 67. *See also* Employers/masters, Madras
Bunster, Ximena, 4, 83n. 1
Butler, Judith, 2

Calagione, John, 224, 240
Cameron, John, 90, 93
Canada, 290
Capitalism, 4–5, 11, 152, 276
Caplan, Lionel, 32, 33
Caplan, Patricia, 33–34

Caring, Madurai (India), 47, 49
Caste, 4; Madras (India), 64, 66, 67, 84n. 8; Madurai (India), 31, 32, 37, 38–39, 40, 50, 53, 57n. 2; Nepal, 91–92, 102, 104, 107, 110; Sri Lanka, 181. *See also* Brahmans
Castles, Stephen, 249, 250
Catholic Institute for International Relations, 227
Cebuano vernacular, 121, 123–27, 133nn. 8, 9
Central Bureau of Statistics (CBS), 93
Chaney, Elsa M., 4, 56n. 1, 83n. 1
Character, Madurai (India), 37–52, 54
Charity, Madurai (India), 44
Charlton, Joy, 209
Chatterjee, Partha, 223
Chettiars, 50–52
Chicago Tribune (newspaper), 285
Child Workers in Nepal (CWIN), 94
Children, as servants: Java, 142, 144, 145, 150, 152; Nepal, 93–94, 95–100, 111; Toraja (Indonesia), 161. *See also* Mothering/motherhood
Chin, Christine B. N., 290
China, 4, 20n. 3
Chinese-American men, 3–4
Chinese-Indonesians, 171, 277
Ching, Linda, 238–39
Christianization, Toraja (Indonesia), 160–61
Churman, Imam, 260
Class, 2, 3, 4, 5, 10, 283–84
Class, and feminist theory, 252; Filipino, 222–25, 240, 240; Indonesia, 270; Java, 139; Madras (India), 64, 65–66, 67, 68, 75, 78–80, 81–82, 83nn. 1, 2; Madurai (India), 31, 32–33, 37–40, 42–46, 47–50, 53–54, 55–56; Middle East, 187; Nepal, 93, 102, 103, 104, 109, 110, 111, 112;

Toraja (Indonesia), 164–65, 166–67. *See also* Hierarchies; Status
Clifford, James, 9, 10, 112, 159
Clinton, William Jefferson, 63
Cock, Jacklyn, 4, 56n. 1, 83n. 1, 159
Code-switching, 124, 145
Cohen, Colleen Ballerino, 235, 240
Colen, Shellee, 3, 4, 5, 6, 8–9, 19n. 1, 56n. 1, 89, 90, 158, 174n. 1, 186, 210, 225
Colonialism, 4, 5, 64, 208, 252
Colonization, 6, 160, 209
Comaroff, Jean, 8
Comaroff, John L., 8
Communication. *See* Language
Compensation, 89, 101
Connerton, Paul, 103
Connolly, Clara, 252
Constable, Nicole, 4, 6, 10, 11, 16, 133n. 6, 180, 288; "Dolls, T-Birds, and Ideal Workers," 221–47
Consumption, Madras (India), 78, 80
Contemplacion, Flor, 285
Contrast sets. *See* Other; Self; We-they distinctions
Cooke, M. T., 3, 6, 83n. 1, 102
Coser, Lewis, 19n. 1
Council of Religious Scholars. *See* Majelis Ulama
Cremer, Georg, 160, 254, 255, 275
Crisis borrowing, Nepal, 94

Damron, John, 232–33
Daniel, E. Valentine, 36
Darsih, 271
Dasta, Pascuala, 237
Debt: Java, 146; Nepal, 93, 94; Philippines, 225; Polwatta (Sri Lanka), 182
Democracy, Indonesia, 267
Dependency: India, 208–9, 210–12, 213–16, 218–19; Java, 142; Nepal, 92–94, 102–3, 104

"Dependents in the Master's House" (Kidder), 207–20
Derrida, Jacques, 152
Dias, Malsiri, 6, 190–91, 201n. 6
Dickey, Sara, 4, 10, 12, 17, 20n. 6, 32, 54, 55, 56, 67, 209, 210, 212, 214, 289, 290; "Mutual Exclusions," 31–62; "Negotiating Homes, Hegemonies, Identities, and Politics" (coauthor), 1–29
Differences. *See* Social differences
Dill, Bonnie Thornton, 19n. 1, 56n. 1
Dirks, Nicholas, 32
Discourse, Malaysia, 139
Disease, 11
Disposition, Madras (India), 73
Distant Companions (Hansen), 284
Distinction (Bourdieu), 66
Diwaliwan (magazine), 228, 229, 234, 236, 239, 243nn. 9, 11
Djajdiningrat-Niewenhuis, 154n. 9
"Dolls, T-Birds, and Ideal Workers" (Constable), 221–47
Domestic helper doll, 224, 232–33
Domestic workers/servants, 2, 4, 8, 10, 11; and expatriate employers/masters (India), 208–19; Filipinos in Hong Kong, 221–44; Indonesian, 228, 249–79; Java, 138, 139–40, 141–53, 154nn. 6, 7, 8; Madras (India), 64–65, 66, 67, 68–80, 81–82, 83nn. 3, 4, 6; Madurai (India), 33–37, 40–52, 53–54, 55, 56; Nepal (kamgarnes/nokars), 87, 88, 89–100, 101–2, 103, 104–10, 111; politics, 285–86; Sri Lankan housemaids in Middle East, 179–201; Toraja (Indonesia), 157–58, 159–70; Ujung Pandang (Indonesia), 170–72; Visayas (Philippines), 120, 121, 123–31
Domination, 90, 95, 208, 217, 218–19
Dorde, Vickei, 230

"Doulati the Bountiful," 276
Dowry, Madurai (India), 46
Dress, Madras (India), 73, 78
Dumont, Jean-Paul, 10, 13–14, 11,
    132n. 3, 174n. 1, 287, 288;
    "Always Home, Never Home,"
    119–35
Dumont, Louis, 67
Dutch Reformed Church, 174n. 5
Duty Free Philippines, 234

East Timor, 277
Economics, 8
Economy, global, 4–5
Education: Madras (India), 66; Madu-
    rai (India), 33, 39, 46; Nepal, 87,
    97–98, 99–100
Eelans, Frank, 190
Ellison, Ralph, *Invisible Man*, 218, 219
Emigration, 5
Employees. *See* Domestic workers/
    servants
Employers/masters, 2, 4, 8-9, 10, 11;
    expatriates (India), 208–19; Hong
    Kong, 224, 227, 228, 231, 232,
    235–36, 237, 238–39, 240, 241,
    242nn. 3, 5, 243n. 15; Indonesia,
    258; Java, 138, 139, 140, 141–53;
    Madras (India), 64, 65–66, 67,
    68–80, 81–82; Madurai (India),
    34, 35–40, 41–42, 47–52, 53, 54,
    55–56; Middle East, 187, 252;
    Nepal (malik or sahu), 87, 88–89,
    90–92, 94–95, 95–96, 101–3,
    104–7, 111; Saudi Arabia, 255,
    256–57, 260–61, 265, 274; Toraja
    (Indonesia), 158, 159, 161–72;
    Visayas (Philippines), 120,
    128–29, 130
Employers of Overseas Domestic
    Helpers Association, 237,
    238–39, 242n. 6
Employment agencies, Philippines,
    239, 240, 241

Engagement, Java, 148
Engels, Friedrich, 89
English language, 74–75, 84n. 7, 123,
    124, 126, 127
Enloe, Cynthia, 285–86, 290
Equality, 5
Errington, Shelly, 165
Escher, M. C., 207–8
Ethnicity, 2, 3–4, 9, 10, 11, 20n. 5, 64,
    83n. 1; and feminist theory, 252;
    Madras (India), 66; Middle East,
    187; Nepal, 110, 112; Toraja
    (Indonesia), 168, 174n. 5
Ethnoscapes, 251
Euphemisms, 9; Nepal, 88, 90–92, 111;
    Toraja (Indonesia), 161
Everett, Jana, 110
Expatriates, In India, 208–19
Exploitation, 274; and Indonesian
    migration, 250; Java, 149; Madu-
    rai (India), 47–48; Nepal, 93, 94,
    112; Saudi Arabia, 261

Fairchilds, Cissie, 19n. 1, 132n. 2
Familial identity, 10, 11. *See also*
    Kinship/family
Fausto-Sterling, Anne, 20n. 5
Fe, Aquarius, 229–30
Feith, Herbert, 250
Feminism, 5
Feminist theory, 252
Fernandes, Leela, 32
Fischer, Michael M. J., 88
Flueckiger, Joyce B., 6
Foucault, Michel, 90, 103, 288
Frank, Arthur W., 20n. 6
French, Carolyn, 227
Funerals, Toraja (Indonesia), 165–66,
    167–68

Gaitskill, Deborah, 19n. 1, 83n. 1
Gamburd, Geraldine E., 180, 183
Gamburd, Michele Ruth, 10, 11, 15,
    179–205, 210, 289

García Castro, Mary, 4, 56n. 1, 83n. 1
Garis Besar Haluan Negara (GBHN), 250
Gatmaytan, Dan, 290
Gaw, Kenneth, 20n. 2, 227
Gee, James P., 36
Geertz, Clifford, 20n. 5, 137
Geertz, Hildred, 145, 146, 153n. 4
Gellner, Ernest, 223
Gender, 2, 4, 5, 10–11, 20n. 5, 64, 83n. 1, 120, 179, 283–84, 287; expatriates and servants (India), 216–17; Filipino, 235, 237–40; and Indonesian migration, 249–79; Java, 143; Madurai (India), 33–34; Mothering/motherhood, 196–97; Nepal, 92, 95–96, 102, 110, 111, 112; Polwatta (Sri Lanka), 184–86, 192, 196–97, 200; and Sri Lankan migration, 183; Toraja (Indonesia), 158
"Gender, Islam, and Nationality" (Robinson), 249–82
Generational identities, 11, 120
Generosity/gifts: expatriates and servants (India), 217; Java, 14, 141, 145–51, 152; Madurai (India), 41, 43, 44, 47
Genet, Jean, The Maids, 119, 131
Gerard, Jessica, 289
Gergen, Kenneth J., 20n. 6
Gergen, Mary M., 20n. 6
German expatriates, in India, 209
Gibson, Gloria D., 20n. 6
Giddens, Anthony, 37, 66
Gifts. See Generosity/gifts
Gill, Lesley, 3, 4, 5, 56n. 1, 90, 102–3, 109, 159, 180, 187, 284
Gin, Ooi Keat, 20n. 2
Ginsberg, Faye, 31
Glenn, Evelyn Nakano, 4, 56n. 1, 83n. 1
Godelier, Maurice, 106, 109

Goffman, 288
Gold, Ann Grodzins, 37
Goldstein, Judith, 173
Gordon, Suzanne, 109–110
Graham, Susan Lauderdale, 19n. 1, 132n. 2
Gramsci, Antonio, 7, 90, 95, 159, 287
Grandmothers, Polwatta (Sri Lanka), 197–98
Greed, 42
Gregson, Nicky, 19n. 1
Group identities, 9–10
Gulf War, 285
Gumperz, John, 74, 84n. 8
Gunatilleke, Godfrey, 190
Gurgka, 93
Gutierrez, Eddie, 234

Habits, Madras (India), 73
Habitus, 66, 276
Hall, Kenneth R., 6
Hall, Stuart, 179
Hancock, Mary, 54
Hansen, Karen Tranberg, 3, 4, 7, 10, 17, 33, 56n. 1, 83n. 1, 154nn. 7, 9, 158, 181, 187, 208, 286; "Ambiguous Hegemonies," 283–92; Distant Companions, 284
Hart, Gillian, 138
Harun, Lukman, 256–57, 258, 259, 260, 262, 263, 264, 265, 266
Hefner, Robert, 139
Hegel, Georg, Phenomenology of Spirit, 104
Hegemony, 2, 4, 7–9, 286–88
Helpers, 11, 13, 119–32, 142, 161, 171, 174n. 1, 242n. 1. See also Domestic workers/servants
Heston, Alan, 57
Heyzer, Noeleen, 255, 290
Hierarchies, 3, 4, 5, 7, 9, 10, 11, 180, 207; expatriates and servants (India), 208, 209, 210, 219; Java, 139, 144–45; Madurai (India),

Hierarchies (continued)
57n. 2; Middle East, 187; Nepal, 101; Polwatta (Sri Lanka), 200; Toraja (Indonesia), 159, 160–62, 164; Ujung Pandang (Indonesia), 170, 172; Visayas (Philippines), 127, 129. See also Class; Status

Hill, Bridget, 289

Hill, Hal, 141, 154n. 5

Hill, Willard W., 174n. 3

Hinduism, 91

Hobsbawm, Eric J., 89, 223

Holmström, Mark, 33, 65

Hong Kong, 4, 11, 83n. 1, 122, 133n. 6, 249, 271, 290; Census and Statistics Department, 225, 242n. 5; Filipino identity negotiation in, 221–44; Immigration Department, 227, 228

Hong Kong Employers of Overseas Domestic Helpers Association, 237, 238–39, 242n. 6

Hospitality, Madras (India), 71, 73–74

Householders. See Employers/masters

Household worker, 8–9. See also Domestic workers/servants

Housemaids, Sri Lankan, in Middle East, 179–201. See also Domestic workers/servants

Hugo, Graeme, 254, 269

Humanitarianism, 5

Humor, 14, 174n. 2; and identity negotiation, 172–73; Philippines, 222, 243n. 13; Toraja (Indonesia), 157–58, 159, 162, 163–64, 166, 167–70; Ujung Pandang (Indonesia), 170–72

Husbands, 11. See also Kinship/family

Identities, 2, 3, 4, 5, 8, 9–11, 20n. 6, 179–80; Filipino, in Hong Kong, 223, 224; Java, 138; Madras (India), 66, 67; Madurai (India), 31, 32, 55; Nepal, 87, 98–99, 109,

111; Polwatta (Sri Lanka), 186; Toraja (Indonesia), 158, 159, 162–67; Visayas (Philippines), 131. See also Age; Caste, Class; Ethnicity; Gender; Nationality; Rank; Social identity

Identity negotiation, 5, 7, 12–19; Filipino, in Hong Kong, 221–44; and humor, 172–73; Madurai (India), 31; Nepal, 90; Toraja (Indonesia), 158–59, 167–70; Visayas (Philippines), 120

Identity politics. See Identities; Politics

Immigration, 210

Indebtedness, Nepal, 93

Indentured labor, Nepal, 91

Independent, The (magazine), 285, 290

India, 110, 227; expatriates in, 208–19; Madras, 63–84; Madurai, 31–57

Indian Railways, 63–84

Indonesia, 11, 227, 228; Five Year Plans, 253–54; Java, 137–54, 254, 277–78; Labor Department, 277; Manpower Department, 254, 261, 262, 264, 267, 268, 269, 272; migrant workers in Middle East, 249–79; Religious Affairs Department, 261; Toraja, 157–75; Ujung Pandang, 160, 161, 170–72, 173

Indonesian domestic workers, 4

Indonesian Manpower Suppliers' Association (IMSA), 258, 259, 262, 267

Industrialization, 4

Inequalities, 2, 3, 63, 180, 283–84

Inferiority, 3

Inner Life of a Javanese Woman, The (Linus), 153n. 1

"Inside the Home and Outside the Family" (Weix), 137–56

International Labor Organization (ILO), 273

Interviews. See Narratives

Invisible Man (Ellison), 218, 219

Islam, 138, 143, 147, 150, 160, 161, 171, 172, 249–79, 285
Israel, 285
Italy, 228, 238, 290

Jacobson, Doranne, 185
Jakarta Post (newspaper), 264, 265, 268, 272, 273
Japan, 20n. 3, 154nn. 8, 10
Japanese-American men, 3–4
Jaschok, Maria, 226
Java, 137–54, 254, 277–78
Jay, Robert, 146
Jelin, Elizabeth, 19n. 1
Joshi, Savita, 102

Kabayan (newspaper), 225, 228, 229, 234, 236–37, 239, 243nn. 11, 14
Kainz, Howard P., 104
Kamgarnes. *See* Domestic workers/ servants, Nepal
Kapadia, Karin, 32, 34
Katzman, David M., 19n. 1, 132n. 2
Keesing, Roger, 10
Kessler, Suzanne, 20n. 5
Kidder, Louise H., 10, 15–16, 18, 55, 83n. 6, 208, 209, 211, 217, 288; "Dependents in the Master's House," 207–20
Kinship/family, 153–54n. 4; Indonesia, 257–58, 264, 271; and Indonesian migration, 250, 251; Java, 138, 139–41, 144, 145, 146, 151–53; Madurai (India), 35, 55; Nepal, 87, 88, 94, 97, 104–7, 111–12; Polwatta (Sri Lanka), 184–86; rhetoric, 14; Toraja (Indonesia), 157–58, 161–62, 163, 167–70, 174n. 8; Ujung Pandang (Indonesia), 171–72
Kipp, Rita, 9, 56
Kiribamune, Sirima, 184, 185, 191, 196
Kleinman, Arthur, 20n. 6

Knowledge, 64, 66, 68–77, 80, 81
Kompas (newspaper), 252, 254, 255–56, 257, 258–59, 260–61, 262, 263, 264, 265, 266, 267, 268–69, 272, 278n. 5
Kondo, Dorinne, 87
Korale, R. B. M., 185, 190
Korea, 20n. 3, 270
Kshetriyas, 91
Kumar, Nita, 32
Kuwait, 20on. 3, 285

Labor, 2, 8, 9; as export commodity, 250; Foucault on, 103; Java, 143, 150, 153; Madras (India), 64; Madurai (India), 31, 32, 33–34, 37–52, 53; Nepal, 88, 90, 93, 94, 102, 108, 111; Sri Lanka, 180; Toraja (Indonesia), 162. *See also* Work
Labor migration. *See* Migration
Labor Movement Between Countries, 253
Labov, William, 35
Langellier, Kristin M., 36
Language, 8–9, 11; expatriates and servants (India), 208, 210, 212–13; Filipino, in Hong Kong, 221–22, 223; Indonesia, 270; Java, 139, 144–45; Madras (India), 66, 67, 70–71, 73, 74–75, 84n. 7; Madurai (India), 31, 33; Nepal, 88–89, 90–92, 99, 103–4, 105–6, 111; Toraja (Indonesia), 161, 174n. 1; Visayas (Philippines), 121–27, 130, 132n. 5, 133nn. 8, 9
Latief, Abdul, 269
Latin America, 83n. 1
Lave, Jean, 66, 68, 72, 76
Lavie, Smadar, 8
Learning, Madras (India), 68–77
Legal Aid Institute (LBH), 271
Lerner, Melvin J., 217
Lerner, Sally C., 217

Lesbians, Filipino domestic work-
ers (T-birds), 11, 237–40,
243nn. 16, 18
Leupp, Gary P., 20n. 2, 145, 153n. 2,
154nn. 8, 10, 11, 289–90
Lewandowski, Susan, 38
Liberties, Madurai (India), 49–50
Lifestyles, Madras (India), 72, 75,
77–80
Ling, L. Huan-Ming, 253, 255, 261
Linguistics. See Language
Linnekin, Jocelyn, 10, 159
Linus, Suryadi A. G., Inner Life of a
Javanese Woman, The, 153n. 1
Lorfing, I., 253
Lowe, Michelle, 19n. 1
Loyalty, Java, 146, 152, 154n. 11
Lycklama, Geertje Lycklama à, 255

Madamba, Vady, 231
Madras (India), 63–84
Madurai (India), 31–57
Magazines. See specific magazines
Maids. See Domestic workers/servants
Maids, The (Genet), 119, 131
Maids and Madams (documentary
film), 284
Majelis Ulama (Council of Religious
Scholars), 261–67
Makassarese, 160, 170, 171
Malaysia, 4, 139, 249, 268, 271
Malik. See Employers/masters, Nepal
Mananwatte, Sarath, 200n. 4
Manners: Filipino, in Hong Kong, 230;
Madras (India), 73–74
Manor, James, 32
Marcus, George E., 88
Marecek, Jeanne, 185
Marginalization: Middle East, 187;
Nepal, 92, 94
Margold, Jane A., 6
Marks, Carole C., 278n. 3
Marriage: Madurai (India), 46; Nepal,
100, 112

Martens, Margaret, 109, 110
Martin, Mike W., 174n. 2
Marx, Karl, 89, 106, 109
Masters. See Employers/masters
Materialism: Madurai (India), 47, 49,
50, 54
Maternalism, 154n. 9, 159
Mauss, Marcel, 140
Maza, Sarah C., 19n. 1, 132n. 2, 208
McKenna, Wendy, 20n. 5
Mecca, 251, 254–55, 260, 263
Media, 4, 11, 133n. 7, 285; Indonesia,
252; Nepal, 107–8; Philippines,
243n. 12. See also specific maga-
zines and newspapaers
Medick, Hans, 145
Mehta, Alan B., 90, 91, 113n. 1
Memmi, Albert, 211, 219
Mendoza, Jennifer, 234
Mexico, 110
Michaels, Sarah, 36
Middle East, 16, 286; Indonesian domes-
tic servants in, 249–79; Sri Lankan
housemaids in, 179–201, 210
Migration, 4, 5; Filipino OCWs in
Hong Kong, 221–44; Indonesian
servants in Middle East, 249–79;
Nepal, 94; Sri Lankan housemaids
in Middle East, 179–201; Toraja
(Indonesia), 174n. 9. See also
Overseas contract workers
Miller, Jean Baker, 209
Miller, Mark J., 249, 250
Mishler, Elliot G., 36
Mishra, Chaitanya, 90, 94
Mission for Filipino Migrant Workers,
221
Mitchell, William E., 158, 174n. 3
Mitter, Swasti, 109, 110
Mixmix, 124
Moore, Henrietta L., 112
Morals/morality: Filipino, 231, 235;
Java, 151; Madurai (India), 44,
49, 53, 54, 56; and narratives, 36

Moran, Mary H., 8
Mothering/motherhood, 179, 184–86, 199–200; fragmentation, 186–87; grandmothers, 197–98; Kamala, 192, 196, 197–98, 199; long-distance, 190–91; money management, 194–96; Priyanthi, 193–94, 195, 196, 199, 201n. 13
Muhammadiyah, 256, 264, 266
Murdock, George Peter, 133n. 10
Murray, Stephen O., 11
"Mutual Exclusions" (Dickey), 31–62

Nagata, Judith, 10, 159
Nahdatul Ulama, 256
Namibia, 110
Nannies. See Housemaids
Nannygate, 63
Narayan, Kirin, 36
Narrative analysis, 36
Narratives, 20n. 6; Madurai (India), 31, 32, 35–36, 37–56; Toraja (Indonesia), 162–67
Nasr, Julinda Abu, 253
Nationalism, 222–25, 234, 240, 241
Nationality, 2, 10; and Indonesian migration, 249–79; Middle East, 187
"Negotiated Identities" (Adams), 157–78
"Negotiating Homes, Hegemonies, Identities, and Politics" (Adams and Dickey), 1–29
Neo-Marxism, 106
Nepal, 3, 87–113
Ness, Sally, 127
Netanyahu, Benjamin, 285
Netanyahu, Sara, 285
Netherlands, 160
New Order government (Indonesia/Java), 141, 152, 153, 154n. 5, 258, 263, 269–70, 273, 274, 275, 277–78
Newspapers. See specific newspapers

Nijehold, Geertje Lydama à, 290
Noire de . . . (film), 283, 284
Nokar (servant), 91. See Domestic workers/servants, Nepal
Nongovernmental organizations (NGOs), 270–74, 275
Nooy-Palm, Hetty, 160, 162, 174n. 6
Norton, Anne, 9
Nostalgia, 4
Nugent, Daniel, 224, 240
Nurture. See Mothering/motherhood
"Nurture for Sale" (Gamburd), 179–205
Nyishang (Nepal), 3

Occupation, Madurai (India), 39
O'Leary, Elizabeth, 290
Organization of Petroleum Exporting Countries (OPEC), 181, 253
Origin of the Family (Engels), 89
Ortega, Michelle, 234
Ortner, Sherry, 7, 112, 180
Other, 2, 3; Hegel on, 104; Madurai (India), 31, 54. See also Self; We-they distinctions
Outhouse people, 67. See also Domestic workers/servants, Madras
Outhouses (servants' quarters), Madras (India), 64
Overseas contract workers (OCWs), 4, 122, 225, 228, 234; Filipino, 221–44; Indonesian, 249–79. See also Migration
Overseas Workers Welfare Administration, 234
Overtime, 98

Pakistan, 254
Palmer, Phyllis, 19n. 1
Parents, of servants: Java, 150; Nepal, 95; Toraja (Indonesia), 174n. 7
"Pariyem's Confession" (Suryadi), 137–38
Parthans, Swat, 101

Part-time workers, Madurai (India), 34
Paternalism, 270, 273
Patriarchy, Indonesia, 263, 264, 270
Patriotism, Philippines, 225
Patron, 8–9. *See also* Employers/
  masters
Peacock, James, 174n. 3
Perera, P. D. A., 190
Persecution, 11
Personal Narratives Group, 20n. 6, 36
Personal space. *See* Private space
Philippine National Bank, 234
Philippines, 249, 253, 254, 255; over-
  seas contract workers, 221–44,
  261; unemployment, 225; Visayas,
  119–33
Politics, 8, 9–11, 285–86; Madurai
  (India), 56, 68–77; Toraja
  (Indonesia), 158
Polkinghorne, Donald E., 36
Polwatta (Sri Lanka). *See* Sri Lankan
  housemaids
postcolonialism, 123
Poverty, 11, 57n. 3; Indonesia, 273;
  Madurai (India), 31, 32, 34, 37, 39,
  42, 43–45, 46–47, 53; Nepal, 92,
  93, 94; Polwatta (Sri Lanka), 181
Power, 3, 7, 8, 9, 90, 180; Hong Kong,
  225; Indonesia, 263; Madras
  (India), 68, 76, 81; Malaysia, 139;
  Nepal, 87. *See also* Hegemony
Practice(s): Madras (India), 66, 67,
  68–80, 81, 82; Nepal, 103
Precarious Dependencies (Gill), 284
Preston-Whyte, Eleanor, 83n. 1
Primordialists, 20n. 5
Private schools, Madurai (India), 46
Private space, 5, 8, 142–43
Promiscuity, 11
Prostitution, indentured, 276
Public space, 5, 8

Race, 2, 3–4, 5, 64, 83n. 1, 283–84;
  and feminist theory, 252; Madras

(India), 64, 66; Middle East, 187;
  United States, 218
Radin, Paul, 174n. 3
Ragus, Evangeline, 231
Raheja, Gloria Goodwin, 32
Raju, Saraswati, 33–34
Ram, Kalpana, 32
Ramos, Fidel, 235
Rand McNally, 200n. 2
Rank, 10, 11; Java, 138; Madras
  (India), 66; Madurai (India),
  31; Toraja (Indonesia), 161, 162,
  163, 164, 165, 167, 174n. 10,
  175nn. 11, 12; Ujung Pandang
  (Indonesia), 170
Rape, 272, 277. *See also* Sexual
  abuse/harassment
Recruitment, 271; Indonesia, 253, 255,
  256, 257, 259, 260, 265, 272;
  Java, 143; Nepal, 94–95
Regionalism, 222–25
Regmi, Mahesh Chandra, 94
Relationships, 2, 3, 8, 207
Relationships, Hegel on, 104
Relationships, India, expatriate-
  servant, 208–9, 211–12, 213–16,
  218–19; Java, 138, 139, 140–41,
  142, 146, 147, 150, 153n. 2;
  Madras (India), 66, 68, 76; Madu-
  rai (India), 35, 36–37, 46–56;
  Nepal, 87, 90–91, 95, 101, 108–9;
  Toraja (Indonesia), 158, 159,
  161–62, 167
Republika (newspaper), 273
Resistance, 107, 108, 159, 287
Respect, Madras (India), 78, 79
Respectability, Nepal, 101–2
Rey, P., 106
Rice Paddy Babies Ltd., 232–33
Ricoeur, Paul, 36
Riessman, Catherine Kohler, 36
Risseeuw, Carla, 181, 192, 195, 196–97
Robinson, Kathryn M., 6, 10, 11,
  16–17, 160, 174nn. 4, 8, 175n. 14,

250, 251, 257, 258, 263, 277, 278n. 4, 288, 289; "Gender, Islam, and Nationality," 249–82
Robison, Richard, 139, 154n. 5
Rogers, Susan Carol, 112
Rollins, Judith, 3, 4, 56n. 1, 83n. 1, 101, 104, 145, 154nn. 6, 8, 9, 159, 180, 210
Romero, Mary, 3, 4, 55, 56n. 1, 144, 145, 154n. 9
Romula, Carlos P., 231
Rosaldo, Michelle Zimbalist, 112
Rosaldo, Renato, 36, 37
Roseberry, William, 7
RPB (HK) Ltd., 232
Rubbo, Anna, 19n. 1
Rueda, Oly, 231
Ruhunage, L. K., 200n. 4
Russell, Sharon Stanton, 268, 279n. 6

Sabean, David W., 145
Sahu. See Employers/masters, Nepal
Salaff, Janet, 226
Samarasinghe, Gameela, 190, 201n. 6
Sanjek, Roger, 3, 4, 5, 6, 8–9, 19n. 1, 56n. 1, 89, 90, 158, 174n. 1, 225
Sankar, Andrea, 225, 226
Sannad, June Laggawan, 230–31
Saudi Arabia, 200n. 3, 210, 252, 253, 254–57, 258–61, 263–66, 267–69, 271, 275, 276, 277, 290
Savera, Mira, 110
Scandinavian expatriates, in India, 209
Schampers, Toon, 190
Schenk-Sandbergen, Loes, 109
Scheper-Hughes, Nancy, 191
Schooling. See Education
Scott, James C., 108, 139, 159, 173, 187, 189–90, 224, 287
Scott, William Henry, Slavery in the Spanish Philippines, 127
Sears, Laurie J., 6, 11
Seddon, David, 90, 94, 95, 106

Self, 2, 3, 179–80; Hegel on, 104; Java, 138; Madurai (India), 31, 54; and narratives, 36. See also Other; We-they distinctions
Sembene, Ousmane, 283, 284
Servants. See Domestic workers/servants
"Service or Servitude?" (Shah), 87–117
Servitude, 63, 287
Servitude: Java, 138, 139, 141–45, 149, 154n. 8; Toraja (Indonesia), 162–67
Sexual abuse/harassment, 271, 274; Indonesia, 271, 272, 277; Saudi Arabia, 260–61, 269, 276
Sexuality, 2, 10, 11; Nepal, 107; T-birds, 237–40, 243nn. 16, 18; Toraja (Indonesia), 158
Shah, Saubhagya, 9, 10, 11, 13, 96, 288, 289; "Service or Servitude?," 87–117
Sherbiny, Naiem A., 254
Shiraishi, Saya, 146
Siblings, 11. See also Kinship/family
Siegel, James, 150
Singapore, 4, 133n. 7, 249, 271, 285, 290
Situated practice, 66
Situationalists, 20n. 5
Slavery in the Spanish Philippines (Scott), 127
Slaves/slavery, 4, 89; Madurai (India), 41; Nepal, 91; Toraja (Indonesia), 161, 162, 163, 164–65, 166–67, 174nn. 6, 10; Visayas (Philippines), 127
Smith, Anthony, 223
Smith, Margo L., 19n. 1
Social differences, 63, 64; Java, 139, 141; Madras (India), 65, 70
Social identity, Java, 138, 139, 140, 146
Social learning, Madras (India), 68–77

Social mobility, Madras (India), 65, 77, 81, 82

Social stratification, Toraja (Indonesia), 161

Social structure/setting, 2, 3, 8, 11, 36–37

Solidaritas Perempuan (SP), 270–74

Sombrio, Rose, 239

Somers, Margaret R., 20n. 6

South Africa, 83n. 1, 109–10, 284

Southall, Aidan, 9

South Asia, 6–7. *See also specific countries*

South China Morning Post (newspaper), 232

Southeast Asia, 6–7. *See also specific countries*

South Sulawesi, 157–75

Spanish-American War (1898), 125

Spanish language, 125

Spivak, Gayatri Chakravorty, 276

Sri Lanka, 227

Sri Lankan Bureau of Foreign Employment (SLBFE), 183, 200nn. 3, 4

Sri Lankan housemaids, in Middle East, 179–201, 210

Stahl, Charles W., 253

Stasilius, Daiva, 252–53, 290

Status, 2; Madras (India), 78; Nepal, 92, 102; Toraja (Indonesia), 161, 165; Ujung Pandang (Indonesia), 172; United States, 210. *See also* Class; Hierarchies

Stereotypes, 4; Filipino, in Hong Kong, 229; Indonesian, in Saudi Arabia, 263

Stockard, Janice, 225

Stoeltje, Beverly, 235

Stoler, Ann Laura, 4, 20n. 2

Strathern, Marilyn, 112

Suara Karya (newspaper), 268

Suardiman, Siti Pardini, 160, 255

Subardjo, H. N. Bambang, 260

Subjection, India, expatriate-servant, 208

Subordination: India, expatriate-servant, 217, 218–19; Nepal, 95

Subramanian, Pavoorchatram Rajagopal, 83n. 5

Sudomo, 258, 259, 263, 264, 265, 266, 267, 268

Sudras, 91

Sullivan, Norma, 150

Suryadi, Linus, "Pariyem's Confession," 137–38

Susilo, 271

Swami, Laxmi, 285

Swedenburg, Ted, 8

Tagalog language, 121, 125, 132n. 5, 221–22

Taiwan, 228

Tamil Nadu (India). *See* Madurai

Taussig, Michael, 19n. 1

Taylor, Jean Gelman, 20n. 2

T-birds, 237–40, 243nn. 16, 18

Technology, Madras (India), 71

Tellis-Nayak, V., 6

Tempo (magazine), 259, 260, 268

Tenaga Kerja Wanita (TKW), 270

10/10 celebration, 224, 233–40, 241, 243n. 11

Thailand, 20n. 3, 227, 249, 253, 254, 255

Thunderbirds, 237–40, 243nn. 16, 18

Tien, Ibu, 261

Tilly, Louise, 4

Tinig Filipino (magazine), 224, 228–32, 237, 240, 241, 243nn. 10, 18

Tokagawa period (Indonesia/Java), 154n. 10

Tolen, Rachel, 10, 12–13, 55, 56, 65, 285, 288; "Transfers of Knowledge and Privileged Spheres of Practice," 63–86

Toraja (Indonesia), 11, 14, 157–75

Torture, 261, 271

Training: Indonesia, 271, 274; Nepal, 101–2

"Transfers of Knowledge and Privileged Spheres of Practice" (Tolen), 63–86

Transnationalism, 234. *See also* Migration

Triwijarti, Endah, 270

Tsing, Anna Lowenhaupt, 31

Tucker, Susan, 4, 83n. 1

Ujung Pandang (Indonesia), 160, 161, 170–72, 173

Unemployment: Nepal, 93; Philippines, 225; Polwatta (Sri Lanka), 180–81, 195

Unicef, 92, 93

Unions: Filipino, 238; Madurai (India), 50–51; Nepal, 88, 109

United Arab Emirates (UAE), 192, 197, 200n. 3, 285

United States, 4, 83n. 1, 125, 210, 218, 284, 285

Untouchables, 57n. 2

Utomo, Y. Priyo, 269

Vacati, 70–71, 74, 76–77, 78, 79, 80, 83n. 5

Vaishyas, 91

Values, 9; Filipino, 228–29; Islamic, 264; Madras (India), 67, 78; Madurai (India), 33, 40, 50; Nepal, 103

Van den Berghe, Pierre, 20n. 5

Van der Veer, Peter, 181

Visayan vernacular, 121, 124

Visayas (Philippines), 119–33

Volkman, Toby, 162, 170, 174n. 9

Wadley, Susan S., 184

Waletzky, Joshua, 35

Wanita Islam Indonesia, 262

Wansekara, W. M. V., 200n. 4

Watson, James L., 4

Watson, Rubie S., 4, 20n. 2, 83n. 1, 226

Wealth, 4; Madras (India), 67; Madurai (India), 31; Madurai (India), 42–46

Weerakoon-Gunawardene, Nedra, 6, 190–191, 201n. 6, 290

Weinrich, Anna K. H., 83n. 1

Weix, G. G., 10, 11, 14, 153–154n. 4, 174n. 8, 257, 287, 288; "Inside the Home and Outside the Family," 137–56

Westwood, Sally, 94

We-they distinctions, 2, 10. *See also* Other; Self

White, Geoffrey, 10, 20n. 6, 159

White, Sarah C, 31

Whitmore, John K., 6

Wilk, Richard, 235

Williams, Raymond, 7, 180

Wilmsen, Edwin N., 165

Wives, 11, 20n. 3. *See also* Kinship/family

Wolf, Diane, 151, 158

Wolff, John U., 124, 125, 133n. 9

Women, expatriates, 216–17. *See also* Domestic workers/servants, Madurai; Gender

Women's Solidarity for Human Rights. *See* Solidaritas Perempuan

Work, Madurai (India), 38–39. *See also* Labor

Workers. *See* Domestic workers/servants

Working students, 128

World Bank, 93

World War II, 200n. 2

Yabes, Jesus, 232

Yalman, 200n. 2

Yanagisako, Sylvia Junko, 112

Yes Ma'am (documentary film), 284

Yuval-Davis, Nira, 252–53, 278n. 2

Zambia, 284